T0256555

ENHANCED VISUALIZATION

ℰach generation has its unique needs and aspirations. When Charles Wiley first opened his small printing shop in lower Manhattan in 1807, it was a generation of boundless potential searching for an identity. And we were there, helping to define a new American literary tradition. Over half a century later, in the midst of the Second Industrial Revolution, it was a generation focused on building the future. Once again, we were there, supplying the critical scientific, technical, and engineering knowledge that helped frame the world. Throughout the 20th Century, and into the new millennium, nations began to reach out beyond their own borders and a new international community was born. Wiley was there, expanding its operations around the world to enable a global exchange of ideas, opinions, and know-how.

For 200 years, Wiley has been an integral part of each generation's journey, enabling the flow of information and understanding necessary to meet their needs and fulfill their aspirations. Today, bold new technologies are changing the way we live and learn. Wiley will be there, providing you the must-have knowledge you need to imagine new worlds, new possibilities, and new opportunities.

Generations come and go, but you can always count on Wiley to provide you the knowledge you need, when and where you need it!

WILLIAM J. PESCE
PRESIDENT AND CHIEF EXECUTIVE OFFICER

PETER BOOTH WILEY
CHAIRMAN OF THE BOARD

ENHANCED VISUALIZATION

Making Space for 3-D Images

Barry G. Blundell

BICENTENNIAL
1807
WILEY
2007
BICENTENNIAL

WILEY-INTERSCIENCE
A JOHN WILEY & SONS, INC., PUBLICATION

Published by John Wiley & Sons, Inc., Hoboken, New Jersey.
Published simultaneously in Canada.

For general information on our other products and services please contact our Customer Care
Department within the U.S. at 877-762-2974, outside the U.S. at 317-572-3993, or fax 317-572-4002.

Wiley also publishes its books in a variety of electronic formats. Some content that appears in print,
however, may not be available in electronic format.

For more information about Wiley products, visit our Web site at http://www.wiley.com.

Library of Congress Cataloging-in-Publication Data:

Blundell, Barry, 1956-
  Enhanced visualization: making space for 3-D images / by Barry G. Blundell.
     p. cm.
  ISBN: 978-0-471-78629-0
  1. Computer graphics. 2. Three-dimensional imaging. I. Title.
  T385.B592 2007
  006.6′93−dc22

                                                        2006027649

Printed in the United States of America.

10 9 8 7 6 5 4 3 2 1

To
Jandy, Alys, Quintus

Jasper

Gryphon

And absent friends

The untold want by life and land ne'er granted,
Now voyager sail thou forth to seek and find.

Walt Whitman (1819–1892)

Contents

Preface

At last they found — his foragers for charms —
A little glassy-headed hairless man,
Who lived alone in a great wild on grass;
Read but one book, and ever reading grew
So grated down and filed away with thought,
So lean his eyes were monstrous; while the skin
Clung but to crate and basket, ribs and spine.

The origins of modern three-dimensional (3-D) computer graphics can be traced back with certainty to the Renaissance period that flourished in Italy between the fourteenth and sixteenth centuries. Critical to this era of cultural rebirth was the coalescence of scientific and artistic thinking, and this provided the synergy needed to bring about an age of remarkable intellectual enlightenment. During this period the systematic techniques needed to accurately represent 3-D scenes on two-dimensional (2-D) media were derived, disseminated and gradually refined. By adopting an accurate perspective framework and through the incorporation of a range of pictorial depth cues, artists developed the techniques whereby they became able to create works that possess, surpass, and even transcend photorealism.

The flat-screen computer display via which we interact with the digital world represents the electronic rendition of the traditional artist's tableau, and pictorial depth cues are used to convey the form and spatial relationships of three-dimensional images to the human visual system. However, in our everyday lives when judging spatial relationships, our eyes are each presented with a slightly different view of the scene under observation. Using mechanisms of which we have little understanding, the visual system interprets such disparities as cues to depth, and this provides a means by which we can more accurately judge both absolute and relative distances. It was not until the first half of the nineteeth century that Charles Wheatstone and David Brewster independently discovered this effect and developed stereoscopic display systems. The emergence of photographic techniques provided great impetus to this approach and when appropriately prepared image pairs are correctly viewed, scenes no longer appear to reside on a 2-D plane but demonstrate a remarkable sense of 3-D *relief*. This powerful cue to depth is, however, absent from images depicted on the standard computer screen, and so scenes that are inherently 3-D remain locked within the 2-D confines of Flatland.

Standard stereoscopic images provide only a single view onto a scene (it is not possible to move the head from side to side and obtain a new vantage point). However, from the beginning of the twentieth century researchers began to develop display techniques that would not only support a "look around" capability, but would also enable 3-D images to be viewed directly without recourse to special viewing apparatus (e.g., the stereoscope). This work has resulted in a great diversity of 3-D display paradigms. Approaches differ not only in terms of the techniques that are used in their implementation, but also in respect of the characteristics of the images that they are able to depict, and their impact on the human visual system.

Within this book we focus primarily on two general classes of 3-D display: volumetric systems (via which images may be depicted within a transparent physical volume), and varifocal systems (which support the formation of images within a virtual space). Both classes of display are able to interface with the human visual system in a natural manner and therefore depth cue conflict is largely avoided.

Despite the immense effort applied to the development of 3-D display systems able to more naturally interface with the human visual system, and the excellent results that have been obtained, relatively little progress has been made in applying these results to the advancement of the computer interface. Some believe that major changes in the interface are unnecessary, and that by judicious fine tuning, it can continue to be developed to keep pace with ever more complex computer applications. Others feel that in the case of certain applications (i.e., involving the creation, visualization and manipulation of complex 3-D images), radically new approaches are necessary. This type of debate generally focuses on the visualization opportunities offered by the current flat screen display, as compared with those that may be supported by alternative creative 3-D display technologies. However, even if we are willing to accept that the mathematically based perspective techniques put in place some 700 years ago provide the optimal means by which image data that is inherently 3-D should be presented to the visual system, we are still left with the question of the impact of this display modality on interaction. Bidirectional communication underpins the modern computer interface and the display plays a crucial role not only in the visualization of computer-processed data but also in defining the ways in which we can interact with the digital world. Consequently, we need to consider whether the traditional image rendition technique also provides optimal support for efficient and intuitive interaction.

During the decades in which creative 3-D displays have been researched, the main thrust of this work has been to develop systems able to significantly advance the visualization process. Relatively little emphasis has been placed on the interaction opportunities that may be supported by new display modalities. As in a previous work [Blundell and Schwarz, 2006], within this book we attempt to begin to address this imbalance and consider both the visual characteristics of display systems and the natural and intuitive interaction opportunities that they may support. In this respect, volumetric systems are particularly interesting since many architectures impose little restriction on viewing freedom and, as with a goldfish bowl, the image scene can be viewed from practically any orientation. Furthermore, since images are depicted within a physical volume, the volumetric approach may be considered to provide the electronic rendition of the traditional sculpted image rather than the image rendered on a 2-D tableau. This provides us with many exciting opportunities and also gives rise to some interesting challenges.

The advancement of the human-computer interface to enable the efficient and effective use of new forms of display and interaction techniques and the development of synergistic interaction modalities, requires an indepth understanding of a broad range of disciplines spanning both the arts and sciences. Consequently, as in the case of the previous work cited, I have attempted to adopt (wherever possible) a transdisciplinary approach, thereby making the material available to the widest possible audience. Where possible, acronyms have been avoided, reliance on technical jargon has been minimized, and the necessary mathematics has been presented in an approachable manner. An extensive set of references are provided by means of which more indepth discussion may be obtained, and various questions are presented at the end of each chapter. A number of these are intended to provide opportunities for group discussion.

In Blundell and Schwarz [2006], the concept of a "suspension of disbelief" as applied to various forms of creative media is discussed. It appears that English poets William Wordsworth and Samuel Taylor Coleridge were the first to use this phrase in the late eighteeth century. This concept retains its relevance and is a critically important consideration (or should be) in the design and implementation of the human-computer interface. It was in connection with this idea that Coleridge wrote his remarkable poem, *The Rime of the Ancient Mariner*. This was illustrated by Gustave Doré and a number of his images were used in the previous work. In keeping with this tradition, in this book I again draw upon Doré's illustrations—this time from those that he produced for the verse written by Alfred Lord Tennyson, Tennyson's *Idylls Of The King*. Images and associated verse are presented alongside each other. Sadly, it is impossible to do justice to Doré's evocative woodcuts when they are reduced in size and the interested reader is referred to the Dover Publication entitled *Doré's Illustrations for Idylls Of The King* [1995] in which the images are reproduced at a size of 300 mm by 220 mm.

Despite the care that has been taken in the preparation of this book, errors and omissions will undoubtedly have occurred. I would very much appreciate feedback from readers, especially concerning ways in which future editions could be improved and in relation to any work that has been omitted or incorrectly attributed. I can be reached at barry.blundell@physics.org.

I sincerely hope that you will enjoy this book and that its content may be of use to you in your endeavors.

BARRY G. BLUNDELL

Courcelle, France
November 2006

Concerning the Front Cover Image

Frank Hurley (1885–1962) was an Australian photographic artist renowned for capturing evocative and highly potent images on film. One of his works is reproduced on the front cover. This depicts the "Endurance" (the ship used by Ernest Shackleton[1] for his ill-fated 1914–1916 expedition) mortally trapped in the Antarctic icepack. Despite the use of a 2-D medium, Hurley employs cues mainly provided by the ship to convey the extent of a vast three-dimensional space. Indeed he was remarkably skilled in his craft and was described by the First Officer of the Endurance as "... *a warrior with his camera who would go anywhere or do anything to get a picture.*" Hurley's photographs tell stories and strongly support a suspension of disbelief. In viewing the image, we momentarily forget that we are looking at a photograph and become captivated by, and immersed within, the scene. Hurley's skills enabled him to convey an image that transcends the medium of expression—complex human emotions are stimulated and within our imagination a tale unfolds. For example:

Its wooden legs crack through the ice-capped snow
and are anchored so the monster's eye
is where your eye fringed with ice finds its eyepiece.
The light, you say, the dark, blue light.

The ship lists and cracks,
its masts long shadows.
The shrouds hang heavy with ice
making the yards live.

So little light, the plates must be exposed
while the heart beats blindly on.
The silver slowly changes
on the glass taking on the black
of waiting while the inevitable
is prefigured.

From *Pictures of the Floating World*, by Professor Koenraad Kuiper[2]

---

[1] Perhaps researchers working on the development of 3-D display and interaction technologies for applications in areas such as medicine would do well to bear in mind Ernest Shackleton's family motto: "*By endurance we conquer!*"

[2] Reproduced by kind permission of Professor K. Kuiper, © 2006 Koenraad Kuiper.

Acknowledgments

*Then to her own sad heart mutter'd the
Queen,
"Will the child kill me with her innocent
talk?"
But openly she answer'd, "must not I,
If this false traitor have displaced his lord,
Grieve with the common grief of all the
realm?"*

The preparation of this book began early in Spring 2005. The calendar has now turned full circle and today I come to the last task before submitting this manuscript—the production of this brief section.

I would like to begin by expressing my appreciation to those people who have undertaken remarkable pioneering research in relation to the development of display system technologies. Without the efforts of so many highly motivated, creative researchers this book would indeed be impoverished. Despite my best efforts however, it has not proved possible to communicate with all those who have worked within this community. As will become apparent during the course of the book, this area of research spans many decades, and even researchers move on. Hopefully in future editions it will be possible to include contributed material from other pioneer workers.

I should like to express my thanks to all those who have provided direct help in the production of this book. Firstly, thanks to Professor Rüdiger Hartwig not only for providing Figures 1.4(b) and 7.12, but also for the encouragement and kindness he has shown over the years, and for his advice which has invariably been sound. My appreciation also to Professor Malcolm Baird for supplying the photograph of his father, John Logie Baird (Figure 6.2). Professor Eric Korevaar has been kind enough to provide material in connection with his pioneering work in relation to the development of the static-volume display technology employing a gaseous medium, which is discussed in Section 5.6.1. Particular thanks to him for supplying photographs of his experimental apparatus (Figures 5.8 and 5.9). Dr. Alan Sullivan and Dr. Gregg Favalora have also kindly supplied material and images in connection with the excellent display technologies that they have created and made available as commercial products.

Obtaining permissions to use artwork from other sources has been a time-consuming occupation. A number of people have been extremely helpful in facilitating this process. I should particularly like to mention Dr. Claus Ascheron at Springer-Verlag, Elizabeth Sandler of *Science*, Jenny Needham of the Society for Information Display, Catherine Belanger at the Louvre in Paris, Maria Luisa Nava at the National Archaeological Museum in Naples, and Susannah Lehman of the Optical Society of America. My appreciation also goes to the Institute of Electrical Engineers for dealing with permissions quickly and efficiently, similarly the SPIE and Elsevier. My thanks to Jerry Kuehl for pointing me in the direction of the Imperial War Museum reguarding WWII images, and to David Bell at the IWM who provided assistance in connection with Figure 1.4(a)—indeed, I shall miss our somewhat lengthy correspondence! In terms of general assistance, many thanks go to John Copeland at the IEE both for library facilities and for providing most helpful information. Thanks to Dover Publications which gave informal advice about copyright and allowed the use of Gustare Doré's images from its excellent edition of *Idylls of the King*, (1995). Thanks also to the Royal Geographical Society for permission to use the Frank Hurley image of "Endurance" Frozen in the Ice' on the front cover, and to Professor Kon Kuiper for permission to use lines from "Pictures of the Floating World" (previously published in Sport V34).

At John Wiley Hoboken, I should like to express my thanks to Paul Petralia and Whitney Lesch (particularly for her efficient, prompt and ever-cheerful responses). Thanks also to Dean Gonzalez who has done so much to facilitate the production of high-quality artwork, and to Lisa Van Horn who has managed production. Additionally, I much appreciate the work of the typesetters in India.

This book represents, as always, the culmination of the efforts of many people. Those mentioned above have provided direct support and assistance during the book's preparation. Of equal importance are those whose influence provided me with the necessary inspiration. To refer to all who have paved the way would be impossible, but I should like to briefly mention one period of my academic career which, over the years, has not receded into the mists of time but has grown in significance and continues to be a source of great inspiration.

When I first entered the Schuster Laboratory at the Victoria University of Manchester in the mid-1970s to embark upon a degree in physics, little did I know that this would be my home for some ten years. Professor John Willmott CBE, the head of department, drew the short straw in becoming my director of studies. Sitting behind his desk, his face often obscured by clouds of smoke rising from his pipe, John did not in those days suffer either fools or shrinking violets gladly. But I have never known him to be anything other than scrupulously just, and on his watch the Physics Department flourished and an environment for individualistic creativity prospered.

Some of those who presented lectures were rather shy and self-effacing characters, and one could only feel sorry that they had been dragged from their research and placed before large and daunting student audiences. Others were more flamboyant characters, and here a professor of astronomy springs to mind whose lectures generally began on-topic, before invariably diverting within minutes on to his most recent exploits at NASA, or his enthralling account of the way in which the solar system would end. Others spoke very little, preferring to begin formulating mathematic proofs on one blackboard and end the activity some six or eight panels later. During these occasions, students could do little more than watch with awe while frantically attempting to copy the hieroglyphics for understanding at a later time. In short, lectures did not necessarily directly convey knowledge of the subject matter (after all, such knowledge is relatively easy to gain), but rather provided inspiration and an insight into genius. These were the often unsung heroes, and perhaps their ultimate accolade should be that they never inflicted death by Powerpoint on their students!

My Ph.D. supervisor was also strongly individualistic. I was one of the first to develop microprocessor technologies within the department, and when in the first year of my Ph.D. I built a microprocessor system able to control a spectrometer and acquire, process, and display its output, the work was regarded as a seven-day wonder although many came to see this fascinating sight. Festooned with wires, that small microprocessor system was empowered to drive motors and solenoids, and in response to its efforts spectral lines would mystically appear on a display screen. When my supervisor finally arrived for his viewing he looked on silently for seemingly several minutes. He then placed his hands around the metallic frame containing the microprocessor system and lifted it some thirty centimetres into the air before triumphantly impacting it onto the polished mahogany table. As he walked away he mentioned that it didn't seem to work anymore. Perhaps he was—like Merlin—seeing a machine attempt to match his own magical powers; perhaps he had an insight into what such technologies could bring; or, more likely, perhaps I was simply an irritating student who needed bringing into line... His approach to dealing with unreliable instrumentation was similarly individualistic. In his office he maintained a large hammer that he would soundly apply to offending equipment. The result was that much of it looked as though it had been involved in a major air crash—on the other hand on many occasions I observed at first hand that faulty apparatus could be brought into line by means of this technique.

I should certainly not overlook the technical staff who provided the means and the skills for turning ideas into reality. Furthermore, they served the invaluable function of developing student communication skills. Sadly, today the concept of the personal technician is fading into oblivion, and one can only feel that as a consequence today's students are being impoverished. The administrative support staff are also remembered with great fondness. Particular thanks to Joan Blackburn whose kindness (particularly during the turmoil of those sepia days) is always remembered. Indeed she is a very remarkable lady.

It was not until I briefly returned to the UK nearly 20 years later, that I fully appreciated the freedom I had enjoyed during those formative years. I was soon to find that within the university environment I was no longer allowed to fit mains plugs, change defective lightbulbs, or take a clock down from a wall to update the time. Major changes had occurred and any experimental work that I intended to perform would have to be accompanied by screeds of "risk assessment" documentation. Furthermore, and perhaps even more importantly, the regulations appeared to preclude any significant student participation in traditional forms of experimental development. I confess I found the issue of taking down a clock from a wall a little puzzling, until it was pointed out that there was the possibility of my falling off a chair or stepladder whilst undertaking the task...

Thanks should go to friends in many countries who have supported and encouraged my efforts a special mention of Rosemary Russo, Iwan Pekerti, Bob Craig, Robin Ramsey, Peter Walker, Guy and Maïte Beaufils, and our good friends at LaCourcelle, also remembering the support and patronage of a number of New Zealanders (especially David Powell, Bob Young, and many others, not forgetting the many students who worked on technologies and of course B.H.). I should particularly like to mention Richard Wood for his vision, faith, and support.

I should also like to express my deep gratitude and affection to all my family. Particular thanks go to Jandy and Alys for all their support and the work they have undertaken in the preparation of this book. A special thanks to Quintus for allowing his ageing father to again experience the joys of youth, namely "Thunderbirds," "Stingray," and "Fireball XL5." I have earnestly assured him that once the first royalty check from this book arrives, I will track down a "Supercar" video.

It would perhaps be inappropriate not to mention Gryphon, the destroyer of worlds. Certainly, it is difficult to believe that a puppy can be the source of so much chaos and mindless destruction. Possibly he should be thanked for not eating this manuscript, but I suspect that there are certain things even Gryphon would find indigestible.

Finally, a special thanks to Jasper who has faithfully kept watch at my side throughout every minute of the preparation of this book. The fact that he has quietly snored throughout the proceedings perhaps says something about his views on its content...

B.G.B.

e-mail: Barry.Blundell@physics.org

1 Setting the Scene

And high above a piece of turret stair,
Worn by the feet that now were
silent, wound
Bare to the sun, and monstrous ivy-stems
Claspt the gray walls with hairy-fibred
arms.

1.1 INTRODUCTION

In this chapter we present various background discussion, introduce a number of key concepts that will be further developed elsewhere in the book, and briefly outline the volumetric and varifocal display paradigms. We begin by focusing on issues relating to the evolution and adoption of the flat screen display as the primary means of viewing electronically processed signals. Here, we briefly consider the development of the conventional television display and the subsequent adoption of this display paradigm as a means of depicting computer-processed data. Within this context we refer to some of the remarkable work undertaken during the early 1940s in developing displays linked to analog systems, which were able to portray perspective views of three-dimensional (3-D) data sets and were also able to support real-time interaction activities. In fact, as we will discuss, in a number of specialized areas the need to interact in real time with electronically displayed information pre-dates the modern computer. Here, as in a previous work [Blundell and Schwarz, 2006], we emphasize the point that the visualization opportunities offered by new types of 3-D display technology represent only one facet of their potential. Of equal importance are the interaction opportunities that a display is able to properly support.

One important historical landmark in the development of the modern computer display concerns the transition from vector to bitmapped (pixmapped) graphics. The former approach bears certain important similarities to the "dot graphics" technique employed in many volumetric and varifocal display systems. Consequently, in Section 1.2.4, we briefly review these two approaches and discuss their potential strengths and weaknesses.

In Section 1.3, we outline some of the attributes associated with the conventional flat screen display that have contributed to its widespread adoption across a diverse range of applications. Here, we also introduce the essential characteristics of a range of creative 3-D display technologies that are the subject of ongoing research and development. These approaches are discussed in greater detail in Chapter 3. In fact, the volumetric and varifocal display systems that are the main subject of this book represent two classes of "creative" 3-D display.

Having laid various foundations in connection with the visual representation of data, we turn our attention to issues relating to the interaction process (Sections 1.4 and 1.5). Here we refer to the development of the event-driven graphical user interface (GUI) in the 1970s, along with problems that are arising in certain key applications as a consequence of the integration of the flat screen display and event-driven user interface. Within this context, we refer to the synergy existing between the human visual and motor systems which, if properly supported, can significantly advance our ability to interact with the digital world. We also introduce the concept of an interaction space and discuss the mapping that exists between it and the image space. In the case of, for example, the conventional flat screen computer display, both the image and interaction spaces are usually two-dimensional (2-D); as we will discuss, this can hamper our interaction with image data sets that are inherently three-dimensional. On the other hand, volumetric display systems provide a 3-D image space and thus, by "making space" for the third dimension, can, in principle, more readily support direct 3-D interaction.

In Section 1.6 we introduce the volumetric and varifocal display paradigms. As we will discuss, the conventional computer display may be regarded as an electronic version of the traditional artist's canvas, able to provide the human sense of sight with a set of "pictorial" depth cues (for example, shading and perspective) through which we obtain a sense of three-dimensionality. On the other hand, various "creative" display technologies extend the traditional canvas by conveying various additional cues to the observer. In the case of some approaches, this is achieved through a computational process by means of which two or more views on an image scene are created. Although the image(s) continues to be depicted on a flat screen, the visual system perceives an image that lies on one or both sides of this imaging plane; that is, the image appears to occupy a 3-D space. Some of the depth cue information is, however, synthetic and depth cue conflict (or visual inconsistency) can arise. Volumetric and varifocal systems offer to provide depth cue information in a more natural manner; therefore, in principle, there is more chance of the display meeting the visual requirements of the human observer. In fact, as discussed in Section 3.7, the volumetric image represents the electronic equivalent of the physically sculpted object, and provided that the display and interaction spaces can be properly configured, volumetric displays are likely to give rise to some interesting interaction opportunities.

As with other chapters in this book, we conclude with a brief "investigations" section where various issues relating to the content of the chapter are presented for further consideration or discussion.

1.2 HISTORICAL BACKGROUND

> *... can it be said that Watt and Stephenson, Davy and Faraday,*
> *have done more to change both the course of history*
> *and the material conditions of life*
> *than did Napoleon or Wellington, Walpole or Pitt?*[1]

Pioneering research into both cinema and television dates back to the nineteenth century, and while the former (in terms of its ability to support the capture and playback of animated image sequences) made the transition from experimental form to commercial product in only ~6 years, the gestation period of the latter was very much longer. In an excellent book dealing with the early history of television, Albert Abramson [1987] writes:

> *Television took a long time gestating. It grew with the technology of the times; its disciplines came from a broad spectrum of the arts and sciences that were more often than not unrelated.... The early history of television is made up of discoveries that at the time seemed absolutely unrelated to each other. To find a bridge for them was impossible. Time was needed to fit the pieces together into a sort of jigsaw puzzle.*

Interestingly, as will become evident during the course of this book, these comments could equally be applied to the evolution of creative 3-D display systems in general, and particularly to the efforts that have been made to develop viable volumetric and varifocal systems. Consequently, it is instructive to briefly consider aspects of this history because it will enable us to put into perspective the difficulties that have been experienced in introducing new types of 3-D display technologies. It also provides us with a framework within which we can better understand the architecture of some of the early volumetric techniques that we will discuss in other chapters.

The motion picture paradigm and television may be perceived as representing two forms of visual experience that possess some distinctly different characteristics.

---

[1] Campbell Swinton [1912] giving the Presidential Address to the Röntgen Society at which he laid out his ideas for 'all electronic' television.

For example, traditionally in the case of cinema, images are captured on film and, after processing the storage media, are physically transported to the locations at which they are to be viewed. As such, this does not represent a medium of direct communications, able to portray events in real time, but rather one in which the audience views imagery at some time after its recording. In short, this approach does not support simultaneity. The quest for television was rather different inasmuch as techniques were sought which would enable image capture, transmission, and display to take place in real time, thus supporting instant communications across large distances. In this sense, early pioneers often perceived television as providing the audience with an electronic telescope through which they would be able to view distant events as they occurred. Indeed, the ability of television to support real time (or close to real time) broadcasting was not only a goal of pioneers from the earliest days, but also appears (at least in Germany) to have been a major driving force behind the development of national broadcasting in the 1930s and early 1940s. Here the televising of the 1936 Olympic Games, and subsequently of large-scale state-sponsored political rallies, seems to have provided an ideological impetus for the development of a technology that could be used for propaganda purposes and strongly influence an audience[2]:

> *Imagine that you see before you, for example, a close-up of the Führer giving a speech that at the very same moment is taking place a thousand kilometres away! Isn't that fantastic? The filmed newsreel has to be edited and corrected before, many hours after the event, it can finally be shown. But television broadcasting brings an unmediated experience that is stronger than being there![3]* [Wehr, 1940][4]

The quest to develop workable television in fact began decades earlier. In the second half of the nineteenth century, a great variety of techniques were proposed and often prototyped, although it appears that not until August 25, 1900 was the term "television" first publicly used.[5] The diversity of the proposed techniques is indicated by the range of names that were coined—for example, Telephotograph, Phantascope, Dussaud Telescope, Telephone, Phoroscope Telectroscope, and so on (this latter name seems to have been quite popular, clearly relating the approach to the concept of the electrical telescope referred to here). Many of the techniques employed used a diverse range of electrical and electromechanical systems—for example, displays comprising a 2-D array of image elements (each of which was individually addressable)[6] and others that made use of a variety of often ingenious

---

[2] Indeed, the power of this medium to influence opinion must have been well-recognized in Germany, because research and development into the development of television for general broadcasting continued for some time during World War II (despite its primary use being for propaganda purposes rather than direct military application). In contrast, television broadcasting in the United Kingdom was suspended from September 1, 1939 through until 1946. During this period, however, research into various display and interaction systems continued.

[3] Also see discussion of the "suspension of disbelief" in Blundell and Schwarz [2006].

[4] Originally published in "Die Sendung," English translation taken from Uricchio [1996].

[5] By Constantin Perskyi at the International Electricity Conference held in Paris [Abramson, 1987].

[6] For a brief example, see the letter by J. Perry and W. E. Ayrton [1880].

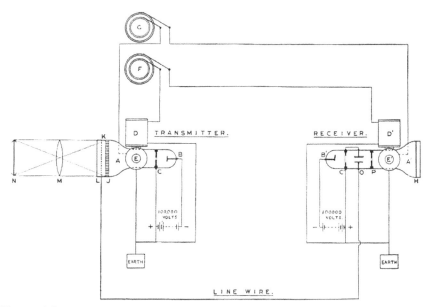

Figure 1.1 In 1912, A.A. Campbell Swinton described his ideas for the implementation of an electronic image capture and display system. He suggested the use of a CRT (Crookes tube) for the depiction of the image together with a raster scan. Video was to be transmitted via the 'line wire'. However, some twenty years were to pass before the move from electromechanical to purely electronic systems was made and many of his ideas came to be realized. (Reproduced from Campbell Swinton [1912].)

scanning techniques (this parallels past and ongoing research into volumetric display systems). The book by Albert Abramson [1987] is recommended to the reader interested in learning something of the diversity of systems that were explored. See also Gordon [1880], Middleton [1880], *The Telegraphic Journal* [1881], and the *York House Papers* [1880].

It appears that it was not until 1911 that the first fully electronic television system was proposed. In a speech given before the Röntgen Society, Alan Archibald Campbell Swinton described a system in some detail that included both image capture and display hardware [Campbell Swinton, 1912]. Interestingly, the display employed a cathode ray tube (CRT) for image depiction (see Figure 1.1). He recognized that his ideas represented little more than a vision that could not at that time have been readily realized:

> *My object has not, however, been to show you a really worked-out scheme for distant electronic vision. . . . my desire has been merely to put on record certain ideas that have occurred to my imagination in the hope that they may lead others to the invention of a more practicable method of arriving at what is wanted.*
>
> *In conclusion, if it is objected that ideas of this kind should not be presented naked and unashamed in this manner, but should be kept to one's self till they can be put forward respectably clothed in practically worked-out garb, I can quote the example of*

our Honorary Member Sir William Crookes, who some four years prior to the first of Signor Marconi's patents, and two years previous even to Sir Oliver Lodge's celebrated Royal Institution lecture gave ... a complete idea of how wireless telegraphy might be carried on over great distances by means of the Hertzian waves.

John Logie Baird's[7] "Televisor" appears to have been the first television system to be publicly marketed [Geddes and Bussey, 1991], and it went on sale in early 1930. This was a low-definition electromechanical system, central to which was a rotating Nipkow disc some 20 inches in diameter. The disc contained a series of 30 holes that spiraled from its periphery to the center, and behind the disc was a neon lamp. Video signals that for a time were broadcast by the BBC were received using a standard radio ("wireless"), the output from which was used to drive the neon lamp (rather than the radio's loudspeaker). Thus, the illumination provided by the neon lamp was modulated by the transmitted signal. The lamp illuminated only a small portion of the disc's surface such that only one hole was at any time illuminated by the lamp. The result was that the disc/lamp combination provided a scan comprising a series of 30 vertical arcs 12.5 times per second, and by synchronizing the rotation of the receiver's Nipkow disc with one used by the image capture hardware, visible animated images could be formed. A lens was used for magnification purposes and provided a final image some 4 inches in height and 2 inches in width. Naturally, definition was limited and a second radio receiver was needed if both sound and video imagery were to be simultaneously supported.[8] The text by Geddes and Bussey [1991] provides an excellent introduction to the history of live broadcasting, although it perhaps underestimates the importance of the contribution made by Baird, who spent many years promoting television and thus facilitated the subsequent introduction of the all-electronic systems that employed the CRT for image depiction and offered superior resolution. In fact, from research undertaken by the author, it appears that Baird may well have been the first to propose and prototype swept-volume volumetric display systems (and associated image capture hardware). See Section 6.3 for further discussion on Baird and the volumetric display systems that he patented in 1931 and 1942.[9]

[7] Early in Baird's difficult life, this remarkable individualist and pioneer (see Figure 6.2) left England for Trinidad; there, surrounded by citrus fruits and sugar cane, he embarked on the establishment of a jam factory. It must have seemed to him that his fortune was made—nothing could go wrong... *"The first thing to do was to find a suitably large pot in which to boil the jam. A scrap merchant in the Port of Spain sold me ... a wash-tub big enough to hold one hundredweight of jam. Underneath this we built a brick fireplace... and started off with a cauldron filed with sugar and orange cuttings... Sweet-smelling clouds of vapour rose from the pot and floated into the jungle. They acted like a trumpet call to the insect life and a mass of insects of all shapes and sizes appeared out of the bush in terrifying numbers. They flew into the steam above the cauldron in their thousands, and scorched, fell lifeless into the boiling jam. I dropped my stirrer and ran.... Hundreds of enormous ants invaded us, and in one night, made away with one hundredweight of sugar... great spiders ran up and down the walls... whilst mosquitoes continually enfolded me in a cloud"* [Moseley, 1952].

[8] For an excellent discussion of Baird's life and work, see, for example, Kamm and Baird [2002].

[9] For additional and interesting discussion on the history of early television, see, for example Myers [1936].

Some promoted the view that television would replace radio and so threaten the existing industry, and even as late as around 1935, *The Wireless and Gramophone Trader* indicated that *"The public must, if possible, be made to forget all about television for the time being"* [Geddes and Bussey, 1991]. In describing the difficulties of introducing television, these authors go on to add: *"The RMA circulated a confidential statement ... that to enjoy even the limited transmissions envisaged '... the televiewer will have to sit in a semi-darkened room and concentrate his vision on a small square of glass for two hours.'"* Despite considerable skepticism, visionary individuals provided the drive to create appropriate electronic components and circuits, and advances were rapidly made. However, it would appear that surmounting the many considerable technical problems was less difficult than the challenges faced in gaining general acceptance of this new form of medium. Publicity often sought to glamorize emerging television systems and was intended to appeal to the affluent (see, for example, Figure 1.2). Not only did this new piece of domestic furniture have to be promoted in its own right, but also (and perhaps more importantly) it would have to become a centerpiece around which viewers could conveniently gather (see, for example, Figure 1.3).

1.2.1 Interaction

> *Gentlemen, you have invented the biggest time-waster of all time.*
> *Use it well.*[10]

Traditionally (and generally even today), neither the cinema nor television support audience interaction, and so we can regard these as normally providing a uni-directional means of communication. Effective bi-directional communication is, of course, fundamental to the modern human–computer interface, and the importance of supporting interaction with various forms of electronically processed and visually presented image data has long been recognized. Consider, for example, the oscillograph that was pioneered in mechanical form in approximately 1891 and provided a means of depicting time-varying waveforms.[11] Essential to any device of this type are controls that permit image manipulation, thereby enabling the operator to more readily extract information from the data depicted on the flat screen display.

Similarly, the development of radar systems prompted research into user interaction with a variety of display paradigms. For example, in a remarkable publication that appeared in the 1940s, a range of display techniques are evaluated for use in the

---

[10] Regarding television. Attributed to Isaac Shoenberg, appointed as Head of Research of the EMI television development team in ~1931. EMI developed the Emitron camera tube and played a leading role in the development of high-definition television (the 405-line standard that was used in the United Kingdom and many other countries until the late 1960s). On perusing current TV offerings, it appears to the author that Shoenberg must have been a true visionary!

[11] This was the precursor to today's oscilloscope (and its more specialized derivatives).

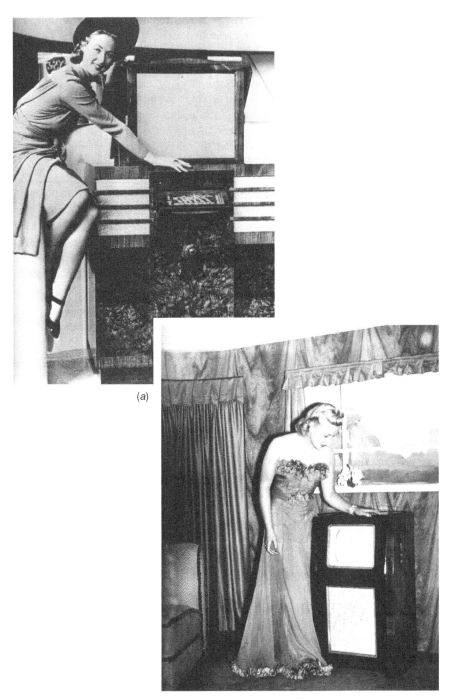

(a)

(b)

depiction of radar signals returned from airborne objects [Parker and Wallis, 1948, 1949]. As we will discuss in Section 1.2.3, the authors of this work considered not only the creation of perspective displays (based on standard flat screen display technologies), but also several approaches to volumetric display system implementation (see Sections 6.4.3 and 7.2) and the incorporation of head tracking to enable an operator of a stereoscopic display to view images from different orientations. In this early publication, the importance of accommodating user interaction with the depicted image is given some emphasis.[12] Early real-time interaction with television imagery was used, for example, in a number of military applications such as the piloting of unmanned aircraft and missiles. By way of example, consider the German Hs293D "guided bomb" that was in development during the closing stages of World War II (see Figure 1.4).

Launched and controlled from a plane, this represented an early rocket-propelled[13] air-to-ground missile. Fitted with a camera system in its nose (referred to as the "Tonne A" and employing a Super Iconoscope LS 9 imaging tube), video

Figure 1.2 In the 1930s, television quickly developed (despite considerable scepticism) and was soon able to offer large screen capabilities. Marketing material often sought to stylize and glamorize an embryonic (and often unreliable) technology that was primarily targeted toward an affluent audience. It appears that in the UK television was promoted for domestic use, whereas in Germany (specifically in Berlin) televisions were, in the main, located in public halls.[14] (a) At Radiolympia in 1937, Philips demonstrated a TV employing a 4-inch CRT (with a final anode voltage of 25 kV). A lens etched onto the face of the CRT enabled images to be projected onto a screen measuring 20 by 16 inches—a remarkable feat for the period (unfortunately, the CRT proved to have a short lifetime). (b) A Philips television demonstrated at Radiolympia in 1939 (the end of this show marked the end of public broadcasting in the UK for some seven years). Although (b) provides a smaller and more compact display system than does (a), neither were especially portable as the CRT voltages (including the final anode voltage) would have been generated using a physically large transformer operating at mains frequency (50 Hz). Often located at the bottom of the apparatus, these became quite warm during use and were inviting to domestic pets. Over time these lethal transformers became known as "cat killers"... (Images Reproduced from Geddes and Bussey [1991].)

---

[12] This paper does not cite either the earlier or the parallel work undertaken by John Logie Baird. See Section 6.3.

[13] The rocket motor used hydrogen peroxide as fuel. A catalyst (an aqueous solution of calcium peroxide) promoted the rapid decomposition of the hydrogen peroxide into steam released at very high speed. The motor produced a peak thrust of 600 kg and ran for some 12 s [Pocock, 1967].

[14] Uricchio [1996] quoting from "Die Sendung," indicates that in January 1940 six such halls operated with ~10,000 people attending. By April of the same year, this grew to twelve halls with an attendance of ~16,000 in that month.

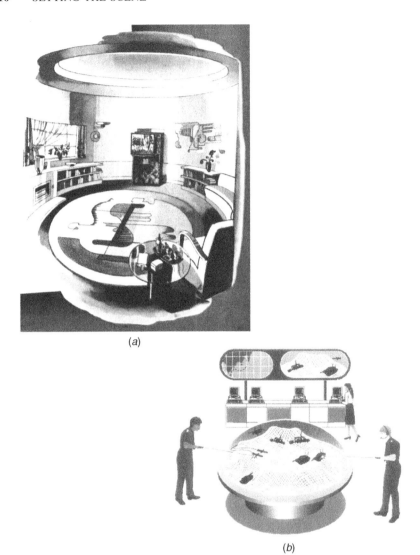

(a)

(b)

Figure 1.3   (a) Promoting television in the 1930s: a stylistic point of focus. The purchase of early televisions had a great impact on room layout; they became a centerpiece around which viewers would gather, and toward which viewers would gaze. This is in contrast to radio, which, when introduced, was far less obtrusive. Many volumetric display systems impose little restriction on viewing direction, and they too form a centerpiece. (Image reproduced from Geddes and Bussey [1991].) (b) Although the television is suited to being located against a wall or in a convenient corner, the volumetric system must be placed more centrally, thus enabling a set of viewers to gaze inwardly. As such, volumetric displays (that provide almost unlimited viewing freedom) are invasive and, as with television, a willingness to adapt our behavior is a prerequisite to general acceptance. Although the illustrations were created some 70 years apart, the artists seek a common goal: the placement of the technology within a stylistic and futuristic environment (Image supplied and reproduced by kind permission of Dr. Mark Lasher.)

(a)

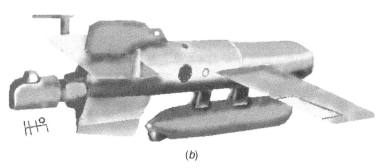

(b)

Figure 1.4 The German Hs293D rocket propelled air-to-ground missile. Under development towards the end of WWII, this missile provides us with an early example of user interaction with the electronically processed image. An on-board camera system was used to transmit video imagery to a controller who remotely piloted the missile. The operation of such a system would have been far from easy. Images (a) and (b) show the Hs293—the upper photograph provides an indication of the size of the missile and in the lower image the general architecture is shown. [Image (a) courtesy of the Imperial War Museum, London. Image (b) drawn by and reproduced by kind permission of Professor Rüdiger Hartwig.]

could be sent back to the parent aircraft via either a cable or wireless link. The controller was provided with a joystick and had the task of maneuvering the missile to keep the transmitted image of the target in the correct location on the display screen. The screen provided a vertical raster scan comprising 224 lines, was 8 cm × 9 cm in size, and supported a refresh frequency of 50 Hz [Pocock, 1967]. There can be little doubt that to use such a system the operator would have required considerable skill, and given a maximum speed of 375 miles/hour ($\sim$167 ms^{-1})

and a maximum range of 10 miles, the operator would have needed to react very quickly to the changes in the transmitted image.[15]

In fact, the history of electronic display systems provides us with a diverse range of specialist applications in which interaction with the depicted image plays a vital role, and in the next subsection we briefly consider aspects of the traditional and current relationships that exist between the display, the image data source, and the interaction tool(s).

1.2.2   The Display, Data Stream, and Interaction Tool Interface

In Section 3.2, various subsystems that comprise a 3-D display are identified and these are subsequently used to provide a framework by which the operation and characteristics of a variety of displays can be readily described (see Figure 3.1 in which these subsystems are summarized). For the moment, it is not necessary to discuss these individual subsystems and it is sufficient to note that they are often considered independently of the image acquisition systems that may be used in conjunction with a display and any interaction tools that may be incorporated within a system. In short, today the display is often treated in isolation, and this arises as a direct consequence of the underlying hardware and software systems to which the display, the interaction tools, and any image capture systems are usually interfaced. This is summarized in Figure 1.5 Here, for example, it may be seen that computer-based technologies act as the intermediary between hardware used for data capture and the display; no direct link exists between the two. The ways in which the computer hardware may process the input data stream are generally only limited by our ability to specify the actions that are to be taken and by the time that these actions may occupy. Thus when designing a display, we often consider it in isolation—reassured by the prospect that its characteristics can be mated to those of the image acquisition hardware via flexible computer-based technologies.[16] However, in the case of display systems that were developed prior to the general proliferation of digital computer technologies (or components able to perform analog computation), the designer had to focus not only on the visual characteristics of the display but also on the way in which the display would mate with other components, such as the image capture hardware. This situation is illustrated in Figure 1.6, where it may be seen that, for example, a direct link exists between the data acquisition hardware and the display (at the time when some of the early displays were prototyped, even simple tasks such as the buffering of data could not be easily

---

[15] Uricchio [1996] refers to a demonstration of a rocket-propelled missile equipped with an on-board camera system which is said to have been held outside Berlin just after World War II. He refers to this as *"the German 'Tonne' missile"* and writes *"... the German developers of the rocket targeted its guidance system at the photographic image of a young girls face so that their interrogators could see, from the point of view of the rocket's television camera, how the missile could be steered."* To date, the author has not been able to confirm that such an odd demonstration took place. However, in the case that it did, it is likely that it in fact involved the Hs293D, because the term "Tonne" is more likely to have referred to the imaging system.

[16] Whether this is an optimal approach is a matter for debate.

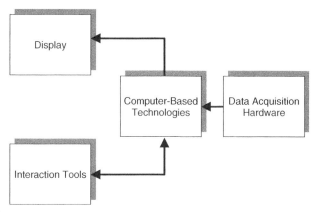

Figure 1.5   The design and implementation of display and interaction hardware is greatly facilitated by the use of computer-based technologies. As may be seen, the display, data acquisition hardware and interaction tools do not directly interface with each other, but communicate via the computer hardware. Often therefore these subsystems are considered in isolation, for we have almost unlimited flexibility in the way that the computer-based technologies may be made to operate. This contrasts with the situation illustrated in Figure 1.6. (Diagram © A. R. Blundell 2006.)

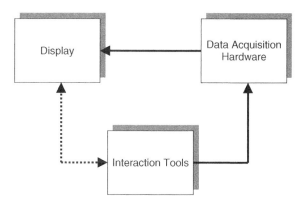

Figure 1.6   In the case of early systems, subsystems such as the display, the data acquisition hardware and interaction tools had to be 'directly' connected. Although this situation was ameliorated by the development of more advanced analog components (offering to support, for example, analog computation techniques), early pioneers had to consider a display's visual characteristics alongside its ability to directly link to other subsystems (on occasion, to satisfy the latter it was necessary to compromise the former). This contrasts with the situation illustrated in Figure 1.5. (Diagram © A. R. Blundell 2006.)

achieved). In some cases, a display's visual characteristics were compromised in order that it could match the constraints imposed by the data acquisition hardware.

> Today, as far as the display itself is concerned, we generally adopt a "one size fits all" approach.

When in later chapters we review some of the pioneering work carried out in connection with volumetric display systems, it is therefore necessary to readjust our thinking so as to continually bear in mind that without computer technologies, and before the advent of more advanced analog components, a display's design was strongly influenced by the nature of the hardware used for data acquisition. By way of example, see discussion in Section 3.3.1 on the proposal for a stereoscopic display dating back to 1930 [U.S. Patent Number 1,876,272], and see Section 6.3 in connection with early volumetric displays described in a patent filed in 1931 by John Logie Baird [British Patent Number 373,196].

1.2.3   The Conventional Display

> *The release of atom power has changed everything*
> *except our way of thinking ... the solution to this problem*
> *lies in the heart of mankind.*
> *If only I had known, I should have become a watchmaker.*[17]

As we have seen, systems able to convert appropriate electronic signals into some form of visible image are by no means new, and many of the computer graphics techniques in use today were originally employed by displays linked to circuitry able to perform analog computation.[18] The seminal paper written by Parker and Wallis [1948, 1949], which was mentioned in Section 1.2.1, provides one of the first accounts concerning the creation and depiction of perspective images on the conventional flat screen display. In this respect, the authors first consider the projection of a volume (that may, for example, be cubic) representing the extent of a radar scan onto a standard CRT display. The transformations needed to permit this volume to be displayed at any orientation (see Figure 1.7) were achieved by means of three "magslip resolvers."[19] In the context of the displayed image they write:

> *There is an ambiguity in the display, in that the volume can be "turned inside out"*
> *mentally. This is due to the lack of perspective. The effect of perspective can be obtained*

---

[17] Attributed to Albert Einstein (1875–1955).

[18] Display-based systems supporting significant analog calculation began to emerge in the 1940s. It would appear that prior to that time the usual situation was as depicted in Figure 1.6.

[19] See, for example, Williams and Parker [1952].

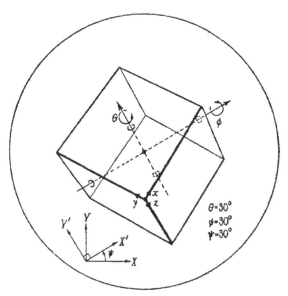

Figure 1.7   In this illustration, the cube represents a volume scanned by radar. A perspective representation of this volume was projected onto a flat screen display and the graphics engine (implemented by means of analog components) employed by Parker and Wallis enabled the orientation of the volume to be adjusted so that it could be observed from any viewpoint. (Reproduced by permission from Parker and Wallis [1948] © 1948 IEE).

by enlarging parts of the cube which are supposed to be nearer, and reducing those parts supposed to be further away.

Consequently, they created a perspective view (see Section 2.3.1) by the standard approach of employing a scaling factor to gradually reduce the size of those portions of an image that should appear to be located further away from the observer. Here they assigned a right-hand coordinate system such that the x and y axes lie in the plane of the display screen, with the z axis normal to its plane (the positive direction being toward the observer). Given that X represents the location of a point measured along the x axis in the nonperspective image, then, for the perspective image, this is mapped to a location X_0 such that

$$X_0 = \frac{X}{1 - \frac{Z}{d}}. \tag{1.1}$$

Here, Z indicates depth within the image scene and d, the viewing distance (as measured from the surface of the screen). A similar calculation is performed for the y coordinates of each point in the image (see Section 2.3.1 for related discussion).

In their publication, Parker and Wallis present a photograph of an image depicted on a conventional display to which a perspective enlargement factor has been applied. This is reproduced in Figure 1.8, and an overview of the early graphics

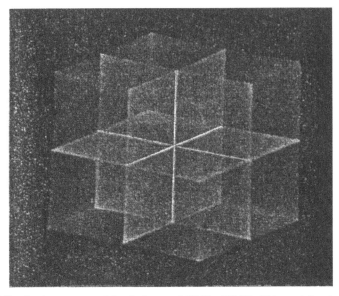

Figure 1.8   An image created by Parker and Wallis [1948]. This pertains to a volume swept out using a 'rectangular' radar scan. The image is depicted on a flat screen display and a scaling factor is applied to create a perspective view. Within the volume, cross wires and two reference planes can be seen. The inclusion of the former implies that a user could interact with the displayed image. Unfortunately, the author has been unable to locate a higher quality version of this remarkable image. (Reproduced by permission from Parker and Wallis [1948] © 1948 IEE.)

engine that they used is provided in Figure 1.9. They also suggest the use of "perspective shading". In this respect they write:

> *In addition to perspective, the brilliance of the display can be modulated according to Z, so that the nearer portions of the volume are always brighter. This will be called "perspective shading".*

The creation of a perspective image assumes a certain viewpoint. In the case of the flat screen display and most 3-D display techniques, the perspective is computed for a defined viewing position and the image should be viewed from this position in order that the perspective is optimally preserved. In the case of volumetric displays, the image is created within a volume and consequently its three-dimensionality is naturally perceived. As a result, linear perspective automatically changes with viewing position.

During the 1940s, other researchers reported work undertaken in connection with the creation of systems able to depict the results of an analog calculation process.

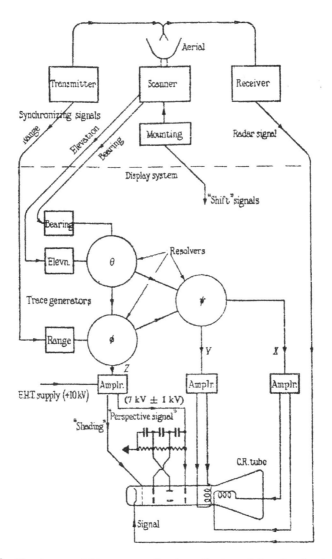

Figure 1.9 The data acquisition system (for the collection of aircraft radar data) and the graphics engine described by Parker and Wallis in their seminal 1948 publication. This system performed analog computation, central to which are the three resolvers. Adjustment of these enabled the orientation of the perspective view of the volume scanned by radar signals (see Figures 1.7 and 1.8) to be changed with respect to the observer. This was a remarkable achievement given the technologies available at that time. (Reproduced by permission from Parker and Wallis [1948] © 1948 IEE.)

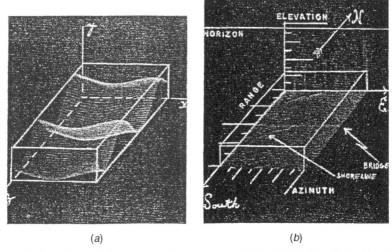

(a)   (b)

Figure 1.10 Electronically generated images reported by Carl Berkley in 1948. Illustration (a) shows a perspective view of a waveform depicted on a flat screen display. In (b) a simulated radar pattern is illustrated. Here a terrain map is generated above which airborne objects may be represented. (Reproduced by permission from Berkley [1948] © 1948 IEEE.)

These include Carl Berkley [1948], who investigated the depiction of functions with up to three variables on a standard flat screen display (see, for example, Figure 1.10). In this paper, Berkley discusses the potential application of displays of this type in areas such as the visualization of aircraft radar data (aircraft depicted over an electronically generated terrain map), the visualization of mathematical functions, meteorology, and so on.

1.2.4 Raster and Vector Graphics

One key advance in the implementation of computer display systems was the transition that occurred in the 1970s from vector to bitmap (and subsequently pixmap) graphics.[20] This involved creating a display screen in the form of a 2-D array of picture elements (pixels) and associating to each a unique memory location. Thus, in the case of the bitmapped display, each pixel can be individually addressed and so illuminated—or otherwise. This contrasts with the vector graphics technique in which image components are represented as a series of lines or polylines. Since several approaches to the implementation of volumetric systems employ a

---

[20] Although the term "bitmap" is commonly used in this context, this strictly applies to systems in which each pixel is represented by one bit (and is therefore illuminated or otherwise). In the case where each pixel has associated with it a number of bits (defining gray scale, color, etc.), then it is more accurate to use the term "pixmap" [Foley et al. 1997]. In this book, we generally adopt this approach.

dot graphics technique for image generation (this being a special case of the vector display method), it is instructive to briefly consider aspects of the vector and bitmapped display.

1. *The Vector Technique:* As indicated above, in the case of a vector display an image comprises a series of lines or polylines. In fact, the image screen is not exhaustively scanned and due to timing constraints, a large portion of the screen will normally be void. A simplified outline of elements used within the relevant part of the graphics pipeline is given in Figure 1.11. Central to this approach are the display list and display list controller. The former takes the form of random access memory in which the starting coordinates (and other attributes) of the line segments comprising each polyline within a frame

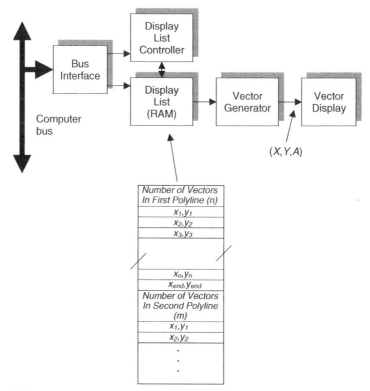

Figure 1.11 Functional elements of the vector graphics paradigm. Here, the display list provides the starting coordinates of each vector, end coordinates can clearly be deduced. However, this is not the case for the last vector within each polyline. We therefore assume an additional final entry for each polyline (x_{end}, y_{end}) which indicates the end coordinates of the last vector to be drawn within the polyline. Computed deflection coordinates (and additional information such as vector color) are passed to the display. Various additional processing may be performed—in order to, for example, remove the bright spots that form when two vectors cross. (Diagram © Q. S. Blundell 2006.)

are stored. The vector generator is responsible for rapidly reading this data and forming the deflection signals (and associated attribute information (A) such as vector intensity) that will be passed to the display. The electron beam within the CRT-based display responds to these signals by drawing each line segment, and hence the visible image is constructed. The total number of vectors that may be drawn during each image update period (as determined by the frame rate) provides an indication of the system's performance. However, this value is influenced by the average length and spatial distribution of vectors which comprise an image, together with the order in which the vectors are drawn on the display. Consider a simple numerical example in which we assume that the display and drive circuitry are able to achieve the full-scale deflection of the electron beam in 5 μs. Then for a display screen with typical dimensions, we can assume a rate of deflection on the order of 140 ns·cm^{-1}. For a frame update rate of 30 Hz, the total distance that a beam can travel per frame is approximately 2 km. However, because this distance includes the time spent in moving the beam between polylines, not all of this time is devoted to the production of light. In comparison, in the case of a raster-scanned CRT-based display of approximately the same size (we assume a horizontal dimension of approximately 35 cm) offering 800 scan lines per frame, the beam would move a total distance of approximately 560 m per image update.[21] Clearly, from these rough figures, it would appear that the vector display should, at least in principle, be able to fill an entire display screen. However, for a given image data set, the order in which the vectors are drawn will determine the total distance moved by the electron beam(s), and this in turn will impact on the total time that the beam spends in moving between polylines. To maximize the number of vectors per frame, it is desirable to minimize this total move time, but this is not without difficulty because as we briefly discuss in Section 4.4.2 (in the context of the volumetric dot graphics technique) the computational cost associated with the ordering process grows rapidly with the extent of the input data set (i.e., the number of polylines that comprise a frame).[22] Thus, in the case of a vector display, a considerable amount of the time available during each image update period is generally occupied with moving between lines and polylines and is consequently wasted.[23] Furthermore, the above does not include time penalties that can arise when drawing a polyline. Here, in order to avoid

[21] Including the retrace between lines.

[22] Also see Blundell and Schwarz [2000] and Schwarz and Blundell [1997].

[23] Furthermore, a vector display able to support the deflection speed indicated here would necessitate the use of electron guns able to support post deflection acceleration and deflection magnification (see Section 12.3). Such displays are expensive and since a shadow mask is not employed, full color image depiction is problematic. Typically, such displays are able to provide two-color image depiction by means of a phosphor penetration technique (see, for example, Boff et al. [1986]). On the other hand, the absence of a shadow mask ensures very high efficiency (in terms of the production of visible light).

visible overshoot, it may be necessary to pause between the outputting of connected vectors that have significantly different orientations.

The essential weakness of the vector graphics approach relates to the random order in which individual lines and polylines are created on the display screen. This results in significant time wastage because voltages are continually established on the deflection plates in order to move from one part of the screen to another. Thus a major difference between the vector and raster approaches relates to the form of the deflection signals. In the case of the former, deflection signals are determined by the image content and the order of vector creation. However, for a raster approach, deflection signals are repetitive and independent of image content.

The vector graphics technique is well-suited to the depiction of wire frame images, but becomes less efficient when "solid" images are to be displayed. This is because solid area fills are achieved through the use of multiple closely spaced vectors that are oriented parallel to one another. These may not be drawn in sequence and consequently may have significant "move time" overheads.

Further useful reading in connection with the vector graphics approach may be found in most of the older computer graphics texts; those by Salmon and Slater [1987] and Demel and Miller [1984] provide useful starting points.

2. *The Bitmap/Pixmap Technique:* The development of this highly ordered method of display implementation (in which all pixels can be addressed during each image update period) was reliant on advances in random access memory technologies—particularly in terms of price, performance, and storage density. In the 1970s, workers at Xerox Palo Alto Research Center (PARC) pioneered this important development and produced a display paradigm in which all pixels forming the display could be addressed during each image update period via a raster-scanning technique. Furthermore, as we will briefly discuss in the next subsection, they also pioneered the event-driven graphical user interface, which is a vital part of the modern personal computer.

Pivotal to the pixmap display technique is the ability to update each and every image element (pixel) within a fixed image update period. Consider a raster-scanning technique (in which interlacing is not employed) where the display is able to depict x pixels horizontally and y pixels vertically. Then the time to address all the pixels comprising a line (t_{line}) is given by

$$t_{\text{line}} = x \cdot t_p + T_h,$$

where t_p denotes the time needed to address and activate each pixel and T_h denotes the flyback time for the horizontal retrace (which may include other timing components). The time to draw a complete frame (t_{frame}) is therefore

$$t_{\text{frame}} = y \cdot t_{\text{line}} + T_v = y(x.t_p + T_h) + T_v,$$

where T_v is the flyback time for the vertical retrace (this is assumed to encompass any additional time components). Thus, assuming a refresh frequency of R frames per second, it follows that

$$t_p = \frac{1}{Rxy} - \frac{T_v}{xy} - \frac{T_h}{x}.$$

It is convenient to define a "pixel frequency" ($f_p = 1/t_p$) that can be used to indicate the performance of display hardware needed to support a particular display resolution [Salmon and Slater, 1987]. Thus,

$$f_p = \frac{Rxy}{1 - T_v R - T_h R y}, \tag{1.2}$$

For example, if we assume a noninterlaced monitor able to display 1000×800 pixels per frame with a 50-Hz refresh frequency and for which $T_h = 4$ µs and $Tv = 20$ µs, then we obtain a pixel frequency of approximately 50 MHz. Interlacing makes it possible to increase the time available for addressing all screen pixels (without introducing image flicker problems) and so reduces the demands placed upon the display hardware in terms of bandwidth.[24]

1.3   WORKING WITHIN A 2-D SPACE

> *"If a picture's worth a thousand words,*
> *a sculpture's worth a million."*[25]

The flat screen computer display (based on either CRT or thin panel technologies) has gained widespread acceptance, providing the window through which we view and interact with the digital world. In Figure 1.12, we illustrate some of the key characteristics associated with the traditional flat screen display, which have enabled it to be usefully employed across a very wide spectrum of computer-based applications. Below, we summarize several issues of particular relevance to our subsequent discussions in relation to volumetric systems (for more detailed discussion, see Blundell and Schwarz [2006]).

1. *Traditional Considerations:* Interaction with some form of 2-D medium is pivotal to many forms of human creativity (such as drawing, painting, engineering design, and geometry). Consequently, the flat screen computer display

---

[24] The only additional overhead incurred relates to the introduction of one or more additional vertical flyback intervals.

[25] Attributed to Bernardo Torres. Quoted from Hesselink and Downing [1993].

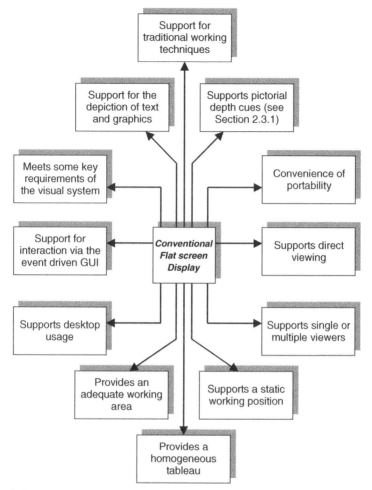

Figure 1.12 Various characteristics associated with the traditional flat screen computer display paradigm. The ability of this general display technique to satisfy (to a greater or lesser extent) these features have favored its usage across a broad spectrum of applications. However, as discussed in the text, the increasing complexity of many applications coupled with increased user expectations are resulting in the need to significantly advance this display paradigm. (Diagram © Q. S. Blundell 2006.)

augments our endeavors by providing a natural and convenient extension to traditional tableaux, such as paper or canvas. The techniques needed to depict 3-D scenes, objects, and structures within the confines of a 2-D space took many years to evolve, and several of the techniques that are used in 3-D computer graphics can be traced back to pioneers such as Giotto di Bondone (~1267–1337), Filippo Brunelleschi (1377–1446), and Leon Battista Alberti (1404–1472). The work of such individuals enabled great artists to employ a

2-D media in such a way as to not only be able to create photorealistic images but to ultimately transcend the bounds of photorealism and be restricted only by the limitations of human imagination. This history is briefly discussed by Blundell and Schwarz [2006], and more detailed discussion may be found in texts such as those by Edgerton [1976, 1991] and Kemp [1978].

Consider a mechanical engineering design process. Here, the creation of realistic 3-D images of objects and/or structures on a *conventional* 2-D screen is generally only of limited use. Although they may serve to provide an important insight into the aesthetic form of an object, they do so from only one viewing position[26] and do not readily lend themselves to the incorporation of measurements and general production detail. Most importantly, as we will discuss in the next subsection, interaction with such images cannot be achieved in a natural manner.

Gaspard Monge (1746–1818) is credited with the development of modern engineering drawing techniques by which objects are depicted by means of 2-D orthogonal views. His ideas for the use of a double orthographic projection technique whereby objects and/or structures are represented by means of plan and elevation views were expounded in a textbook that he wrote in support of his teaching [Géometrie Descriptive, 1989] (see Carl Boyer [1991] for further discussion).

The techniques that permit a 2-D medium to be used in support of the portrayal of 3-D imagery have in fact been in place for many years; the development of an active (electronic) 2-D medium was simply a natural extension of the traditional passive surfaces upon which humans have expressed their creative ideas throughout the centuries.

During the 1980s and early 1990s, computer technologies (in the form of the personal computer) rapidly proliferated and impacted, to a greater or lesser extent, on practically every form of human endeavor. Working practices had to be adapted to enable the use of these digital tools, and even those with many years of experience in the use of traditional methods had to learn new ways of working. However, we are often reluctant to change those ways that have served us well over the years and move away from the security of a working environment within which we are empowered by our own knowledge (often based on years of experience). Consequently, in many areas, traditional techniques for performing tasks were ported to the computer, thereby enabling first-generation computer users to maximize the use made of their knowledge and experience and at the same time minimize the scale of the adoption process. At that time, users often encountered computers later in life, and so they were initially far more confident in the use of traditional media. This situation has now greatly changed; in many countries, children from the earliest age are simultaneously exposed to the use of both digital

---

[26] As discussed in Section 3.4, the display may be augmented by a head-tracking system, thereby enabling support for motion parallax. However, in the main the object or structure is repositioned using interaction tools such as the mouse. Consequently, in general we cannot simply move our head from side to side or up and down and so change the viewpoint.

and traditional media. However, we are left with a legacy in which many of the approaches used in the depiction of computer processed information (and for its manipulation) are nonoptimal. Clearly, for example, the traditional engineering drawing techniques described by Gaspard Monge at the time of the French Revolution are unlikely to represent the optimal framework through which we can exploit the power of digital technologies for creative design activities!

2. *The Homogeneous Tableau:* This is a facet of the conventional flat screen display that is often taken for granted and, in the case of volumetric displays, it is particularly problematic. We expect the computer screen to provide a uniform tableau such that when an object is moved from one screen location to another, the number and spatial distribution of pixels that comprise the object will remain essentially unchanged. Furthermore, we take it for granted that when an object is repositioned on the screen, its color or intensity will not, as a result of display hardware deficiencies, be arbitrarily altered in some way. The regularity of pixel spacing and the invariance of pixel attributes underpin screen homogeneity. In the case of the conventional flat screen, computer display pixels are regularly spaced and are of the same size, and the attributes that may be applied to each (color and intensity) do not vary with the physical location of the pixels on the screen. However, when we attempt to extend the 2-D display screen to provide a 3-D tableau for image depiction (as is the case with volumetric systems), architectures seldom properly support isotropy and homogeneity. As will be seen in later sections, this is a major problem associated with many types of volumetric display and is a consideration that is often given insufficient attention during the design and implementation phases.

3. *Support for Graphics and Text:* Although vector graphics displays were able to support the coexistence of graphics and text, they were expensive and were therefore not generally available to average computer users. However, with the advent of the bitmapped display, the human–computer interface was greatly advanced and we now take for granted the benefits derived from the ability to bring together pictorial and written forms of communication. Nonetheless, text is inherently two-dimensional, and this poses problems when we consider its depiction within a volume (image space) that does not significantly restrict viewing position. A range of alternative display paradigms have, for many years, been the subject of considerable research activity, and a large number of approaches have been proposed and prototyped (although the number that have actually been commercialized is quite small). These systems can support additional depth cues—particularly binocular parallax (stereopsis) (see Section 2.3.4). In line with previous work (see Blundell and Schwarz [2006]), we will refer to these as "creative" 3-D display systems and attribute to them one or more of the characteristics indicated in Figure 1.13.

From this illustration it is apparent that in the case of creative 3-D display systems, uncertainty generally exists as to the benefits that may be

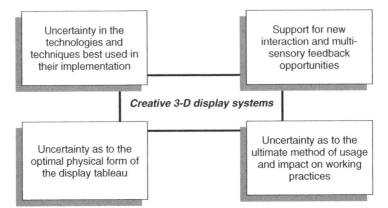

Figure 1.13   Creative 3-D display systems will be defined as having the ability to satisfy the binocular parallax (and possibly motion parallax) depth cues and exhibit some of the characteristics indicated here. (Adapted from Blundell and Schwarz [2006] © 2005 A. R. Blundell.)

derived from new approaches and their ultimate potential for advancing the human–computer interaction process. Perhaps, given the length of time over which many of these techniques have been researched, this may appear to be surprising. However, it reflects that most of the research effort has been directed toward the technologies themselves and much less work has been undertaken in the application and evaluation of systems. Further, researchers have generally focused on the new visualization opportunities that displays may offer while overlooking the importance of the pivotal role that a computer display plays in the interaction process. We consider this further in the next subsection.

1.4   CONCERNING INTERACTION

As discussed previously, systems able to support a user's interaction with electronically generated images have been researched and used in various specialized applications for at least 60 years. These early systems were underpinned by analog computation, and to date the author has not located any detailed discussion of interactive graphics applications based upon digital computation prior to the work of Ivan Sutherland, who developed an interface system he called "Sketchpad" in the early 1960s.[27] He introduces this in the following way:

> *The Sketchpad system makes it possible for a man and a computer to converse rapidly through the medium of line drawings. Heretofore, most interaction between man and*

---

[27] However, it would be most surprising if during the 1950s, work had not been undertaken in this area in conjunction with digital systems. The author would be keen to hear from any reader who has knowledge of such work.

computer has been slowed down by the need to reduce all communications to written statements that can be typed; in the past we have been writing letters to rather than conferring with our computers. [Sutherland, 1963]

Sutherland goes on to illustrate the power of this approach by providing various examples of the way in which image primitives may be created though direct interaction techniques. For example:

> *If we point the light pen at the display system and press a button called "draw," the computer will construct a straight line segment which stretches like a rubber band from the initial to the present location of the pen . . . .*

In the mid-1960s, William English and co-workers undertook research that was to have a major impact on the way in which we now interact with the computer. Not only did they research the efficiency of various existing interaction tools (such as the light pen and joystick), but they also prototyped for use in their trials other devices, such as the mouse [English et al., 1967]. Constructed in a small wooden case,[28] this was somewhat different in appearance from the mouse that we use today.[29] In the early 1970s, the mouse was refined for use with the Alto. This computer was developed at Xerox PARC and was the precursor to the Xerox Star workstation. The Star was introduced in 1981 and represented the first commercially available workstation to offer a bitmapped display and the graphical user interface (GUI) that is the basis for today's human–computer interaction activities. (For further reading see, for example, Johnston et al. [1989], Smith and Alexander [1999], and Blundell and Schwarz [2006].)

- *The event-driven graphical user interface places the conventional flat screen display at the heart of all interaction activities and the ability of this display paradigm to support interaction activities in which bi-directional communication is closely coupled has augmented the usefulness of the 2-D display tableau.*

- *Pivotal to practically all human creative processes is the synergy existing between our sensory and motor systems. Consequently, the human–computer interface should facilitate and promote natural synergistic interaction. Furthermore, it should aim to take advantage of the richness of our human communication skills.*

---

[28] Measuring $2 \times 3 \times 4$ (inches), the mouse used two orthogonally mounted potentiometers (driven by wheels rather than a ball) to measure movement. The mouse was equipped with one selection button (switch). Position measurements were based on the analog signals derived via the potentiometers.

[29] For a brief review of the work carried out by English et al., together with others who have investigated models that may be used to gauge the efficiency of a range of interaction tools, see Blundell and Schwarz [2006].

The GUI paradigm developed at Xerox PARC during the 1970s provided the foundations for the modern interface; during the intervening years, advances have tended to represent refinements of the original approach rather than major new developments. On the other hand, computers are now employed across a far wider range of applications and software systems have become more complex. In turn, this has led to increasingly complex interfaces that are largely designed using the techniques pioneered more than 25 years ago. It is therefore not surprising that benefits originally derived from the event-driven GUI are gradually being eroded; despite the advances made in computer technologies during the intervening years, the user must adapt to the machine: unfortunately highly evolved human communication skills are of little value when interacting with the digital world. Quoting from a previous work [Blundell and Schwarz, 2006]:

> *... it is interesting to stand back for a moment and speculate on the number of hours per week that we now spend bound to our computers, attempting to convey our emotionally-driven thought processes via imprecise communication skills to machines that operate solely upon logic, and are utterly oblivious to the richness of human dialogue.*

This book focuses on display techniques that support the depiction of objects and structures within a 3-D space. The use of an imaging *volume* provides considerable opportunities for not only the visualization of computer-processed imagery, but also for the development of new interaction paradigms. In order to most readily appreciate the possible benefits that may be derived from such technologies, it is instructive to briefly consider potential weaknesses of the conventional GUI when employed in, for example, 3-D design applications where it is necessary to visualize and manipulate objects that are inherently 3-D or which are separated in a 3-D space.

Some of the factors that have eroded the usefulness of the conventional GUI within the context of creative 3-D design applications are summarized in Figure 1.14. Here, the area of the screen in which the user is able to interact with the image is referred to as the "workspace," and the remainder of the screen contains the menu system. The use of a flat screen display will at times make it necessary for a user to carry out interactive operations upon the orthogonal 2-D views, which, as discussed previously, have played a pivotal role in engineering for several hundred years. Alternatively, the user may be able to directly manipulate 3-D primitives rendered for depiction on the 2-D screen. In either case, the user is often unable to carry out even simple operations in a way that mimics real-world practices. Consequently, one must continually adapt to the software system and learn the techniques devised by the software designer to permit objects that are inherently 3-D to be manipulated within Flatlands.[30]

As software packages become more advanced, user interfaces become increasingly complex and contain an ever-greater number of options and features. The architect of an applications program must therefore continually devise the means

---

[30] For amusing discussion of life within an imaginary 2-D world, see Abbott [1884]. *Envisioning Information* [Tufte, 1990] provides much relevant and interesting discussion.

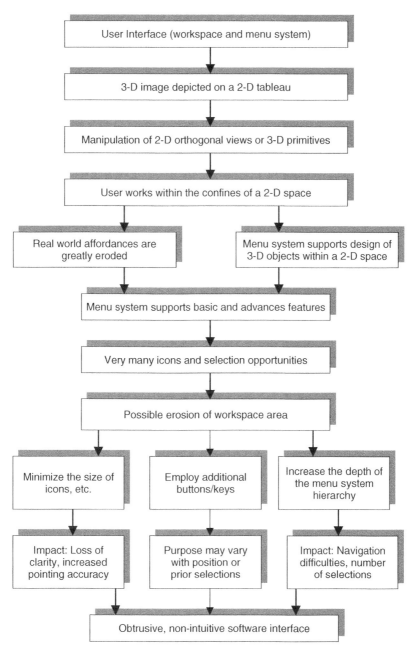

Figure 1.14   Issues relating to the implementation of a GUI for creative 3-D design applications. The area of screen in which the operator is able to manipulate the image is referred to as the 'workspace'. See text for discussion. (Diagram © A. R. Blundell 2006.)

of incorporating an ever-larger menu system, without increased erosion of the workspace. As indicated in Figure 1.14, the three most frequently used approaches (which are generally adopted in combination) involve either (a) a reduction in the size of each menu icon, (b) the adoption of more layers within a hierarchical menu system, or (c) the use of additional mouse (or other) buttons (e.g., a selection operation followed by a 'right click'). However, each has associated problems:

1. *Reduced Icon Size:* As icons become smaller, it is increasingly difficult to insert legible text labels within them; thus, in order to indicate functionality, pictorial symbols (whose meaning is often obscure and/or ambiguous) are frequently used. Furthermore, reducing the size of icons necessitates greater accuracy in cursor positioning prior to a selection operation.

2. *Increasing Hierarchical Depth:* Increasing the depth of the menu hierarchy can cause the user to experience problems in terms of navigation through the various layers. This is exacerbated in the case of operations in which tasks often cannot be performed in a "natural" (real-world) manner—such as the manipulation of 3-D objects within a 2-D space.[31] Furthermore, this approach increases the number of selections that must be correctly made in order to accomplish a particular task.

3. *The Use of Additional Buttons:* This becomes problematic when button functionality varies with either cursor position or as a consequence of the previous operation; as with increasing the hierarchical depth of a menu system, this increases the user's conscious awareness of the interface's presence between the user and the task.

In summary, as software complexity increases it is very difficult for the designer to produce an interface that remains unobtrusive to the end user and does not impact negatively on the creative tasks that the user is performing. Various forms of creative 3-D display offer to ameliorate this problem by:

1. Supporting the depiction of 3-D objects and structures within a volume, thereby enabling tasks that are inherently 3-D to be carried out in a manner that more closely mimics real-world activities.

2. Providing support for new interaction devices, techniques and software interfaces.

> Within this book we emphasize not only the importance of considering the visualization opportunities that may be offered by a display paradigm, but also the ways in which the display will augment the interaction processes

---

[31] The user is then left with the last resort; the "Help" facility. When battling with the interface, confidence is often gradually eroded, even to the extent of attempting to gain help from a dancing paperclip . . . .

1.5 IMAGE AND INTERACTION SPACES

> *I believe it is in our nature to explore*
> *... to reach out into the unknown.*
> *The only true failure would be not to explore at all.*[32]

It is useful to loosely distinguish between various forms of image space that may be produced by display systems. These can be divided into five general categories as described below[33]:

1. *The Planar Image Space:* In the case of the conventional flat screen computer display, images are depicted on a 2-D surface and although such images are able to convey depth information through the use of pictorial depth cues (see Section 2.3.1), the important binocular and motion parallax depth cues are absent.[34] Furthermore, the eyes converge and focus on the plane of the screen rather than on details of an image scene that we interpret (from the data provided by the pictorial cues) as lying at different distances. The "image space" (comprising the workspace and menu system) provided by displays of this type is represented by a 2-D surface whose dimensions are determined by those of the size of the screen. We do not assign to these systems an *imaging volume* within which images may be positioned.

2. *Physical 3-D Image Space:* As discussed in Section 1.6, volumetric display systems employ a physical material or arrangement of materials which occupy a physical volume and within which image components may be depicted. Consequently, an image is able to occupy three spatial dimensions, and as such the depth cues of binocular and motion parallax (see Sections 2.3.3 and 2.3.4) are satisfied. Furthermore, since image components may be physically positioned at different distances from an observer, both convergence and accommodation occur in a natural manner. Thus the physical and perceived images are (at least in principle) spatially similar. For the purposes of this book, we assume that a physical image space is bounded (by, for example, a containing vessel) and so a physical interaction tool cannot penetrate and pass through this type of image volume.

3. *Free Image Space:* In Section 9.3.2 we briefly describe a volumetric display that employs an image space comprising dust particles which are able to scatter incident light. By measuring the instantaneous location of these particles and directing the voxel activation mechanisms appropriately, it is possible to create images within an *unbounded* volume. Since the 3-D image

---

[32] Sir Ernest Shackleton (1874–1922).

[33] *Note*: These differ from those previously employed in Blundell and Schwarz [2006] and are intended to more closely support our discussion of volumetric and varifocal systems.

[34] However, as we will see in Section 3.4, it is possible to equip systems that employ the conventional flat screen display with additional hardware so that both binocular and motion parallax are conveyed to the user.

space has no physical boundary, an interaction tool may pass through the volume occupied by the image opening up interesting interaction opportunities. Alternatively, by means of an appropriate optical arrangement, it is possible to project an image (located, for example, within a physical image space) so that it appears in free space and is positioned between the projection apparatus and the observer. For the purposes of this book, we will consider both of these scenarios as giving rise to a "free" image space. This matter is discussed further in Sections 11.6.1 and 11.6.2, where we refer to Michael Halle's "Projection Constraint," and for the moment it is sufficient to note that such images may satisfy the binocular and motion parallax cues and also the cues of accommodation and convergence. Additionally, physical objects may (in principle) "touch" the image.[35] A free image space may also be formed using holographic techniques.

4. *Virtual Image Space:* As indicated in category 3 above, we assume that when a free image space is formed by means of an optical projection system, the image space resides between the observer and the optical component into which the observer looks. However, an optical system may also be used to project an image that appears to lie *behind* the optical component. Generally, varifocal mirrors systems (see Section 1.6.3 and Chapter 10) have been used to create images of this type; for the purposes of this book, we will refer to such images as being located within a virtual image space. In the case that a transparent component is used to produce such images,[36] it is possible to achieve no-parallax between a physical interaction tool and image components. Advantageously, and unlike the free space image technique, the presence of the interaction tool cannot impact on image formation.

5. *Apparent Image Space:* In the case of stereoscopic display techniques, although the image is usually generated on a 2-D surface, it is *perceived* as occupying a 3-D volume. Consequently, in the case of systems whose operation is based on the principle of the stereoscope, the physical image and the perceived image are spatially disparate[37] and the sense of an image's three-dimensionality is derived from the binocular information presented to the human visual system, rather than from the reality. Displays of this type are able to satisfy the binocular parallax (and possibly motion parallax) cues. However, accommodation and convergence cues are decoupled (see Section 2.3.2). In this book, we will define the depth of such an image

---

[35] However, the introduction of physical objects into such an image space may have a negative impact on image formation (see Blundell and Schwarz [2006]).

[36] For example, images reflected in an angled sheet of glass—the classic Pepper's Ghost illusion; see Sections 9.6 and 11.6 and also Blundell and Schwarz [2006].

[37] The image may appear to lie above or beneath the surface upon which the stereoscopic images are presented or may span both sides of this surface.

space as that perceived by the human visual system as a consequence of the satisfaction of the binocular parallax depth cue.[38]

In categorizing image spaces in this way, we are able to gain a useful insight into the characteristics of the images formed by means of various display paradigms. However, this represents only one approach: A variety of other schemes are equally valid. Furthermore, it is important to remember that all display technologies provide (to a greater or lesser extent) the "illusion" of three dimensionality. For example, displays based on the stereoscopic approach employ images depicted on 2-D surfaces from which the visual system derives a sense of 3-D *relief*. Equally, although a volumetric image is depicted in a physical image space, all visible points (voxels)[39] that comprise an image are generally not simultaneously illuminated, and in fact each of these points may emit light for only brief (but regular) intervals. However, as a consequence of the temporal response characteristics of the visual system (see Section 2.4), this transient light output may not be detected in the illusion that we experience.

As well as defining the extent of the image space, it is also instructive to refer to an interaction space. Many interaction tools operate within the confines of a certain physical region—although the concept of an interaction space is not universally applicable. For example, a joystick may operate by movement, in which case the interaction space is defined by the extent of motion, or alternatively the device may sense and respond to the pressure applied by the user. In this latter case, it is not possible to define an interaction space. In the case of interaction tools such as the joystick (when this is used in "absolute" mode), the interaction space may be directly mapped into the image space via a simple scaling factor. Thus, the total displacement ($\mathbf{D}$) of a cursor on a conventional flat screen from a central rest position would be given by

$$|\mathbf{D}| = \sqrt{(a\mathbf{x})^2 + (b\mathbf{y})^2}, \qquad (1.3)$$

where x and y represent the horizontal and vertical components of the joystick movement, and a and b are the horizontal and vertical scaling factors. Alternatively, the joystick may be used in "rate" mode whereby the speed of cursor motion is determined by the magnitude of the joystick deflection (e.g., the cursor velocity (v), is given by $v = kx$ and so the displacement of the cursor in the horizontal direction is $D = kxt$, where t denotes the duration for which the joystick is held at position x).

---

[38] Although such systems satisfy binocular parallax (and also possibly motion parallax), the accommodation and convergence combination is not correctly satisfied (see Section 2.3.2).

[39] "*A voxel (volume element) is the 3-D equivalent of a pixel (picture element) and forms the fundamental 'particle' from which volumetric images are constructed. A voxel should take the form of a sharply defined source of visible radiation, and ideally is spherical in shape. Furthermore, voxel attributes... should be invariant with respect to viewing direction*" [Blundell and Schwarz, 2000]. For discussion on the voxel and relating to volumetric data sets, see, for example, Blundell and Schwarz [2000, 2006].

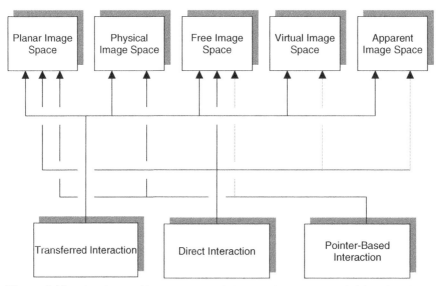

Figure 1.15 Five forms of image space and the three interaction modalities identified in the text. Connecting lines indicate the interaction opportunities that are *typically* available for each form of image space. (Diagram © Q. S. Blundell 2006.)

The mouse provides a further example of an interaction tool for which there is no defined mapping between the image and interaction spaces. In fact, although the mouse itself imposes no restriction on the size of the interaction space, we find it convenient to greatly confine the extent of its interaction space.[40]

The five forms of image space referred to above are summarized in Figure 1.15, together with three general interaction paradigms. These were previously introduced in Blundell and Schwarz [2006] and are briefly reviewed below:

1. *Direct Interaction:* In the case of this interaction modality, a physical interaction tool (and this may include the hand) is able to enter the image space and so directly "contact" the image.[41] This approach brings together the image and interaction spaces. In the case where a physical 3-D image space is employed, then either the material comprising the image space, the motion of components sweeping out the image space, or the bounding vessel will prevent the insertion of a physical interaction tool, and so this interaction modality is precluded from such an image space.

[40] Usually we employ a scrolling action (whereby the mouse is frequently lifted and repositioned) in order to achieve the desired cursor motion without the need for extensive lateral reposition of the wrist (which generally rests on the table).

[41] In the case of the planar image space associated with the conventional flat screen display, this interaction technique may be implemented using, for example, a light pen able to "touch" the screen.

Difficulties may arise if this interaction modality is employed in conjunction with display systems based on the stereoscopic technique (the "apparent image space" scenario). As previously indicated when viewing stereoscopic images, the accommodation and convergence cues become decoupled with the eyes focusing on the 2-D image plane and converging on features of regard within the perceived 3-D image (see also Section 2.3.2). However, if a physical interaction tool is inserted into the image space[42] then when this is viewed, the eyes will correctly focus and converge upon it. Constantly switching between the view of the image scene and that of the pointer may exacerbate depth cue conflict. Furthermore, the presence of the tool may interfere with image formation. In a previous work [Blundell and Schwarz, 2006], essential conditions for the use of the direct interaction technique are identified.

Through the use of a physical interaction tool able to support haptic feedback, image components may appear to have substance.

2. *Transferred Interaction:* Here, the interaction and image spaces are separated and the mapping from one to the other is achieved by means of some form of computer-generated cursor. Thus, moving the interaction tool gives rise to a corresponding (and hopefully intuitive) movement of the cursor. In principle, this interaction modality may be used with all five of the forms of image space summarized in Figure 1.15.

3. *Pointer-Based Interaction:* In this case, an interaction tool is used to project a visible collimated beam (generated by, for example, a laser diode) into an image space, and this may be used to provide a visual cue as to the orientation of the pointer with respect to the image space. Additionally, the location and orientation of the beam as it projects through the image space may be sensed by the host computer and used to support more advanced interaction opportunities. This interaction technique is most suitable for use with some of the forms of display that produce a physical 3-D image space. For example, the use of conventional laser pointers may be particularly helpful when a number of people are viewing and discussing an image scene created by a swept-volume volumetric display (see Chapter 4). In this case, laser beams can be readily seen as they impinge on the moving screen, and therefore image features that are of interest can be readily indicated (also see Section 11.6).

1.6 INTRODUCING VOLUMETRIC AND VARIFOCAL TECHNIQUES

In this section, we turn our attention to some of the basic characteristics of volumetric and varifocal display systems. We begin by discussing the volumetric approach, and here we largely confine our comments to issues that are of a general nature

---

[42] Assuming that this is possible, as a consequence of the image space being located in front of, rather than behind, the stereoscopic window.

and independent of the underlying architecture used in the implementation of the display. In Section 1.6.3, we briefly describe the varifocal technique and introduce the basic principle of operation of this display paradigm.

1.6.1   The Volumetric Technique

> *Men wanted for hazardous journey.*
> *Small wages, bitter cold,*
> *long months of complete darkness,*
> *constant danger, safe return doubtful.*[43]

Common to all volumetric systems is a transparent physical volume ("image space") within which visible images may be created. Since these images are depicted *within* a volume, they are able to occupy three physical dimensions and therefore satisfy a number of pictorial, oculomotor, and parallax depth cues (see Section 2.3). A definition of the volumetric approach was provided in a previous work. This reads as follows:

> *A volumetric display device permits the generation, absorption, or scattering of visible radiation from a set of localized and specified regions within a physical volume.* [Blundell and Schwarz, 2000]

In the next subsection we present an alternative definition that focuses on the nature of the image rather than on the image creation process. Practically all volumetric architectures proposed to date have produced images that emit light. However, this is not an inherent feature of the volumetric approach; also, as indicated in the above definition, the possibility exists for the creation of volumetric architectures that give rise to images that are made visible by means of external illumination (see, for example, Section 5.7). In such a case, removal of the external light source would render the image invisible.

The volumetric display's image space may be likened to a fish tank or spherical goldfish bowl. The fish, weeds, and other objects within the water are equivalent to the image components created in the image space under computer control, and the observer has considerable freedom to view the scene from different orientations (see Figure 1.16). In fact, many volumetric embodiments impose little restriction on viewing freedom, and so one or more observers may simultaneously view the image scene from different directions. However, most volumetric images are translucent and lack the "solidity" of the aquatic scene. This can impact on the suitability of such display systems for particular applications.[44]

---

[43] Newspaper recruitment advertisement said to have been placed by Sir Ernest Shackleton in 1914 prior to his ill-fated Antarctic expedition.

[44] For general discussion on volumetric systems, see, for example, Blundell [1998] and Blundell and Schwarz [2002].

Figure 1.16   When explaining the nature of a volumetric image space, an analogy to a gold fish within a bowl or fish tank is often useful. This photograph shows fish "swimming" within such an image space using the cathode ray sphere (CRS) volumetric display. Unfortunately, as discussed in the text photographing such images by conventional means results in a loss of clarity—the nonpictorial depth cues are lost (and the 3-D image is compressed onto a 2-D surface). Here, this difficulty is exacerbated by noncolor reproduction. Central in the image are two fish, and lower down are weeds. (Original image copyright © B. G. Blundell 2006.)

The majority of volumetric architectures give rise to translucent images in which the depth cue of opacity depth is absent. In such cases, one part of an image cannot occlude another part located at a greater distance from the observer. Furthermore, because of the practically unrestricted range of viewing positions associated with many volumetric architectures, computer graphics techniques cannot be readily used for hidden line removal (a part of an image component that should be occluded from one viewing position may not be occluded when the image is viewed from a second position). In practice, when volumetric images are viewed directly, the depth cues of accommodation and convergence ameliorate difficulties that may be caused by the lack of image opacity.

The depth cues of accommodation and convergence[45] permit the visual system to direct its greatest attention on object(s) lying at a certain distance from the eyes, with less attention being given to objects that are in closer or more distant proximity.

---

[45] Accommodation refers to the focusing of the eyes on an object of interest, and convergence relates to the location at which the visual axes of the two eyes are made to meet. Thus, when we examine a pen held vertically at arm's length, our eyes focus on the pen and the visual axes converge upon it. Other objects positioned at lesser or greater distances are then less distinct. See Section 2.3.2 for further discussion.

However, although when images are viewed directly these cues ameliorate the lack of image opacity, they are not available when volumetric images are photographed by conventional means.

> When volumetric images are photographed by conventional means, all non-pictorial depth cues are lost. These include accommodation, convergence, and binocular parallax. In the case of translucent images, this is particularly problematic: The entire image scene is compressed onto a 2-D plane and essential strengths of the volumetric approach are no longer conveyed to the viewer.

In Figure 1.17 a photograph of a volumetric image is presented which illustrates the loss of clarity that occurs when even a simple image is photographed conventionally. In Figure 1.18, we provide a stereoscopic photograph of a stick figure depicted on the cathode ray sphere (CRS) (see Sections 4.6, 7.2.1, and 12.3). When either of the two photographs comprising the stereopair are viewed independently, only pictorial depth cues are present and there is a loss of three-dimensionality. However, when this pair of images is viewed correctly, the binocular parallax cue provides a clear sense of *relief,* enabling the viewer to gain a better insight into the volumetric approach.[46] Conventional photographs that depict only the volumetric image (and do not include additional background information) are of little value (see Figures 1.16 and 1.19). However, in the case of simple volumetric images, clarity is enhanced through the inclusion of additional context information (such as a view of the location of the image within the confines of the image space—that is, when the image and the containing vessel can both be seen). Such an image is depicted in Figure 1.20.

In Table 1.1, various general strengths and weaknesses of the volumetric approach are summarized. The characteristics listed in this table should be considered as indicative; they are not equally applicable to all volumetric embodiments. Furthermore, some of the potential weaknesses arise not as a result of fundamental problems associated with the volumetric approach, but rather as a consequence of the considerable viewing freedom offered by many of these systems. Such weaknesses are indicated in bold typeface. In subsequent chapters we examine in greater detail a number of the characteristics summarized in Table 1.1 and place these in context by reviewing the characteristics of other approaches to the implementation of 3-D display system technologies.

1.6.2   The Essence of the Volumetric Paradigm

It is instructive to briefly review the definition of the volumetric approach presented at the beginning of Section 1.6.1. This emphasizes the image creation process

---

[46] However, the stereopair fails to support motion parallax (see Section 2.3.3).

Figure 1.17   A wire frame image of the satellites in orbit around the Earth [image depicted on the cathode ray sphere (CRS)]. When viewed directly, the image has great clarity and the form of the elliptical orbits can be clearly seen. The photograph captures only pictorial depth cues and the entire image is compressed onto a 2-D plane. Inherent spatial content is therefore lost. Generally, this problem is greatly exacerbated by the lack of image opacity. (Original image copyright © B. G. Blundell 2006.)

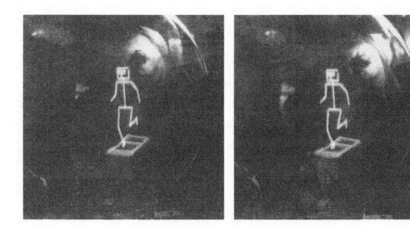

Figure 1.18   A stick figure able to run around a cylindrical image space in a natural manner. Despite being a very simple geometric image, the natural movement of the limbs that may be observed when the figure is viewed directly provides startling realism. The inherent three-dimensionality of the volumetric image may be perceived by fusing these images. Although with practice this may be done directly, it is more easily achieved by means of a pair of stereoglasses. The image is depicted on the cathode ray sphere (CRS) and was photographed using two conventional cameras, each viewing the image from a slightly different perspective. (Original image copyright © B. G. Blundell 2006.)

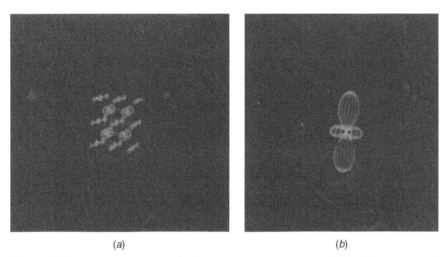

(a)   (b)

Figure 1.19   Volumetric images depicted on the CRS are shown in isolation. (a) Cubic atomic lattice. (b) S and P electron orbitals. When photographed, spatial content is lost as a result of the compression of the image onto a 2-D surface, and the lack of any backdrop (such as the containing vessel or surrounding room) further exacerbates the difficulty of image interpretation. This compares to the image depicted in Figure 1.20, where the visibility of the containing vessel improves image interpretation. (Original image copyright © B. G. Blundell 2006.)

rather than the interface between the display paradigm and the visual system. Consequently, although the previous definition of the volumetric technique remains valid, for the purposes of this book we prefer to use an alternative description:

> A volumetric display device enables visible images to be formed within a transparent physical volume. Light that emanates from this volume may be viewed directly by the human visual system and since a range of depth cue information can be naturally extracted from any image displayed in this way, there is, at least in principle, no disparity between the location and form of the physical and perceived images.

This focuses on our perception of the volumetric image and emphasizes that most depth cue information is supplied in a natural manner consistent with our visual perception of the real world. Furthermore, the lack of disparity between the physical and perceived images assists in distinguishing between the volumetric technique and other 3-D display techniques (see Sections 3.3–3.6). In reality, in the case of many volumetric display embodiments, the physical and perceived images are disparate. Generally, this is caused by the medium forming the image space (or by the vessel that contains the image space) and through which light propagates from the image to the observer(s). Clearly, variations in refractive index within the image

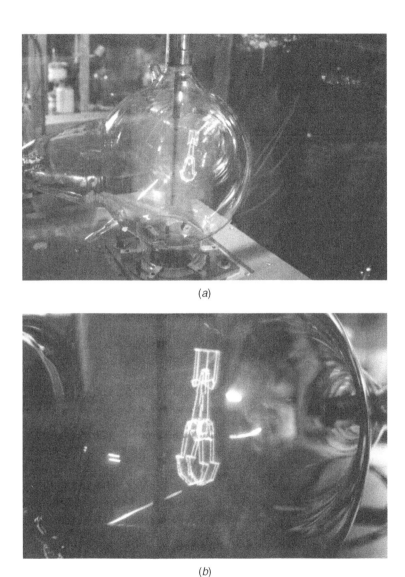

(a)

(b)

Figure 1.20 A simple animated wire frame image comprising a piston, connecting rod and crankshaft depicted on the cathode ray sphere (CRS). Image clarity is improved by the visibility of the containing vessel (cf. Figure 1.19). In the case of both (a) and (b), the photographic images look unremarkable. However, when viewed directly, the sight of these virtual mechanical components operating in unison and seeming to float within space takes on a magical quality. (Original images copyright © B. G. Blundell 2006.)

TABLE 1.1 A Brief Summary of Various Strengths and Weaknesses that May be Associated with the Volumetric Approach[a]

General Strengths of the Volumetric Technique	Potential Weakness of the Volumetric Technique
The majority of spatial information is presented to the human visual system in a natural manner.	**The depth of the image space may determine the distance over which perspective information may be naturally presented.**
Considerable viewing freedom.	Translucent images are generally produced.
Support for multiple viewers.	"God's eye" view—nonimmersive.
Support for both accommodation and convergence (these cues are not decoupled).	Optimal image space form and dimensions may vary with the nature of the intended application.
Low-cost display technology.	**Most suited to the depiction of images—the visibility of text is affected by viewing location.**
The observer(s) may readily perceive the spatial form and/or separation of objects lying within the image space.	**The clarity of spatial relationships may vary with viewing direction—necessitating image rotation or user mobility.**
New interaction opportunities.	Usually an observer cannot physically enter an image space.
Relatively low computational overheads.	An image space may exhibit anisotropic and non-homogeneous characteristics.

[a]Although some are inherent characteristics (such as the "God's eye" view), others are commonly associated with specific embodiments. A number of potential weaknesses arise or are exacerbated by the very wide viewing freedom that is supported (at least in principle) by many volumetric architectures. Thus, constraining viewing freedom may ameliorate these problems. Such weaknesses are indicated in bold typeface

space volume, or the change in refractive index at the image space boundary, will cause distortion/displacement of the perceived image. Furthermore, the degree of distortion may also vary with viewing angle. The designer must therefore consider not only the transparency of the image space but also its uniformity with respect to the propagation of light. This is discussed further in subsequent chapters.

1.6.3 The Varifocal Approach

As discussed in later chapters, a broad range of approaches may be adopted in the implementation of volumetric displays. Consequently, to simplify the introductory discussion on these systems, we have described concepts that are of a general nature, preferring to defer more detailed discussion until later chapters. However, in the case of varifocal systems, the general techniques that may be brought to bear in their implementation are more limited, and so it is appropriate to introduce this class of display by means of a general hardware description.

As we have seen, we have associated with the volumetric display a physical 3-D image space within which computer-processed data may be depicted. Furthermore, we have assumed that there is, no inherent disparity between the location and form of the physical and perceived images. In fact, in the case of most other forms of 3-D display technology, the physical and perceived images are disparate. Varifocal systems are no exception, because the physical image is cast onto a mirrored surface whose continually changing curvature determines the extent of a volume (image space) within which the perceived image resides or appears to reside.

The basic principle of operation of a varifocal display is illustrated in Figure 1.21. Here, a reflective (mirrored) coating is deposited on one side of a thin and flexible membrane. The periphery of the membrane is held within a rigid frame, and the membrane itself is continually flexed. As indicated in Figure 1.21, this may be achieved by "stretching" the membrane across the outer edge of a large loudspeaker. By applying an appropriate signal to the loudspeaker, the pressure difference across the membrane will cause it to continually change curvature, thereby producing a mirror of varying focal length. Appropriately computed slices of an image data set are depicted on a 2-D display screen and are projected onto the varifocal mirror. The user views their reflection.

As discussed in further detail in Chapter 10, an image space of useful dimensions can be produced by small (and readily achievable) deflections of the mirror.

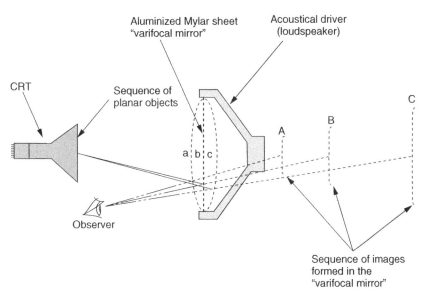

Figure 1.21 The basic principle of operation of a varifocal display. A flexible membrane with mirrored surface is attached to a large loudspeaker. Through the application of a suitable signal to the loudspeaker, the mirrored surface continually varies its curvature and forms a mirror with variable focal length. Image slices are depicted on a 2-D screen and reflected by the mirror. Consequently, a 3-D image is formed within a virtual image space. (Reproduced from Rawson [1969], with permission from IEEE.)

Unfortunately, as the mirror changes its focal length, the magnification that it provides also varies, and this impacts on the shape of the image space and causes "anomalous perspective" (see Section 10.5.2). However, this difficulty can be solved by scaling the image slices prior to their depiction. Unlike many volumetric approaches, the varifocal technique provides only a single window onto the displayed image. Consequently, as with volumetric techniques that significantly restrict viewing position, the varifocal approach is readily able to support the depiction of both text and graphics.[47] In Chapter 10, we discuss the operation of varifocal systems in greater detail and review some of the displays that have been developed over the years. This discussion includes a brief outline of a varifocal technique developed by Lawrence Sher in which the membrane mirror is replaced with a stiff resonant structure (see Section 10.5.3).

1.7 DISCUSSION

> *Why does this applied science,*
> *which saves work and makes life easier,*
> *bring us so little happiness?*
> *The simple answer runs;*
> *Because we have not yet learned to make sensible use of it.*[48]

In this chapter we have laid various foundations that will provide a basis for subsequent discussion. Our brief consideration of the history of television provides us with a useful reference by which we can begin to gauge the difficulties associated with the introduction of 3-D display technologies. Certainly, the technical problems that we may encounter in the implementation of these displays (and associated interaction tools) are more easily dealt with than are the difficulties in relation to taking a prototype display from the laboratory and turning it into a successful and widely used commercial product (see Blundell and Schwarz [2006] for related discussion).

In Section 1.2.2, we briefly discussed changes that have taken place in the interface between the display and the data acquisition/interaction systems. Here—for example, in the very early proposals for television—we encounter designs in which an image is converted into electrical signals by a 2-D array of elements. Each element is then directly connected to a corresponding element in the display apparatus. However, the impracticality of such an arrangement was soon recognized (in terms of the number of wires needed for the link between "camera" and display), and techniques that would support serial (rather than massively parallel) interconnects were proposed (see, for example, Figure 1.1). However, as components and devices were refined, it became possible to connect data acquisition hardware to the display via circuits able to perform analog computation, and this facilitated

---

[47] Although the inclusion of text may cause the image space to become cluttered.
[48] Attributed to Albert Einstein (1875–1955).

interaction opportunities (see, for example Figure 1.9).[49] During the course of the last 30–40 years, the development and proliferation of computer-based technologies has made it possible to interconnect data acquisition devices, display hardware, and interaction tools by means of digital systems that offer almost unlimited flexibility. No longer is it necessary to focus on the ways in which the display can be directly coupled to the data acquisition hardware; such issues can be dealt with within the digital domain. However, while this has made the designer's work much simpler, it has meant that data acquired from practically any source is processed in such a way as to enable its depiction on the conventional flat screen display. In certain applications, this is far from an optimal arrangement and can result in reduced visualization and interaction opportunities.

Finally, in this chapter we have provided an insight into the nature of volumetric and varifocal systems. These two display paradigms will be discussed in some depth in subsequent chapters.

1.8 INVESTIGATIONS

1. Discuss, within the context of image distortion, the impact of employing *solid* spherical, cylindrical, and cubic image spaces.

2. A volumetric image is confined within a physical image space. Discuss the impact that this may have on interaction opportunities.

3. Discuss the acoustic noise that may be associated with the varifocal technique.

4. Volumetric images are normally constructed using voxels (a voxel is the 3-D equivalent of the pixel employed by the conventional flat screen computer display). Why is a raster graphics approach often not adopted (i.e., the exhaustive scanning of an image space)?

5. Discuss the difficulties faced during the 1930s in relation to the development and introduction of television. In what ways do these parallel the problems faced by those attempting to develop and introduce creative 3-D display systems for computer-based applications?

---

[49] Prior to the early 1960s, the majority of patents describing volumetric displays also include designs for appropriate data capture hardware. However, in the case of more recent patents, researchers tend to focus on either data acquisition or data display—but not both. This reinforces the notion that with the introduction of computer hardware it has become possible to clearly separate the subsystems and leave the computer to deal with their union.

2 Aspects of the Visual System

And Vivien follow'd but he marked her not.
She took the helm and he the sail; the boat
Drave with a sudden wind across the deeps.
And touching the Breton sands, they disembark'd.

2.1 INTRODUCTION

In order to effectively design, develop, and apply creative 3-D display systems, it is vital for researchers to possess a well-founded knowledge of the technologies that may be brought to bear in their implementation. However, this knowledge in itself is insufficient and we must be equally aware of many aspects of the complex human visual system. Consequently, in this chapter we focus on some issues relating to our sense of sight. However, within the available space we can do little more than touch on this fascinating subject, so references to additional literature are provided throughout the chapter.

In Section 2.2 we briefly discuss the human eye, which, in itself, is a remarkable optical device and as a component within the visual system exhibits superlative performance. Here, we concern ourselves with some of its basic characteristics and provide a number of key references for further reading. From the perspective of the design and application of 3-D displays, it is vital to have an understanding of the basic mechanisms by which we interpret the form of 3-D imagery and by which we are able to accurately judge both the absolute and relative distances of objects comprising an image scene. Excellent texts such as Schiffman [1990] and Kandel et al. [2000] provide introductions to the Gestalt[1] Theory of visual perception and so provide an excellent starting point in understanding mechanisms by which we interpret the form of 3-D imagery. In Section 2.3 we consider a number of depth cues by means of which we are able to judge both absolute and relative distance. The cues that we discuss highlight aspects of the mechanisms by which we are able to interpret and so interact with a 3-D space.

Finally, in Section 2.4 we consider temporal aspects of the visual system. These impact on display design in terms of the minimum image refresh rate needed to avoid both conscious and subliminal flicker and the minimum image update rate needed to support the smooth depiction of dynamic image sequences.

2.2   SOME CHARACTERISTICS OF THE EYE

> *When Emperors, Kings, Pretenders, shadows all,*
> *Leave not a dust-trace on our whirling ball,*
> *Thy work, oh grave-eyed searcher, shall endure,*
> *Unmarred by faction, from low passion pure.*[2]

The eye is an extraordinary optical instrument, and in this context O'Shea [1985] writes:

> *All in all, the eye is a formidable optical system providing zoom focusing, adaptation to a wide range of light levels, central and peripheral imaging, and dual responses to provide both high-level and low-level detection—all in a one-inch diameter sphere! Any optical designer worth his or her salt would be proud to design a system like that. Of course, they wouldn't have the luxury of millions of years of field trials.*

Below, we briefly consider some facets of the eye:

1. *Spectral Response:* The human eye is responsive to electromagnetic radiation with wavelengths ranging from ~400 nm to ~700 nm. However, as illustrated by the spectral luminous efficiency curves depicted in Figure 2.1, its sensitivity varies with wavelength. As may be seen from this illustration, the eye's response has two distinctly different profiles: one corresponding to the operation of photoreceptors (known as cones) which operate most efficiently in daylight conditions, and the other corresponding to the operation

---

[1] Gestalt—from the German, which approximately translates to "shape" or "form".

[2] Published in *Punch* in 1894 and republished the same year in *Nature* following the death of Hermann von Helmholtz (1821–1894).

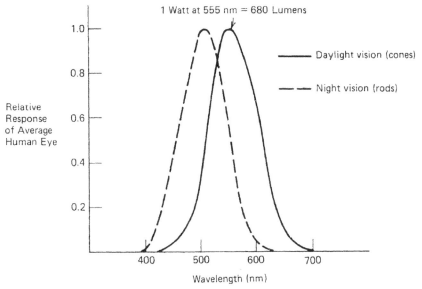

Figure 2.1 Spectral luminous efficiency curves for the photoreceptors in the human eye. The cones operate most efficiently in stronger lighting conditions whereas the rods are more sensitive and support our night vision. The rods and cones have peak wavelength sensitivities of approximately 500–510 nm and 555 nm respectively. The presence of three classes of cone (each of which has a different absorption spectrum) provides support for color vision. The rods and cones are equally sensitive to light with a wavelength of ∼650nm (red). However this is not indicated in this diagram, as both curves are depicted as normalized. (Reproduced by permission from O'Shea [1985] © 2006 John Wiley & Sons.)

of photoreceptors (rods) that exhibit greater sensitivity and are dominant under lower levels of illumination.[3] The former response profile is known as the "photopic curve" and the latter is called the "scotopic curve". The two peak sensitivities occur at ∼555 nm (yellow-green)[4] and ∼500–510 nm (blue-green), with the rods and cones being equally sensitive at ∼650 nm.[5]

---

[3] Under "normal" lighting conditions, both rods and cones contribute to the visual process.

[4] Color is not a property of light, but of the visual system.

[5] In radiometry, the radiative energy per unit time (radiation flux or power) is usually quoted in watts (1 W = 1 Joule/s). However, a source may have a high power output but, as a consequence of its wavelength, may be either invisible or only dimly perceived by the visual system. In the field of photometry, the detector is assumed to be the eye and photometric units (such as the Lumen) provide us with a measure of the output from a source as indicated by the response of the eye. Conversion between watts and lumens is readily achieved by means of the spectral luminous efficiency curves depicted in Figure 2.1. By definition, 1 watt of radiant energy at 555 nm equals 680 lumens. We can then use the spectral luminous efficiency curves to scale other wavelengths. For example, a 100-mW helium-neon laser emitting light at 633 nm has a photometric power output of $100 \times 10^{-3} \times 680 \times 0.25 = 17$ lumens (the value of 0.25 being obtained from the spectral luminous efficiency curves and corresponds to the wavelength emitted by the laser).

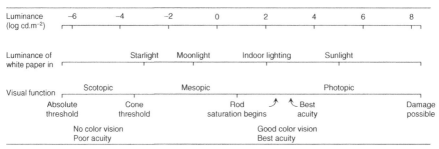

Figure 2.2   The eye can operate over a tremendous range of lighting conditions—as indicated by the logarithmic scale provided on the top row of this diagram. Below this, corresponding exemplar levels of luminance are provided. Here the illuminance of white paper under different conditions is used—at one extreme the paper reflects starlight and at the other extreme bright sunlight. Finally, the diagram indicates the role played by the rods and cones under these different conditions. At low levels of luminance, reliance is placed on the rods (scotopic viewing) and at high levels of luminance on the cones (photopic viewing). Between these extremes both rods and cones contribute to the visual process (mesopic vision). (Reproduced by permission from Boff et al [1986] © 2006 John Wiley & Sons.)

2. *Dynamic Range:* The human eye is able to operate over a wide range of lighting conditions (luminances[6]). For example, on a bright sunny day, the photon flux is $\sim10^{20}$ photons $m^{-2}s^{-1}$ whereas the photon flux provided at night by the stars[7] is $\sim10^{12}$ photons $m^{-2}s^{-1}$. Thus between these two extremes the photon flux differs by eight orders of magnitude and the eye is able to operate over this tremendous range (although within an image scene the differences in luminance are relatively small). In Figure 2.2 the range of luminances over which the eye is able to operate are indicated using a logarithmic scale.

The sensitivity of the human eye is indeed remarkable and in the 1940s, Hecht et al. [1942] undertook experiments to determine the smallest photon flux that could be detected by the eye (under optimal conditions). In this fascinating and informative publication, it is shown that a rod can be activated by a single incident photon. However, since the photoreceptors randomly fire even in the absence of a visual stimulus (giving rise to "retinal noise"—see, for example, Cameron et al. [1999]), this does not cause a visual event—for which a small number of rods must be stimulated.

3. *The Photoreceptor Array:* The conventional computer screen typically comprises an array of some 800,000 pixels distributed on a surface of, say, 1000 cm^2 (giving an approximate pixel density of $\sim$800 pixels cm^{-2}); by

---

[6] When referring to the amount of light energy incident on a surface, we use the term "illuminance". Alternatively, when considering the amount of light energy reflected by a surface, the term "luminance" is used.

[7] This does not represent the minimum threshold for vision. In fact, the visual system, when properly adapted, is able to operate down to $\sim10^{10}$ photons $m^{-2}s^{-1}$.

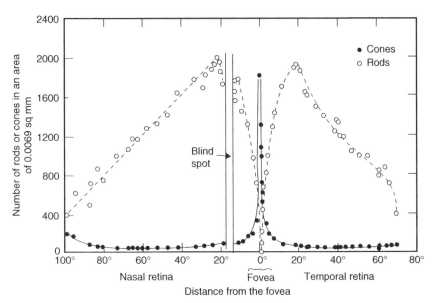

Figure 2.3 The distribution of rods and cones across the central horizontal plane of the retina. A very high density of cones occurs in the *fovea* (the central region of the retina which is able to support super-high-resolution imaging). (Reproduced with permission from Chapanis, A., Garner, W. R., and C. T., *Applied Experimental Psychology*, John Wiley [1949]; Copyright © 1949 John Wiley & Sons.)

means of this, images are presented to the human eye. Within the eye are some 126 million photoreceptors, which in the *fovea* (the central region of the retina onto which the region of regard is projected) reach a density of ~150,000 mm^{-2}! Thus the *fovea* is able to support super-high-resolution image acquisition; in this respect, its capabilities far surpass the image resolution provided by the typical flat screen display. The distribution of the rods and cones across the retina is indicated in Figure 2.3. As may be seen from this illustration, the fovea comprises a very high density of cones. In contrast, the density of rods gradually increases toward the fovea and then rapidly falls away. Various capabilities and characteristics of the eye are therefore determined by the location on the retina, onto which an image component is cast. In this context, writing more than 130 years ago, Helmholtz noted:

> So that the image which we receive by the eye is like a picture, minutely and elaborately finished in the centre, but only roughly sketched in at the borders. [Helmholtz, 1873][8]

However, in practice, this does not detract from our visual experience as the central region of fixation is automatically projected onto the fovea.

---

[8] See Warren and Warren (eds.) [1968]. Much of Helmholtz's discussion on perception retains its relevance and is highly recommended to the interested reader.

Measurements of the resolution capabilities of the eye are generally referred to as acuities. These are briefly summarized in Blundell and Schwarz [2006], and for our present purposes it is sufficient to mention one exemplar measure: detection acuity. This acuity considers the angle subtended at the eye by a single isolated object located normal to visual axis. Naturally, the object size and its distance from the eye determine this angle. Under somewhat idealized conditions, Hecht and Mintz [1939] measured this acuity and found that participants could perceive a single dark line (viewed against a well-illuminated background) when its thickness subtended a mere 0.5″ at the eye. Consequently, under appropriate conditions and for an *emmetropic* eye, it is possible to perceive a retinal image that is only 0.04 μm! Under less optimal conditions, a detection acuity of $\sim 1'$ may be assumed.[9]

In this section we have briefly touched upon various aspects of the human eye. Together with the references cited in the above text, the following publications are recommended to the interested reader: Lindsay and Norman [1972], Coren et al. [2004], and Schiffman [1990], together with numerous other psychology texts, provide informative and well-presented discussion on aspects of the human visual system (see also Dember and Warm [1979], which provides sound discussion on human visual perception and Osgood [1953]). Purves and Lotto [2003], Bruce et al. [2003], and Tovee [1996] provide excellent reading and many valuable references, and Banchoff [1996] discusses visualization issues associated with multidimensional geometry. Both Sherr [1998] and Biberman (ed.) [1973] discuss issues relating to the interface between the electronic display and the visual system. Land and Nilsson [2002] provide an insight into the diversity of eyes within the animal kingdom—and here, once reading begins, is a book that is difficult to put down! See also references cited in Blundell and Schwarz [2006] and Boff et al. [1986].[10]

2.3 DEPTH CUES

Our perception of the three-dimensionality of our surroundings is based on a variety of cues that are made available to the visual system. These cues to depth are usually subconsciously interpreted and provide us with an impression of both the absolute location of objects within a 3-D space and their relative positions. Detailed discussion on depth cues can be found in many texts, for example, Boff et al. [1986], Howard [2002], Howard and Rogers [2002]. Books such as those by Schiffman [1990] and Coren et al. [2004] provide excellent general coverage. In this section we provide a brief overview of key cues and emphasize issues that are especially important in the development of 3-D display systems.

Depth cues may be grouped in various ways, and for simplicity we will categorize them as "pictorial," "oculomotor," and "parallax" cues. In the subsections that follow, we consider cues in each of these categories.

---

[9] Corresponding to 0.3 mm at a distance of 1 m.

[10] The two volumes edited by Boff et al. are unfortunately out of print and becoming increasingly difficult to obtain. However, they remain definitive and indispensable works.

2.3.1 Pictorial Cues

As this title implies, these cues underpin traditional painting techniques and permit an accurate perspective (and even photorealistic) view on a 3-D scene to be created upon a 2-D surface. Naturally, such cues are monocular in the sense that in the case of, for example, the traditional painting or conventional flat screen display, the same image is presented to the two eyes. The pictorial cues are derived from information contained within the image that is cast onto the retina. For example:

(a) *Occlusion (Interposition):* Opaque objects within the visual scene may partially block our view of other, more distant objects. When viewing a scene, we continually anticipate the shape and visual content of objects and so if only a portion of an anticipated shape is present, we are likely to conclude that other closer objects are blocking our view. This is illustrated in Figure 2.4, where two simple shapes are shown. If these two objects existed within a 3-D space, then, as the circle is partially occluding our view of the square, we would generally assume that the circle is the closer of the two. Of course, this may be an incorrect interpretation, since a portion of the square may in fact have been cut away. This raises the possibility that the two objects lie at the same distance or that the circle is the more distant component. Fortunately, other depth cues assist in resolving this possible ambiguity, and here it important to note that although we tend to discuss cues in isolation, in reality they act together, thereby providing a range of

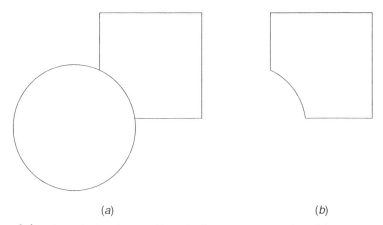

(a)   (b)

Figure 2.4 The occlusion (interposition) depth cue. In (a) a portion of the square *appears* to be occluded by the circle and so we will probably conclude that the circle lies between the square and the observer (this is reinforces by the different height of the two objects in the visual field). In this case, we are anticipating that the square is actually complete. However, this may not be the case—a portion of it may have been cut away [as shown in (b)]. This leads to the possibility of the shapes presented in (a) existing at the same distance from the observer—or even that the circle is the more remote of the two. Other depth cues assist in the resolution of such ambiguity. (Diagram © A. R. Blundell 2006.)

information that enables us to create a true mental picture of the organization of a 3-D scene.

> Our interpretation of a 3-D scene relies on information that is gained from a combination of depth cues. Furthermore, the relative emphasis that we subconsciously place on these cues varies according to the nature of the scene under observation.

In general, volumetric display systems do not support image opacity. This is not an inherent weakness of the volumetric approach but rather a facet of many of the techniques that have been adopted in the implementation of volumetric systems (see Section 5.7 for an example of a volumetric technique that provides support for image opacity).

(b) *Aerial Perspective:* During its passage through the atmosphere, light impinges upon small particles (such as water and dust particles). These scatter the light, and this causes more distant objects to appear less well defined. Furthermore, the color content of such objects is often lost and they take on a bluish tint (e.g., the bluish haze that we commonly see when looking toward a distant mountain).

Volumetric displays often impose very little restriction on the orientation from which an image may be viewed. In such cases, the aerial perspective cue is not appropriate for inclusion.

(c) *Shadowing:* Shadows and shading can provide us with a strong indication of the shape of objects. In everyday life, our judgment is generally based on an assumed light source position which is usually from above. In the case of images depicted on flat-screen-based displays, it is possible to artificially introduce both shadows and shading during the processing of an image data set. However, in the case of volumetric systems that support considerable freedom in viewing direction, there is little scope for the introduction of artificial shadows. An alternative would be to develop a display technology able to create images that exhibit opacity and which can be illuminated by external light sources. In this way, natural shadows could be cast within the image space. However, in the case of practically all existing volumetric displays, the voxels[11] that comprise an image emit light and are translucent: They do not reflect ambient light, nor can they block its passage. There is therefore an important need to develop volumetric systems that support the formation of opaque voxels which reflect rather than emit light (see Section 5.7).

(d) *Height in the Visual Field:* This cue is readily apparent when we look out to sea or across a flat landscape that extends to the horizon. Here the sea

---

[11] A voxel is the three-dimensional equivalent of the pixel and represents the fundamental 'particle' from which volumetric images are constructed.

(or land) appears to gradually ascend toward the horizon while at the same time the sky appears to descend. In this way the sea eventually seems to meet with the sky at the horizon. In general terms:

- *For an object that is located below the horizon:* More distant objects appear to be positioned higher in the lower portion of the visual field.
- *For an object that is located above the horizon:* More distant objects appear to be positioned lower in the upper portion of the visual field.

This is illustrated in Figure 2.5, and the impression is caused by the optical arrangement within the eye—specifically the finite separation of the eyes lens and retina. This is in contrast to the three other cues described above, these occur as a consequence of the physical disturbance of the light as it passes through a 3-D space prior to reaching the eye.

(e) *Linear Perspective:* This provides a remarkable and powerful cue to depth. Consider two objects of equal size and that are located at distances x_1 and x_2 from an observer (as illustrated in Figure 2.6). Light emanating from the more distant object subtends a smaller angle at the eye and therefore creates a smaller image on the retina. Thus, as with the height in the visual field cue, linear perspective occurs as a consequence of the separation of lens and retina within the eye. It is because of this geometry that, for example, railway lines appear to converge in the distance (and the "sleepers" to which the tracks are fixed appear to become more closely spaced).

Figure 2.5 This illustration demonstrates the relation between distance and height in the visual field. Here, the South Pacific Ocean appears to gradually rise toward the horizon while the sky sinks; eventually, they appear to meet at the horizon. (Original image copyright © Q. S. Blundell 2006.)

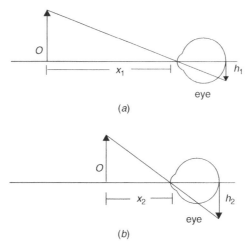

(a)

(b)

Figure 2.6 In (a) an object located at a distance x_1 from the eye produces a retinal image of height h_1. However, as illustrated in (b), when the object is brought closer to the eye the size of the retinal image increases to h_2. The dependence of the size of the retinal image on distance gives rise to linear perspective.

The development of the mathematical techniques that enable our real-world perception of linear perspective to be reproduced on a 2-D medium (such as an artist's canvas) underpinned the Italian Renaissance, and the first demonstration of the use of an accurate mathematical based perspective is generally attributed to Filippo Brunelleschi. This probably took place early in the fifteenth century.[12]

In creating a painting that accurately records our perception of the three-dimensionality of a scene, the artist is mimicking aspects of the image projection mechanism within the human eye. As we observe our surroundings, the 3-D imagery is mapped onto a 2-D surface (the retina) forming an image that is in many ways equivalent to the scene rendered on canvas or conventional flat screen computer display. Interestingly therefore, when we observe a scene that is physically 3-D the eye forms a perspective projection of this scene on the retina, but when we view a 3-D scene already rendered on a surface, the image formed on the retina is simple a copy of it (although scaled in size). Our visual perception of the 3-D world around us contains both factual and illusionary information. For example, the occlusion of one part of an image component by another object that is in closer proximity is factual, but on the other hand both linear perspective and the associated height of objects within the visual field are illusionary. Consequently, although we know that railway tracks are parallel, we do not question the perceived image in which tracks are

---

[12] There is some uncertainty associated with this demonstration (see Blundell and Schwarz [2006] together with references cited therein).

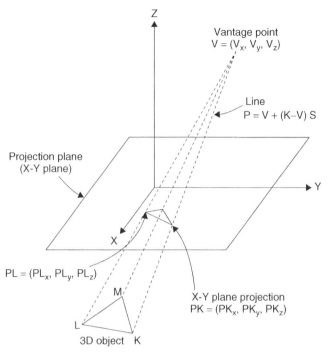

Figure 2.7   A 3-D object with vertices denoted by K, L and M is projected onto a 2-D plane (P). This projection is carried out for a specific viewpoint (V). The projection of a 3-D scene onto a 2-D plane as illustrated here is fundamental to computer graphics and the geometrical technique was delineated during the Renaissance which flourished in Italy from the fourteenth to the sixteenth century. The eye performs an equivalent process as it projects images of the physical world onto the surface of the retina. (Reproduced by permission from Boff et al [1986] © 2006 John Wiley & Sons.)

no longer parallel. However, although an artist who ignored illusionary cues by (for example) depicting tracks that remained parallel would be creating a factual rendition, the completed work would not be perceived as being visually accurate. Both the artist who accurately projects a 3-D scene onto a surface and the eye which projects a 3-D scene onto the retina are in essence undertaking a similar mapping process. Consequently, it is instructive to briefly examine the simple geometry associated with this task.

Consider Figure 2.7, which shows an object in 3-D space, a viewpoint (denoted V), and a projection plane (P), onto which we wish to map the object. This scenario is equivalent to the creation of a 2-D rendition of a 3-D object on a traditional flat screen display. By rearranging the diagram so that the projection plane lies on the other side of V, a drawing that more intuitively depicts image formation in the eye is created (due to symmetry, the projection plane can be located on either side of V and an equivalent result is obtained in both cases). Consider a point P that moves on the line VK. The coordinates of P may be expressed by the parametric equations as[13]

$$P_x = V_x + s(K_x - V_x), \tag{2.1}$$
$$P_y = V_y + s(K_y - V_y), \tag{2.2}$$
$$P_z = V_z + s(K_z - V_z). \tag{2.3}$$

The parameter s indicates the fractional distance of the projection plane along the line VK. If, for example, $s = 0$, then the equations indicate that the viewpoint lies on the projection plane. Alternatively, when $s = 1$, the point K lies on the projection plane. Given that the projection plane corresponds to $z = 0$, it follows that $P_z = 0$ and thus from Eq. (2.3) at the point of intersection we obtain

$$s = \frac{V_z}{V_z - K_z}.$$

Substituting this value into Eqs. (2.1) and (2.2), we obtain the x and y projections of K:

$$PK_x = V_x + \frac{V_z(K_x - V_x)}{V_z - K_z}, \qquad PK_y = V_y + \frac{V_z(K_y - V_y)}{V_z - K_z}.$$

These equations may be simplified by arranging the coordinate system such that the z axis passes through the viewpoint. In this way, both V_x and V_y equal zero and therefore we have

$$PK_x = \frac{V_z.K_x}{V_z - K_z}, \qquad PK_y = \frac{V_z.K_y}{V_z - K_z} \tag{2.4}$$

The point L indicated in Figure 2.7 may be similarly mapped onto the projection plane:

$$PL_x = \frac{V_z.L_x}{V_z - L_z}, \qquad PL_y = \frac{V_z.L_y}{V_z - L_z}.$$

Thus each point from which the object is formed may be cast onto the projection plane (and line segments such as KL may be mapped simply by computing their end-point projections). Each point within the image that is cast onto the projection plane is calculated not only in accordance with its x and y values (which lie parallel to the projection plane) but also in such a way as to take into account the depth of the point relative to the projection window, and hence the viewpoint. Here it is important to note that the perspective scene created on the projection window is calculated for a particular viewing position.

By dividing both the numerator and denominator of Eq. (2.4) by V_z, we obtain an equation equivalent to Eq. (1.1), which was employed by Parker and Wallis [1948, 1949]. Alternatively, the perspective transformation can

---

[13] Here, we follow the simple analysis presented in Boff et al. [1986].

be expressed in the form of a matrix multiplication that can then be conveniently combined with other homogeneous transformations. Thus for point K we obtain

$$
\begin{bmatrix} PK_x \\ PK_y \\ 0 \\ 1 \end{bmatrix} = \left(\frac{1}{V_z - K_z} \right) \begin{bmatrix} V_z & 0 & 0 & 0 \\ 0 & V_z & 0 & 0 \\ 0 & 0 & 0 & 0 \\ 0 & 0 & -1 & V_z \end{bmatrix} \begin{bmatrix} K_x \\ K_y \\ K_z \\ 1 \end{bmatrix}.
$$

2.3.2   Oculomotor Cues

The difference between stupidity and genius
is that genius has its limits.[14]

Accommodation and convergence relate to physiological changes within the eye. The former is a monocular cue and is therefore commonly grouped with the cues mentioned above (in this case these cues are generally referred to as "monocular" rather than "pictorial" cues). On the other hand, convergence is underpinned by the action of the two eyes and could therefore be discussed alongside other binocular cues. For our purposes, it is convenient to categorize accommodation and convergence together because these two cues share various common properties: Both are said to relate to physiological changes within the visual system, both operate most effectively for objects that are at close range, and both interactively influence each other [Okoshi, 1976]. In this latter respect, Okoshi indicates that as the eyes converge on a point of fixation, this "*automatically brings about a certain degree of accommodation.*" Similarly, "*. . . information on accommodation influences convergence, though it is a weaker effect.*" This is discussed in more detail by Howard [2002, Chapter 9], who writes:

A change in accommodation is normally accompanied by a change in vergence—an increase in accommodation evokes convergence and a decrease evokes divergence. This is known as accommodative convergence (AC). . . . Since accommodative convergence is evoked by accommodation rather than by disparity, it can be evoked by a stimulus presented to only one eye.

He goes on to add:

A change in horizontal vergence, however it is evoked, is accompanied by an appropriate change in accommodation, a response known as convergence accommodation (CA).

As we discuss in Section 3.3, the stereoscope provides support not only for the pictorial cues but also for binocular parallax. When a stereoscopic image is viewed, accommodation and convergence are decoupled; this can cause discomfort for those who only occasionally view stereo images. Both accommodation and convergence are briefly discussed below.

---

[14] Attributed to Albert Einstein (1879–1955).

(a) *Accommodation:* This cue relates to the tension that must be applied to the ciliary muscle to bring into focus the feature upon which we are fixated. Contraction of this muscle results in a deformation of the crystalline lens (mainly in the anterior surface[15]) and hence a change in its focal length. Boff et al. [1986],[16] quoting the findings of Campbell and Westheimer [1960], report an accommodation reaction time to a visual stimulus of $\sim$0.3 s and a duration of $\sim$0.9 s from the onset of the stimulus to the completion of the accommodation adjustment.[17] Interestingly, when viewing a stimulus that is at a fixed distance, the accommodation system is not at rest but exhibits oscillations (the amplitude of which can exceed 0.5 diopters[18] within a frequency band centered on 2 Hz) [Campbell et al., 1959].

The accommodation cue is not supported by the conventional monocular display or by the various creative 3-D display technologies that are underpinned by the traditional stereoscope. In both cases, the entire image scene is simultaneously in focus and as an observer's gaze shifts between image components that appear to be located at different depth, the eyes essentially remain focused on the display screen.

(b) *Convergence:* The optical axes of the two eyes meet at the point of fixation. This is achieved by muscles that exert forces on the eyes, causing them to swivel slightly inward. The degree of force that must be exerted on the eyes may provide an indication of the distance of an object from the observer. Thus in viewing our surroundings, accommodation and convergence operate together: The eyes focus on, and their axes meet at, the point within an image scene that is under scrutiny.

The visual system may obtain an indication of distance using a process of triangulation, although the baseline is limited to the interocular distance ($\sim$6.3 cm for adults) and consequently the cue would be most effective for objects that are in close proximity to the observer. Consider the diagram presented in Figure 2.8, where the eyes fixate on a point (*A*) lying at a distance *s*. Given a convergence angle of α, it is apparent that

$$\tan\frac{\alpha}{2} = \frac{x}{2.s}.$$

Using the small-angle approximation $\tan\alpha \approx \alpha$[19] and for an interocular distance of 6.3 cm, we obtain

---

[15] Changes in shape of the posterior surface are resisted by the presence of the vitreous humor.

[16] Volume 1, page 4.6.

[17] Trials carried out on young adults with 'normal' vision.

[18] "Diopters"—the reciprocal of distance (where distance is measured in meters). Thus for an object placed at a distance of 0.5 m from the eye, this would correspond to 2 diopters. Similarly an object at infinity would correspond to zero diopters. The power of a lens may be quoted in diopters where this is determined as the reciprocal of the focal length.

[19] Here α is measured in radians.

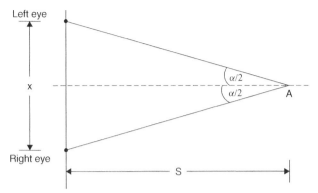

Figure 2.8 The two eyes are separated by a distance x and fixate on a point A which is at a distance s. In principle, a process of triangulation may be used to indicate distance.

$$\left| \frac{d\alpha}{ds} \right| \approx \frac{x}{s^2} \approx \frac{6.3}{s^2}, \tag{2.5}$$

thus indicating the rapid decrease in sensitivity with increasing distance. The theoretical effectiveness of the convergence angle cue with distance may be further demonstrated by way of a simple example. Consider an object that is moved from infinity to a position 4.3 m from an observer. This will produce approximately the same change in the vergence angle (α) as a closer object that is moved from a position of 20 cm by a distance of just 1 cm!

When focusing on an object located at a distance in excess of approximately 3 m, the crystalline lens is fully relaxed and reaches its maximum curvature when we regard objects that are located within approximately 20 cm of the eye. This limits the range over which the accommodation cue could operate. As indicated above, the focusing of the eyes occupies a significant time, and there is considerable debate as to the reliance that we place on this cue in our everyday lives [Coren et al., 2004]. The importance of convergence as a means of judging absolute distance is also a matter of debate. In this context, Coren et al. write:

> *Feedback from such vergence movements could be useful in determining the distance of objects, although there has been some controversy about how useful and reliable such information is as a depth cue.*

In trials in which an image comprises two point sources of light located at different distances from the observer, it has been shown that accommodation and convergence of the eyes alone has enabled participants to determine which light source is the more distant. This is clearly an artificial situation and reflects the adaptive ability of the visual system. Coren et al. [2004] write:

> *Perhaps one reason why convergence and accommodation are somewhat weaker cues for depth is that the eye will use other depth cues preferentially to adjust the eye. Thus*

there is some evidence that the eyes will attempt to converge and accommodate as if they were looking at objects at various distances in response to the available depth cues from other sources (e.g., Takeda, Hashimoto, Hiruma, and Fukui, 1999) even when these cues are in paintings and line drawings (Enright, 1987a, 1987b).

If we assume that depth cues represent content that is contained within the image scene presented to the visual system from which relative and absolute depth information may be derived, then accommodation and convergence as introduced above would not in fact represent depth cues at all. It is usual to consider accommodation and convergence as being represented by physiological changes in the eyes—the extent of which are fed back to the visual cortex. However, these changes are not initiated and controlled by the eyes themselves, but rather are determined by the underlying processing of the visual scene. Thus they originate indirectly.

> In short, accommodation and convergence as described above represent an observable (and measurable) outcome of the processing of the image scene.

2.3.3   Motion Parallax

In the case of motion parallax, relative movement between the observer and an image scene enables the visual system to derive additional depth information. Here, as an observer moves—for example, to the left—objects that are closer than the point of fixation will appear to move to the right and those further away will appear to move to the left. (This can be readily observed by means of three pointers—for example, pens balanced on a tabletop—at different distances.)

Let us consider for a moment the issue of absolute motion parallax whereby the visual field contains only a single object as indicated in Figure 2.9. Here, an object O is located at a distance d from an observer (positioned at A). The observer moves a distance x to location B. From this vantage point, the object lies at a distance d'. The angles θ and θ' denote the angles subtended by the object O relative to the direction of observer motion. Using the Sine Rule for triangles, it is apparent that

$$\frac{x}{\sin \beta} = \frac{d'}{\sin \theta} = \frac{d}{\sin(180 - \theta')}.$$

where $\beta = \theta' - \theta$. Thus,

$$d = \frac{x \cdot \sin \theta'}{\sin(\theta' - \theta)}$$

and

$$d' = \frac{x \cdot \sin \theta}{\sin(\theta' - \theta)}.$$

Following discussion in Boff et al. [1986], in the simplest case where we restrict movement to lateral head motion, then for an object lying directly in front of

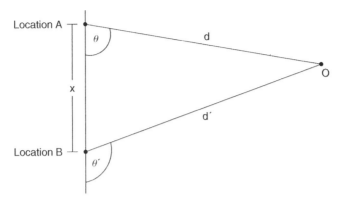

Figure 2.9 The determination of the distance of a single point (O) by means of absolute motion parallax. For simplicity we assume monocular vision. The observer moves with translational motion between points A and B and may in principle determine both d and d'. This process relies on proprioception. See text for discussion.

the observer, both $\sin\theta$ and $\sin\theta'$ can be approximated to unity. Furthermore, since in this situation $\theta' - \theta$ is small, we can make the small-angle approximation $\sin(\theta' - \theta) \sim \theta' - \theta$.

$$x \approx d(\theta' - \theta).$$

Differentiating with respect to time provides us with an expression relating the speed of an observers translational motion (v) to the angular velocity of the change in angular direction of the object (ω):

$$v \approx d\omega. \tag{2.6}$$

To determine either d or d', an observer must perceive both v and ω. In the case that only a single object is visible, the information must be derived from proprioception.[20] For details of some experimental findings in this area, see Boff et al. [1986] and references cited therein. However, by way of summary:

> *Overall, it appears that absolute motion parallax can exert some influence on distance perception, but is most effective at very close distances (i.e., less than 1 m) and when combined with other information such as accommodation and perspective transforms.*

Our surroundings usually contain numerous objects that are located at different distances from our viewpoint. In this situation as we move, so to does the image that each object casts onto the retina, with the relative motion of these image components being determined by the distance of the corresponding object from the observer. This relative motion is referred to as relative motion parallax or simply motion parallax. Let us consider the case of two objects located at distances

---

[20] A knowledge of the position, orientation and movement of our limbs within a 3-D space. Proprioception from the Latin *proprius* — "own" (see, for example, Blundell and Schwarz [2006]).

x_1 and x_2 approximately directly in front of the observer. From Eq. (2.6) and assuming that the observer moves with a translational speed v, then if the angular velocities of the images projected on the retina are denoted as ω_1 and ω_2, we obtain

$$\frac{x_1}{x_2} \approx \frac{\omega_2}{\omega_1}.$$

Consequently, if the angular velocities of the images cast onto the retina can be measured, it is possible to determine their relative distances. Furthermore, this can be done independently of the speed of motion of the observer. Trials have demonstrated that motion parallax can be useful in judging relative distances of objects (i.e., identifying which objects within a scene are closer or further away) but is less valuable in determining absolute distances. However, when we consider judgment of absolute distances in our everyday lives, cues do not operate in isolation but rather provide the visual system with a range of sources that can be brought together to often provide remarkable accuracy in distance estimation.

There are various forms of motion parallax. These are discussed in some detail by Howard and Rogers [2002], and several are briefly summarized below:

1. *Absolute Parallax:* Consider the image projected onto the retina by a single point in space. As discussed above, the location of the retinal image will move when either the point moves (and the eye is stationary) or when the eye moves and the point is stationary. The extent by which the retinal image will shift is determined by both the distance of the point from the eye and the distance over which the point (or eye) moves.

2. *Linear Parallax:* Consider a 3-D object or collection of objects in 3-D space. As the eye moves from side to side (or as the image components pass before the observer), more distant parts of the scene will appear to move more slowly. Although this cue is naturally satisfied by both volumetric and varifocal displays, in the case of the conventional flat screen display it cannot be realized through head movement. As discussed in Section 3.4, the standard stereoscopic display may overcome this limitation through the inclusion of head tracking.

3. *Looming:* By changing the size of a stationary object, we can provide a sense of motion toward or away from the observer. For example, as an object gradually grows larger, we may obtain an impression that it is traveling toward us.

4. *Kinetic Depth Effect:* Consider a 3-D structure (such as a cube) constructed using matches, straws, or the like. When the shadow of this physical 'wire frame' structure is cast onto a 2-D surface, the image generally fails to convey a sense of the object's inherent three-dimensionality. However, when the structure is made to rotate and this gives rise to corresponding changes in the shadow, its 3-D form is immediately apparent. This is known as the kinetic depth effect.

2.3.4 Stereopsis (Binocular Parallax)

When we view our surroundings, the images cast onto the two retinas are not identical but in fact provide us with two slightly different views on the scene under observation. This is due to the physical separation of the two eyes (in the case of adults the eyes are approximately 63 mm apart) and under normal circumstances, the visual system fuses these images in such a way that differences (disparities) between them are interpreted as providing an indication of depth. This depth cue was first exploited in the development of the stereoscope during the first half of the nineteenth century, and many of today's the creative 3-D display technologies continue to be based on this principle. For details of this history see, for example, Howard [2002], Wade [1983, 2003], and summary discussion in Blundell and Schwarz [2006].

In this subsection, we do not consider stereopsis in detail because this subject is given excellent and detailed coverage in other works. However, for our current purposes, it is useful to have an insight into the basic geometry concerning the formation of the two retinal images. Therefore we briefly discuss this aspect of stereopsis and provide useful references for more detailed discussion on this fascinating and powerful depth cue.

As indicated above, due to the physical separation of the two eyes, the images projected onto their retinas contain both vertical and horizontal disparities, each representing the image scene as viewed from a particular location. Careful study of the stereoscopic image pairs presented in Figure 2.10 will reveal very small geometric disparities; when these pairs are fused, the disparities will result in the perception of three-dimensionality. In the text that follows, we consider only horizontal disparity.

Given that when viewing a collection of objects located within a 3-D space, the images formed on the retinas are not identical, it is natural to ask if there exists a locus of image points that will create identical images on the two retina. In fact, this was the subject of investigation for many centuries, and Howard [2002] discusses this interesting history. Such a locus of points does exist and is referred to as the horopter. There are in fact various forms of horopter, and in this brief account we focus on a theoretical horizontal horopter that is known as the Vieth–Müller circle.

Consider Figure 2.11, in which O denotes the point of fixation upon which the visual axes of the two eyes converge such that lines Om and On are equal in length. We assume that the optical nodes of the two eyes are located at positions m and n and the circle represents the theoretical Vieth–Müller horopter. We now consider two arbitrary points on this circle denoted as x and y. Basic geometry tells us that *"angles on the circumference of a circle and which are erected on the same cord are equal."* Thus angles α, β, and γ are equal (since they are erected on the same cord and lie on the same circumference). In Figure 2.12, we add two additional cords (Ox and Oy). From the former, it is apparent that angle P is equal to angle Q. Thus the angle subtended by point x relative to the optical axis of each eye is the same. Similarly, for point y, cord Oy indicates that angle R equals angle S and so both points x and y are projected onto corresponding points within each

(a)

(b)

Figure 2.10   Close and careful comparison of the two images comprising each of the stereo pairs presented here reveals small disparities resulting from the images having been captured from different vantage points. When the image pairs are fused, the disparities result in the perception of a single 3-D image. [Image (a) Cathedral Square, Christchurch, New Zealand, kindly supplied to the author by Robin Ramsey.]

retina (i.e., there is—at least in principle—no disparity between the projections of either point x or point y onto the retinas). This applies for the locus of points that lie on the Vieth–Müller circle and that are within the visual field. However, if we now consider a point J that does not lie on the circle, we find that the angle that it subtends relative to the visual axis of each eye will not be the same, and this will give rise to a disparity in the two retinal images.

In Figure 2.13, we illustrate a series of Vieth–Müller circles, each corresponding to a different fixation distance. It should be noted that such circles provide only an approximate indication of the locus of points that will give rise to zero disparity in the projected retinal image. For points located close to the horopter (with a region known as "Panum's fusional area"), it is still possible to fuse the two retinal images

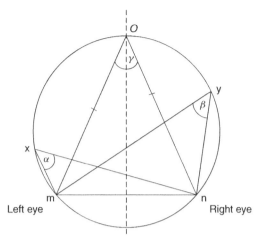

Figure 2.11 Angles on the circumference of a circle and which are erected on the same cord are equal. Thus angles α, β, and γ are equal in size. This diagram illustrates the theoretical Vieth–Müller circle. Point O represents the point of fixation and points m and n the optical nodes of the two eyes. Points x and y are two arbitrary points that lie on the Vieth–Müller circle and are within the visual field.

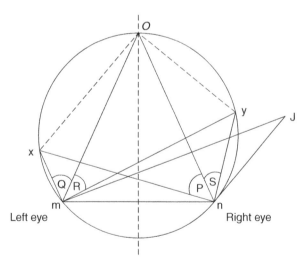

Figure 2.12 Here we build on the diagram presented in Figure 2.11 by adding two cords (Ox and Oy). From cord Ox, it is evident that angles P and Q are equal in size. From cord Oy, angles R and S are also equal in size. Thus both points x and y are projected onto corresponding points within each retina (i.e., there is (at least in principle) no disparity between the projections of either point x or point y onto the retinas). However for point J (which does not lie on the circle), the angle subtended relative to the visual axis of each eye will not be the same and this will give rise to a disparity in the two retinal images.

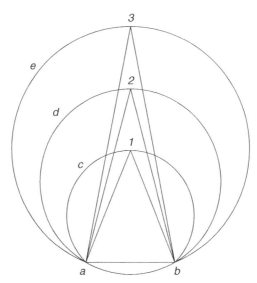

Figure 2.13 A series of Vieth–Müller circles (*c*, *d*, and *e*), each corresponding to a different fixation distance (*1*, *2*, and *3*). Each of these provides an approximate indication of the locus of points in the horizontal plane that will give rise to zero disparity. [Reproduced from the *Encyclopaedia Britannica*, Adam and Charles Black, Edinburgh (1879).]

despite the disparity contained within them. This binocular disparity is interpreted by the visual system as providing an indication of depth.[21]

2.4 CONSIDERATIONS ON IMAGE REFRESH

> *All, that I know*
> *Of a certain star*
> *Is, it can throw (like an angled spar)*
> *Now a dart of red,*
> *Now a dart of blue*
> *Till my friends have said*
> *They would fain see, too.*[22]

Volumetric displays may be broadly classified as either "swept" or "static" volume systems. For the moment, we need not concern ourselves with the architectural differences between these two general approaches; also, it is sufficient to note that in the case of the former class of display, voxels which comprise an image do not

---

[21] In this discussion, we have not considered vertical disparities which may be used by the visual system in a variety of ways: "*including the perception of absolute distance, depth scaling of horizontal disparities, and the perception of 3-D shape*" [Howard, 2002].

[22] Robert Browning (1812–1889), "My Star."

continuously emit light but rather exhibit transient light emission. This is an inherent characteristic of the swept-volume technique. Similarly, the majority of static-volume systems also give rise to voxels that do not continuously emit light. However this is not an inherent characteristic of the static-volume approach and in the case of this class of display, there is the *possibility* for continuous light output. The temporal characteristics of voxels activated by means of the varifocal technique exhibit similar temporal characteristics as those associated with the swept-volume approach.

In general terms, volumetric and varifocal systems interface in an harmonious manner with the human visual system. However, all varifocal displays and the majority of volumetric architectures give rise to images that are not continuously present but which are repeatedly illuminated for only brief periods of time. This can adversely impact on the visual system.

Below we briefly discuss typical temporal characteristics of light output from voxels activated by means of these different techniques:

1. *Swept-Volume and Varifocal Systems:* In the case of such displays, voxels are activated for brief periods of time. As we will discuss, the designer seeks to employ methods that minimize the time required for a voxel to reach the desired level of light output and the time taken for an activated voxel to return to the nonvisible state following the removal of the activation stimulus. It is convenient to define a duty cycle (κ) such that

$$\kappa(\%) = \frac{\text{The time for which a voxel within an image scene is visible}}{\text{The time for which a voxel within an image scene is nonvisible}} \times 100.$$

This duty cycle is illustrated in Figure 2.14. For swept-volume and varifocal systems, although the duty cycle is usually quite small, we may still consciously view such a light source as being continuously illuminated.

2. *Static-Volume Systems:* As indicated above, in principle it is possible to develop static-volume architectures in which each visible voxel comprising an image scene operates in a bi-stable mode such that when it is activated, it remains in this state until a deactivation signal is applied to it. In such a case, the image update rate would be determined solely by the need to support the smooth depiction of dynamic image sequences ($\sim$10 Hz). This contrasts with the higher update rate needed to prevent image flicker when the voxel production paradigm is based upon transient optical phenomena.

For the majority of static-volume systems, the visibility of each voxel decays after the removal of the excitation stimulus. Here, the rate of decay is determined by the underlying techniques that are used for the production of the visible change. A long decay period is not desirable because this may have a negative impact on image quality when dynamic image sequences are displayed.

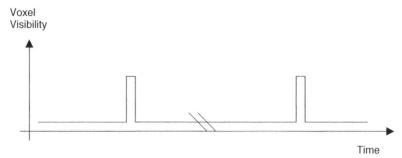

Figure 2.14 An idealized representation of the temporal nature of light output from voxels associated with the swept and varifocal classes of display. In the case of display systems that exhibit a low parallelism in voxel activation a voxel may emit light for a time on the order of a microsecond and subsequently remain nonvisible for some 20 to 40 milliseconds before being re-illuminated.

Consider for a moment a light source emitting pulses of light. The minimum frequency at which these pulses must occur in order that they are consciously perceived as a continuum is referred to as the critical flicker frequency (CFF). This frequency is influenced by a number of factors, including the level of adaptation to the lighting conditions, the wavelength composition of the source, the distance of the source from the eye, and its luminance [Coren et al., 2004]. The Ferry–Porter Law (which is empirically determined) is often used to relate the CFF to the luminance (L) and is approximately valid over a wide range of image intensities:

$$CFF = a + b\log(L),$$

where a and b are constants. For a dimly illuminated display viewed under low levels of lighting, the CFF may be as low as 15 Hz.[23] When high levels of luminance are involved, flicker can still be consciously observed even when refresh frequencies of up to 60 Hz are employed Boff et al., 1986 (see Figure 2.15).

Unfortunately, support for higher refresh frequencies places greater demands on the display technology and the output stages of the graphics engine (see Chapter 11). In the case of volumetric displays employing transient optical phenomena in the voxel production process, a refresh frequency of ~25 Hz may be sufficient provided that the images are not viewed continuously for protracted periods of time. However, it is preferable to support a minimum refresh frequency of 30 Hz.

2.5 DISCUSSION

The conventional flat screen computer display provides support for the pictorial depth cues but not for the binocular and "oculomotor" cues. However, the

---

[23] Here we refer to our conscious perception of flicker. Subliminal perception of flicker may result in discomfort and will often dictate that a display system that is to be used for protracted periods be refreshed at a significantly higher frequency than that indicated by the conscious CFF.

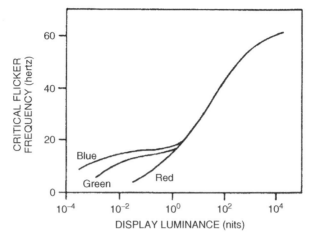

Figure 2.15 Measurement of the minimum refresh rate needed to provide the perception of a flicker free image for different levels of luminance. Note that at high levels of luminance, the CFF is relatively high. (Reproduced from Boff et al [1986] © 2006 John Wiley & Sons. Original source: Raster Graphics Handbook, Van Nostrand Reinhold Company, Inc. [1980].)

development and application of displays that are able to support a broader range of cues is not in itself automatically a panacea, and one must carefully judge the nature of the benefits that may be derived through the use of such systems. These may be grouped into three broad categories: augmented realism, augmented information content, and alternative interaction opportunities [Blundell and Schwarz, 2006]. Without a doubt, support for the binocular cues can dramatically impact on realism, and it was for this reason that the stereoscope became so popular during the Victorian era. As far as augmented information content is concerned, many of us experience great difficulty when attempting to mentally construct 3-D models corresponding to either geometric shapes or spatial relationships. By way of example, consider a high school student attempting to solve a simple geometry problem in which angles within a 3-D wire frame structure are to be calculated, or who must visualize the structure of even a relatively simple molecule. In both cases, students often find themselves grappling with the visualization process, and the construction of a simple model using (for example) wires or straws will usually greatly facilitate the exercise. In this context, creative 3-D displays may be of great assistance, enabling user(s) to more readily perceive shapes, structures, and spatial relationships.

In terms of the alternative interaction opportunities referred to above, creative displays offer to support a broad range of alternative (and hopefully more intuitive) interaction paradigms). In this chapter we have briefly reviewed some facets of the human eye and have commented on its formidable characteristics. However, to gain a meaningful insight into the visualization process, we need to look beyond the eye and consider the visual system as a whole. Here, at best we can gain an insight into some of the techniques that it employs so as to enable us to process vast amounts of image data in real time and without conscious effort. However, if we are to properly understand the ways in which a display paradigm may advance the interaction process, then consideration of the visual system is in itself insufficient and it is also necessary to examine the human somatosensory and motor systems. In this way we may obtain considerable benefits as we draw upon the synergy that may be catalyzed by properly bringing together complex human sensory systems.

In the next chapter, we consider general issues relating to 3-D display systems and briefly review a number of classes of creative 3-D display. This paves the way for subsequent discussion on the volumetric and varifocal paradigms.

2.6   INVESTIGATIONS

1. Suppose that the spectral response of the photoreceptors within the eye was constant across the range of visible wavelengths. How would this impact on our perception of color, and how would this affect the view out of a near by window?

2. Estimate the size of the retinal image projected onto the retina when we view (a) a television screen and (b) a computer display. In each case you should assume a typical viewing distance. Does the projected image extend beyond the *fovea*?

3. Consider a fine strand of a spider's cobweb viewed at a distance of 60 cm. Estimate the width of the image that this casts onto the retina.

4. Using, for example, light-emitting diodes (LEDs) connected to a variable-frequency square-wave generator, determine the CFF for different observers. Repeat the exercise with LEDs emitting different wavelengths and under different ambient lighting conditions. Interesting results may be obtained by including in your trials "super bright" LEDs.

3 Creative 3-D Display Techniques

A storm was coming, but the winds were still
And in the wild woods of Broceliande,
Before an oak, so hollow, huge and old
It look'd a tower of ruin'd masonwork,
At Merlin's feet the wily Vivien lay . . .

3.1 INTRODUCTION

In this chapter we focus on various display techniques that can support the binocular and, in some instances, the motion parallax cues and provide further insight into various characteristics of the volumetric approach. We begin by introducing a number of subsystems that comprise a display. Here, we discuss the image space creation, voxel generation, voxel activation, and re-imaging/projection subsystems (this latter subsystem may be used to form the free space image). These provide a useful framework around which we can structure our discussions in later chapters.

In Section 3.3 we consider systems based on the principle of the stereoscope that are able to support the binocular parallax depth cue. Charles Wheatstone and David Brewster originally pioneered this technique in the mid-nineteenth century and, as we shall discuss, the principle of the stereoscope underpins many of today's "creative" 3-D display systems. In this section we also consider two early exemplar displays dating back to the 1930s and 1940s, which employed the stereoscopic principle for the depiction of electronically processed imagery.

Having outlined the operation of displays employing the principle of the stereoscope, we discuss the extension of this technique for the support of the motion parallax depth cue, and in Section 3.5 we consider fundamental differences between the real physical image scene and the electronically processed rendition. Multi-view display techniques are briefly outlined in Section 3.6. Many of today's creative 3-D display systems build on the methods formulated by artists during the Italian Renaissance and consequently have much in common with traditional painting techniques. On the other hand, volumetric systems that support considerable freedom in viewing orientation provide images that more closely resemble the traditional sculpted rendition. Consequently, in Section 3.7 we discuss aspects of painting and sculpture, and here we draw on some of the remarks made by Leonardo da Vinci in connection with these two forms of expression.

This chapter provides only summary discussion of various creative 3-D display techniques. However, appropriate references are provided to publications containing more detailed information.

3.2   DISPLAY SUBSYSTEMS

> *It has become appallingly obvious*
> *that our technology has exceeded our humanity.*[1]

Any creative 3-D display may be considered as comprising several basic subsystems. In this section we build upon previous discussion [Blundell and Schwarz, 2006] and provide a subsystem model (see Figure 3.1) able to embrace the majority of creative 3-D display systems and which is particularly suited to both the volumetric and varifocal approaches.

1. **"Basic" Image Space Creation:** We define this subsystem as relating to the physical techniques that are brought to bear in the production of a region over which some form of image may be physically depicted. In the case of, for example, the conventional flat screen monocular display, this subsystem is 2-D and corresponds to the rectangular screen via which images are directly presented to the visual system. Alternatively, as we discuss in the next section, coding techniques may be used to extend the traditional monocular display to support binocular parallax. In this case, the human visual system

---

[1] Attributed to Albert Einstein (1879–1955).

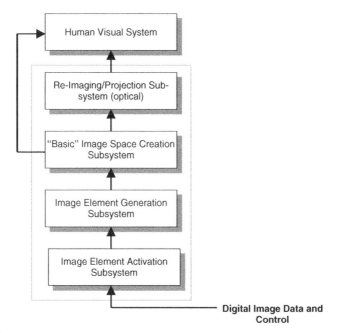

Figure 3.1 A creative 3-D display system comprises a number of subsystems. For the purposes of this book, we will assume that the display may be considered in terms of the four subsystems that are depicted within the broken rectangle. We consider that these subsystems may give rise to four possible forms of image space: physical, free, virtual, or apparent, see text for details (we neglect the 'planar' image space associated with the conventional flat screen display). (Diagram © Q. S. Blundell 2006.)

perceives an image that no longer lies in the plane of the screen but rather that exhibits a striking sense of *relief* and *appears* to exist within a volume (the apparent image space model that was introduced in Section 1.5). This three-dimensionality is not a physical reality but an illusion wholly created by our interpretation of the visual stimulus. In contrast, the volumetric approach gives rise to images that exist within a 3-D volume, and so the visual system faithfully interprets their inherent three-dimensionality.[2]

Thus we view the "basic" image space as corresponding to the region in which image elements are physically, virtually, or apparently located. This image space may be viewed directly or indirectly:

(a) **Direct Viewing:** In the case of an image depicted within a volume, the human visual system derives spatial information from the natural 3-D form of the image. We consider that the image is perceived as occupying a

---

[2] As indicated in the next chapter, in the case of many volumetric techniques, images exist in a volume only when viewed over time (when considered instantaneously, only a partial image exists), most frequently on a plane. In this sense, volumetric images are often illusionary.

"physical" image space. On the other hand, although an image may be physically depicted on a surface, we can present it to an observer in such a way that the visual system perceives an image which seems to occupy a volume. In this case we refer to the image as being located in an "apparent" image space (see discussion below on the terminology adopted in this book in connection with various forms of image space).

(b) **Indirect Viewing:** In the case of some display architectures, light emanating from the "physical" image space may pass through some form of optical system (referred to in Figure 3.1 as the "re-imaging/projection" subsystem) prior to reaching the observer. As discussed in subsequent sections, this may take various forms such as special-purpose viewing glasses or an optical arrangement fitted to a planar screen on which images are depicted. This subsystem in some ways modifies the passage of light and typically enables certain display configurations to support stereopsis and possibly motion parallax.

For the purposes of this book we will assume four possible forms of 3-D image space. These were previously introduced in Section 1.5 and for convenience are summarized below[3]:

(a) **Physical Image Space:** As indicated in (a) above, images may be formed within a physical volume and may be viewed directly. In the case that the volume is bounded by a containing vessel or contains static/moving components that preclude the insertion of a physical interaction tool into the image space, we refer to this as a "physical" image space/display volume.

(b) **Free Image Space:** We may create an image within a physical image space and view it indirectly (via a re-imaging/projection subsystem; see Figure 3.1). The perceived image may then appear to emanate from a region located between the optical system and the observer. Alternatively, it is possible to implement a volumetric display volume that is not bounded and into which interaction tools may be inserted (see Section 9.3.2). We consider both scenarios to represent the formation of a "free" image space. A primary difference between the free and physical image spaces is therefore the ability to physically enter the display volume (which enables us to employ direct interaction techniques). Other differences may also exist (for example, a free image space may be more restrictive in viewing freedom). In this context, the primary purpose of the re-imaging projection subsystem is to project an image into "free space," however it may also provide image magnification.

(c) **Virtual Image Space:** As with (b) above, we may create an image within a physical image space and view it indirectly (via a re-imaging/projection

---

[3] The descriptions provided here of "physical," "free," "virtual," and "apparent" forms of image space need on occasion to be adapted to encompass special cases. They are not therefore intended to be definitive. The fifth form of image space introduced in Section 1.5 (the "planar" image space) is not considered here.

subsystem). The perceived image may then appear to emanate from *behind* the optical component into which the observer gazes and is therefore classed as virtual rather than real. Consequently, we refer to such an image as existing within a "virtual" image space. In the case that the optical component is transparent, direct interaction techniques may be supported. As discussed in Chapter 10, the majority of varifocal systems developed to date give rise to virtual image spaces. In this case a re-imaging projection subsystem may, in principle, be used to form a free image space.

(d) **Apparent Image Space:** Images depicted on a surface may be presented to the visual system in such a way that we perceive an image that occupies a 3-D space (e.g., the stereoscopic techniques, see Section 3.3). In this case we refer to image production within an "apparent" image space. An apparent image space may also be formed by a re-imaging/projection subsystem that is used in conjunction with a flat screen display—see, for example, the discussion on the parallax stereogram and on lenticular techniques, presented in the next section; also, the parallax barrier technique is outlined in Section 3.6. (Note that the physical and perceived images are disparate.)

In the case of images that occupy a physical or free image space, the image is formed or brought to focus within a volume. In the case of a virtual image space, the location of the image is determined by the path along which the light "appears" to have traveled and is therefore, to an extent, illusionary. The apparent image space is also illusionary.[4]

Reference to the physical, free, virtual, and apparent forms of image space is particularly helpful when considering interaction opportunities.

2. **Image Element Generation (Voxel Generation):** This subsystem concerns the physical processes that give rise to the emission of light (or some other visible optical change) and so permit the formation of a visible image. In the case of the conventional flat screen cathode ray tube (CRT)-based display, the image element generation subsystem is represented by the phosphor coatings which, by a process of cathodoluminescence, are able to convert a portion of the energy imparted by one or more incident electron beams into visible light. Within the context of volumetric and varifocal displays, images are formed from voxels and therefore we will sometimes refer to this as the voxel generation subsystem.[5]

---

[4] This is perhaps a contentious assertion since all displays are illusionary. However, in the case of both the physical and free image space scenarios, we can employ a simple measuring device to detect the emission or focusing of light at points in space. In principle, the actual and perceived location of such points in space should be identical. However, in the case of the apparent image space, such physical measurements cannot be directly made—it is within the "mind's eye" that a stereogram's three-dimensionality is perceived.

[5] Either voxels or pixels may be employed as the fundamental elements that comprise an image. In general discussion we therefore refer to "image element generation" and "image element activation" subsystems.

3. **Image Element Activation (Voxel Activation):** This subsystem is responsible for stimulating the image element generation subsystem to cause the emission of light or some other form of visible optical change. In the case of the conventional CRT-based display referred to in (2) above, this subsystem is represented by the electron beams scanned across the phosphor coating(s) which impart energy, thereby enabling visible image formation. Within the context of volumetric and varifocal displays, images are formed from voxels and so we will sometimes refer to this as the voxel activation subsystem.

Although it is convenient to discuss a display system in terms of these various subsystems, it is important to remember that they are highly interdependent and should not be considered in isolation. For example, the selection of a particular image element generation technique will limit the approaches that may be employed for image element activation. In turn, this will greatly influence the characteristics of the "basic" image space and, in the case of volumetric and varifocal system, will determine the voxel activation capacity (voxel bandwidth) that may be supported by the display.

3.3 STEREOSCOPIC TECHNIQUES

Charles Wheatstone and David Brewster pioneered the stereoscope in the nineteenth century [Wheatstone, 1838, Wade, 1983, 1987, 2003, Blundell and Schwarz, 2006], and the basic principle of its operation underpins the majority of today's creative 3-D display technologies. The traditional stereoscope supports not only the standard pictorial depth cues, but also binocular parallax (stereopsis), so that objects and scenes exhibit a strong sense of three-dimensionality. This is achieved by capturing an image scene from two different perspectives (either by photography or, in the case of computer-generated stereoscopic images, by rendering a scene for two different orientations). As discussed in Section 2.3.4, disparities in the images received by the two eyes provide a strong sense of depth, and so the perceived image appears to be located on either side of (or to span) the surface on which the stereo pair are displayed.

Examples of stereo images are provided in Figures 1.18 and 2.10. These are most easily viewed via a stereoscope (or stereoscopic glasses), although, with a little practice, it is possible to observe the stereoscopic content naturally without the need for recourse to any viewing apparatus.[6]

The stereoscope was produced in various forms and gained great popularity during the Victorian and Edwardian eras, enabling the "armchair traveler" to experience a greater sense of realism and also enabling the military planner to benefit from the increased information content contained within the stereoscopic image pair. It appears that it was not until the 1930/1940 period that photographic images were replaced with electromechanical/electronic displays.

---

[6] For excellent discussion on stereoscopic display techniques, see, for example, Valyus [1962] and Lipton [1982, 1991, 1997].

Creative 3-D display systems whose operation is underpinned by the stereoscopic principle employ various techniques for the depiction of the images that form the stereo pair and for directing each image to the appropriate eye. In this latter respect, some form of coding technique is commonly employed. This may necessitate the use of special viewing glasses that decode the images prior to viewing. Three general approaches may be adopted for image coding; and following previously introduced terminology [Blundell and Schwarz, 2006], we refer to these as temporally, spatially, and chromatically coding techniques. Each approach provides the user with the pictorial cues we associate with the conventional flat screen display, although these are presented to each eye from a different viewing location (thereby providing the human visual system with the information needed to better interpret spatial relationships). The provision of this additional information places extra demands on the bandwidth that must be supported by both the display and graphics hardware. If the bandwidth is not increased, but maintained at the level employed by the monocular approach, a reduction in image quality will ensue. Below, we briefly discuss the three coding techniques referred to above and indicate their impact on both display performance and image quality (this is summarized in Table 3.1).

1. **Temporal Coding:** In the case of this approach, the two images forming the stereo pair are alternately depicted as separate frames on a flat screen display. The observer employs special viewing glasses containing eyepieces that can be individually switched between transparent and opaque states. The switching of these shutters is controlled by the hardware driving the display so that each eye sees only alternate frames and hence only one of the two images that comprise the stereo pair. Early embodiments employed a viewing apparatus that used cumbersome mechanical shutters (for example, US Patent Numbers 2,273,512, 1,1506,524, 1,658,439 and Lipton [1982, 1991, 2001]). Lightweight liquid-crystal-based active shutter glasses are now commonly employed, with switching signals typically being transmitted from the display to the glasses via a wireless link.

   Each eye is only presented with alternate frames and so, in order to avoid image flicker, the refresh frequency of the display must be increased. Naturally, this increases the bandwidth that must be supported by the graphics hardware and monitor (in terms of the pixel frequency—see Eq. (1.2)).

   In this scenario, the two images comprising the stereo pair are not passed to the visual system simultaneously—in fact, only one image is present at any time. It may therefore be somewhat surprising that this does not interfere with the extraction of disparities from within the stereo pair by the visual system and thereby interfere with our ability to properly perceive depth information.

2. **Spatial Coding:** Unlike the temporal coding technique, this approach does not necessitate the use of viewing glasses: Images may be viewed directly, although in the simpler embodiments a certain viewing position is assumed

TABLE 3.1 Summary of the Impact of Three Stereoscopic Image Depiction and Coding Techniques Upon the Bandwidth that Must Be Supported by the Display and Graphics Hardware Together with Their Potential Effect on Image Resolution and Color Pallet[a]

Parameter	Temporal Coding	Spatial Coding	Chromatic Coding
Display bandwidth	Approximately doubled	Unchanged	Unchanged
Graphics pipeline	Approximately doubled	Unchanged	Unchanged
Image resolution	Unchanged	Resolution reduced	Unchanged
Color pallet	Unchanged	Unchanged	Generally bi-color (restricted range of additional colors possible)

[a]This comparison is made relative to the performance of a conventional flat screen display offering only monocular support and is simply intended to be indicative.

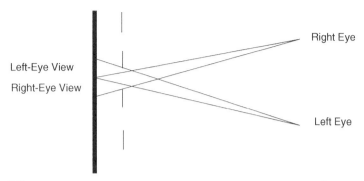

Figure 3.2   The parallax stereogram technique proposed by F. E. Ives in 1903. Here a plate comprising a series of slits is placed in front of a specially prepared photograph (or conventional 2-D display screen). The left and right eye views of a stereopair are divided into a series of fine strips and interleaved. Thus the slit plate ensures that only one set of strips are visible to each eye. Naturally this approach assumes a certain viewing position.

and therefore user mobility is restricted.[7] Systems of this type may be implemented in a number of ways; perhaps the simplest embodiment is the parallax stereogram illustrated in Figure 3.2. Here, the left and right views of the stereo pair are produced as a series of fine strips that are alternately depicted on a photograph or 2-D display. In front of these there is a "slit plate". The slits within this plate and the image strips have approximately the same pitch and as may be seen from the illustration, the plate ensures that image strips corresponding to the left and right views are visible only to the appropriate eye. This approach was first proposed by F. E. Ives in a patent filed in 1902 (US Patent Number 725,567). In this patent the inventor outlines the display technique in the following way:

> *The stereogram consists of a single transparent photographic image divided into lines, each alternate one of said lines corresponding to a portion of the respective element of a double stereogram, the photograph having the appearance that would be obtained by printing the two halves of an ordinary double stereogram in superposition upon one surface. In front of this stereogram is placed a transparent-line screen, consisting of opaque lines with clear spaces between them, there being as many clear spaces as there are lines in the photograph belonging to a single element of the stereogram .... The result is that when using the two eyes as in ordinary vision, from a suitable viewpoint, the right eye seeing only the lines of the photograph which belong to the right-hand element of the stereogram . . . the objects photographed appear to stand out solidly as in a stereoscope.*

---

[7] When viewed from the correct location, the "*orthoscopic*" (normal) image is seen. However, when the user moves away from this position, the image intended for the right eye is seen by the left and *vice versa*. In this case, the "*pseudoscopic*" image is observed in which depth information is reversed. As the observer moves further away from this position, the correct image will again be observed, and so on. [McAllister, 1993].

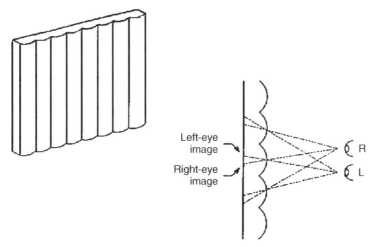

Figure 3.3 The use of a lenticular sheet comprising a series of cylindrical lenses that replace the slit plate used for the parallax stereogram technique (see Figure 3.2). When viewed from the correct location, the lenses direct left and right views to the appropriate eye. This approach may be extended to support motion parallax—but only in one direction (usually horizontally). (Reproduced from Blundell and Schwarz [2000].)

Alternatively, a "lenticular sheet" comprising a set of cylindrical lenses may be fixed to the front of a conventional display (see Figure 3.3). The thickness of the sheet is such that its rear surface corresponds to the focal plane of the lenses [Okoshi, 1976]. As with the "slit plate" described above, the lenses are able to direct left and right views to the appropriate eye (see Figure 3.3). Both the "slit plate" and lenticular approach may be adapted to provide support for motion parallax (see Section 3.6).

The use of a lenticular sheet for the creation of a spatially coded stereoscopic display is in fact a simplification of a technique reported in 1908 for integral photography Lippmann, 1908.[8] This employed a fly's eye lens sheet and provided a means of capturing and displaying photographs that provide both vertical and horizontal parallax. Naturally, in the case of the lenticular sheet, the use of cylindrical lenses means that parallax can only be supported in a single direction.

Fundamental to any stereoscopic display system is the provision of binocular disparity through the use of a pair of images that depict a scene or object(s) from two viewpoints. In the case of the temporal coding technique outlined above, the inclusion of the additional binocular cue necessitates an increase in the bandwidth of both the graphics engine and the display hardware. In contrast, the use of the spatial coding technique does not impact on the bandwidth that must be supported by the graphics hardware, but does lead

---

[8] For relevant reading see Ives [1928, 1929, 1930a, 1930b, 1931].

to a reduction in image resolution. This is because both images within the stereo pair are simultaneously displayed in each image frame and therefore share the available number of pixels supported by the screen.

3. **Chromatic Coding:** As with the spatial coding technique, chromatic coding allows both images within the stereo pair to be depicted simultaneously on a conventional flat screen display. Each of these images is depicted in a different color (e.g., red and green) and in order that the observer's left and right eyes are presented with the appropriate images, glasses containing appropriate eyepiece filters are used.[9] As we have seen, in the case of both the temporal and spatial coding techniques, the extension of the conventional flat screen display to support stereopsis has associated overheads: In the case of the former, this impacts upon display bandwidth, and in the latter case reduced image resolution. Chromatic coding of the stereo pair also has an associated overhead which in this case impacts on the pallet range that may be supported by the display technique. Indeed, chromatically coded images are generally only depicted in two colors although it is possible to provide additional (although limited) color capability (see Girling [1990]).

The three approaches outlined above employ some form of coding that enables the stereo pair to be properly presented to the visual system. An alternative approach provides a separate display for each eye via which the two images comprising the stereo pair are depicted. This technique more closely mimics the traditional stereoscope, and the use of two separate display screens makes a coding scheme unnecessary. As with the traditional stereoscopes, each eye is prevented from seeing the image intended for the other eye. This technique is used in the implementation of the immersive virtual reality (IVR) head-mounted display (HMD).[10]

As indicated in a previous work Blundell and Schwarz [2006], it appears that the first research undertaken in connection with the development of a stereoscope in which traditional photograph-based stereo pairs were replaced by two CRT displays able to depict the output from an analog computation system dates back to the 1940s [Schmitt, 1947]. For convenience, one form of apparatus used is illustrated in Figure 3.4; as may be seen, the output from each CRT was made visible only to the appropriate eye. This represents perhaps the first all-electronic immersive 3-D display. Subsequent developments were undertaken by a number of researchers including Morton Heilig (see US Patent Number 3,050,870, which was filed in 1962) and Sutherland [1968]. As with the system developed by Otto Schmitt, these systems also employed two cathode ray tubes via which stereoscopic images were depicted.

To make practical HMDs, it is necessary to reduce the size of the electronic displays (here, miniature CRT displays have given way to those based on

---

[9] This approach dates back to the mid-nineteenth century.

[10] This is also employed in various augmented reality headsets (see, for example, Blundell and Schwarz [2006] and Burdea and Coiffet [2003]).

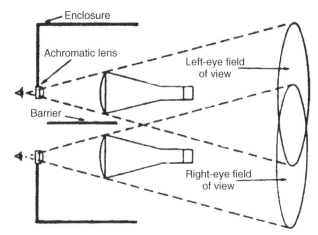

Figure 3.4 An immersive 3-D display described by Otto Schmitt in a publication that appeared in 1947. Here, electronically processed stereo pairs are depicted by means of two CRTs, which are arranged so that each CRT is only visible to the appropriate eye. (Reprinted with permission from Schmitt [1947]; Copyright © 1947, American Institute of Physics.)

LCD technologies). At the same time, in order to enhance the impact of the display paradigm, developers have attempted to ensure that the images occupy a large portion of the visual field. This, and the close proximity of the displays to the eyes, necessitates the insertion of an optical arrangement between the eyes and display screen, thereby enabling the user to readily focus on the stereo images.

The work described by Otto Schmitt in his 1947 publication does not represent the first attempt to develop an electronic form of stereoscope. An electromechanical system was proposed in a patent filed by Joseph Bayer in 1930. Aspects of this patent are briefly discussed in the next subsection.

3.3.1 A "Fog Penetrating" Televisor

Although it is unlikely that the approach outlined by Joseph Bayer in 1930 (US Patent Number 1,876,272) could have been successfully implemented, it is instructive to briefly consider aspects of his proposal. The patent begins as follows:

> *This invention relates to new and useful improvements in a fog penetrating televisor for seeing through fog, clouds, rain and smoke . . . invisible infra-red rays are translated into visible light . . . This invention is designed to eliminate these hazards by allowing the pilot to see through them.*

The essential weakness of this patent concerns the detection of infrared radiation. However, had the inventor slightly modified the approach described in the patent so as to detect visible light, it would have perhaps offered an electromechanical television system able to support the binocular parallax depth cue.

Plan and end elevation views of the image capture system are provided in Figure 3.5a. In brief, radiation entering the apparatus is focused by two lenses (14)

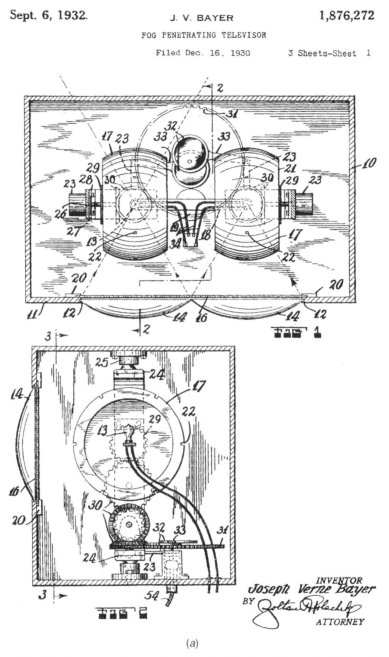

Sept. 6, 1932.   J. V. BAYER   1,876,272

FOG PENETRATING TELEVISOR

Filed Dec. 16, 1930   3 Sheets-Sheet 1

(a)

Figure 3.5   The fog penetrating televisor described by Joseph Bayer in 1930. In (a) plan and end elevation views of the image capture system are provided. In (b) an observer views the stereoscopic images via a stereoscope and in (c) a plan view of the display apparatus is provided. (Reproduced from US Patent Number 1,876,272.)

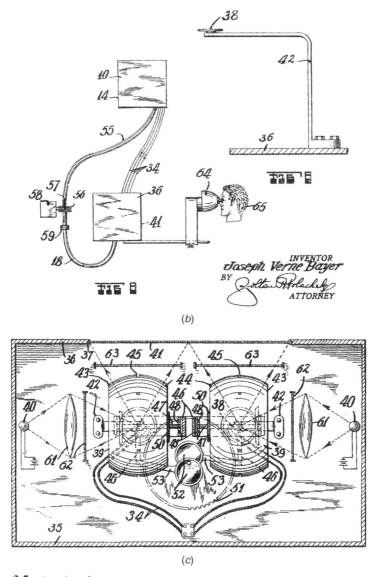

Figure 3.5 (*continued*)

onto the two detectors (labeled (13) in the illustration), with each detector capturing the image scene from a different location and thereby supporting stereoscopic imaging. The detectors are each located at the center of a rotating barrel (17) that performs the scanning function. As may be seen from the side elevation diagram, a series of holes are machined into the barrel at its widest circumference; and as the barrels rotate, the detectors are able to sample the illumination stimulus at regular intervals. This provides a 1-D scan of the image scene. This is extended to a 2-D scan by enabling the barrels to oscillate in the horizontal plane (i.e., normal to the direction of rotation). The output from the detectors is sent via a serial link to the display.

A plan view of the internal components within the display apparatus is provided in Figure 3.5c. As with the image capture system, this again employs two rotating/oscillating barrels, each equipped with a series of holes around its broadest circumference. The output from the two light sources (40) is projected onto two mirrors (38) whose angular position may be changed in accordance with the signals received from the image capture device (via an electromagnetic arrangement).[11] In short, the light emanating from the two sources is scanned in synchronism with the image capture scan and is modulated in accordance with the signals produced by the detectors. The stereoscopic images are cast onto a ground glass screen where they are viewed using the arrangement illustrated in Figure 3.5b.

This approach reinforces earlier discussion (Section 1.2.2) concerning the difficulties faced by designers prior to the proliferation of computer-based technologies that can be used to readily interface image capture and image display hardware. Although the scan technique described in this patent is interesting, the detection system is impractical and, as described, the system could not have operated. As with many other patented data capture and display systems, it is difficult to clearly assess the extent to which the system was prototyped. The impracticality of the detection technique suggests that this system simply represents a concept and that the inventor was more experienced in the mechanical and optical domains and less so in electrical techniques. On the other hand, at times the inventor is authoritative and there is an indication of sound experience:

> *Clearer images and more details are possible when scanning is done so that the images are scanned slightly different from each other with both the angles and the direction of scanning being different, when viewed by the operator through a stereoscope.*

3.4   EXTENDING THE STEREOSCOPIC APPROACH

Support for the binocular parallax depth cue gives rise to images that demonstrate a remarkable sense of *relief*. Such images generally provide an observer with a greater impression of realism and may enable spatial relationships to be more readily discerned. Furthermore, in some situations, features that may be difficult to perceive in the case of a monocular image may be made readily visible through the support for stereopsis. Consequently, in many situations, stereoscopic imaging offers considerable benefits. However, in the case of the basic stereoscopic technique, a user will quickly become frustrated since unlike our real-world experience, it is impossible to change viewing position and see objects from different locations. Thus the

---

[11] Optimistically, the inventor anticipates that the detectors will provide a high-frequency response for the sampling of the signal and that their sensitivity will be such that they are able to directly drive these electromagnets (without signal amplification). Furthermore, the detection process is achieved without any stable reference ....

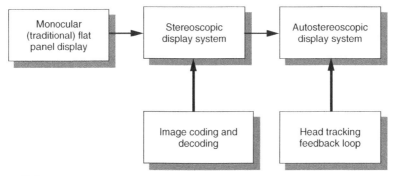

Figure 3.6   Through the use of additional hardware and software systems, the conventional flat panel display may support both binocular and motion parallax. The inclusion of motion parallax necessitates hardware that can track changes in a user's head position in accordance with which the display is suitably updated. However, any discernible latency occurring between the movement of the observer and the update of the image can be problematic. (Diagram © 2005 A.R. Blundell.)

changing perspective seen when, for example, we move our head slightly relative to a real-world scene does not occur when we attempt to change our viewing location relative to a traditional stereoscopic image. The absence of this powerful motion parallax depth cue (see Section 2.3.3) reduces realism, makes it more difficult to accurately determine spatial relationships, and hampers interaction.

Fortunately, in the case of computer-based stereoscopic display systems it is possible to support this depth cue in several ways. In the case of one approach, additional hardware is used to track the position of the user's head relative to the display screen (see Figure 3.6). This information enables the graphics engine to update the stereoscopic image in accordance with changes in viewing location.

> Motion parallax derived by head movement relative to a 3-D scene provides a simple, intuitive, and rapid method for interacting with spatial images. In its most basic form, the stereoscopic technique does not support this interaction modality and therefore a user must employ some form of interaction tool in order to make even minor changes in viewing perspective.

The earliest publication located by the author which suggests the use of head tracking as a means of updating the perspective view on a scene depicted on a flat screen display is contained in the extensive paper by Parker and Wallis [1948].[12] These researchers write:

> *Since the use of parallax in everyday life most commonly occurs when one is moving relative to a large number of stationary objects, it may be preferable for the operator*

---

[12] Also see Section 1.2.3.

to move his head rather than give him aspect controls to turn manually. The aspect controls would then be operated by movements of the operator's head, a joystick device being used as a coupling, for example. The operator will then move his head around and look into an apparently stationary three-dimensional volume. In order to remove any ambiguity and improve realism, the perspective and/or perspective shading described previously could be added to the display. This could be made adjustable, arranged to follow automatically any head movements, by the incorporation of a telescopic device . . . . It is clear, however, that this could be arranged for only one observer at each display.

In the 1960s, Ivan Sutherland described work undertaken in the development of a HMD that incorporated head tracking by means of both mechanical and wireless systems. This work is briefly overviewed by Blundell and Schwarz [2006] and is described in some detail in Sutherland's original and informative publication [Sutherland, 1968].

Today, head tracking systems are commonly based on ultrasound transmission. For example, three ultrasonic transmitters may be located at the corners of a triangular frame that is typically situated above a flat screen display. Similarly, three ultrasonic receivers are arranged in a triangular configuration and are attached to a user's stereo viewing glasses. A triangulation technique based on the time taken for a signal transmitted from each ultrasound transmitter to reach each of the three receivers may then be used to measure the position and orientation of the plane containing the three receivers (and hence the observer's head location) relative to the plane containing the three transmitters. The propagation speed of sound in air (v) is dependent on temperature such that

$$v \propto \sqrt{T},$$

where T denotes the temperature in kelvin. Consequently, if we represent the speed of sound in air at $0°C$ (273 K) as v_o, then

$$v = v_0 \sqrt{\frac{T}{273}} = v_0 \sqrt{1 + \frac{\theta}{273}}.$$

Where θ is the temperature expressed in degrees centigrade. Using the binomial expansion, we may write this in an approximate form:

$$v \approx v_0 \left(1 + \frac{\theta}{546}\right)$$

Assuming a velocity of sound at $0°C$ of 331 ms^{-1}, then

$$v \approx 331 + 0.6\theta.$$

Consequently, for an ambient temperature of $27°C$, the velocity of sound is ~ 347 ms^{-1}. Thus in the case of a user located at 50 cm from a display, the propagation time for a signal is ~ 1.4 ms. If each of the transmitters broadcast in sequence, then a single set of position measurements cannot be made in less than ~ 4.2 ms.[13]

---

[13] Employing an electromagnetic position sensing system may effectively eliminate this measurement time. Alternatively, the method referred to in the text may be modified so that each transmitter

In practice, this time is often increased by delays that are inserted between signal transmissions to avoid any interference that may arise as a consequence of echoes from the previous transmission. Additionally, the brief time needed to process measurements and pass the updated information to the graphics processor in order to initiate the creation of the stereoscopic image from the new viewing direction must also be taken into account. Thus, changes in viewing position cannot result in an instantaneous image update, and any lag that is either consciously or subconsciously perceptible may cause discomfort to the user. Factors that contribute to this lag are summarized in Figure 3.7.

The problems associated with the implementation of affordable systems able to offer accurate and rapid position sensing are offset by the computational efficiency of this approach. Indeed, the use of head tracking as a means of incorporating the motion parallax cue within a stereoscopic display system offers efficiency in terms of the demands placed on the display system and graphics engine. By way of comparison, consider the case of the volumetric display that permits an image to be viewed from practically any orientation. In this case the image content is visible from all possible orientations necessitating the entire image to be output during each image update period—irrespective of whether or not the image is being viewed from a particular location. On the other hand, in the case of the stereoscopic approach that incorporates head tracking, only a single view on an image data set is output during each frame, with this view corresponding to the observer's viewpoint.

> Volumetric embodiments that impose little, if any, restriction on viewing position require that, during the course of each image update period, all views on an image scene be displayed—irrespective of whether or not a scene is being observed from a particular position. However, in the case of the stereoscopic approach incorporating head tracking, only one view is output, with this corresponding to the viewing perspective of the user.

Certainly, the natural ability of many volumetric embodiments to provide freedom in viewing direction without the need to monitor observer location (and so introduce inherent latencies associated with the head tracked stereoscopic approach) coupled with support for multiple simultaneous observers[14] may, in the case of certain applications, be advantageous. In the next subsection, we discuss the ability of a display system to satisfactorily supply depth cues to the human visual system.

broadcasts at a different frequency, in which case the receivers would be equipped with filters enabling each to only detect the transmission of one particular source. This would reduce position measurement time. Various other approaches are possible.

[14] Some stereoscopic display embodiments that employing head tracking can also support a plurality of observers (e.g., the CAVE and its derivatives; see, for example, Blundell and Schwarz [2006], Cruz-Neira [1992, 1993]). However, the view is optimal for one observer (whose viewing position is monitored) while other observers obtain an inferior (but generally acceptable) view.

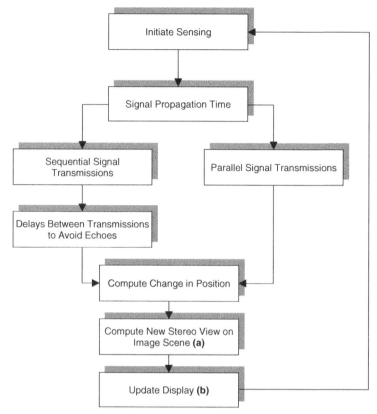

Figure 3.7   The time components associated with sensing changes in observer position and updating the display to provide support for motion parallax. The designer strives to minimize the lag that occurs between movement and corresponding image update. Component (a) may be reduced by only providing support for horizontal parallax, and (b) may be reduced by maximizing the refresh frequency of the display hardware. (Diagram © Q. S. Blundell 2006.)

3.5   THE PHYSICAL 3-D IMAGE AND ITS ELECTRONIC RENDITION

*'I paint objects as I think them,
not as I see them.*[15]

Architects and engineers have devised construction techniques enabling us to live and work within controlled environments in which pleasant conditions are continually maintained. Even in temperate lands where power-hungry domestic air conditioning is generally not used, windows are often sealed and power savings in winter are enhanced through the use of double and even triple panels of glass. And

---

[15] Attributed to Pablo Picasso (1881–1973).

so we become increasingly insulated from our surroundings and from the natural extremes of temperature and humidity that come with the hour of the day and season of the year. We move between artificial environments and accept without question those sealed windows that cannot be thrown open to allow admittance to fresh air, bird song, and the giant moths, bats, and other life forms that are attracted by the room lighting . . . .

Since we now so often accept that a window need often do no more than provide a means by which we can gain a visual impression of the outside world, perhaps we would not be surprised to encounter within a futuristic novel reference to homes constructed entirely of insulating nontransparent materials. Electronic "windows" would be provided in the form of wall-mounted thin panel displays providing a remarkably flexible means of viewing our geographic surroundings or supporting an illusion that we live elsewhere.

Fortunately, such a claustrophobic Orwellian vision has little chance of becoming a reality, for there are *inherent* differences between the visual characteristics of the natural and artificial image. By way of example, let us suppose that the electronic display paradigm can satisfy (without recourse to viewing glasses) the binocular parallax depth cue and that motion parallax is also supported without the introduction of update latencies.[16] Despite these assumptions, we are still left with a number of fundamental issues that distinguish between the naturally observed scene and its electronic equivalent. These are summarized in Table 3.2, and below we briefly consider the issues relating to accommodation and convergence:

TABLE 3.2 Attributes of the Physical Image as Compared to an Equivalent Image Viewed by Means of an Electronic Window

Physical Window	Electronic "Window"
Nonquantized	Quantized (in terms of picture elements and color pallet)
Continuous image update	Noncontinuous image update
Continuous light emission	Light emission is often noncontinuous
Continuous motion	Motion occurs in discrete steps
Accommodation/convergence—no decoupling	Accommodation/convergence—decoupling
All image components can be brought into focus in accordance with changes in our direction of fixation. Consequently, accommodation is scene-dependent	If the image data is acquired by imaging a physical scene focusing issues are likely to be problematic. Consequently, accommodation is scene-independent

[16] To avoid the latencies associated with the head tracking technique discussed in the previous section, we may for example assume the use of a multi-view approach (see Section 3.6).

1. **Accommodation:** In the case of the natural scene, the focusing of the eyes changes as our gaze moves between objects located within a 3-D space. However, for objects that lie at distances beyond several meters, the ciliary muscles are relaxed and the eyes are effectively focused at infinity. In the case of the electronic "window" (flat screen display supporting binocular parallax), despite the three-dimensionality of the perceived scene, the eyes focus on the screen itself. They do not refocus as our attention moves between scene components that appear to be located at a greater or lesser distance.

2. **Accommodation/Convergence Breakdown:** Although the eyes focus on the screen (stereo window), the eyes converge on the apparent location of the image component to which our attention is directed. This contrasts with our observation of a physical 3-D scene where accommodation and convergence operate together: The eyes focus upon, and their axes meet at, the point of interest. The decoupling of accommodation and convergence is an inherent characteristic of some creative 3-D display technologies and is briefly discussed by Lipton [2001], who refers to it as A/C breakdown.[17]

Even if we neglect issues that relate to the quality of an image and its refresh, and assuming that a display technology is able to properly support binocular and motion parallax,[18] A/C breakdown remains an inherent characteristic of a number of display paradigms. Both holographic, volumetric, and varifocal techniques provide us with examples of approaches in which accommodation and convergence remain coupled in a natural manner.

> The volumetric approach supports the natural operation of the human visual system's accommodation and convergence mechanisms. However, as with the linear perspective cue, the range over which the volumetric display can faithfully support these cues is defined by the depth of an image space.

3.6 MULTI-VIEW DISPLAYS

As discussed in Section 3.4, the incorporation of a head-tracking system enables the standard stereoscopic technique to be extended to support the motion parallax depth cue. In this case the display depicts only a single perspective on

---

[17] It should be noted that by interposing an appropriate optical arrangement between the display screen and the observer or by reducing the extent of parallax in a stereoscopic image, the degree to which these cues are decoupled can be reduced. Furthermore, the decoupling may be ameliorated by positioning the perceived stereoscopic image so that it spans both sides of the stereo window.

[18] Many creative 3-D display paradigms support only horizontal motion parallax. In this case, one cannot view images from different perspectives by moving the head vertically. Limiting a system's ability to the provision of only horizontal parallax reduces computational cost; further, in the case of some of the display techniques (such as the simple lenticular sheet introduced in Section 3.3), the optical arrangement simply cannot support both vertical and horizontal parallax.

Pitch (*p*)

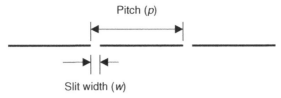

Slit width (*w*)

Figure 3.8   The parallax barrier approach that can be used to support motion parallax. Okoshi [1976] suggests a width to pitch ratio of ∼1/10. This compares to a value of ∼0.5 for the parallax stereogram. Unfortunately, as the width to pitch ratio is reduced the parallax barrier increasingly blocks the passage of light and so image brightness is reduced. Further, as the slit width is reduced, diffraction of light will ultimately become problematic.

a scene, corresponding to an observer's viewpoint. Multi-view systems offer an alternative solution by simultaneously providing a number of stereoscopic views, each of which is visible from a certain viewing location (viewing zone). Thus the observer may move between these zones and see the image scene from different positions.

A range of techniques may be used in the implementation of multi-view systems, with these differing most significantly in the way in which the image perspectives are directed into the viewing zones. The Parallax Barrier Method provides a simple example of this approach[19] and is an extension of the technique discussed in Section 3.3 for the formation of the parallax stereogram.

In order to support motion parallax, the barrier is fabricated so that the ratio of the slit width to pitch is much smaller than that used for the depiction of parallax stereograms (see Figure 3.8). Rather than dividing a single stereo pair into strips and interleaving them (as is the case with the parallax stereogram), a plurality of such pairs are divided into strips and interleaved, with each providing a view on the image scene from a slightly different location. Thus from a particular viewing position, the observer sees pairs corresponding to a certain viewpoint.

A weakness commonly associated with the parallax barrier concerns the loss of image brightness caused by the physical presence of the barrier, a problem that is exacerbated by the reduction of the slit width (w) and an increase in pitch (p). Okoshi [1976] indicates that typically $p < d/3500$, where d represents the viewing distance. Thus for $d = 50$ cm, $p < 0.14$ mm. In the case where $w \sim p/10$, then $w \sim 14$ μm.

In an alternative scheme, a lenticular sheet or the "fly's eye" lens sheet[20] may be used, thereby overcoming the loss of image brightness. As with the volumetric approach, where there is considerable freedom in viewing position, during each image update period all views on the 3-D scene must be depicted, irrespective of

[19] See a patent filed by Clarence Kanolt in 1915 (US Patent Number 1,260,682) for details of the "parallax panoramagram".

[20] This is able to support both vertical and horizontal parallax [Okoshi, 1976].

observer location. The total number of pixels that comprise the screen are equally shared between these views, and so the number of pixels that may be devoted to each view (N_v) is given by

$$N_v = \frac{N_x \dot{N}_y}{V},$$

where N_x and N_y denote the number of pixels that may be illuminated horizontally and vertically on a rectangular screen and V represents the number of stereoscopic views to be depicted [Blundell and Schwarz, 2006].

The following additional references provide useful discussion on a range of multi-view techniques: Inoue et al. [2000], Hamagishi et al. [2001], Perlin et al. [2000, 2001], Lippman [1908], Kollin [1988]. Discussion of the related "moving slit" approach can be found in Collender [1967] and Tilton [1988]. See also Travis [1990], Lang et al. [1992], Travis et al. [1995], and Dodgson et al. [1999]. Summary discussion is provided in a number of books such as McAllister [1993] and Blundell and Schwarz [2006].

3.7   ON PAINTING AND SCULPTURE

> *If you call painting dumb poetry,*
> *the painter may call poetry blind painting.*
> *Consider then which is the most grievous defect,*
> *to be blind or dumb?*[21]

The systematic techniques needed to permit the accurate depiction of a 3-D scene on a 2-D canvas were formulated and disseminated during the Renaissance period, which flourished in Italy between the fourteenth and sixteenth centuries (see, for example, Edgerton [1976, 1991] and Blundell and Schwarz [2006]). These techniques enabled artist to create accurate renditions of a 3-D scene on the canvas panel or other planar surface and ultimately led to works that possess and even surpass photorealism.

The conventional monocular flat screen computer display is the electronic equivalent of the traditional artist's canvas, and so many of the techniques used in modern computer graphics are based on the principles that were laid down during the Renaissance period. As discussed in Chapter 2, this conventional display paradigm is able to satisfy the range of pictorial depth cues, and the creative 3-D display systems introduced in the previous sections extend the capabilities of this approach, enabling binocular parallax (and, in some cases, motion parallax) to be supported. These displays build upon and extend the traditional image depiction techniques formulated during the Renaissance and therefore retain many of the characteristics associated with the 2-D tableau.

---

[21] *The Notebooks of Leonardo da Vinci* [Richter, 1998].

Volumetric display systems that support considerable freedom in viewing orientation give rise to images that from a visual perspective may be considered to represent an electronic equivalent of the traditional sculpted image.[22] Consequently, when we compare such volumetric architectures with other forms of creative 3-D display systems that are based on some form of static flat screen display technique, we must bear in mind that we are in essence making a comparison between two markedly different display modalities.

Some 500 years ago, Leonardo da Vinci highlighted various basic differences that exist between traditional perspective painting techniques and sculpture. Some of his comments reflect the limited understanding of the visual processes (especially with respect to nonpictorial cues) that existed at that time. He does not allude to the natural way the eyes are presented with binocular and motion parallax information when a sculpted image is viewed, nor to the manner in which the eyes automatically converge and focus upon a feature of interest. Furthermore, and perhaps surprisingly, he does not appear to allude to the canvas as providing a single view on a scene in contrast to the sculpted image that supports freedom in viewing direction. However, some of his other remarks are directly applicable to today's volumetric and stereoscope-based imaging techniques and highlight differences between these two general approaches. Several of his comments are reproduced in the subsections that follow (quotations are taken from Richter [1998]).

3.7.1   Information Content

Consider an artist wishing to employ paints and canvas in order to record a three-dimensional real-world scene. If sufficiently skilled, the artist will be able to employ the techniques formulated during the Renaissance to form a monocular window onto the scene, capturing a wealth of detail and placing this within a framework that accurately records the various pictorial depth cues. This depth cue information is, in fact, encoded within the image and decoded by the visual systems of those who subsequently view the completed work. To achieve "photorealism" within a perspective painting requires great talent, as the artist must capture not only the content of the scene that is to be recorded, but also the cues that form the framework and that extend the 2-D canvas to provide the illusion of three-dimensionality. In this context, Leonardo da Vinci writes:

> *Painting requires more thought and skill and is a more marvellous art than sculpture, because the painter's mind must of necessity enter into nature's mind in order to act as an interpreter between nature and art; it must be able to expound the causes of the manifestations of her laws, and the way in which the likenesses of objects that surround the eye meet in the pupil of the eye transmitting the true images; it must distinguish among a number of objects of equal size, which will appear greater to the eye; among colours that are the same, which will appear darker and which lighter; among objects*

---

[22] Here we refer to images that primarily convey the form of a 3-D object. The analogy becomes less meaningful when we consider volumetric displays used to show the spatial arrangements of a set of objects (e.g., a collection of aircraft in flight).

all placed at the same height, which will appear higher; among similar objects placed at various distances, why they appear less distinct than others.

The artist is responsible for every detail depicted on the canvas—the finished work represents the coalescence of the artist's ability to accurately observe a 3-D scene and to properly map these observations onto a 2-D space. Indeed the window created by the artist has a profundity that surpasses photographic recording, for the artist depicts a perspective corresponding to the scene as it is perceived after being processed by the human visual system—as it appears in the "mind's eye". The rendered scene therefore not only encodes imagery within a perspective framework but also is likely to contain detail of the artist's cognitive processes.

The artist can control a range of depth cues, each of which may, in general terms, be adjusted independently of the others. When sculpting an object, the opportunities for adjusting the cues are more limited since they may be implicitly defined by aspects of the image. For example, the extent of a sculpted image[23] will define linear perspective and its form (coupled with the location of external lighting sources) and will automatically determine the location of shadows and degree of shading. In this context, Leonardo da Vinci writes:

The art of painting includes in its domain all visible things, and sculpture with its limitations does not, namely the colour of all things in their varying intensity and the transparency of objects. The sculptor simply shows you the shapes of natural objects without further artifice. The painter can suggest to you various distances by a change in colour produced, by the atmosphere intervening between the object and the eye. He can depict mists through which the shapes of things can only be discerned with difficulty; rain with cloud-capped mountains and valleys showing through; clouds of dust whirling about the combatants who raised them; streams of varying transparency, and fishes at play between the surface of the water and its bottom; and polished pebbles of many colours deposited on the clean sand of the river bed surrounded by green plants seen underneath the water's surface. He will represent the stars at varying heights above us and innumerable other effects whereto sculpture cannot aspire.

The image rendered on a display employing some form of static planar screen can offer the flexibilities described by Leonardo da Vinci, whereas the volumetric technique is somewhat more limited in its capabilities (especially when there is little restriction on viewing position). This is compounded by the inability of the majority of volumetric architectures to support image opacity, which causes particular problems when we seek to incorporate within the volumetric image a sense of shading and/or distinct shadows. One possible approach to the inclusion of opacity makes use of voxels that scatter incident light (see Section 5.7), and this would enable light and shade to be readily associated with an image through the use of external light sources. In connection with illumination, Leonardo da Vinci writes:

In the first place, a statue is dependent on certain lights, namely those from above, while a picture carries its own light and shade with it everywhere. Light and shade are essential to sculpture. In this respect, the sculptor is helped by the nature of the

---

[23] Here, we assume a sculpture that may be viewed from any direction.

relief, which produces them of its own accord; while the painter has to create them by his art in places where nature would normally do so.

3.7.2   Working within a 3-D Space

> The secret of life is to have a task,
> something you devote your entire life to,
> something you bring everything to,
> every minute of the day for the rest of your life.
> And the most important thing is,
> it must be something you cannot possibly do.[24]

The extent to which the Italian Renaissance denoted a period of discovery or redis-covery of the techniques needed to support the geometrically accurate recording of 3-D imagery upon a 2-D canvas is a subject of interesting debate (see, for example, Figure 3.9). Certainly our perception of the abilities of classical artists to accurately capture perspective views on 2-D media is likely to be influenced (and perhaps distorted) by the numerous works of pictorial art that have been lost during the intervening centuries. Leonardo da Vinci writes:

The one advantage which sculpture has is that of offering greater resistance to time....[25]

And so, perhaps after the passage of several millennia, the diversity and number of surviving sculptures coupled with the range of architectural works remaining in existence (or that have been reconstructed) provide us with a firmer basis upon which we can discuss the ability of our ancestors to appreciate facets of a 3-D space. Consider the artist creating a sculpture such as the one illustrated in Figure 3.10. Putting to one side the physical difficulties of working with materials such as marble, it is apparent that the artist's task would be greatly facilitated if both the physical person who is to be sculpted and the tableau from which the image is formed exist in close proximity and *within the same spatial dimensions.* In such a situation, the artist is able to make physical measurements and use these directly to assist in the creative task.[26] As the sculpted image takes form, various depth cues will become inherently associated with it. Of course, in the case of the image shown in Figure 3.10, the artist must strive for unrestricted viewing freedom (cf. many volumetric techniques). This contrasts with the traditional painting that provides only a single view on a scene.

---

[24] Attributed to Henry Moore (1898–1986).

[25] Leonardo da Vinci also writes: "*As I practise the art of sculpture as well as that of painting, and am doing both in the same degree, it seems to me that without being suspected of unfairness I may venture to give an opinion as to which of the two is of greater skill and of greater difficulty and perfection.*" Given his confidence in the greater durability of the of the sculpted image, it is therefore perhaps surprising that he is better known for the paintings that he created. He writes; "*Painting is more beautiful, more imaginative and richer in resource, while sculpture is more enduring, but excels in nothing else.*"

[26] Although the artist may wish to scale measurements.

Figure 3.9   This remarkable fresco fragment was located in Pompeii and dates back to the first century A.D. Here, the artist demonstrates a superb ability to capture detailed imagery and realistic perspective upon a 2-D tableau. The facial expressions are captivating and transcend time, despite the passage of two millennia, the fresco provides us with an insight into the character and personality of this couple—it is as though we know them. Mount Vesuvius erupted in 79 A.D. and we are left to ruminate on their fate. (Reproduced by kind permission of the National Archaeological Museum, Naples.)

3.7.3   Display Capability

The creation of the perspective painting formed on a surface and the crafting of the sculpted image represent two forms of markedly different outlets for creative expression, and although images created by these two techniques possess

Figure 3.10 Venus de Milo. This remarkable sculpture is some 1.8 m in height and was crafted from Parian marble. The work dates back to the second century B.C. and was discovered on the Aegean island of Melos in 1820 by a peasant named Yorgos. The ability of the artist to work within a 3-D space is demonstrated by the flawless excellence of the sculpture. (Reproduced with kind permission of the Musée du Louvre, Paris.)

several similarities, there are also key differences (see Figure 3.11). Broadly these differences relate to:

1. The range of depth cues that may be associated with the image.
2. The ability of the artist to control and/or manipulate these depth cues.
3. The freedom in viewpoint supported by the depiction modality.

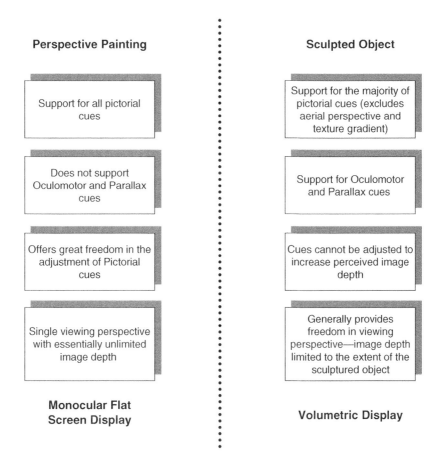

Figure 3.11 Here we summarize key differences in the visual characteristics of the perspective painting created on a planar surface, and the sculpted image which occupies three physical dimensions. In terms of their interface with the human visual system the former equates to the monocular flat screen display, and the latter to the volumetric approach. (Diagram © A.R. Blundell 2006.)

Some five centuries ago, Leonardo da Vinci wrote:

In fact, painting is adorned with infinite possibilities which sculpture cannot command.

Certainly, as a consequence of our interpretation of the range of pictorial cues that may be incorporated and manipulated within a perspective painting, the artist has great freedom in controlling the depth at which image components are perceived to be located. In this respect, Leonardo da Vinci would have been focusing on the pictorial cues and not those that we now refer to as parallax and oculomotor cues and which are not supported by traditional painting techniques—but which are inherently associated with the sculpted image.

In the 1990s, immersive virtual reality was often perceived as having unbounded potential and therefore was frequently deemed to be superior to other forms of interface to the digital world. From the perspective of the image depiction technique, the world presented to the IVR user is entirely synthesized, with no artifact or feature existing unless created by the host computer. In principle, this offers the "infinite" possibilities that da Vinci attributed to the traditional painting technique. However, in the case of both modalities we have come to recognize inherent limitations. Similarly, limitations exist in the case of the sculpted image and, just as the traditional painting and the image scene depicted on the conventional monocular computer display do not support natural accommodation and convergence, nor provide binocular information, so the sculpted image (and volumetric system offering great freedom in viewing location) fails to properly support several pictorial cues (particularly texture gradient or aerial perspective). Moreover, the depth occupied by the perceived image is restricted. In relation to aerial perspective, da Vinci writes:

> *The effects of aerial perspective are outside the scope of sculptors' work; they can neither represent, . . . nor mists, nor dull weather, nor an infinite number of things which I forbear to mention lest they be wearisome.*

The ability of many volumetric display architectures to allow great freedom in viewing direction and to permit simultaneous viewing by a number of observers can be most advantageous. On the other hand this freedom means that it is not possible to adjust the depth cues associated with an image scene to increase the depth that we perceive the scene to occupy, nor can a sense of image opacity be promoted by means of the standard computer graphics technique of hidden line removal. Some of the ways in which viewing freedom impacts on our ability to manipulate the volumetric image are summarized in Figure 3.12.

A range of depth cues are inherently associated with both the traditional physically sculpted image and the image created within a volumetric image space. These provide the human visual system with the ability to accurately gauge the image size. Any attempt to manipulate depth cues to create an illusion by which the image appears to occupy a depth greater than is the physical reality cannot be sustained across a wide range of viewing positions.

3.8 DISCUSSION

The majority of creative 3-D display systems (including the varifocal approach) provide only a single window onto an image space and do not support "all-round" viewing. The volumetric paradigm offers considerable flexibility in this respect. Although some of the volumetric displays that we will encounter restrict viewing freedom to a single window (see, for example, display units described in Chapter 6), other architectures enable the user(s) to look onto the image space from practically

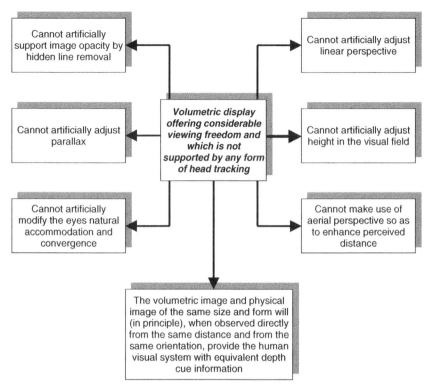

Figure 3.12   When considered from the perspective of the way in which their inherent three-dimensionality impacts on the human visual systems, the physical sculpted image and the volumetric image (depicted on a system which offers very considerable freedom in viewing position and which is not augmented by any form of head tracking technology) exhibit many similarities. As discussed in the text, some five hundred years ago Leonardo da Vinci recognized various limitations associated with the sculpted image and the greater freedoms provided by the traditional 2-D canvas. In the case of the former, the depth cues cannot be artificially modified to enhance the perceived image depth, whereas in the case of the traditional image depicted on a planar surface, the artist is able to create images of essentially unlimited depth (depth being indicated only by the range of pictorial cues). However an important strength of both the physically sculpted image and electronically rendered volumetric image is that depth cues (pictorial, oculomotor, and parallax cues) are naturally satisfied across the actual dimensions of the image. (Diagram © Q. S. Blundell 2006.)

any orientation. Although such viewing freedom can be advantageous, it can also result in difficulties, especially since in order to employ such systems we must move away from the traditional single window display paradigm with which we have great familiarity. To take full advantage of viewing freedom, we must rethink the ways in which displays are best used and tasks most effectively carried out (and here it is important to note that viewing freedom gives rise to new interaction opportunities).

In the next chapter we turn our attention to the techniques that may be used in the implementation of volumetric systems and focus on the "swept-volume" approach. In Chapter 5 we turn our attention to "static-volume" systems.

3.9   INVESTIGATIONS

1. An ultrasonic technique based on the time of flight technique discussed in Section 3.4 is used to measure the distance of an observer from the display screen. Assuming a typical viewing distance, estimate the error in position accuracy that may be caused by a change of $5°C$ in room temperature.

2. What factors determine the slit width and pitch of a parallax barrier that is to be used in the implementation of a multi-view display?

3. Consider the "fog penetrating televisor" outlined in Section 3.3.1. Based on this summary or by examination of the patent, what do you consider to be the strengths and weaknesses of this proposal?

4. Discuss the quotation provided at the end of Section 3.3.1 beginning "*Clearer images and more details* . . .". Do you consider this to be valid, and if so, why?

5. In Section 3.4 we discussed the extension of the stereoscopic approach to provide support for motion parallax, and in Section 3.6 we considered multi-view displays that are able to provide support for both binocular and motion parallax. Is support for binocular parallax a prerequisite for supporting motion parallax?

6. Some volumetric architectures provide only a single window onto an image space while others support practically unrestricted viewing (thus enabling users to view 3-D images from practically any orientation). Discuss the advantages and disadvantages of employing a display that provides "all-round" viewing. How do you believe such displays could be most effectively used? Identify applications that may benefit from unrestricted viewing freedom, and also identify applications in which this would be detrimental.

4 The Swept-Volume Approach

Thence to the cave: so day by day she past
In either twilight ghost-like to and fro
Gliding, and every day she tended him,
And likewise many a night.

4.1 INTRODUCTION

All swept-volume displays employ a mechanical system that causes a surface (or 3-D structure) to rapidly and repeatedly sweep through a physical volume and also utilize transient optical phenomena in the production of visible voxels. Some, or all, of the volume swept out forms the physical image space within which computer-processed data may be depicted. Many volumetric systems proposed or constructed to date may be classified as swept-volume systems, and great ingenuity has been applied to devising appropriate forms of motion for a range of possible

Enhanced Visualization: Making Space for 3-D Images. By Barry G. Blundell

surface geometries (or 3-D structures), as well as to the creation of mechanisms permitting visible voxel production. Although the basic principles of operation of swept-volume systems are easily understood, the subsystems forming the display can interact in subtle ways and so it often proves difficult to assess in advance all possible weaknesses that may be associated with a particular approach.

In the next section we introduce three exemplar swept-volume systems. The first of these employs the rapid rotational motion of a planar screen, the second relies on translational motion, and the last utilizes the rotational motion of a 3-D structure. These systems have been selected to best highlight various aspects of this general approach and will be referred to during our subsequent discussions. Having introduced (in a general way) some of the basic principles of operation that may be used in the implementation of swept-volume systems, we turn our attention in Section 4.3 to a more detailed discussion on aspects of the three key display unit subsystems previously introduced in Section 3.2. In Section 4.4 we focus on the important issue of the degree of parallelism supported by the voxel generation and activation subsystems and introduce the "voxel activation capacity," "voxel location capacity," and "fill factor" parameters. These provide an important indication of one aspect of a display unit's performance and may also be applied to the static-volume displays introduced in the next chapter. In Section 4.5 we classify swept-volume systems according to the types of subsystem used in their implementation and so provide a useful framework within which display embodiments may be described.

As indicated above, all swept-volume displays employ some form of rapid cyclic motion for the formation of an image space. Reliance upon mechanical movement is often considered to represent a weakness of the swept-volume approach. This matter is discussed in Section 4.6, and here we emphasize that many pivotally important technologies also place reliance on motion.

Finally, in Section 4.7 we introduce various forms of "dead zone" which may be associated with swept-volume systems and that may negatively impact on a display system's effectiveness. Throughout the chapter, we highlight aspects of our discussions by making reference to swept-volume display embodiments that are covered in more detail in Chapters 6, 7, and 8.

4.2 EXEMPLAR SWEPT-VOLUME TECHNIQUES

The swept-volume approach is most easily understood by examining the operation of particular embodiments. In this section we introduce three systems, each of which has been selected to highlight different facets of this general technique. These systems are described loosely without undue recourse to precise terminology. In subsequent sections we will introduce various more formal terms and concepts that may be used to more rigorously describe the implementation of systems, their principles of operation, and their performance characteristics. However, for the moment, we will describe systems in general terms and leave the reader to gauge inherent strengths and weaknesses of each implementation.

In the Appendix, an overview of some of the characteristics of the various display embodiments discussed in this book is provided. Within this tabulated summary, we indicate the section(s) where each technology is discussed. However, some sections refer to more than one display embodiment; therefore, so as to improve clarity and facilitate cross-referencing, each display type is identified by a code. Such codes are included in the descriptions that follow.

(a) System 1: The Rotational Motion of a Planar Screen (Ref. 8A).   A system employing the rotational motion of a rectangular planar screen is illustrated in Figure 4.1. As may be seen from this diagram, the axis of rotation lies in the plane of the screen. As the screen rotates, it sweeps out a cylindrical volume that forms a transparent image space. Provided that no visual obstructions are imposed by the surround or other apparatus, images created within this volume may be

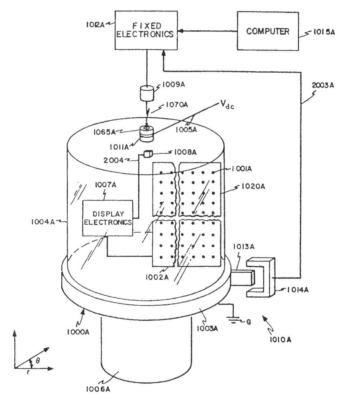

Figure 4.1   A swept-volume technique that utilizes the rotational motion of a planar array of opto-electronic elements (Ref. 8A). During a single rotation of the screen, each element is responsible for the creation of voxels along a circular track. The screen rotates at a rate sufficient to allow the human visual system to fuse the image, and so image flicker is not consciously perceived. For the moment, we neglect issues concerning the passage of signals to the rotating opto-electronic devices and note that in order for the host computer to generate meaningful images, it must be able to continually track screen position. See also Sections 8.2 and 11.5. (Reproduced from US Patent Number 4,160,973.)

viewed from practically any orientation. In terms of this simple embodiment, we assume that a rectangular array of opto-electronic elements [such as light-emitting diodes (LEDs)] is bonded to the screen's surface and that each of these may be individually addressed (activated).[1] Naturally, causing a diode to emit light for a brief interval will result in the generation of a visible "point" or "trail" of light within the image space. The period of rotation of the screen (T) relative to the duration of light emission (t), along with the radius from the axis of rotation of the element responsible for the production of the light (R), determines the elongation of the light trail formed (S) (as measured in the direction of the screen's motion).[2] Thus,

$$S = \frac{2\pi R t}{T}. \tag{4.1}$$

The minimum rate of rotation of the screen is determined by the critical flicker fusion frequency (see Section 2.4). In the case of the display configuration (outlined above) which is intended to depict images of only a single color, optical elements located on each of the two regions of the screen (i.e., on either side of the axis of rotation) may generate voxels during a single refresh. As a consequence, an image may be updated twice during each rotation of the screen, and so it is possible to reduce the rate of screen rotation. However, if we put this case to one side and suppose that an image is updated only once per rotational cycle, we can assume a minimum rotational frequency of $\sim$25 Hz. Consider a voxel that is generated at a distance (R) of 200 mm from the axis of rotation. Assuming that the voxel has a diameter of 0.4 mm (in the plane of the screen), then we can suppose that to maintain an approximate degree of symmetry in its form (i.e., to avoid undue voxel elongation which may degrade image quality—recall that the display will support viewing from practically any orientation), the voxel "length" (S) as measured in the direction of the screen's motion should also be approximately 0.4 mm. Equation (4.1) provides a duration of light emission (t) of $\sim$13 µs. Clearly, to maintain uniform voxel form, it is necessary (at least in principle) to vary t according to the radial position at which each voxel is located.[3]

As the screen rotates, its motion is divided into a number of sectors (see Figure 4.2) to each of which a radial slice of the image data set is written, and in this way the overall 3-D image is formed. Clearly, this relies upon the host computer continually maintaining track of the position of the screen and establishing its entry and exit from each sector position. Although the computer may accurately locate voxels within the plane of the screen, this approach does not

---

[1] For the moment, we will not concern ourselves with the problems associated with the passage of electrical signals to the rotating diodes.

[2] Here we assume that the opto-electronic devices may be turned on and off instantaneously.

[3] In practice, the degree of voxel elongation is determined by various factors. For example, in the case where LEDs are used, fast turn-on and turn-off can be assumed. However, if phosphors are employed, then after the removal of the excitation stimulus, light output will not instantaneously fall to zero. In other situations, to maximize the total number of voxels that may be activated during each update period, the shortest possible activation times are employed. In general, we tolerate some small degree of voxel elongation.

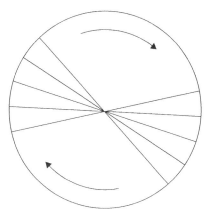

Figure 4.2   A plan view of a planar screen rotating about a central axis. The image space is divided into a number of sectors. As the screen passes through each of these, a corresponding radial slice of the image data set is drawn upon it. Although this is a convenient technique, it is not without weaknesses. These vary according to the particular embodiment but may include voxel positioning inaccuracies in the direction of screen motion, the inability to create voxels along the axis of rotation (dead image space, see Section 4.7.4) and the formation of a visual dead zone (see Section 4.7.3).

facilitate equally accurate voxel positioning within the direction of the screen's motion—unless each opto-electronic element can be individually and simultaneously addressed. Any form of addressing scheme that restricts the number (or combination) of elements that can be simultaneously activated within a sector will result in voxel positioning errors. The extent of such errors becomes more acute as the degree of parallelism exhibited by the voxel activation mechanism is reduced. This is an issue that we discuss further in Section 4.4.

(b) System 2: The Translational Motion of a Planar Screen.   Having briefly considered an approach employing rotational screen motion, we now turn our attention to an embodiment that uses a rapid and regular reciprocating (translational) movement. Such an arrangement is shown in general terms in Figure 4.3. Here we can see that the planar screen sweeps out an image space by moving back and forth. Naturally, such movement cannot result in the screen maintaining a constant velocity throughout the entire range of its motion. Therefore we are faced with two options:

- We maximize the distance through which the screen moves with constant velocity by using the highest possible acceleration at either end of its travel. In this case we confine the image space to that region in which the velocity is uniform.

- We design the system to accommodate a nonuniform velocity profile (typically sinusoidal motion).

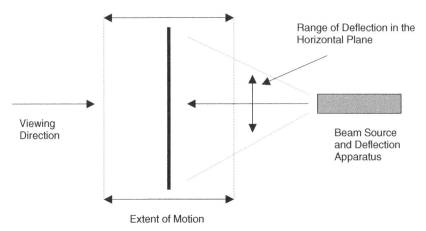

Range of Deflection in the
Horizontal Plane

Viewing
Direction

Beam Source
and Deflection
Apparatus

Extent of Motion

Figure 4.3 An example display employing the translational motion of a planar screen. We assume that voxels are created upon the screen using a single beam source that can be directed (under computer control) to any point on its surface. Naturally the viewing freedom associated with this embodiment would be considerably less than in the case of the first exemplar system. (Diagram © A. R. Blundell 2006.)

As will be discussed shortly, both these options have associated strengths and weaknesses. Below we briefly examine image update considerations and the calculation of beam deflection angles.

In the case of System 1 introduced above, which uses rotational motion, we discussed the possibility of achieving two image refreshes during each cycle of the screen's movement, thereby reducing the frequency of rotation. In the case of an approach that uses translational movement, although we can achieve two image refreshes per cycle of screen motion, this does not enable us to reduce the frequency of movement. This can readily be understood by reference to Figure 4.4. Consider a plane P that lies midway in the screens range of movement. If the screen completes a full cycle of movement in a time T (i.e., sweeps back *and* forth during this interval), then we are able to refresh points within the plane P at regular intervals of $T/2$. On the other hand, consider plane Q that is located at an extreme of the screen's motion. The refresh of points in this plane will occur at intervals of time T. Therefore if $T = 40$ ms, voxels located in the plane denoted as P in Figure 4.4 can be refreshed every 20 ms. On the other hand, voxels in the plane denoted by Q can only be refreshed every 40 ms—that is, at the rate of screen's cycle of motion. Hence, reducing the frequency of screen motion by a factor of two would be possible for voxels located in planes close to P, but voxels lying at a greater distance would appear to flicker (this problem becomes more acute toward the extremes of screen movement).

The creation of visible voxels could be achieved by equipping the screen with a rectangular array of opto-electronic elements as used in the embodiment introduced previously, which employed rotational motion. In order to demonstrate an alternative approach, we will consider that a stationary beam source and appropriate

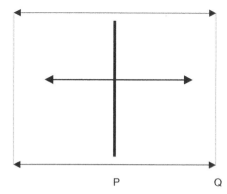

Figure 4.4 Although in the case of an embodiment employing the translational motion of a planar screen, voxels may be addressed twice per cycle of screen motion, the screen must move with a frequency that is no less than the critical flicker frequency ($\sim$25 Hz). Consider that the screen has a period of motion denoted T. At the mid-point of its movement (P), voxels can be refreshed at regular intervals of $T/2$. However, at other positions, voxels cannot be refreshed at this rate. For example, at position Q (corresponding to one extreme of movement) voxels can only be refreshed at intervals of T.

beam deflection apparatus, are employed, as indicated in Figure 4.3 (both electron and laser beams could be used for this purpose). If an electron beam is used, beam deflection can be achieved at low cost and at high speed. In this scenario the screen would be coated with a material able to convert electron beam energy to visible light through a process of cathodoluminescence (see, for example, Ozawa [1990]). The use of a directed laser beam requires more complex deflection apparatus, and deflection speeds may ultimately limit performance.

Let us assign a rectangular coordinate system to the image space. Here we will assume that the X and Y axis' are in the plane of the screen and the Z axis is parallel to the direction of the screens motion. Furthermore, we will assume that the origin is located on the beam deflection apparatus. In order to produce a visible voxel at an arbitrary point (x, y, z) within the image space, it is necessary to compute the required deflection angles (θ_x, θ_y) and to turn on the beam for a short duration as the screen passes through the appropriate location within the Z plane. The basic geometry is shown in Figure 4.5, and from this illustration it is apparent that

$$\tan \theta_x = \frac{x}{\sqrt{y^2 + z^2}} \tag{4.2}$$

and

$$\tan \theta_y = \frac{y}{\sqrt{x^2 + z^2}}. \tag{4.3}$$

Let us suppose that at time $t = 0$, the screen is passing the central part of the image space (i.e., position P in Figure 4.4). Assuming that the amplitude of the screen's motion is denoted by A, then for a sinusoidal velocity profile, at time t,

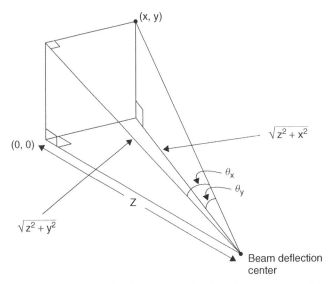

Figure 4.5 The geometry associated with the activation of a voxel at an arbitrary location (x, y) on the surface of a planar screen moving with translational motion. The deflection angles are identified as θ_x and θ_y.

the position of the screen relative to the mid-position of its travel is given by

$$z(t) = \frac{A}{2} \sin \omega t,$$

where $\omega = 2\pi/T$. Consider the movement of the screen from P to Q (i.e., a one-quarter cycle of its motion). If we assume the creation of k equally spaced image planes within this space, then we may express the separation of each image plane (ζ) as[4]

$$\xi = \frac{A}{2(k - 1)}.$$

Let each image plane be denoted by j, where $j = 0, 1, 2, \ldots$ as illustrated in Figure 4.6. Thus the time (t_j) at which the screen enters the jth image plane is

$$t_j = \frac{1}{\omega} \arcsin\left(\frac{j}{k - 1}\right) = \frac{T}{2\pi} \arcsin\left(\frac{j}{k - 1}\right). \tag{4.4}$$

For each slice, the deflection angles are calculated by substituting the appropriate value of z into Eqs. (4.2) and (4.3). Clearly, should the motion of the screen be nonuniform (e.g., sinusoidal motion) and if each image plane is to be equally spaced, then the time available for the formation of each image slice (τ) will vary.

---

[4] For simplicity, we assume that the first of these planes lies at P and the last at Q.

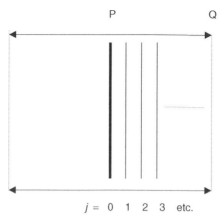

Figure 4.6 The region of image space lying between P and Q is divided into k image planes. These are denoted by $j = 0,1,2,3$ etc. See text for details.

For the motion of the screen between planes P and Q, we may express this time as

$$\tau = |t_j - t_{j-1}| = \frac{T}{2\pi}\left(\arcsin\left(\frac{j}{k-1}\right) - \arcsin\left(\frac{j-1}{k-1}\right)\right). \qquad (4.5)$$

The minimum slice duration occurs at the mid-position of the screen's motion. If, for example, we divide the image space formed between planes P and Q into 15 image planes and assume a frequency of motion of 25 Hz, then we obtain a minimum value for τ of $\sim$0.46 ms (corresponding to the screen's motion between planes $j = 0$ and $j = 1$). In the case of the previous exemplar system, we employed a matrix of voxel generation elements, each member of which could be individually addressed thereby providing a high degree of parallelism in the voxel activation process. In the case of the current embodiment, we have chosen to use a single beam source for the creation of each visible voxel, and therefore voxel activation is entirely sequential—parallelism is not supported. Consequently, all the voxels to be displayed within a slice must be illuminated sequentially within the time τ. If we assume that the activation time for each voxel is on the order of 0.5 μs, then, continuing with the numerical example used above, we would be limited to a maximum of $\sim$900 voxels in the slices for which the screen's velocity is at its greatest. On the other hand, consider the situation where the screen speed is at its slowest. This corresponds to the greatest amplitude of travel. From Eq. (4.5), we obtain a value for τ of $\sim$2.4 ms, enabling some 4800 voxels to be illuminated.

If the maximum number of voxels that can be illuminated within each slice is allowed to vary, this will lead to (or certainly contribute to) a nonuniform image space tableau. In this case, imposing uniformity requires that we populate each slice with the maximum number of visible voxels as defined by the worstcase population. However, in doing so, we are imposing worst-case performance across the entire depth of the image space. An alternative strategy is to seek a nonsinusoidal velocity profile, and this returns us to the possibility of defining the extent of the image space as that portion of screen motion in which the velocity can be maintained at a constant level.

As we will discuss in subsequent sections, the great majority of volumetric technologies proposed to date exhibit a variety of nondesirable image space characteristics. However, these do not necessarily compromise a display system's usefulness.

(c) System 3: The Rotational Motion of a 3-D Structure.   In the case of this exemplar swept-volume system, we move away from the notion of a moving surface and consider the use of a 3-D structure. Briefly returning to the first of our example systems, we can foresee the potential weakness, illustrated in Figure 4.7*a* and which may occur when the plane of the screen lies edge on to the observer. In this case a "visual dead zone" (a region of diminished image intensity) is generally observed, as depicted in Figure 4.7*b*. Although we will discuss this phenomenon in more detail in Section 4.7.3, it is apparent that it may be caused by presence of opto-electronic elements bonded to the screen impinging on the propagation of light. One possible solution is to locate the elements throughout a rotating volume rather than on a rotating surface, as illustrated in Figure 4.8. Here, a solid, transparent and cylindrical volume is employed. As with the first of the example systems, a rotational motion is used. The opto-electronic devices retain their relative positioning normal to the direction of rotation, but are dispersed in the direction of rotation. This approach can ameliorate the severity of the visual dead zone, but due to the increasing density of opto-electronic elements as we approach the axis of rotation, problems can still occur.[5]

4.3   SWEPT-VOLUME SUBSYSTEMS

As we have seen in the previous section, all swept-volume displays employ the mechanical motion of either a surface or 3-D structure upon which (or via which) visible voxels may be formed. Within the swept-volume category, we exclude systems in which a surface is subjected to regular deformation—displays of this type are commonly referred to as varifocal systems and are discussed separately in Chapter 10. We assume that in the case of swept-volume displays the surface is rigid and is not deformed during its cyclic motion. In the following subsections we review the subsystems that comprise a swept-volume display and which were previously introduced in Section 3.2.

4.3.1   Image Space Creation

*Science is a wonderful thing
if one does not have to earn one's living at it.*[6]

---

[5] For brief discussion, see (5) in Section 12.6.
[6] Attributed to Albert Einstein (1879–1955).

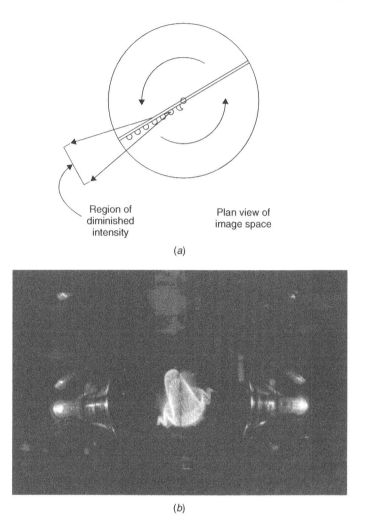

Region of
diminished
intensity

Plan view of
image space

(a)

(b)

Figure 4.7 The opto-electronic elements illustrated in (a) and which were employed in the first example system disrupt the passage of light and give rise to a "visual dead zone" (the size of the elements relative to the size of the screen is exaggerated for clarity). This dead zone takes the form of a region of diminished image intensity. The finite thickness of the rotating screen may also cause or exacerbate the extent of this visual dead zone (see Section 4.7.3). The 3-D image of a math function presented in (b) provides an illustration of such a dead zone. This image is displayed on a cathode ray sphere prototype (see Sections 1.6.1, 4.6, and 12.3). The impact of the visual dead zone is generally ameliorated by binocular vision. [Diagram (a) © Q. S. Blundell 2006, (b) © B. G. Blundell 2006.]

The physical image space is formed by the rapid and regular motion of a surface or 3-D structure. We may elect to define the image space by the dimensions of the surface and the extent of its motion, or may confine the image space to a portion of the volume swept out. This latter approach is generally intended to improve various

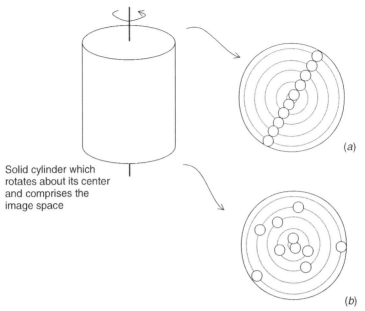

Figure 4.8 In the third example system, the opto-electronic elements no longer lie in a plane [as indicated in (a), but are dispersed, as in (b)]. As the cylindrical volume rotates, each element is responsible for voxel creation along a circular track. However, unlike the first of our example systems, the relative location of each element on each track is no longer the same. By analogy, we can loosely compare this approach to runners racing along a circular course. Each runner is confined to a particular track, and all runners have a different starting location. (Reproduced from Blundell and Schwarz [2000].)

image space characteristics at the expense of image space dimensions. Here we can introduce a useful measure: the sweep efficiency (ξ), which is expressed as

$$\xi(\%) = \frac{V_I}{V_P} \cdot 100, \qquad (4.6)$$

where V_P represents the volume physically swept out and V_I the volume actually available for image production (image space).

Few swept-volume embodiments exhibit a 100% sweep efficiency, although many come quite close to achieving this. By way of example, let us consider the three example systems introduced in the previous section. System 1 is likely to exhibit adverse voxel depiction characteristics along (or close to) the axis of rotation. This arises as a consequence of the presence of any central shaft that supports the rotating screen, or because of the finite thickness of the screen itself. Consequently, at or around the axis of rotation, voxel production is generally not possible, and this gives rise to a volume of "dead image space" (see Section 4.7.4). Such a display will therefore have a sweep efficiency of a little less than 100%. In the case of System 2, the sweep efficiency may be influenced by the screen's velocity profile. If we use a sinusoidal motion, then the sweep efficiency is optimal—although this is achieved at the expense of either uniformity (in terms of the maximum number of voxels that may be illuminated in each slice) or the total number of voxels that can be activated within the image space during each cycle of screen movement. Alternatively, we may employ a linear velocity profile, in which case the sweep efficiency is significantly lowered as we do not include within the image space those portions of the screen's motion during which it is accelerating. For System 3, the sweep efficiency may (in principle) be 100%.

Example Embodiment (Ref. 4A): The display unit illustrated in Figure 4.9 provides us with an example of an ingenious approach that provides excellent image space characteristics at the expense of a very low sweep efficiency. This system mimics our example System 2, effectively creating a translational motion with a constant velocity profile (however, this is achieved by means of rotational movement). As may be seen, the display (prototyped in the early 1970s) employs a number of small screens arranged around the periphery of a rotating cylinder [Szilard, 1974]. Each is displaced from its neighbors and so follows a helix around the cylinder. The imaging system projects image slices onto these screens as they pass through a particular location, each screen being illuminated in turn. Thus the size of the image space within which visible voxels may be formed is determined by the dimensions of each screen and by their total offset (i.e., the depth of the helix which they sweep out). If we assume that j square screens with sides of length X cm are employed, then the radius of the wheel (r_{wheel}) on which they are mounted is approximately

$$r_{wheel} = \frac{jX}{2\pi}.$$

We assume that each screen is offset from its neighbour by k cm providing an image space depth $d = jk$ cm. Thus the volume swept out by the screens (V_P) may be expressed as:

$$V_P = jk\pi X^2 \left(\frac{j}{\pi} + 1 \right). \tag{4.7}$$

By way of a numerical example, we assume that each of 15 screens with sides of length 10 cm are offset by 2 mm. The resulting physical image space has a depth of 3 cm and volume 300 cm^3. However, the physical volume swept out by the rotating structure is $\sim$5400 cm^3. In this case the sweep efficiency (ξ) is only $\sim$6%![7]

In the discussion that follows, we put to one side the use of a 3-D structure and focus on the motion of a surface upon which visible voxels are created. In the next subsection,

---

[7] Naturally, careful design (e.g., the use of tapered screens) can improve this efficiency—a little.

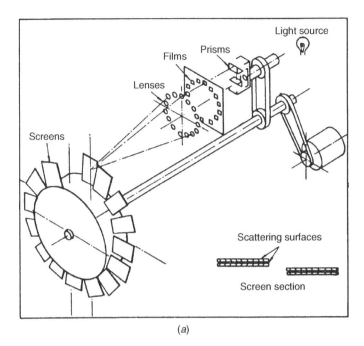

(a)

(b)

Figure 4.9 A swept-volume display pioneered in the early 1970s by John Szilard. The small screens form blades around a central wheel or cylinder. Each is offset from its neighbors, thus forming a helical arrangement. The pitch of this helix determines the image space depth. This embodiment offers sound image space characteristics, but this is achieved at the expense of a very low sweep efficiency. (Reproduced from Szilard [1974] with permission from Elsevier, © 1974 Elsevier.)

we consider the voxel generation subsystem in more detail, and for our present purposes it is sufficient to note that visible voxels may be formed by means of an array of elements (e.g., System 1 in Section 4.2), or by a coating which is caused to emit visible light (e.g., System 2). Such an array of elements or surface coating will be referred to as a 'surface of emission' (SOE) and represents the underlying technique employed for the generation of visible voxels. This surface must be supported in some way—it cannot exist in isolation. The screen therefore comprises two components: (1) the surface of emission and (2) the supporting structure which ensures that despite rapid cyclic motion the surface of emission remains undistorted.

All too often the impact of the supporting structure on the visible image has been given insufficient attention, and this has negatively impacted on perceived image quality. Generally, the supporting structure may be subdivided into two parts: the "substrate" and the "framework". The substrate represents the material upon which the surface of emission is constructed/deposited. In the case of systems employing the rotational motion of a screen and which impose very little restriction on viewing orientation, this must be transparent, and its thickness must be minimized to reduce image distortion and the severity of the visual dead zone (resulting from refraction of light as it passes through the substrate). The second part of the supporting structure takes the form of additional hardware that provides increased rigidity and may connect the screen to the drive mechanism responsible for screen motion. This may include a framework placed around the screen—or perhaps in the case of a system employing rotational motion, a shaft passing through the center of the image space.[8] In designing the supporting structure, various issues must be considered with care. For example:

1. *The Nature of the Forces Acting on the Screen:* In the case of a system employing translational motion, from the perspective of forces imposed on the screen sinusoidal motion is preferable to a linear velocity profile. For either translational or rotational movement, forces can be greatly reduced by effecting screen movement within an evacuated vessel. Alternatively, in the case of rotational motion we can employ, for example, a transparent cylindrical framework that co-rotates with the other screen components, as illustrated in Figure 4.10. This ensures that the air contained within the cylinder co-rotates with the screen and prevents the screen from exhibiting a pumping action (with associated turbulence). Furthermore, the cylinder serves to increase the rigidity of the screen (thereby enabling the substrate thickness to be reduced) and provides a convenient structure to which the motor drive may be attached. In such an embodiment, the use of an axial shaft may be avoided.

2. *Thickness of Supporting Structure:* Irrespective of the choice of translational or rotational motion, as the image space volume is increased, the screen is subject to greater forces (which increase as the square of the rotational

---

[8] In the case of swept-volume displays that employ the rotational motion of a planar screen within an evacuated vessel, a flexible screen may be employed. In this case rigidity could, for example, be derived from the centripetal force acting on the screen.

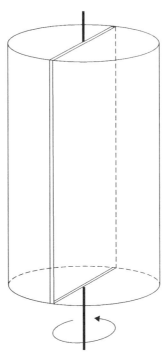

Figure 4.10   The use of a transparent cylindrical framework provides not only additional rigidity but also, because the air is contained and therefore co-rotates with the screen, reduces turbulence. This arrangement is suitable for use with either planar or helical screens. Such an arrangement is likely to have minimal impact on image visibility. (Diagram © A. R. Blundell 2006.)

rate). However, increasing the thickness of the substrate or adding additional framework is likely to adversely impact on perceived image quality. Although the use of transparent components will generally avoid image occlusion, the refraction of light as it travels through different media will result in image distortion. This point has been given insufficient attention in the design of a number of volumetric embodiments, and it is vital that the designer places equal emphasis on both (a) the creation of the volumetric image and (b) the propagation of light from the image to the observer(s). In short:

Even the most perfectly crafted volumetric image may take on a poor visual appearance. As the light passes through, and emerges from the image space, it may experience refraction and anisotropic attenuation. Images are then likely to appear distorted and image quality will vary with viewing position. Optimal image quality then occurs when an image is of a certain size, is created in a certain position within the image space, and when it is viewed from a particular location.

As discussed in the previous section (in the context of the third exemplar system), the combination of components forming the screen (including the surface of emission) will often result in a "visual dead zone." This can degrade image appearance, especially when images are photographed (when images are viewed directly, human binocular vision slightly ameliorates this effect). Various types of "dead zone" that may be associated with swept-volume displays are discussed in Section 4.7.

3. *Screen Vibration:* It is critical that screen vibration be minimized. Vibration is directly transferred to the visual image and impacts on both image stability and image sharpness. Consequently, in the case of rotational motion, the screen must be carefully balanced. Avoiding screen vibration can be particularly challenging when no center shaft is used.

In the context of rotational motion, we have so far considered only the use of a double-bladed planar screen. A helical form of screen provides an alternative solution and is particularly well suited to the creation of a cylindrical image space having a small height-to-radius ratio. Various forms of helices may be employed, although care must be taken in considering the formation of dead zones (see Section 4.7.4). This may arise when a portion of the helix lies between activated voxels and the observer—or, in the case where voxels are created by a directed beam source, when a portion of the helix obstructs the beams passage to its intended location on the helix.

The geometry of a rotating screen is essentially limited to planar and helical configurations. Other screen profiles tend to have inherent weaknesses; in general terms, the screen should satisfy the following criteria:

1. Provide an image space with a suitable form and with appropriate dimensions.

2. Should not give rise to "dead image space"—regions within the volume within which voxels cannot be created. Here we note that in the case of rotational motion, both the planar screen and helix give rise to a small region of dead image space about the axis of rotation.

3. Should not obstruct the passage of light from regions of the image space to the observer.

4. As indicated above, in the case of systems employing a directed beam the presence of portions of the screen should not obstruct its passage to an intended location on the surface of emission.

An alternative screen geometry is illustrated in Figure 4.11. This approach was reported by Yamada et al. [1984] and employs two Archimedes spirals rotating around a common center.[9] Unfortunately, this configuration exhibits a low sweep efficiency, a problem that is exacerbated as the depth of the image space is increased. See Section 6.5.4 for another similar embodiment; also, in Section 7.5.2

---

[9] This technique is also discussed in Blundell and Schwarz [2000].

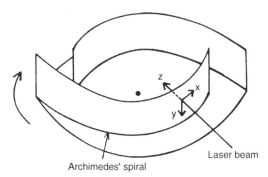

Figure 4.11   An alternative swept-volume image space creation geometry. Here, two Archimedes spirals rotating around a common centre are employed. As they rotate, an image space is created—the depth of which is determined by the difference between the maximum and minimum distance of the spirals from the axis of rotation. This approach was pioneered by Yamada et al. [1984]. (Reproduced by permission © 1984 Laser Institute of America.)

a further example is provided of a swept-volume architecture employing an unusual screen shape (Ref. 7O).

4.3.2   Voxel Generation

> *If you give me six lines written by the hand of the most honest of men,*
> *I will find something in them which will hang him.*[10]

The voxel generation (image element generation) subsystem represents the underlying physical processes used in the production of visible voxels. Two general approaches may be adopted:

1. *Active Voxel Generation:* Here, a matrix of elements are employed and through the application of an appropriate stimulus, each element is able to undergo a visible change. The first of the exemplar systems introduced in Section 4.2 provides us with an instance of this approach. Most frequently, the visible change corresponds to the emission of light (and so gives rise to the production of emissive voxels), although, as discussed in Section 5.7, elements may also interact in a controllable manner with ambient lighting (thereby producing nonemissive voxels). In this latter case there is the possibility of producing opaque voxels and thereby the potential to satisfy the depth cue of opacity (see Section 2.3.1).[11]

---

[10] Attributed to Cardinal Richelieu (1585–1642).

[11] Opaque image formation through the use of the nonemissive voxel technique cannot usually be achieved by means of the swept-volume technique. In fact, the author is only aware of one swept-volume technique able to support image opacity (see Patent Number US 2005/0180007 A1 filed by Oliver Cossairt and Joshua Napoli). However, this approach may be considered to represent a hybrid swept-volume–multi-view technique.

2. *Passive Voxel Generation:* In this case, the surface of emission takes the form of a coating deposited on the screens supporting substrate or may be produced by treating the surface of the substrate in an appropriate manner. The former approach was employed in the second example system introduced in Section 4.2. Here, the surface of emission takes the form of a phosphor coating (see, for example, Sections 7.2.1 and 7.3.1 for other embodiments employing this approach). Treatment of the surface of the screen substrate is most frequently associated with systems that employ laser beams for voxel activation. In this case, the laser light is scattered when it impinges upon the surface (a suitable scattering surface may be produced by sand-blasting glass). Voxels created by means of the passive voxel generation technique are emissive.

As a consequence of the screen's motion, swept-volume displays must employ transient optical phenomena for the production of visible voxels. Therefore only a proportion of the voxels that comprise an image are activated at any one time (although the human visual system may not consciously be aware of this). As a result, even if we were able to assign to the activated voxel a degree of opacity, temporal activation characteristics would preclude the satisfaction of the occlusion depth cue. A "ghostly" translucent image is a characteristic of nearly all swept-volume display architectures.

The underlying phenomena used in the implementation of the voxel generation subsystem must be selected with care. Basic selection criteria include:

1. *Rapid Activation:* The mechanism should be able to rapidly react to the voxel activation stimulus. The time required for the mechanism to reach an arbitrary 90% of its intended visual change will be referred to as the dwell time (T_{dwell}).

2. *Conversion Efficiency:* The mechanism should be efficient in terms of its ability to convert the activation energy into a visible change. This is particularly important in the case of embodiments employing cathodoluminescence, because different phosphors exhibit considerably different conversion efficiencies and must therefore be selected judiciously.

3. *Maximum Light Output:* In the case of embodiments employing emissive voxels, the light output should be sufficient for good voxel visibility under the typical lighting conditions employed within the environment in which the display is to be operated. The maximum light output may be determined by the saturation of the physical process used for voxel generation, or by the maximum energy that can be practically supplied in the activation process (e.g., the energy of an electron beam). Since swept-volume systems use transient phenomena for voxel generation, individual voxels are visible for only brief periods of time and therefore the average illumination that each supplies to the visual system is much less than the peak value.

4. *Rapid Decay:* Once the activation stimulus has been removed, we expect that the mechanism used for voxel generation will rapidly return to its inactive visual state. Should the time required for this transition be excessive, then a voxel will lose definition in the direction of screen motion; in more severe cases, visible voxel elongation may occur. We will refer to this time component as the decay time (T_{decay}) and will arbitrarily define this as the time taken to return to within 10% of the visually inactive state.

5. *Output Wavelength(s):* Aspects of the underlying processes used in the voxel generation mechanism will determine voxel color.[12]

As may be seen from the above, the choice of voxel generation process will impact on the time required to create each visible voxel and the minimum duration of voxel visibility before it returns to its inactive state. In this book, the "voxel visibility lifetime" (T_{decay}) is used to refer to the minimum time for which an activated voxel remains visible after the removal of the activation stimulus and is determined by the voxel generation subsystem. When discussing the temporal components associated with the activation of each voxel, the term "voxel activation time" (T_{act}) is employed and the "voxel time" (T_{vox}) represents the sum of the two:

$$T_{\text{vox}} = T_{\text{act}} + T_{\text{decay}}. \tag{4.8}$$

Thus, the voxel time represents the sum of all time components associated with the creation of each visible voxel and includes the time taken for the voxel to return to its nonactive state. The contribution made by the voxel generation subsystem (δT_{vox}) to the overall T_{vox} may be expressed as

$$\delta T_{\text{vox}} = T_{\text{dwell}} + T_{\text{decay}}.$$

4.3.3 Voxel Activation

The voxel activation (image element activation) subsystem provides the stimulus to the voxel generation process and so gives rise to an optical change resulting in visible voxel formation. The voxel generation and activation subsystems are closely interdependent inasmuch as the choice of one may define or closely restrict options available for the underlying processes that may be used in the implementation of the other.[13] For example, if we employ a phosphor coating for voxel generation, then the use of an electron beam(s) is the most likely choice for voxel activation. Similarly, the use of light-emitting diodes for voxel generation would necessitate electrical signals for voxel activation, and the use of a scattering surface would infer the use of visible light beam(s) (perhaps derived from one or more lasers). However, as will become more evident when we examine a range of swept-volume embodiments (see Chapters 6–8), despite the interdependence of

---

[12] Characteristics of the voxel activation mechanism may also influence/determine voxel color.

[13] Furthermore, the approach adopted in the implementation of image-space creation subsystem also influences the techniques that may be employed in the other two subsystems.

the two subsystems, there is still considerable scope for the designer. By way of example, Figure 4.12 provides a summary of a few of the design options associated with a beam-based voxel activation subsystem used in conjunction with the rotational motion of a planar screen. For clarity, we confine the illustration to a single design route and the diagram is not intended to necessarily infer the order in which design decisions are made. Furthermore, the nature of the intended application(s) will often influence aspects of the display architecture (e.g., the image space form and dimensions, the extent of typical image data sets that need to be depicted, etc.), and this will then restrict the number of techniques suitable for use. It is instructive to briefly consider more closely several of the options available in the implementation of the voxel activation subsystem:

1. *Beam Deflection:* As we have seen, in the case of systems employing a passive surface of emission, voxel activation is achieved by means of one or more beam sources. We may employ a small number of beam sources with additional beam deflection apparatus, thereby enabling each source to create voxels throughout the image space (or throughout a restricted image space volume). We will refer to this as the "directed beam" approach because it assumes that the beam deflection and other control apparatus is able to accurately control the position and time at which the beam(s) impinge on the surface of emission. Alternatively, we may adopt an approach in which we use a large number of individual voxel activation beams. In this scenario, a 2-D array of beam sources are employed, each beam being responsible for the activation of voxels along a track (usually in a single dimension). The Perspecta display discussed in Section 8.3.2 provides an example of this technique.

2. *Static or Dynamic Beam Sources/Deflection Apparatus:* In order for the beam sources and beam deflection apparatus to retain a constant geometry with respect to the moving surface, they must synchronously follow its motion. A number of approaches have adopted this approach through the physical attachment of the beam sources and/or deflection apparatus to the screen (via a supporting framework). This avoids the continually varying geometry associated with systems in which the sources/deflection apparatus are static and which can be particularly problematic in systems employing the rotational motion of a planar screen (see Section 4.7 for further discussion on several forms of "dead zone" that may arise). A display unit employing the co-rotating beam source technique is illustrated in Section 7.3.1.

3. *Number of Beams:* In principle, a single directed beam source may activate voxels throughout an image space:

   - Formed by the translational motion of a passive surface of emission. The beam source/deflection apparatus may be static or dynamic.
   - Formed by the rotational motion of a helical screen equipped with a passive surface of emission. In this case, the beam source/deflection apparatus would be static and usually would be located in-line with the axis of rotation of the helix.

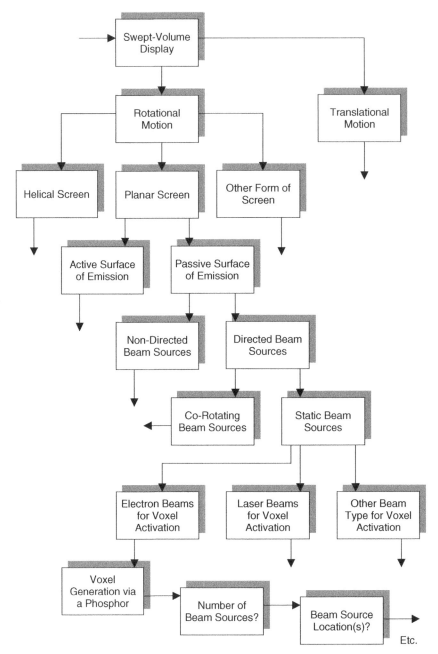

Figure 4.12   Some of the design options that need to be considered in the specification of a swept-volume display. For clarity, we trace only a single path. This relates to a display unit employing the rotational motion of a planar screen and a passive surface of emission that is addressed by several directed beams. Immediately apparent from the illustration is the extent of the options available to the designer. (Diagram © Q. S. Blundell 2006.)

- Formed by the rotational motion of a planar screen. In this case, the beam source/deflection apparatus would co-rotate with the screen.

Other scenarios are likely to necessitate the use of a plurality of beam sources. In each of the cases listed here, voxel activation is sequential and this restricts the number of voxels that can be activated within each image update period. In the next section, we discuss issues relating to parallelism in voxel activation for systems employing both passive and active surfaces of emission.

4.4 PARALLELISM IN VOXEL ACTIVATION

For our purposes, we define the "voxel activation capacity" (N_a) as representing the total number of voxels that may be activated during a single image refresh period (T). This may be expressed as

$$N_a = \frac{P \cdot T}{T_{\text{act}}}, \tag{4.9}$$

where T_{act} represents the average time required to activate each voxel (the "voxel activation time") and P denotes the parallelism supported by the voxel activation subsystem (i.e., the total number of voxels that may be activated simultaneously). In fact, of the three variables indicated in Eq. (4.9), it is P that varies most significantly between the different volumetric technologies, with its value being largely determined by the interaction between the voxel generation and activation subsystems.

In the case of swept-volume displays, the image refresh period usually equals either (a) the reciprocal of the cyclic frequency at which the screen sweeps out the image space (f) or (b) one-half of this value. The first of the example display units introduced in Section 4.2 provides us with an embodiment able (in principle) to support both of these cases. Here, the two blades of the screen (lying on either side of the axis of rotation) sweep out the entire image space during a single rotation and they may therefore be used in conjunction for the production of two-color images (see Figure 4.13a). In this case, $T = 1/f$. Alternatively, each blade may be made responsible for the creation of the entire image, leading to two image updates per cycle of screen motion (and so $T = 1/2f$). Additionally, by exploiting the presence of both surfaces of each blade, it is possible to create opportunities for multi-color image production (see Figure 4.13b). However, as indicated in Section 4.2, in the case of the second example system there is less flexibility and $T = 1/f$.

As we have discussed, for swept-volume systems, voxels may only remain activated for brief intervals, so for the human visual system to perceive a flicker-free image, the image refresh frequency must be greater than the critical flicker frequency (see Section 2.4). This determines the maximum image refresh period, which is on the order of 40 ms. Thus in the case of a configuration supporting only a single image refresh per screen rotation, the minimum cyclic frequency is ~25 Hz.[14]

---

[14] Both image brightness and ambient lighting conditions impact on this minimum value.

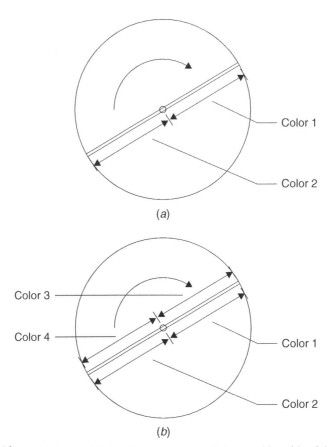

Figure 4.13 In (a) the two blades of a planar screen (lying on either side of the rotational axis) may be used for the production of two-color images. This is achieved by equipping each blade with a voxel generation material able to give rise to voxels of a different color. Alternatively, if the two blades are coated with identical materials (or are equipped with identical voxel generation elements), then each may be used to provide a complete refresh of the image during each full cycle of screen rotation. In this case the rotational frequency of the screen may be halved without any increase in image flicker. In (b) both surfaces of either blade are provided with a voxel generation mechanism able to give rise to voxels of a different color. In this way multicolor images may be produced (other approaches are also possible). For example in the case of the Cathode Ray Sphere (see Sections 1.6.1, 4.6 and 12.3), phosphors able to produce red, green, and blue voxels can be used (the fourth quadrant may be used for the production of white voxels).

The techniques employed within the voxel generation and activation subsystems define the minimum achievable voxel activation time. Consider, for example, the case of a system employing a directed beam impinging on a passive surface of emission and that uses translational motion (an example of this technique is given in Figure 4.14). Here the voxel activation time (associated with a "dot graphics"

NEW MODEL

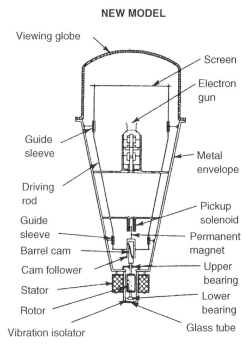

Viewing globe

Screen

Electron gun

Guide sleeve

Metal envelope

Driving rod

Pickup solenoid

Guide sleeve

Permanent magnet

Barrel cam

Cam follower

Upper bearing

Stator

Lower bearing

Rotor

Vibration isolator

Glass tube

Improvements include: induction motor with stator outside vacuum system; barrel-cam screen-drive for true harmonic screen motion; larger screen moving through a greater amplitude; glass dome; and sound isolators

Figure 4.14 The Peritron (Ref 6I)—an exemplar embodiment of a display unit employing the translational motion of a planar screen and a single beam source for voxel activation. This device was pioneered in the 1950s. A high vacuum is maintained so as to enable the use of a directed electron beam for voxel activation in conjunction with a passive surface of emission. Additionally, the vacuum facilitates screen motion. See Section 6.4.4 for further discussion. (Reproduced from Withey [1958], with permission © Penton Publishing.)

voxel activation technique) may be expressed as

$$T_{act} = T_{move} + T_{on} + T_{dwell} + T_{off}. \qquad (4.10)$$

For a display unit employing a directed beam for voxel activation, the components that comprise the voxel activation time are as follows:

1. *The "move time" (T_{move}):* This represents the time needed to direct the beam to the location on the surface of emission at which a voxel is to be activated. Here we assume that the screen is passing through the appropriate region of the image space (i.e., is within the appropriate "slice"). Clearly, the move time varies with the distance over which the beam is to be deflected; as discussed in Section 4.4.2, this can be problematic.

2. *The "on time" (T_{on}):* This represents the time needed to turn on the activation signal and thereby provide the stimulus needed by the voxel generation mechanism for the production of a visible voxel.

3. *The "off time" (T_{off}):* This represents the time needed to turn off the activation stimulus once the visible voxel has been created. It is included in Eq. (4.10) because the beam cannot be moved to the next location at which a voxel is to be activated until the beam has been gated.

4. *The "dwell time" (T_{dwell}):* This represents the duration for which the voxel activation and generation mechanisms must interact to produce each visible voxel. Depending on the physical processes employed in the production of visible voxels, changes in dwell time may possibly be used to produce voxels of varying intensity. Alternatively (and more commonly), the intensity is set by controlling the energy density of the beam.

To maximize the voxel activation capacity, it is desirable that the voxel activation time be minimized. A brief examination of the above time components confirms that for the embodiment under discussion, once we have reached a voxel activation time in the range $0.1-1$ μs, we are somewhat limited in our ability to make further major reductions.

The components that comprise the voxel activation time vary between display unit implementations. For example, if we use a large number of beam sources and avoid the need for beam deflection between active voxel locations (see, for example, the Actuality Systems Perspecta display outlined in Section 8.3.2), then the "move time" component is no longer applicable. Similarly, in the case of an embodiment employing an active matrix of voxel generation elements—each of which is addressed by, for example, electrical signals—the voxel activation time reduces to

$$T_{act} = T_{on} + T_{dwell}. \tag{4.11}$$

Returning briefly to Eq. (4.9). Given a maximum refresh period of 40 ms and a minimum voxel activation time of 0.2 μs, then for a configuration in which $P = 1$, the voxel activation capacity is 200,000. In the case of a system employing a directed beam approach, even this level of performance is not easily achieved because a voxel activation time of 0.2 μs places considerable demands on the hardware systems (especially the beam deflection apparatus).[15] Consequently, to significantly increase N_a, we must introduce parallelism into the voxel activation process.

---

[15] For this configuration, a maximum voxel activation capacity of ~100,000 is more readily achievable. For related discussion concerning techniques that can be employed to increase the voxel activation capacity of systems that employ electron beams for voxel activation, see Sections 7.2.1 and 12.3.

> Unless parallelism is introduced into the voxel activation subsystem (and properly supported by the underlying voxel generation technique), the voxel activation capacity is usually severely restricted. For display units in which parallelism is limited to unity, few approaches are able to support a voxel activation capacity in excess of 500,000. Usually, such systems exhibit voxel activation capacities of 100,000 (or less).

In Chapter 8 we consider techniques that may be adopted to accommodate parallelism in the voxel activation process; in the subsection that follows, we will consider the impact of restrictions in the number of voxels that may be activated during each image refresh period.

4.4.1   Restrictions in Voxel Activation

June was not over
Though past the fall,
And the best of her roses
Had yet to blow.[16]

It is often assumed that the voxel activation capacity directly equates to the total number of pixels that may be depicted on a conventional flat screen display. Consequently, the true significance of this performance metric is frequently misunderstood. If such a comparison is made, it would seem that a volumetric display able to depict a maximum of ~100,000 voxels per frame (or perhaps even less) exhibits quite low performance—after all, a standard low cost computer monitor is able to depict approximately 800,000 pixels per frame! However, such a comparison is not valid since pixels and voxels are not directly equivalent and the characteristics of the 3-D volumetric tableau are quite different from those of the conventional 2-D screen. In the case of a conventional flat screen computer display or television, during each frame all pixels (or areas of the screen) are normally illuminated. However, many of the illuminated pixels provide no information, nor do they contribute to interactive operations. The volumetric approach is somewhat different and the activation of unnecessary voxels is likely to lead to a loss of clarity due to cluttering of the image space (for example, by obscuring depth information).[17]

---

[16] Robert Browning (1812–1889), "Another Way of Love."

[17] The largely unrestricted viewing freedom offered by many volumetric technologies exacerbates this issue. In the case of an overpopulated image space, image clarity is likely to vary considerably with viewing direction.

> In the case of a volumetric display, to avoid needlessly cluttering the image space, the only voxels activated should be those that contribute to the information content, assist in the visualization process, or facilitate interactive operations.

This is evident from our surroundings. The space around us is, from a visual perspective, largely void and if we are to correctly and easily determine spatial relationships, this is a necessary requirement. When, for example, I look out of the window before me to the many trees in leaf nearby, and consciously examine the scene, it looks cluttered. The view appears to be filled with content, color, and fine shading. This enhances the overall visual beauty, but when we analyze this type of view, spatial relationships are often not easily discerned—there is simply too much content for accurate subconscious spatial interpretation.

Clearly, any limitation in the voxel activation capacity should not impact on the ability of a display unit to portray images at the necessary level of detail. In short, limitations in the voxel activation capacity should not adversely impact on image resolution. Consider for a moment a display unit exhibiting a voxel activation capacity of 200,000. For simplicity, we will assume a cubic image space with sides of, say, 20 cm. If the underlying display techniques force a uniform (or approximately uniform) distribution of the voxels throughout the image space (i.e., the case where all activated voxels must lie on a regular lattice), then minimum adjacent voxel separation will be $\sim$3.4 mm (see Figure 4.15). Naturally, such a high minimum inter-voxel separation is likely to result in images of unsatisfactory resolution; at typical viewing distances, gaps between adjacent voxels would be readily evident (unless, of course we were to use overly large voxels to fill in such gaps . . .).

Since most of an image space is void of objects, there is little point in requiring that the total number of voxels that may be activated during each image update period be uniformly distributed through the entire image space volume; as we have indicated, to do so impacts on achievable image resolution (or maximum image space dimensions). The alternative and far more desirable approach is to assign to an image space a closely spaced lattice that specifies possible voxel locations and enables a portion of these potential voxel sites to be populated during each image update period. Following the terminology introduced previously Blundell and Schwarz, 2000, we therefore define a "voxel location capacity" (N_l), which specifies the total number of potential voxel locations and a fill factor (ψ) such that

$$\varphi(\%) = \frac{N_a}{N_l} \cdot 100. \tag{4.12}$$

In this way the achievable image resolution is decoupled from the image space dimensions, and it is possible to depict highly detailed image components. By way of example, let us continue to consider the display unit referred to above, having a voxel activation capacity of 200,000 and cubic image space of volume 8000 cm^3. Here we may seek a maximum adjacent voxel spacing of, say, 0.4 mm, this defining the lattice spacing in relation to potential active voxel locations. This

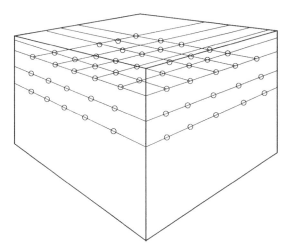

Figure 4.15 In this scenario, the total number of voxels that may be activated during each image refresh period (as indicated by the voxel activation capacity) are spread throughout the image space, being located on a regular lattice. Consequently, the voxel activation capacity coupled with the image space dimensions define the minimum separation of adjacent voxels, which is an undesirable situation. Alternatively, the voxel activation capacity and required minimum intervoxel spacing define the image space volume—which is equally undesirable. See text for discussion.

gives a voxel location capacity of 125×10^6 (note that the voxel location capacity is **not** decoupled from the image space dimensions) and from Eq. (4.12) we obtain a fill factor of 0.16%. Fill factors of less than 1% are a characteristic of most systems in which voxels are activated in a sequential or largely sequential manner [i.e., in which the parallelism (P) indicated in Eq. (4.9) is close to unity]. Putting to one side graphics engine characteristics, the techniques employed in the implementation of the voxel generation and activation subsystems largely determine the degree of parallelism that may be achieved in the voxel activation process. Typically, for an image space of useful dimensions, a 100% fill factor (i.e., a system employing "exhaustive addressing") is associated with systems exhibiting a voxel activation capacity on the order of 100 million. However, as we have seen, these voxels would never be activated in their entirety during a single image update period, and in fact the total number activated for the depiction of a "typical" image scene is likely to be significantly less than 1%. In the next subsection we briefly consider the strengths and weaknesses of the exhaustive addressing and restricted fill factor techniques.

4.4.2 Designing for Predictability

Display units able to depict high-resolution images within an image space of useful dimensions and which support a 100% fill factor normally do so by incorporating a high degree of parallelism within the voxel activation subsystem. Naturally, the voxel generation technique must be amenable to the chosen parallel activation paradigm, and the graphics engine must be able to support the very high bandwidth demanded by the display unit (see Section 11.4.1).

As we have discussed, this exhaustive addressing approach mimics the standard pixel addressing technique employed in a conventional flat screen computer display, and although only a small fraction of voxels will be activated during each image update period, the technique supports the requirement for predictability. In this context, "predictability" refers to our ability to illuminate any subset of the possible voxel locations within an image space. As we move to systems that offer much smaller fill factors, predictability can become an issue. By way of example, consider the second of the example systems introduced in Section 4.2 (a screen moving with translational motion and a single directed beam source for voxel activation). Let us suppose that the depth of the image space is defined by the distance over which the screen moves with constant velocity and denote the time spent in each slice as τ. The total number of voxels that may be activated within a slice (N_s) is the approximately given by

$$N_s = \frac{\tau}{\overline{T}_{\text{move}} + T_{\text{on}} + T_{\text{dwell}} + T_{\text{off}}}.$$

where $\overline{T}_{\text{move}}$ denotes the move time averaged across all voxels to be activated within a slice. This average varies according to the spatial distribution of the voxels contained in each slice and according to the order in which the voxels are drawn. Consequently, both the spatial distribution of voxels within a slice and the order in which they are activated can impact on the total number of voxels that may be included within the slice. We refer to this as "conditional voxel activation".

> "Conditional voxel activation" refers to an adverse condition in which our ability to activate one or more voxels is determined by the spatial distribution of previously activated voxels, or by the order in which these voxels were output to the display unit.

Although conditional voxel activation most strongly relates to display units employing directed beam sources for voxel activation, it also applies to other approaches that exhibit low parallelism within the activation subsystem.[18] To maximize N_s, we may consider ordering the data set within each slice and output it to the display in such a way as to minimize the total move time. This is discussed in previous works Schwarz and Blundell, 1997; Blundell and Schwarz, 2000 and for our purposes it is sufficient to note the following:

---

[18] Here we are assuming that a "dot graphics" technique (rather than a raster scan) is employed.

1. Achieving optimal ordering to minimize the distance moved by a directed beam is the classic "Traveling Salesman Problem" (TSP) and is an example of a combinatorial problem. The computational cost associated with finding an exact solution to a TSP grows rapidly with the extent of the input data set and, for all but quite small input data sets, is unmanageable. Obtaining approximate solutions provides a more practical approach and can result in significant reductions in the total move time within each slice.

2. Reducing the total move time within each slice enables us to accommodate additional voxels. However, the gains that can be made are not known until the ordering process has been carried out, and furthermore they are dependent on the spatial distribution of voxels within each slice. This dependency exacerbates "conditional voxel activation" and may be particularly problematic when dynamic image sequences are to be depicted (also see Section 11.3)

4.5 HARDWARE-BASED CHARACTERIZATION

As discussed in the previous sections, a broad variety of approaches may be adopted in the creation of a swept-volume display, and these generally give rise to systems exhibiting wide ranging visual characteristics. To enable us to more easily distinguish between embodiments and to provide an indicator of their relative performance, it is desirable to develop an effective classification scheme. This may be achieved through the adoption of a bottom-up approach whereby we examine key aspects of the underlying hardware, or by establishing a set of higher-level performance metrics. In this section we briefly discuss the former approach.

Key issues that need to be considered in developing a low-level classification scheme for swept-volume systems are summarized in Figure 4.16, and they concern the techniques employed in each of the three display unit subsystems. The major facets of the image space creation subsystem on which we focus relate to the type of motion employed and the geometrical form of the screen (or the use of a 3-D structure). However, these aspects of image space creation are not necessarily independent: The choice of one may well define (or influence) our selection of the other. For example, if we decide to use a helical form of screen, translational motion is precluded. The use of a passive or active surface of emission (or 3-D structure) provides a convenient way of characterizing the voxel generation subsystem and influences our selection of a voxel activation technique. Naturally an active surface of emission (or 3-D structure) will be directly addressed, whereas a passive surface of emission may be addressed by one or more beams (or may simply reflect image slices).

The implementation of a display unit may therefore be described in terms of a set of simple key terms. For example, the first of the example systems introduced in Section 4.2 could be described as a swept-volume display employing the rotational motion of a planar screen equipped with an active surface of emission (the addressing mode need not be stated because it is implied through the use

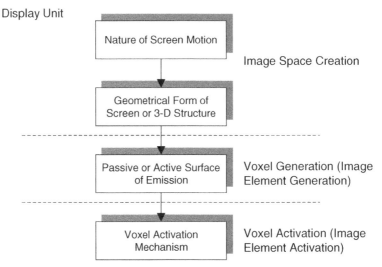

Figure 4.16   Aspects of an apparently simple hardware based classification scheme for swept-volume display units. Each of the facets of the display shown in this diagram can significantly impact on operational characteristics. (Diagram © A. R. Blundell 2006.)

of an active surface of emission). Similarly, the second example system could be characterized as a swept-volume display employing the translational motion of a passive surface of emission, along with a single directed but stationary beam source. Although this approach can be useful, it also has severe limitations; simple display unit descriptions may overlook vital aspects of display performance.

Each of the aspects of a display unit's character that are indicated in Figure 4.16 may greatly impact on a display unit's visual characteristics, and so they should be regarded as being of equal importance. However, when we consider each from the perspective of the diversity of general approaches and technologies that may be adopted in their implementation (and thereby the difficulties we encounter when we attempt to produce a simple classification scheme), we find the image space creation subsystem the simplest to categorize and the voxel activation subsystem the most difficult.

Unfortunately, this simple bottom-up classification scheme may overlook vital aspects of a display unit's character, and attempts to extend it to make it more generally applicable and robust result in schemes that quickly become unwieldy. In Figure 4.17 a more detailed breakdown of facets of a display unit's implementation is provided.

4.6   THE ACCEPTANCE OF MOTION

Could Hamlet have been written by a committee,
or the Mona Lisa painted by a club?
Could the New Testament have been composed as a conference report?

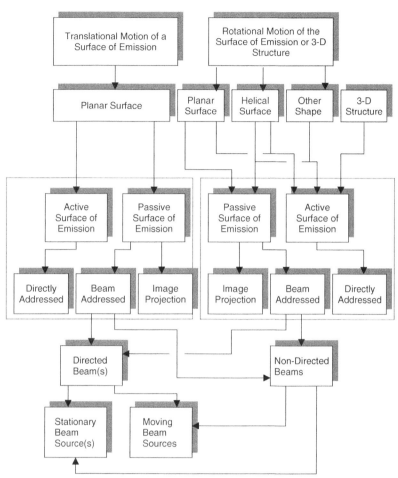

Figure 4.17   A possible (although somewhat unwieldy) hardware based classification scheme encompassing many swept-volume display unit architectures. If an active surface of emission is employed, then implicitly some form of direct addressing scheme must be used. Alternatively, the use of a passive surface of emission provides various options for voxel activation. Some facets of a display's operation may not be included in this scheme (for example, see Section 7.5.5 in which a display unit employing two degrees of freedom in screen motion is briefly described). (Diagram © Q. S. Blundell 2006.)

> *Creative ideas do not spring from groups.*
> *They spring from individuals.*[19]

During the years the author has worked on and researched volumetric displays, he has found that because of the pivotal reliance that is placed on rapid, cyclic mechanical motion, swept-volume systems are often regarded with a degree of

---

[19] Attributed to A. Whitney Griswold (1906–1963), President of Yale.

skepticism. This is perhaps surprising when we consider the prevalence, diversity, and reliability of a wide range of technologies that impact on every aspect of our daily lives and whose operation is underpinned by rapidly moving mechanical components. The reciprocating motion of pistons in a conventional car engine (and from which rotational movement is derived), along with the remarkable rotational speed achieved by components within a jet engine, provide obvious examples of engineering feats that become all the more impressive when we consider the harsh conditions under which these systems operate, and their lifespan.[20]

Mechanical motion underpins the operation of many forms of modern storage media (both digital and nondigital), and, for example, the precise and rapid movements of the read/write heads within a hard disk are generally taken for granted (along with disk reliability). In fact a vast number of appliances and systems that impact on our lives rely on reliable cyclic mechanical movement.[21]

When we examine the design and implementation of the mechanical mechanisms needed for the implementation of swept-volume systems and consider these in the light of other mechanical feats (such as those mentioned above), their implementation would seem almost trivial, and reliability appears to be assured. However, it is important to remember that many of the mechanically based appliances and systems that are now mass-produced and operate with such astounding reliability have, for years, been continually refined and gradually brought to a state of cost-effective perfection.

Certainly, the rate at which we seek to sweep out an image space is not especially great and we are able to tolerate variations in the sweep frequency. Furthermore, the loads imposed on the various mechanical elements can be well-defined and generally the operational environment is not problematic. On the other hand, the optimization of the system involves serious effort,[22] particularly in the design of the elements that comprise the screen.

---

[20] For example, during the typical life of a modern car engine, each piston will be expected to complete some hundreds of millions of cycles of motion within an extremely harsh operating environment. This is achieved with little, if any, maintenance—other than the occasional and generally begrudged oil change. Average operation of such an engine requires rotational rates on the order of two thousand crankshaft revolutions per minute ($\sim$33 Hz), which approximates to the rate at which we seek to sweep out an image space.

[21] The heart must represent one of the most remarkable 'mechanical systems'. If we assume an average pulse rate of 65 min^{-1} then for a person who reaches the age of 80 it will have performed some 2733 million beats (servicing often being unnecessary...).

[22] Optimization of a mechanical system is an extensive undertaking and may lead to a solution that has little similarity to the early prototype. In this context, Sir Frank Whittle describes the early tests on his first jet engine prototype in 1936: *"The apparatus was usually anything but leak-proof and large pools of fuel would collect underneath. Sooner or later, flaming droplets set them alight and we, conducting the tests, would be stepping between the pools of flame like demons in an inferno. ... Some people naturally supposed that we were trying to develop a flame-thrower. Others thought we were merely mad!"* (Whittle F., *Jet: The Story of a Pioneer*, Frederick Muller Ltd., 1953). Thus the jet engine was invented .... The estimation of the force on a jet engine fan blade during the takeoff is an instructive exercise (consider, for example, the case of, a fully loaded 747–400)—although for those nervous about flying, this is a calculation best avoided before takeoff!

By way of example, let us consider the cathode ray sphere (see Sections 1.6.1, 4.4, and 12.3), this being a technology on which the author has worked for many years. As may be seen from Figure 4.18, this display uses the rotational motion of a planar screen. Voxel generation is achieved via one or more phosphor coatings deposited on the substrate, and voxel activation by means of a small number of directed electron beams. Here, the use of electron beams necessitates that a high vacuum be maintained; in all systems developed by the author to date, this has been achieved by continually pumping the display vessel. The motion of the internal components within the display vessel is achieved by a motor that rotates external magnets. Flux from these magnets passes through the vacuum vessel wall and causes the rotation of a steel bar that in turn is connected via a drive shaft to the screen (see Figure 4.18). Naturally, to create portable systems it would be desirable to evacuate and subsequently seal off the display vessel [as is done in the case of the conventional cathode ray tube (CRT)]. However, in order to achieve this objective, it is necessary to heat the system for a few hours during the evacuation process. Consequently, although the conditions under which the mechanical components must operate when the system is in use impose no major difficulties, problems are encountered during the production process. For example, the bearings and any lubricants must be able to withstand high-temperature exposure (and the latter must also have an extremely low vapor pressure). In fact it is preferable that the bearings

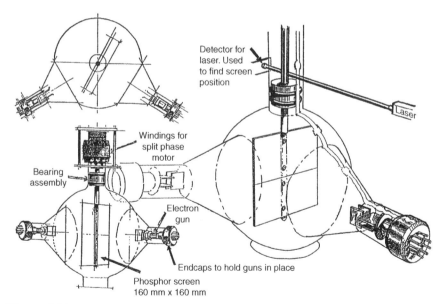

Figure 4.18 The general principle of operation of the cathode ray sphere (CRS). Here, the image space is created through the rapid rotational motion of a planar screen equipped with a passive SOE. A number of electron guns (typically two or three) are positioned around the image space and are responsible for voxel activation. The screen and electron guns are mounted within a spherical glass vacuum vessel. (Original drawing by Warren King.)

should operate without lubrication. The screen must also be able to withstand the high-temperature exposure, and it is critical that it not be distorted during the "bake-out" process.

To date, all cathode ray sphere prototypes have used a glass screen[23] and although a simple and reliable mechanical system has been devised, it by no means represents an optimized solution. Many improvements could be made, including the use of magnetic bearings (to reduce both friction and vibration), the use of a nonrigid screen structure (whereby a very thin flexible material may be used for the screen substrate), and the development of a loading mechanism that precludes the need for a central shaft. However, although such refinements are likely to significantly enhance the quality of this visible image, each in its own right requires considerable effort.

The type of situation in which the mechanical systems exist in rudimentary (far from optimal) form may be seen in the literature concerning many of the swept-volume display units that have, over the years, been prototyped. Consequently, although the basic mechanical mechanisms employed by many swept-volume embodiments are relatively straightforward, the optimization of these mechanisms with respect to image space generation and to their impact on light as it propagates through the image space has generally not been undertaken.

The use of rapid, cyclic mechanical motion within appliances and systems often provides the most cost effective and practical solution and, in some cases, may simply represent the only solution possible given limitations of current technologies. Circumventing the need for electromechanical components can of course be advantageous. In Chapter 5 we discuss the static-volume approach in which image space formation is achieved without recourse to mechanical motion. As we shall see, although this has certain associated advantages, it is in itself no panacea.

> The use of cyclic motion for image space creation should not necessarily be viewed as a weakness inherent in the swept-volume approach but rather as an engineering compromise that permits the production of low cost high performance systems that may be readily implemented using a range of currently available technologies.

4.7   DEAD ZONES

But owl went on and on,
using longer and longer words,
until at last he came back to where he started.[24]

---

[23] Typical screen thickness being in the range 1–2 mm.

[24] From *The Complete Tales and Poems of Winnie-the-Pooh*, by A. A. Milne, Dutton Books (2001).

For the purposes of this book and in accordance with a previous work Blundell and Schwarz, 2000, the term "dead zone" is used to refer to a region or regions within an image space in which, as a consequence of a reduction in one or more image space characteristics, image quality is in some way compromised. In this section, various types of dead zone that may occur in swept-volume display units are summarized, and in Section 5.8 we consider dead zones within the context of the static-volume approach.

4.7.1 The Voxel Placement Dead Zone

This form of dead zone is associated with display units that employ one or more directed beam sources for voxel activation. It is most problematic in systems employing the rotational motion of a planar screen and in which the geometry between the beam deflection apparatus and screen is continually changing (such as in the case of the cathode ray sphere—see Sections 1.6.1, 4.4, 4.6, and 12.3).

Consider for a moment a directed beam source in which the maximum deflection angle in the horizontal plane is denoted by θ—as illustrated in Figure 4.19. We assume that analog signals are used to drive the beam deflection apparatus, with these being converted from the digital domain via a digital-to-analog converter (DAC). The precision of the DAC determines number of voxels that may

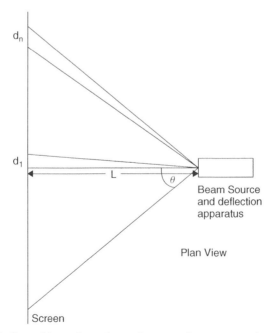

Figure 4.19 A directed beam is used to activate voxels on a screen instantaneously lying normal to the beam axis. The number of voxels that may be activated depends on the precision of the DAC driving the deflection apparatus. The minimum intervoxel separation is nonuniform (i.e. $d_1 \neq d_n$).

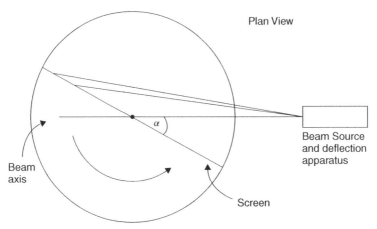

Figure 4.20   As the surface of the screen rotates, the angle (α) between its plane and the beam axis continually varies between $0°$ and $360°$. This impacts on the minimum achievable inter-voxel spacing. Once this minimum exceeds some specified value, we consider the formation of a region in which images cannot be satisfactorily formed and this is termed a "voxel placement dead zone." (Diagram © A. R. Blundell 2006.)

be activated on the screen in the horizontal plane; this coupled with the distance between the deflection apparatus and screen (L), together with the maximum beam deflection angle, will determine inter-voxel spacing. However, as is evident from the illustration, this spacing is not uniform. For example, let us assume the use of an 8-bit DAC, $L = 30$ cm and $\theta = 40°$. In this case the minimum inter-voxel spacing varies from ~0.8 mm (d_1) at the center to ~0.92 mm (d_n) at maximum deflection. Under normal situations, some variation in voxel spacing can be tolerated, however, the problem becomes much more severe when we consider addressing a rotating screen and stationary beam source.

As illustrated in Figure 4.20, as the angle between the plane of the screen and the beam axis (α) becomes more acute, the smallest change in beam deflection angle will ultimately result in an unacceptably large inter-voxel spacing. For example, continuing with the above numerical example, when $\alpha = 10°$, then d_1 increases to ~5 mm).

By increasing the precision of the DAC used to generate the signals supplied to the deflection apparatus, the extent of the voxel placement dead zone may be reduced. However, this cannot help with another form of dead zone which corresponds to unacceptable voxel elongation and that is outlined in the next subsection.

4.7.2   Distortional (Elongation) Dead Zone

In Section 4.2, we briefly considered voxel elongation arising as a result of the finite decay time of the voxel generation mechanism. Voxel shape also depends on the angle of incidence (β) of the activation beam with the screen surface (see

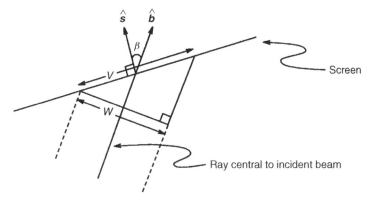

Figure 4.21   Here, a beam of circular cross section (diameter W) is incident on a screen. As the beam impinges on the screen at increasingly acute angles, the activated voxel becomes subject to a greater degree of elongation. Both **b** and **s** are unit vectors corresponding, respectively, to the beam direction and inward normal to the surface of the screen. (Reproduced from Blundell and Schwarz [2000].)

Figure 4.21). This angle is given by

$$\beta = \cos^{-1}(\hat{\mathbf{b}} \cdot \hat{\mathbf{s}}),$$

where **b** and **s** are unit vectors corresponding to the beam direction and inward normal to the surface of the screen, respectively. If we assume that a beam of circular cross section impinges on the screen, then

$$e = \frac{W}{\hat{\mathbf{b}} \cdot \hat{\mathbf{s}}},$$

where W denotes the beam diameter and e the elongated voxel length. Elongation occurs whenever $\beta \neq 0$, and the extent of the distortional dead zone is determined by the criteria that we adopt in our definition of acceptable/unacceptable voxel elongation. In Figure 4.22, the cross-sectional form of a typical distortional dead zone is illustrated for a configuration in which a single static beam source is used for voxel activation by means of a rotating planar screen. The distortional dead zone is associated with display units in which the angle of incidence between beam deflection apparatus and rotating screen continuously varies. It is therefore not limited to display embodiments that employ a planar screen, and it also occurs in systems that use a helical surface. Blundell and Schwarz [2000] provide analysis of this and other forms of dead zone, and additional discussion can be found in Schwarz and Blundell [1994a, b].

To ameliorate the effect of distortional dead zones or eliminate them entirely, various strategies may be adopted. For example:

1. In the case of the cathode ray sphere (see Figure 4.18), more than a single beam source is used. These are arranged so that each is responsible for voxel activation within a certain portion of the image space. Consequently, each

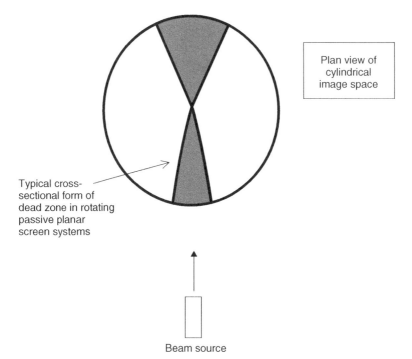

Plan view of
cylindrical
image space

Typical cross-
sectional form of
dead zone in rotating
passive planar
screen systems

Beam source

Figure 4.22 Showing the typical cross-sectional form of a distortional dead zone for a rotating planar screen used in conjunction with a single stationary directed beam. The beam source is assumed to lie in the equatorial plane of the image space. The extent of the dead zone increases above and below this plane. Diagram is not to scale. (Reproduced from Blundell and Schwarz [2000].)

beam achieves voxel activation within that part of image space in which the screen/beam source geometry is such that the voxel placement and distortional dead zone criteria are not exceeded. For beam sources that lie on the "equatorial plane" of the image space, this can usually be achieved with only two sources as indicated in Figure 4.23. However, to reduce the visual obstruction caused by the beam apparatus, it is preferable to arrange the sources below the equatorial plane. This exacerbates the severity of the two forms of dead zone, and so in this case it is likely that a third beam source will be required, as illustrated in Figure 4.24. Although this provides a convenient solution, careful registration of the beam sources is required so that image discontinuities do not arise in the region at which one source takes over from another.

2. An alternative solution is to eliminate the continually varying geometry that occurs between the beam deflection apparatus and screen through the incorporation of a suitable optical arrangement. There are various ways of achieving this goal; see, for example, Section 7.3.2 and discussion on the Perspecta display (Section 8.3.2).

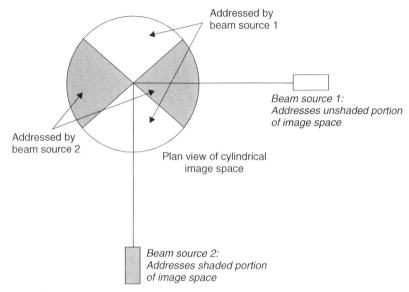

Figure 4.23 To ameliorate the impact of the voxel placement and distortional dead zones, two beam sources may be used. These are arranged so that each is responsible for the activation of voxels within one-half of the image space volume. In this way, neither beam source addresses the screen when the screen/beam geometry is unfavorable. In this scenario, for each beam we have $-45° \leq \beta \leq 45°$. Voxel elongation is therefore restricted to ~40%. The author has adopted this approach for a number of cathode ray sphere (CRS) prototypes. (Reproduced from Blundell and Schwarz [2000].)

3. A further solution is to co-rotate the beam source(s) with the screen. Such an approach is adopted in the display unit introduced in Section 7.3.1.

4.7.3 The Visual Dead Zone

This corresponds to a region of diminished image intensity, and an example of this form of dead zone is provided in Figure 4.7b. The dead zone is usually associated with display units that support considerable freedom in viewing direction. There are a number of possible reasons for the formation of a visual dead zone—for example:

1. *The Impact of the Screen:* This may block or attenuate the passage of light or, as a consequence of refraction, change its direction of propagation. This is most likely to occur to light that is emitted at highly acute angles to the screens surface or that propagates through the supporting structure and will therefore be apparent as a screen rotates so that its plane becomes increasingly parallel to the visual axis of the observer. In Figure 4.7a the impact that a matrix of active voxel generation elements may have on the propagation of light is illustrated.

Figure 4.24   The scheme illustrated in Figure 4.23 assumes that the beam source apparatus lies in the equatorial plane of the image space. If the beam sources are located below this plane (to minimize their impact on viewing freedom), the extent of the voxel placement and distortional dead zones is increased. Consequently, it is likely that an additional beam source would be required. This illustration shows such a configuration adopted for a cathode ray sphere (CRS) prototype. (Original image © 2006 B. G. Blundell.)

2. *Radiation Profile:* The amount of light output from the discrete elements that may be used to form an active surface of emission is unlikely to be omnidirectional. For example, should surface-emitting LEDs be used, the far-field radiation pattern is similar to a Lambertian radiator [Saleh and Teich, 1991] (see Figure 4.25). In this case, as a screen rotates so that its plane becomes increasingly parallel to the observer's visual axis, the image will become dimmer. This may also apply when a passive surface of emission is employed.

3. *Center Shaft:* In the case where a nontransparent center shaft is included within the image space, this may occlude parts of an image.

To reduce the severity of the visual dead zone, it is desirable to ensure that all screen components are transparent, that the voxel generation process exhibits the best possible radiation profile, and that the screen is as thin as possible. In connection with this third factor, a patent filed by Andrew LoRe et al. in 1999 (US Patent Number 6,183,088) includes a proposal for the use of a tapered screen whose thickness is gradually reduced with distance from the axis of rotation (see Figure 4.26). In this way the inventors write the following:

Tapered edges. . . reduce the amount of "edge" in a viewer's line of sight, and thereby reduce the amount of edge-on darkness present in a resulting 3-D image.

See Investigations question number 4.

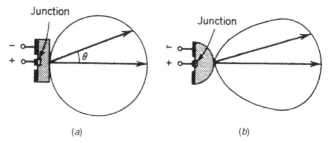

Figure 4.25 In (a) the far field radiation profile for a surface emitting LED approximates to a Lambertian radiator—the output intensity varying with the cosine of the angle from the surface normal. Thus for an angle of 60°, the output intensity has fallen by a 50%. In (b) the LED is equipped with a hemispherical lens. The radiation profile exhibited by the voxel generation mechanism(s) can greatly impact on the severity of the visual dead zone. (Reproduced by permission from Saleh and Teich [1991] © 1991 John Wiley & Sons.)

4.7.4 Other Forms of Dead Zones

A "shadowing" dead zone is associated with some displays in which the image space is formed by the rotational motion of a screen (usually helical in shape) and that use one or more directed beams for voxel activation. The formation of such a dead zone is illustrated in Figure 4.27. As may be seen from this diagram, a portion of the screen obstructs the passage of the beam to a particular location and so causes the voxel to be formed at the incorrect location.

Dead image space refers to regions within an image space in which it is impossible to activate voxels.[25] For example, this may be caused by the failure of a particular screen geometry to sweep through all parts of the image space volume, or may result from the presence of a center shaft. The severity of shadowing and visual dead zones together with the extent of any dead image space must be carefully investigated when considering the form of screen that is to be used in the implementation of a swept-volume display. Generally, the planar screen and helix (possessing no more than a single "twist") may be made to demonstrate the most favorable characteristics in relation to these three forms of dead zone (other screen geometries tend to exhibit particular weaknesses in respect of at least one of the three).

4.8 DISCUSSION

In this chapter, various concepts and terminology relating to swept-volume volumetric systems have been introduced. Several quantitative measures that provide an indication of aspects of performance have been provided; for convenience, these

---

[25] It may appear that the shadowing dead zone is simply a particular form of dead image space. However, it is important to remember that the shadowing dead zone exhibits *two* characteristics: First, it gives rise to a region of dead image space; second, it results in the incorrect placement of voxels.

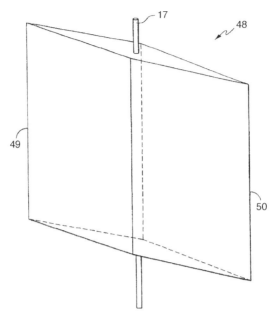

Figure 4.26 A tapered screen profile described in a patent filed in 1999 by Andrew LoRe et al. which is intended to ameliorate the visual dead zone. Also see Section 4.9 (Question 4). (Reproduced from US Patent Number 6,183,088.)

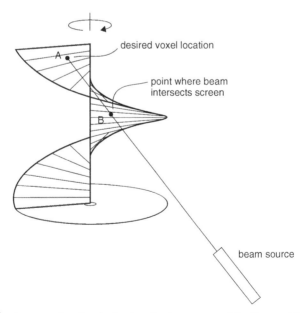

Figure 4.27 An example of a shadowing dead zone caused by the combination of beam direction and screen geometry. Here, we wish to activate a voxel at position A using a directed beam. A portion of the helix obstructs the passage of the beam; as a result, a voxel is formed at location B. (Reproduced from Blundell and Schwarz [2000].)

TABLE 4.1 Measures Introduced in this Chapter Which Provide a Quantitative Indication of Certain Aspects of Performance[a]

Indicator	Summary	Formula for Calculation
Sweep efficiency	The ratio of the image space volume to sweep volume—expressed as a percentage.	$\xi(\%) = \dfrac{V_1}{V_P} . 100$
Voxel activation capacity	The total maximum number of voxels that may be activated during each image update period.	$N_a = \dfrac{P.T}{T_{\text{act}}}$
Fill factor	The ratio of the voxel activation capacity to the voxel location capacity—expressed as a percentage.	$\varphi(\%) = \dfrac{N_a}{N_l} \cdot 100$
Voxel activation time (for the directed beam approach)	The total time required for the activation of each individual voxel. The components vary according to the voxel activation technique.	$T_{\text{act}} = T_{\text{move}} + T_{\text{on}} + T_{\text{dwell}} + T_{\text{off}}$

[a]Although useful, these must be interpreted with care

are summarized in Table 3.1. It should be noted that these are limited in their scope and are therefore not intended to represent general performance indicators. In Section 4.6 we discussed the reliance that swept-volume display units place upon rapid mechanical motion for image space formation. Within this context, we have emphasized that this does not necessarily represent an inherent weakness of the approach and that, as discussed, complex mechanical mechanisms play a critical role in the implementation of many critically important technologies. In fact, the use of motion provides a sound engineering compromise enabling us (in principle) to develop practical, reliable, and useful 3-D displays.

In the next chapter, we introduce various concepts that relate to the static-volume display paradigm, and in Chapters 6, 7, and 8 a range of swept-volume embodiments are discussed.

4.9 INVESTIGATIONS

1. Consider an image space created by means of a circular screen that is inclined with respect to the axis of rotation as illustrated in Figure 4.28. Comment upon the merits and/or deficiencies of this technique.

2. Identify two *inherent* strengths and two *inherent* weaknesses associated with the general swept-volume technique.

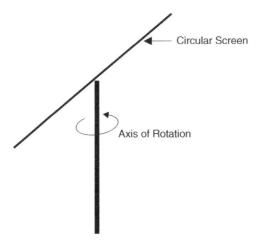

Figure 4.28 A circular screen is inclined to the axis of rotation. See Question 1. This approach was adopted by workers at Texas Instruments (see European Patent Number EPI 0491 284 A1).

3. Consider an image space formed through the rotational motion of a helical screen and that employs one or more directed beams for voxel activation. What, if any, impact would increasing the height-to-radius ratio of the cylindrical image space have on any of the forms of dead zone that were introduced in Section 4.7?

4. Referring to Figure 4.26, what impact (if any) would this screen profile have on an observer's view of voxels lying on the far side of an image space?

5. Referring to Section 4.4.2 and references cited therein, discuss strategies that could adopted for the ordering of voxels within each slice to minimize the total move time (T_{move}).

5 The Static-Volume Approach

And ever in the reading, lords and dames
Wept, looking often from his face who
read
To hers which lay so silent, and at times,
So touch'd were they, half-thinking that
her lips
Who had devised the letter moved again.

5.1 INTRODUCTION

Unlike the swept-volume display paradigm introduced in the previous chapter, static-volume systems place no reliance on mechanical motion for image space creation. Here, the image space is defined by a volume of material or arrangement of materials (that may include electronic and/or opto-electronic components) within which visible voxels may be activated. The absence of moving components may, at first sight, appear to provide a Utopian solution to the implementation of a volumetric system. However, as will become apparent from discussion both here and in Chapter 9 (which provides examples of static-volume implementations), this is not automatically the case.

Enhanced Visualization: Making Space for 3-D Images. By Barry G. Blundell
Copyright © 2007 John Wiley & Sons, Inc.

The first volumetric display the author has uncovered in literature dates back to 1912 (see Section 9.5). This system employed a volume of material within which voxels were activated by the intersection of two spatially modulated nonvisible beams. The approach required no mechanical motion for image space creation and therefore provides the earliest example of a static-volume embodiment.[1] Since the 1940s a broad range of static-volume techniques have been the subject of considerable research activity.

In Section 5.2, we begin by considering a simple static-volume display comprising a 3-D array of light-emitting components. Here, previous discussion concerning the difficulties of building and addressing such an image space is summarized [Blundell and Schwarz, 2000]. In Section 5.3, we review issues relating to the optical qualities of the image space and introduce the "depth efficiency" of an image space (in the case of many static-volume embodiments, the physical and apparent image space volumes differ, and this has important repercussions for both the depiction of images and the ease by which we are able to interact with them).

To facilitate discussion on static-volume systems, a general classification scheme is presented in Section 5.4. This parallels the one adopted in the previous chapter in relation to swept-volume displays, and it is based on the form of the subsystems used for display implementation. Issues relating to the voxel lifetime are summarized in Section 5.5.

In Sections 5.6 and 5.7 we turn our attention to techniques that may be used in the implementation of the voxel generation and activation subsystems, and here several exemplar approaches are introduced. Firstly, we consider the stepwise excitation of fluorescence in both gaseous and nongaseous media whereby visible voxels are produced at the intersection of two beams. Subsequently, we discuss the use of photochromic and thermochromic materials that enable the production of voxels whose visibility is made possible by external illumination. The use of photochromic materials offers to support image opacity and in principle has great potential.

Finally in Section 5.8 we consider dead zones that may be associated with static-volume embodiments and summarize previous discussion Blundell and Schwarz, 2000.

5.2   AN ELEMENTARY STATIC-VOLUME IMPLEMENTATION

Only the foolish visit the land of the cannibals.[2]

The most elementary approach to the implementation of a static-volume display is to construct an image space from a 3-D array of light-emitting components that

---

[1] The earliest swept-volume embodiment that the author has encountered is briefly described in Section 6.3 and dates back to a patent filed in 1931 by John Logie Baird.

[2] Maori Proverb.

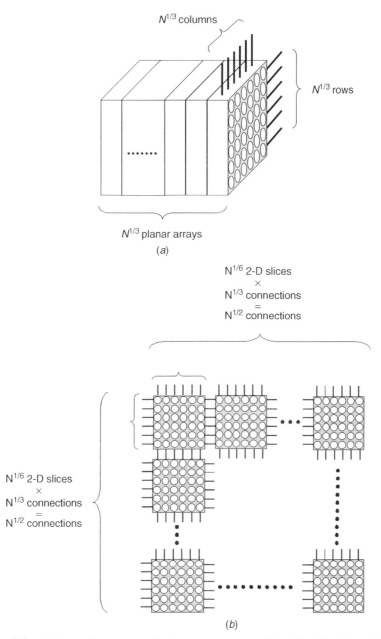

Figure 5.1   In (a) we illustrate a cubic image space comprising $N \times N \times N$ voxel generation elements. This may be considered as N 2-D arrays of N^2 elements. In (b), for convenience we assume that $\sqrt{N}$ is an integer and interconnect the N arrays as illustrated. With this simple addressing scheme, only $2N^{1/2}$ connections are required. (Reproduced from Blundell and Schwarz [2000].)

can be individually addressed as illustrated in Figure 5.1. Schemes of this sort have been proposed in literature by various researchers (see, for example, Nithiyanandam [1975]). Below, some of the problems associated with this general technique are highlighted:

1. *The Number of Voxel Generation Elements Needed:* Consider a swept-volume display unit employing the translational motion (constant velocity) of an active SOE.[3] We assume that the screen comprises an array of $N \times N$ elements and that these are separated (both horizontally and vertically) by a distance ρ. Let the amplitude of motion be ρN (and so a cubic image space is formed); as the screen moves, voxels can be formed at intervals of ρ. The N^2 voxel elements are able to give rise to N^3 voxels during each cycle of the screens movement, and these exist within an image space of volume V such that

$$V = N^3 \rho^3.$$

This contrasts with a cubic static-volume image space (of the same dimensions) in which N^3 voxel generation elements are needed to provide an image space of the same size and in which the inter-voxel spacing (ρ) is preserved. Consequently, the removal of screen motion has resulted in an N-fold increase in the number of voxel generation elements. By way of example, suppose that we wish to create an image space with sides of length 20 cm and that the minimum inter voxel spacing is 2 mm. Then in the case of the swept-volume system alluded to above, 10^4 voxel generation elements are needed and the equivalent static-volume implementation requires 10^6! This impacts not only on the construction of the image space, but also on addressing complexity (i.e., the voxel activation subsystem).

   An alternative approach is to implement a static-volume display unit in such a way that we make use of the same number of voxel generation elements that might be used by a swept-volume system. Thus we redistribute the elements within the static-volume image space. For example, suppose that the swept-volume display employs 10^4 elements with an inter-voxel spacing of 2 mm, then in the case of a static-volume system possessing an image space of the same dimensions and which employs the same number of elements, the inter-voxel spacing would increase to an unsatisfactory value of $\sim$9 mm.

2. *Addressing the Voxel Generation Elements:* As indicated above, the creation of a static-volume display unit possessing an image space of useful dimensions and which exhibits an appropriate voxel resolution requires the use of a very large number of voxel generation elements. Even if we are able to fabricate such an image space, we are still faced with the difficulty of arranging the interconnections between these elements and the graphics engine (i.e., the

---

[3] SOE stands for surface of emission.

implementation of the voxel activation subsystem). In the simplest case, each element could be separately linked to the graphics engine via a "private" data pathway. Thus for a display unit comprising N voxel generation elements, there would be $N + 1$ connections. In principle (depending on the architecture of the graphics pipeline), we could then address all elements simultaneously and the display would demonstrate a parallelism (P) equal to N. Furthermore, such a display would exhibit a 100% fill factor. As we move to larger display volumes and increase the voxel resolution, this approach becomes increasingly impractical and it becomes necessary to reduce the degree of parallelism supported by the voxel activation subsystem.

In the simplest case, we could adopt the row and column addressing scheme commonly employed in thin panel displays. For example, consider a cubic volumetric image space comprising $N \times N \times N$ voxel generation elements. As illustrated in Figure 5.1a, we can consider such an image space to be formed from N 2-D arrays of N^2 elements. Each of these may be addressed using 2N connections. If for convenience we assume that $\sqrt{N}$ is an integer, then (from the perspective of their connectivity), the 2-D arrays may be laid out and interconnected in the manner illustrated in Figure 5.1b. In this case the N^3 elements may be addressed via $2N^{1/2}$ connections.

For example, consider a cubic image space comprising 10^6 elements. If we adopt this simple addressing scheme, then we would require only 2000 connections. However, the parallelism in voxel activation supported by this rudimentary configuration would be unity.

From the perspective of data flow, this addressing scheme may be described as

$$2N^{1/2} \rightarrow N^3.$$

Obtaining a suitable balance between parallelism in voxel activation and the number of data pathways that exist between the display unit and the graphics engine is particularly important because it is likely to impact upon the fill factor (ψ).[4] Let us assume that in the case of the example referred to above, the elements emit light only during the time at which they are addressed (i.e., they switch instantaneously between their two optical states), that the average time needed to address an element is 1 μs, and that the image is completely refreshed in 40 ms. In the case where the addressing scheme exhibits a parallelism of unity, then the maximum number of voxels that may be activated during each image update period is 40,000. In the case that the image space comprises 10^6 elements, this would provide a fill factor of 4%.[5]

---

[4] The fill factor was introduced in Section 4.4.1 and applies to both swept and static-volume approaches.

[5] In practice, a fill factor of 4% is quite satisfactory as long as the technology does not place any restriction on the combination of voxels that may be selected for activation from the total number of possible voxel locations. See Section 4.4.2.

> Increasing the parallelism supported by the voxel activation and voxel generation subsystems will generally increase the fill factor. On the other hand, a parallelism of unity also provides useful opportunities. For example, should an optical sensing device be used in the implementation of some form of pointer based interaction tool, then due to the sequential activation of voxels, the interaction hardware may sense the activation of particular voxel(s) within the image space. This can assist in the determination of pointer location. Furthermore, sequential voxel activation may ameliorate image 'bright spots' that can be caused when two or more voxels located within an observer's line of sight are simultaneously activated.

3. *Optical Characteristics of the Image Space:* Clearly, should the voxel generation elements (or connections to these elements) lack transparency, they will negatively impact on perceived image quality. Even in the case where these elements (and connections) are satisfactorily transparent, we must also consider their refractive indices relative the surrounding image space. For example, so as to arrange the matrix of elements in a rigid manner, one may choose to embed them within a transparent solid medium. Differences between the refractive index of this material and that of the elements will impact on the rectilinear propagation of light and is likely to result in image distortion and/or preferential viewing direction(s).

For examples of static-volume embodiments employing a 3-D array of voxel generation elements, see Section 9.2.

5.3 IMAGE SPACE COMPOSITION

As indicated in the introduction to this chapter, a static-volume display provides a 3-D image space that comprises a material or arrangement of materials within which visible voxels may be activated. The formation of such an image space is achieved without recourse to mechanical motion. This does not necessarily preclude mechanical motion altogether, because it is possible to envisage embodiments in which the voxel activation mechanism(s) rotate with respect to the image space (see, for example, Section 5.4). However, for the moment we will overlook approaches of this sort and simply say that the image space and components therein do not move.

In the previous section, we considered the use of a 3-D matrix of voxel generation elements, with each element being responsible for the production of a single voxel at a fixed location within the image volume. Implementations employing this approach are likely to exhibit an image space that is, from the perspective of light propagation, nonhomogeneous. Below we consider various aspects of such an image space:

1. *Image Space Mass:* Image spaces that employ a 3-D matrix of voxel generation elements that are embedded within a solid or which use uniform liquid

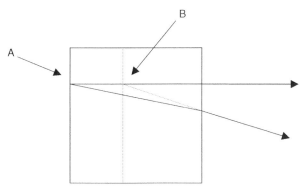

Figure 5.2 The plan view of a cubic image space. When viewed from the position shown, a voxel that is physically located at a point *A* appears to be at point *B* (the scale is exaggerated for clarity).

or solid media may be somewhat difficult to transport. By way of example, consider a hypothetical cubic image space formed from either water or glass. Assuming that the image space has sides of length 40 cm, then for the former the image space would have a mass of ~64 kg and in the latter case the mass would be ~166 kg!

2. *Image Space Dimensions:* In our discussion of swept-volume systems, we introduced the "sweep efficiency" this being the ratio of the usable image space volume to the actual volume swept out (expressed as a percentage; see Section 4.3.1). In the context of static-volume systems we introduce a similar measure that we will refer to as the depth efficiency (χ)[6] where

$$\chi(\%) = \frac{\varsigma}{\sigma} \cdot 100, \qquad (5.1)$$

where ς represents the perceived image space depth and σ the actual (physical) depth. An image space formed from a gas would demonstrate a depth efficiency of 100%. However, this would not be the case for image spaces formed from materials with higher refractive indices because the perceived image space dimensions would be determined by the difference in refractive index between the image space and the surrounding air and by the shape (and dimensions) of the image space boundary. Take the simple case of a cubic image space as illustrated in Figure 5.2 and which has a physical depth of 25 cm. Assuming that the image space has a refractive index of 1.52 relative to the surrounding air, then the apparent depth of the image space would be ~16.5 cm. In this situation, the depth efficiency would be only 66%.

This loss in depth results in image components appearing to be shifted from their actual physical locations within the image space. For the simple example image space and observer location illustrated in Figure 5.2, the shift

---

[6] This also applies to some swept-volume displays that employ the rotational motion of a solid structure. See, for example, Section 4.3.1.

in voxel location (S) is given by

$$S = \sigma \left[1 - \frac{1}{n} \right], \tag{5.2}$$

where σ denotes the true depth of the object within the image space and n the refractive index of the image space relative to the surrounding air. In practice, the situation is somewhat more complex because the extent of the shift is determined by the viewing location relative to the surface(s) of the image space and the profile of the image space boundary.

In certain situations the refraction of light at the image space boundary may be beneficial because it can enable portions of an image to be magnified[7]; this is briefly discussed below.

3. *Image Space Shape:* Consider a spherical image space whose refractive index is greater than the surrounding air:

   (a) To view an image component most readily, the observer can choose a viewing position from where the image component is seen in magnified form (cf. a fish in a goldfish bowl). For some applications, this opportunity may be advantageous but is generally not appropriate in situations where the spatial separations of a collection of objects are of interest.

   (b) Display units that support considerable viewing freedom do not often provide a well-defined backdrop against which images are viewed. Thus, for example, in the case where two observers look into an image space from either side, they are generally visible to each other, and this can reduce image clarity. However, the curvature of the surface of the image space may be used to ameliorate this problem by reducing the visibility of external objects that are located immediately opposite the observer.

5.4 THE CLASSIFICATION OF STATIC-VOLUME SYSTEMS

In this section we briefly consider the classification of static-volume display units. Here, we summarize and build on earlier discussion [Blundell and Schwarz, 2000]. As with the classification of swept-volume display units (see Section 4.5), the approach that we adopt provides a classification paradigm that is based on the general characteristics of the three display unit subsystems and therefore represents a bottom-up rather than a top-down approach. Consequently, although it provides a convenient way of distinguishing between display units, it does not necessarily provide a means by which the overall characteristics of a display may be readily predicted and so is of only limited value in determining the suitability of a display embodiment for use in a particular application.

We begin by considering the image space, which, as we have discussed in the previous section, can comprise a uniform material (in which case we refer to the

---

[7] However, distortions are likely to negatively impact on accurate cursor navigation and therefore hamper interaction.

image space as being homogeneous) or may be formed by bringing together a number of components and materials (in which case the image space is said to be nonhomogeneous). Although homogeneity is desirable, as we have seen from the previous discussion, this characteristic does not in itself guarantee that an image scene can be viewed without distortion.

A homogeneous image space permits the isotropic transmission of light through the volume. Light is thereby able to propagate in a rectilinear manner, and attenuation does not vary with viewing direction. However, homogeneity does not determine effects that occur at the image space boundary.

As may be seen from Figure 5.3, display units that provide a homogeneous image space employ a passive voxel generation subsystem that may be formed from a gaseous or nongaseous material. We use the gaseous and nongaseous categories to emphasize the potential problems discussed above and that are generally associated with the latter (i.e., refraction at the boundary of the image space and image space mass). Display units exhibiting a nonhomogeneous image

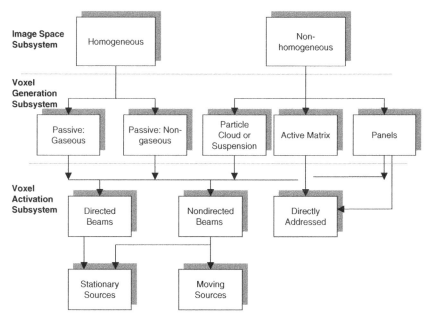

Figure 5.3   A bottom-up classification scheme for static-volume display units. Here, systems are classified according to various subsystem characteristics. This provides a useful way of distinguishing between display unit implementations and is used in Chapter 9. However, it does not necessarily provide us with a basis for accurately predicting overall display unit performance and overlooks any interaction opportunities that a display unit may offer to support. (Diagram © A. R. Blundell 2006.)

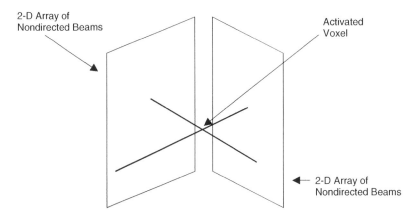

Figure 5.4 A voxel activation technique suitable for use with a static-volume display having a cubic image space and employing a passive voxel generation medium. We assume that voxels are activated when two nonvisible beams intersect. Here, two 2-D arrays of nondirected beams are used, the arrays being orthogonal to each other. In this way, to activate up to N^3 voxels per image refresh, $2N^2$ sources are required. This approach also supports parallelism in voxel activation.

space may use an array of active voxel generation elements (see, for example, Section 9.2) that are directly addressed, or a series of individually addressable panels (see, for example, Section 9.4). Additionally, there is the possibility of employing a particle cloud (see, for example, Sections 9.5.4 and 9.5.5) or suspension.

In terms of the voxel activation subsystem (and putting to one side the active matrix techniques which employs direct addressing[8]) either directed or nondirected beams may be used. In the case of the former, one or more beam sources may be angularly deflected to any location within the image space. For example, in the case of systems that employ the stepwise excitation of fluorescence (see Sections 5.6 and 9.5), a visible voxel may be formed at the point at which two (typically nonvisible) directed beams intersect. Alternatively, rather than scan beam sources, we may, for example employ two 2-D arrays of emissive elements (the arrays being orthogonal to each other as indicated in Figure 5.4). Such an embodiment does not require the use of beam deflection apparatus, and we will refer to this as the nondirected beam approach.

As may be seen from Figure 5.4, in order to activate up to N^3 voxels within the image space, we require $2N^2$ nondirected beam sources.[9] (This compares with the deflected beam approach where, at least in principle, only two beam sources are required.) Suppose the use of a cubic image space with sides of length

---

[8] Display units employing individually addressable panels generally use the direct addressing approach. However, there are also opportunities for beam addressing.

[9] This contrasts with the N^3 voxel generation elements required in the case of the display unit discussed previously and which used an active 3-D matrix.

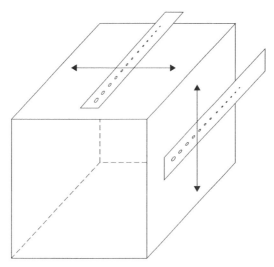

Figure 5.5 Although by definition, static-volume displays do not employ mechanical motion for image space creation, motion is not precluded from the voxel activation subsystem. Here, for example, a static-volume display employs the translational motion of two sets of nondirected beam sources relative to the image space. These each take the form of 1-D arrays and move at different frequencies. This permits a reduction in the number of sources but impacts on the parallelism in voxel activation that may be supported by the display. (Diagram © M. R. B. Blundell 2006.)

25 cm and where the minimum inter-voxel separation is 1 mm. If we were to use the arrangement illustrated in Figure 5.4, then some 125,000 beam sources would be needed. Introducing motion of the beam source apparatus relative to the image space can reduce the number of sources needed. This is illustrated in Figure 5.5, where two 1-D arrays of beam sources move with translational motion. To exhaustively scan the image space, the two arrays must move with different frequencies.[10] As a result, the $2n^2$ number of sources may be reduced (at least in principle) to $2n$.

This hypothetical embodiment employs mechanical motion. However, this movement is restricted to the voxel generation subsystem and does not relate to image space creation. Consequently, display units employing this technique do not fall into our swept-volume category but remain static-volume systems. Returning to Figure 5.3, we further categorize static-volume systems according to the use of motion in the implementation of the voxel activation subsystem. As may be seen from this diagram, a system employing nondirected beams may use either moving or stationary beam sources. In the case of a display unit employing directed beams, we assume that the actual beam sources are stationary.

[10] Also see Question 2 in Section 5.10.

5.5   VOXEL VISIBILITY

The problems of the world
cannot possibly be solved by sceptics or cynics
whose horizons are limited by the obvious realities.
We need men who can dream of things that never were.[11]

By definition, swept-volume display units must employ transient optical phenomena for the production of each visible voxel. Recall Eq. 4.10, which expresses, for a swept-volume beam addressed display unit, the time required for the activation of each voxel (the voxel activation time) as the sum of its temporal components. In the case of a display unit exhibiting a low degree of parallelism in the voxel activation process (such as the one described in Section 7.2.1), it is desirable to make this time as short as possible to maximize the number of voxels that can be output per frame. Even in the case where a very high degree of parallelism is supported (for example, the Perspecta display introduced in Section 8.3.2), the voxel activation time should still be kept quite short. This is because we need to reduce the voxel elongation arising as a consequence of the motion of the screen. In practice, we therefore minimize the "dwell time"; however, in the case of the static-volume approach the dwell time is no longer constrained by any form of screen motion. Consider a static-volume active matrix display in which all potential voxel locations may be simultaneously addressed during each image refresh period. In this scenario, there is no need to minimize the voxel activation time in order to maximize the voxel activation capacity. To ensure the production of "crisp" images, however, we would still seek to minimize the transient components of the "voxel time."[12] Here we note that in the case of an active matrix display, we may (in principle) associate with each potential voxel location circuitry enabling a voxel to continue to retain a constant level of visibility after the removal of the activation stimulus. Although this technique is commonly used in the implementation of thin panel displays, the author has not encountered any active matrix volumetric embodiment that uses this approach. If such a scheme were employed, a voxel could remain at a level of constant visibility until the application of a further signal which would either deactivate the voxel or change its level of activation. Following the onset of this signal we would expect the change in voxel state to occur as quickly as possible. In this case, Eq. 4.8 that provides an expression for the voxel time (T_{vox}) would take the form

$$T_{\mathrm{vox}} = T_{\mathrm{act}} + T_{\mathrm{ss}} + T_{\mathrm{decay}}.$$

Here, T_{act} and T_{decay} continue to represent the voxel activation time and voxel visibility lifetime (although the latter applies only when the activated voxel is to return to its inactive state—otherwise it may be further activated to directly reach an alternative state of visibility). T_{ss} denotes the period of steady-state visibility.

In the case of most, if not all, of the static-volume displays proposed or developed to date, once the voxel activation signal is removed, the light output from the

---

[11] Attributed to John Keats (1795–1821).

[12] This is particularly important in the depiction of dynamic image sequences.

voxel immediately begins to decay ($T_{ss} \sim 0$); also, to maintain image sharpness, we seek to minimize the voxel visibility lifetime.

Although static-volume displays do not employ a moving surface, if an embodiment makes use of "moving sources" such as those referred to in the previous section (see Figure 5.5), voxel elongation (and possibly visible voxel trails) can still occur. In this case, we would endeavor to keep both the dwell time and voxel visibility lifetimes short. In fact, for the majority of static-volume displays, minimization of the dwell time is desirable since this enables more voxels to be activated during each image update period.

5.6 BEAM INTERSECTION AND THE STEPWISE EXCITATION OF FLUORESCENCE

The activation of voxels through the use of beam intersection techniques has attracted considerable attention and was first researched nearly 100 years ago (see Section 9.5). In this section we briefly consider the stepwise excitation of fluorescence—this being the beam intersection technique that has gained the greatest research interest. Most commonly, this approach is based on voxels activated through the use of two directed beams, one or both of which are nonvisible. These pass through a suitable material and intersect at a region where a voxel is to be activated. Whereas the presence of a single beam has in principle no visible effect on the voxel generation subsystem, the combined presence of the two beams stimulates the production of visible light. Following Lewis et al. [1971] (and previous discussion in Blundell and Schwarz [2000]), when referring to each atom, ion, or molecule that contributes to the production of a visible voxel, we will use the term "*fluorescent center*". In the next subsection, we briefly consider some work carried out in relation to the use of a gaseous voxel generation medium, and in Section 5.6.2 we discuss the use of solid materials (also see Chapter 9 for related discussion).

5.6.1 The Stepwise Excitation of Fluorescence in Gaseous Media

Whom the Gods would destroy,
they first make mad.[13]

Simplified (idealized) models illustrating physical processes that may result in the production of visible voxels are provided in Figure 5.6. In Figure 5.6a we show three quantized electronic energy levels associated with an atom. These comprise the ground state (indicated as $|1\rangle$) and two excited states ($|2\rangle$ and $|3\rangle$). A first beam causes excitation from state $|1\rangle$ to $|2\rangle$. The frequency of this beam (ω_1) is resonant with this transition: Beam photons have an energy (E_1) corresponding to the energy difference between these two states. This energy is given by

$$E_1 = h\omega_1 = h\frac{c}{\lambda_1}.$$

---

[13] Attributed to Euripides ($\sim$480–406BC).

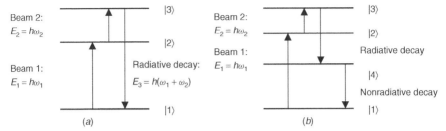

Figure 5.6 Simple models of the stepwise excitation of fluorescence. (a) Illustrates a fluorescent center with three quantized energy states. An incident beam is used to cause excitation from state $|1\rangle$ to $|2\rangle$, and a second beam from state $|2\rangle$ to $|3\rangle$. Subsequently, the system returns to the ground state by radiative decay and so gives rise to a visible photon. In (b) a four-state model is shown. Again, two beams are used in the excitation process, however the radiative decay no longer corresponds to a direct return to the ground state, but rather to an intermediate state ($|4\rangle$). Subsequently, we assume a nonradiative transition to the ground state.

Where, c denotes the speed of light in free space, λ_1 represents the wavelength of the incident beam and h is Planck's constant.[14] Similarly, a second beam (of frequency ω_2 and with photons of energy E_2) is used to cause excitation from state $|2\rangle$ to state $|3\rangle$, and in the case of this simple model the fluorescent center subsequently returns to the ground state by a radiative decay, so emitting a visible photon whose energy (E_3) is given by

$$E_3 = h(\omega_1 + \omega_2).$$

Thus the emitted light has a frequency that is greater than either of the beams used in the excitation process; hence, for this simplified model, these beams would typically lie in the infrared region of the electromagnetic spectrum. In Figure 5.6b, four quantized energy levels of a fluorescent center are shown. Again two beams are used for the excitation process; however, in this system the radiative decay corresponds to a transition to an intermediate state ($|4\rangle$), and is assumed to be followed by a nonradiative transition to the ground state. In this way the energy of the emitted photon no longer corresponds to the combined energy of the incident photons but may have a value that is less than either of their individual values energies. As a consequence the incident beams may, for example, lie in the ultraviolet region of the electromagnetic spectrum.

In practice, a greater number of transitions are likely to be involved in the absorption and/or emission processes, and so the underlying physical processes that give rise to the visible voxel are generally more complex than those indicated by the two models described above. To gain an insight into some of the issues involved in the implementation of a system employing the stepwise excitation process, it is useful to briefly consider an exemplar approach. The work undertaken by Isaac Kim, Eric Korevaar, Harel Hakakha, and Brett Spivey (see US Patent Number

---

[14] Planck's constant $\sim 6.63 \times 10^{-34}$ Js.

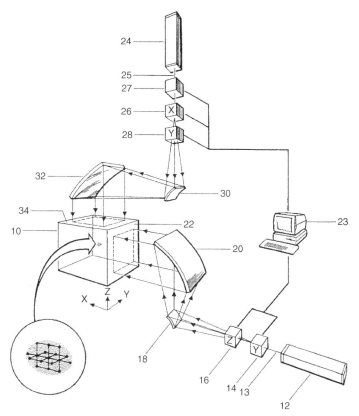

Figure 5.7 An experimental display unit employing the stepwise excitation of fluorescence in rubidium vapor. The two directed beams (13) and (25) enter the image volume normal to surfaces (22) and (34) [thereby avoiding voxel distortion as a result of varying beam intersection geometry (see Section 5.8).] X-Y scanning mirrors (of the galvanometer type) were used to produce a vector scan and thereby create simple images such as the one illustrated in Figure 5.11. In Kim et al. [1996] the researchers report a voxel activation capacity of ∼500 prior to the onset of noticeable flicker—this limit being imposed by bandwidth of the scanning apparatus rather than the voxel generation technique. Beam (13) operates in the IR and beam (25) in the visible part of the electromagnetic spectrum. (Reproduced from US Patent Number 4,881,068.)

4,881,068 and Kim et al. [1996]) provides us with an excellent example. Below we begin by discussing aspects of this work and subsequently related research undertaken by Zito and Schraeder in connection with mercury vapor (see also Section 9.5).

A diagram showing the general setup of the apparatus is provided in Figure 5.7. The researchers formed an image space using a Pyrex chamber equipped with five viewing windows (see Figure 5.8). Within this container a small quantity of

Figure 5.8 The Pyrex cell used to contain the rubidium vapor equipped with five viewing windows and a cold finger. In the photograph the cell is shown inverted, consequently the cold finger appears at the top of the image. In use, this would be below the image space and contain the rubidium. The distance between opposite viewing windows is reported as 7 inches. (Photograph kindly supplied by Professor Eric Korevaar.)

rubidium[15] (1 g) was heated to form a vapor at a density of approximately 3×10^{13} atoms $\cdot$ cm^{-3}. This necessitated the placement of the image space chamber (and some associated apparatus) within an oven operating at $\sim 130°$C (see Figure 5.9).[16] A diagram showing some of the electron energy levels associated with the rubidium atom is reproduced in Figure 5.10. Of particular importance to our current discussions are the $5s_{1/2}$, $5p_{3/2}$, and $7d_{5/2}$ energy levels. These are conveniently placed so that excitation from the $5s_{1/2}$ to the $5p_{3/2}$ states can be achieved by means of an IR laser beam operating at a wavelength of approximately 7800 Å.[17] Subsequently, a second laser operating in the visible portion of the spectrum can be used to excite fluorescent centers to the $7d_{5/2}$ energy levels.[18] Visible radiative decay then occurs

---

[15] The rubidium (Rb) used is reported to have been in the form of its natural isotopic abundance (28% ^{87}Rb, 72% ^{85}Rb). Rubidium is a Group I element (the alkali metals) whose atomic number is 37. It is silvery appearance.

[16] Temperature and density data taken from US Patent Number 4,881,068.

[17] 1 Å = 10^{-10} m.

[18] Although this second beam source lies in the visible portion of the electromagnetic spectrum, it entered the image space from above and passed vertically downwards. If we assume that the light is not reflected by the apparatus located at the bottom of the image space, it would not be visible to an observer. On the other hand, the light produced by the fluorescence process is emitted in all directions and so could be observed from any location.

Figure 5.9 The image space chamber was placed within an oven which, in turn, was located in an insulating housing—illustrated here. Both the oven and its housing were equipped with five windows—these being aligned with those in the Pyrex chamber. The directed beam sources used for the stepwise excitation process entered the image space via two of the windows, with the remainder permitting the observer(s) a view of the images formed within the chamber. (Photograph kindly supplied by Professor Eric Korevaar.)

approximately 73% of the time by the atom relaxing to the $5p_{3/2}$ level.[19] Consider the first beam source which is reported as having a power of 1.2 W and a beam diameter of $\sim$1 mm.[20] The researchers assume that up to 50% of this power is lost in the optical system used to direct and scan the beam and in its entry into the image space. Thus the actual laser power applied to the rubidium (I) is assumed to be $\sim$0.6 W (i.e., a radiant flux density of approximately 0.76×10^6 Wm^{-2}). We can readily calculate the number of photons produced by this beam per second (ρ_p):

$$\rho_p = \frac{I}{h\nu} = \frac{I\lambda}{hc},$$

where, λ represents the wavelength of the beam, h is Planck's constant, and c denotes the speed of light in free space. For $\lambda = 780$ nm and $I = 0.6$ W, we obtain a photon flux density of approximately 2.4×10^{18} photons/second. The beam is reported as being scanned through the volume; by allowing the beam to dwell on particular locations for $\sim$25 µs, columns of rubidium atoms are excited to the $5p_{3/2}$ state. The workers assume the creation of 100×100 such columns (and the

---

[19] As may be seen from Figure 5.10, the second beam source may alternatively be made resonant with the $6d_{5/2}$, $8d_{5/2}$, or $12d_{5/2}$ energy levels and thereby give rise to the production of voxels of other colors.

[20] In the estimations given here, we follow the analysis provided in US Patent Number 4,881,068.

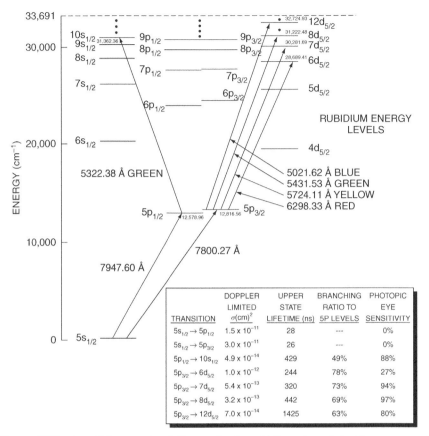

Figure 5.10   A partial energy level diagram for the rubidium atom. A first beam resonant with the $5s_{1/2}$ and $5p_{3/2}$ energy levels excites the atom to the $5p_{3/2}$ state and a second beam is used to stimulate excitation to one of four possible levels. The emission of radiation in the visible portion of the electromagnetic spectrum occurs when the atom relaxes back to the intermediate state. (Reproduced from US Patent Number 4,881,068.)

use of the second beam source to activate up to 100 voxels along each column (thereby providing a theoretical voxel activation capacity of 10^6)). Assuming a column length of 25 cm, a beam diameter of 1 mm, and a density of rubidium of 3×10^{13} atoms $\cdot$ cm^{-3}, then the total number of fluorescent centers per column is approximately 6×10^{12}. The result is that the $5s_{1/2}$ to $5p_{3/2}$ transition becomes saturated (with an estimated two-thirds of the fluorescent centers in the column excited). The second beam source can then be used to further excite these atoms and so produce visible voxels. Assuming that the activation of each voxel occurs in a region approximately 1 mm^3, then some 3×10^{10} fluorescent centers may (in principle) contribute to the production of each voxel. In fact, only approximately two-thirds of these are excited by the first beam source; of these, up to approximately three-fifths can be further excited to the $7d_{5/2}$ state. Thus the number of fluorescent centers that have the ability to contribute to visible light output[21] is approximately $2/3 \times 3/5 \times 3 \times 10^{10} \sim 1.2 \times 10^{10}$. Assuming that some 73% of the atoms in the $7d_{5/2}$ state decay to the $5p_{3/2}$ state (the researchers quote a time constant of 320 ns), then the number of visible photons produced per voxel is approximately $0.73 \times 1.2 \times 10^{10} = 87.6 \times 10^8$. For a refresh rate of 0.25 s, the number of photons emanating from each activated voxel is $\sim 35 \times 10^9$ photons/s. Each photon has an energy given by $E = hc/\lambda$ and for a wavelength of 572 nm, this equals 0.35×10^{-18}J. Thus the total energy emanating from each activated voxel is approximately 12.3×10^{-9}J $\cdot$ s^{-1}. At a wavelength of 572 nm, the efficiency of the eye is approximately 94%[22] of a maximum of around 673 lm/W.[23] Thus the perceived brightness of each voxel can be expressed as being approximately 7.8×10^{-6} lm/voxel. Supposing a typical viewing distance of 30 cm, we obtain an illuminance[24] of approximately 6.7×10^{-6}lm $\cdot$ m^{-2}. By way of comparison, Korevaar and Spivey write:

> *This brightness can be compared to the brightest star in the sky, Sirius, which has a brightness of 9.8×10^{-6} lumen $\cdot$ m^{-2}. The threshold visibility for an achromatic 5×10^{-6} lumen $\cdot$m^{-2} point source occurs at a background luminance of 10^2 candela $\cdot$ m^{-2}. (A chromatic source like ours should be visible in an even brighter background.) A luminance of 10^2 candela $\cdot$ m^{-2} corresponds to a heavily overcast day. Our source of 5×10^{-6} lumen $\cdot$ m^{-2} is 100 times stronger than the threshold visible illuminance in a 10^{-1} candela $\cdot$ m^{-1} background, corresponding to the background light under a full moon. Thus, our 3-D display can be easily viewed in a slightly darkened room.*

In Figure 5.11 we reproduce a simple image depicted on the display prototype developed by Korevaar et al. Without a doubt, an improved scanning system would have significantly advanced the performance of this approach. Both the patent and paper cited above in relation to this work are highly recommended to the interested reader.

This discussion is intended to highlight some of the issues associated with the implementation of a display based on a beam intersection technique in which a gaseous medium is employed for voxel generation. Additional discussion on this general approach is provided in Blundell and Schwarz [2000], where the temporal behavior of the quantum system is discussed and the optimal relative timing of the two beam sources is analyzed (see also Schwarz and Blundell [1993]).

Rubidium provides an example of a material that may be used in the implementation of a display unit employing voxel activation at the intersection of two directed beams; however, various other suitable gaseous and nongaseous materials may be used in the voxel generation subsystem. Drawing on Radzig and Smirnov [1985], Korevaar and Brett provide in their patent a summary of a number of other potentially suitable materials. In Table 5.1, several elements are listed which exhibit an

---

[21] We assume that in the 0.25-μs dwell time, this transition is saturated.

[22] Luminous efficiency function; see footnote 5 in Chapter 2 and, for example, Boff et al. [1986].

[23] Lumens is abbreviated to lm.

[24] Here we divide 7.8×10^{-6} lm/voxel by $4\pi r^2$, the area of a sphere centered upon the activated voxel.

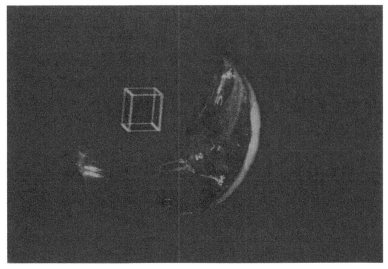

Figure 5.11   Illustrating an image depicted on the prototype system developed by Kore-vaar and co-workers. Reproducing this photograph in black and white greatly detracts from image clarity (in the original the cube appears in vivid red). This and other images are illustrated in color in Kim et al. [1996]. (Reproduced by permission, © 1996 SPIE.)

TABLE 5.1 The Approximate Temperature to Which Various Elements Must Be Heated to Create a Vapor with a Density of Fluorescent Centers of Approximately 10^{14} atoms $\cdot$ cm^{-3}

Element	Approximate Operating Temperature (°C)[a]
Sodium	250
Potassium	175
Rubidium	150
Cadmium	225
Cesium	125
Mercury	25

[a]Temperature data reproduced from US Patent Number 4,881,068.

atomic density (density of fluorescent centers) of approximately 10^{14} atoms $\cdot$ cm^{-3} when heated to an appropriate temperature within the range 25–250°C (naturally, from a practical point of view the avoidance of higher temperatures is desirable). In Table 5.2, we reproduce data on the required wavelength of the directed beam sources to activate visible voxels for the elements listed in Table 5.1. Interest in the use of mercury vapor as a means of implementing a display unit employing the stepwise excitation of fluorescence dates back to the pioneering research

TABLE 5.2 For the Elements Listed in Table 5.1, the Wavelengths of the Directed Beams Necessary to Activate Visible Voxels are Indicated

Element	Laser	Wavelength (transition) [color]		Wavelength (transition) [color]
Cesium:	Laser 1 =	852 nm ($6s_{1/2} \to 6p_{3/2}$) [infrared]	or	894 nm ($6s_{1/2} \to 6p_{1/2}$) [infrared]
	Laser 2 =	621 nm ($6p_{3/2} \to 8d_{5/2}$) [orange]	or	636 nm ($6p_{1/2} \to 9s_{1/2}$) [red]
		585 nm ($6p_{3/2} \to 9d_{5/2}$) [yellow]	or	584 nm ($6p_{1/2} \to 10s_{1/2}$) [green]
		564 nm ($6p_{3/2} \to 10d_{5/2}$) [green]	or	557 nm ($6p_{1/2} \to 11s_{1/2}$) [green]
		550 nm ($6p_{3/2} \to 11d_{5/2}$) [green]		
Rubidium:	Laser 1 =	780 nm ($5s_{1/2} \to 5p_{3/2}$) [infrared]	or	795 nm ($5s_{1/2} \to 5p_{1/2}$) [infrared]
	Laser 2 =	630 nm ($5p_{3/2} \to 6d_{5/2}$) [red]	or	607 nm ($5p_{1/2} \to 8s_{1/2}$) [orange]
		572 nm ($5p_{3/2} \to 7d_{5/2}$) [yellow]	or	558 nm ($5p_{1/2} \to 9s_{1/2}$) [green]
		543 nm ($5p_{3/2} \to 8d_{5/2}$) [green]	or	532 nm ($5p_{1/2} \to 10s_{1/2}$) [green]
		502 nm ($5p_{3/2} \to 12d_{5/2}$) [bluegreen]		
Potassium:	Laser 1 =	766 nm ($4s_{1/2} \to 4p_{3/2}$) [infrared]	or	770 nm ($4s_{1/2} \to 4p_{1/2}$) [infrared]
	Laser 2 =	583 nm ($4p_{3/2} \to 5d_{5/2}$) [yellow]	or	578 nm ($4p_{1/2} \to 7s_{1/2}$) [yellow]
		536 nm ($4p_{3/2} \to 6d_{5/2}$) [green]	or	532 nm ($4p_{1/2} \to 8s_{1/2}$) [green]
		511 nm ($4p_{3/2} \to 7d_{5/2}$) [green]	or	508 nm ($4p_{1/2} \to 8s_{1/2}$) [green]
		480 nm ($4p_{3/2} \to 10d_{5/2}$) [blue]		
Sodium:	Laser 1 =	589 nm ($3s_{1/2} \to 3P_{1/2}$) [yellow]	or	590 nm ($3s_{1/2} \to 3p_{1/2}$) [yellow]
	Laser 2 =	569 nm ($3p_{3/2} \to 4d_{5/2}$) [green]	or	616 nm ($3p_{1/2} \to 5s_{1/2}$) [orange]
		498 nm ($3p_{3/2} \to 5d_{5/2}$) [bluegreen]	or	515 nm ($3p_{1/2} \to 6s_{1/2}$) [green]
		467 nm ($3p_{3/2} \to 6d_{5/2}$) [blue]		
Cadmium:	Laser 1 =	229 nm ($5\,^1S_0 \to 5\,^1P_1^0$) [ultraviolet]	or	326 nm ($5\,^1S_0 \to 5\,^3P_1^0$) [ultraviolet]
	Laser 2 =	644 nm ($5\,^1P_1^0 \to 5\,^1D_2$) [red]	or	480 nm ($5\,^3P_1^0 \to 6\,^3S_1$) [blue]
		466 nm ($5\,^1P_1^0 \to 6\,^1D_2$) [blue]		
		515 nm ($5\,^1P_1^0 \to 7\,^1S_0$) [green]		
Mercury:	Laser 1 =	185 nm ($6\,^1S_0 \to 6\,^1P_1^0$) [ultraviolet]	or	254 nm ($6\,^1S_0 \to 6\,^3P_1^0$) [ultraviolet]
	Laser 2 =	579 nm ($6\,^1P_1^0 \to 6\,^1D_2$) [yellow]	or	436 nm ($6\,^3P_1^0 \to 7\,^3S_1$) [blue]
		435 nm ($6\,^1P_1^0 \to 7\,^1D_2$) [blue]		
		492 nm ($6\,^1P_1^0 \to 8\,^1S_0$) [blue]		

Source: Reproduced with permission from A. A. Radzig and B. M. Smirnov, *Reference Data on Atoms, Molecules, and Ions*, copyright © 2006 Springer Verlag.

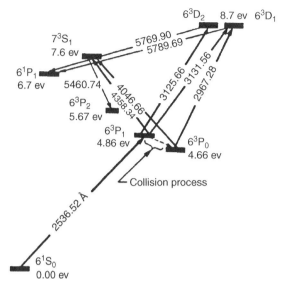

Figure 5.12   A partial electron energy level diagram for a mercury atom. Of particular relevance to the discussion in the text are the ground state (6^1S_0), 6^3P_1, 7^3S_1, and metastable 6^3P_0 state. (Reproduced with permission from Zito [1963], © 1963 American Institute of Physics.)

undertaken by Jack Fajans, who, in 1961, filed a comprehensive patent in relation to this and other voxel generation/activation techniques [US Patent Number 3,123,711]. Subsequently, researchers Zito and Schraeder published papers detailing work carried on the stepwise excitation of fluorescence using mercury vapor for voxel production [Zito, 1963; Zito and Schraeder, 1963].[25] For the moment, we focus on the publications of Zito and Schraeder, and in Section 9.5.1 we briefly discuss aspects of the Fajans patent. A partial electron energy level diagram for a mercury atom is reproduced in Figure 5.12. Zito and Schraeder employed a first beam source to cause excitation from the ground state (6^1S_0) to 6^3P_1 state. For this, a beam operating in the UV portion of the electromagnetic spectrum at a wavelength of 2537 Å is required. Collisions between these mercury atoms in their excited state and diatomic nitrogen molecules (also present) result in the formation of a metastable state (6^3P_0) state. From here, Zito and Schraeder employed a second radiation source (of wavelength 4047 Å) to cause a further excitation to the 7^3S_1 state. Visible fluorescence then occurs by spontaneous decay to the 6^3P_2 which results in the production of green light (of wavelength 5460 Å). From the outset, the work undertaken by these researchers was hampered by the production of suitable beam sources and filters. Zito [1963] discusses the need to minimize the

[25] It appears that Zito and Schraeder [1963] may have been the first to coin the term "image space" in relation to a 3-D display volume.

attenuation of the first beam as it passes through the image space. In this context, he writes:

> In effect, the number of $^3P_0$ atoms produced per unit path length along the beam by the absorption of 2537 Å must be fairly constant throughout the chamber, i.e. independent of the distance from the entrance window of beam 1.

Due to the limitations of the beam source, the issue of beam attenuation was particularly relevant to these researchers.[26] The experimental voxel activation volume is reported to have operated at room temperature with a density of fluorescent centers of approximately 3.95×10^{13} atoms $\cdot$ cm^{-3}. However, and most probably as a result of the limited capabilities of the beam source apparatus, the light output from the fluorescence process was unsatisfactory. Zito writes:

> A value for an acceptable level of visibility for the green 5461 Å line has been given at about 3×10^{13} photons $\cdot$ s^{-1} cm^{-3}. In order to achieve this, it appears at this time that a level of $I_1 = I_2 = 3 \times 10^{15}$ photons cm^{-2} s^{-1} is required. However, a closer examination is required of these excitation processes at such high levels of stimulation and corresponding 6^3P_0 population densities for verification of these extrapolated quantities.

The form of the apparatus employed by Zito and Schraeder is illustrated in Figure 5.13. Since they were simply evaluating the feasibility of the stepwise excitation of fluorescence using mercury vapor, they did not concern themselves with beam scanning apparatus but simply projected the two beams into a cylindrical Pyrex chamber (some 15 cm in length and 11.5 cm in diameter) in such a way that they would intersect. A small amount of mercury was placed within this vessel before it was evacuated to a pressure of approximately 10^{-4} mmHg.

In terms of the incident beams, Zito and Schraeder estimate that the first beam (2537 Å) comprised 6.4×10^{13} photons $\cdot$ s^{-1} cm^{-2} and that the second beam (4047 Å) 10.2×10^{13} photons $\cdot$ s^{-1} cm^{-2} (leading to a fluorescent output (in terms of photon density) of 2.7×10^{10} photons $\cdot$ s^{-1} cm^{-2}). On the other hand, Korevaar et al. were able to employ a far greater photon density (e.g., 2.4×10^{18} photons/second with a beam diameter of 1 mm), and this greatly facilitated improvement in voxel visibility. Zito [1963] provides an interesting and detailed analysis of the excitation and decay mechanisms, and this is highly recommended to the interested reader. See also the publication by Barnes et al. [1974], who describes work undertaken in the stepwise excitation of fluorescence in iodine monochloride vapor.

---

[26] They employed mercury arc lamps built in the laboratory. In respect of these they write "*This lamp is started by tipping the tube, causing the mercury to run along the walls to the anode to establish the arc. The large diameter of the lamp, about 19 mm, necessitated deflecting the arc to the light exit wall of the tube by a magnetic field for maximum unreversed 2537-Å line. When this lamp is hot, the lines are badly broadened; consequently, it was found necessary to water-cool continuously the lower portion of the lamp during operation*' [Zito and Schraeder, 1963]. Laser technologies make life so much easier....

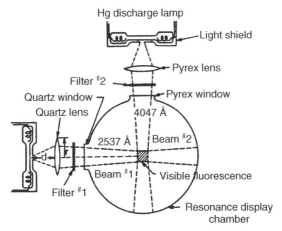

Figure 5.13 Showing the form of apparatus used by Zito and Schraeder in their pioneering investigation concerning the stepwise excitation of mercury vapor for the production of voxels. Mercury arc lamps and filters were used for the production of the two beam sources; the work would have been greatly facilitated had suitable lasers been available. (Reproduced with permission from Zito and Schraeder [1963].)

5.6.2 The Stepwise Excitation of Fluorescence in Nongaseous Media

> *The important thing in science*
> *is not so much to obtain new facts*
> *as to discover new ways of thinking about them.*[27]

The activation of voxels via a stepwise excitation process within a solid has been the subject of research interest for many years.[28] As with the work undertaken by Kaiser and Garrett [1961] (referred to in the previous footnote), calcium fluoride also formed the transparent host material employed by Lewis et al. [1971], but

---

[27] Attributed to William Bragg (1862–1942).

[28] Additionally, work on "two-photon" excitation has also been carried out for many years (see, for example, Goeppert-Mayer [1931]). The process enables the excitation of a fluorescent center to be achieved in a single step. This contrasts with stepwise excitation in which at least one intermediate energy level is required and in which excitation between states is sequential. Experimental studies in this area have been greatly facilitated by the development of maser and laser technologies. See, for example, [Kaiser and Garrett, 1961], who described experimental work carried out in connection with two photon absorption in calcium fluoride crystals in which 0.1% of the Ca^{2+} ions were replaced with europium ions (Eu^{2+}). In this work, the application of a brief pulse of radiation ($\sim$500 μs) with a wavelength of 694 nm (red) is reported to have resulted in a *"brilliant blue fluorescence"*. Two-photon absorption is briefly discussed in Blundell and Schwarz [2000]. See also US Patent Number 3,541,542 filed by Dugay et al., for discussion on the application of two photon absorption for voxel production within a volumetric image space. For introductory material in this and related areas, see, for example, the excellent book by Haken and Wolf [1994].

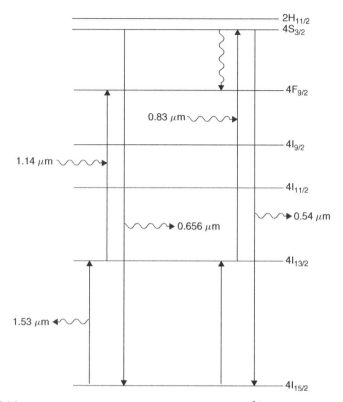

Figure 5.14   A partial energy level diagram for erbium (Er^{3+}) doped into a transparent host material (CaF_2). The second beam source may be used to cause excitation to two different states and so produce voxels of two different colors. In the case that a radiation source with a wavelength of 830 nm is used, the voxel would radiate green light with an additional red component (caused by nonradiative decay to an intermediate state followed by a radiative decay to the ground state). (Reproduced by permission from Lewis et al. [1971] © 1971 IEEE.)

in this case it was doped with erbium[29] (Er^{3+}) rather than europium (used by the earlier researchers). The approach adopted is briefly outlined in Section 9.5.2; for the moment, it is sufficient to confine ourselves to the quantum transitions involved in the activation process. These are illustrated in Figure 5.14. Here it may be seen that a first beam source of wavelength 1530 nm causes the initial excitation and a second beam (with a wavelength of 830 nm) stimulates further excitation. Subsequent radiative decay either directly to the ground state or via a nonradiative transition to an intermediate state (followed by a radiative transition) gives rise to the emission of visible light. The former results in the emission of a photon with a

---

[29] Erbium (atomic number 68) is one of the lanthenides (Rare Earth elements). These elements are highly electropositive.

TABLE 5.3 The Use of ZBLAN as a Transparent Host Material Doped with Rare Earth Lanthanides[a]

Fluorescent Center	Wavelength of First Beam (nm)	Wavelength of Second Beam (nm)	Voxel Color (Wavelength in nm)	Lifetime of Intermediate State (ms)
Praseodymium (Pr^{3+})	1014	840	Red (605 and 636)	0.18
Erbium (Er^{3+})	1550	850	Green (545)	15
Thulium (Tm^{3+})	800	1064	Blue (480)	1.5

Source of Data: Downing et al [1996], (Reproduced by permission Science 273.1185).
[a]See Downing et al. [1996] for details of beam power, types of laser source employed, and so on.

wavelength of 540 nm (green), and the latter results in a photon with a wavelength of 656 (red). Alternatively, the second beam may have a wavelength of 1140 nm, in which case an emission at 656 nm will ensue. In this scenario, the production of a green voxel will result in the inclusion of some red content, whereas a red voxel may be produced without additional color content. Recently, research has been directed to the further development of this general approach. Since the work of Lewis et al., considerable advances have been made in connection with the production of suitable materials and the development of high-performance laser technologies. Consequently, truly solid-state volumetric systems are now feasible (although image space dimensions are likely to be restricted). Researchers at Stanford University and NRAD have explored and developed display devices using ZBLAN[30] as a transparent host material doped with rare earth lanthanides. These include praseodymium (Pr^{3+}), erbium (Er^{3+}), and thulium (Tm^{3+}) [Soltan and Lasher, 1996]. Some excitation and emission wavelengths are summarized in Table 5.3. Further discussion on this approach is provided in Section 9.4.3. For relevant reading on issues related to the stepwise excitation processes associated with Pr^{3+} and Er^{3+}, see, for example, Malinowski et al. [1995], who focus on Pr^{3+}, Tsuboi et al. [1995], who focus on Er^{3+}, and Yokokawa et al. [1995], who consider both Pr^{3+}- and Er^{3+}-doped ZBLAN. [31] See also Eyal et al. [1985].

Regarding the work carried out on the doped ZBLAN display technique, the following additional publications are likely to be of interest: Soltan and Lasher [1996], Glanz [1996], Chinnock [1994], Computer Graphics World [1997], Downing et al. [1994], and Soltan et al. [1992].

---

[30] ZBLAN is a flurozirconate glass and is an acronym for ZrF4–BaF2–LaF3–AlF3–NaF [Soltan and Lasher, 1996].

[31] De Araújo et al. [1994] (and references cited therein) provide interesting reading on investigations into the excitation of Pr^{3+}-doped fluoroindate glasses in which upconversion is achieved via a cooperative energy transfer process involving a pair of Pr^{3+} ions. Here excitation using a wavelength of ~588 nm (orange) produces fluorescence at a wavelength of ~480 nm (blue).

5.7 THE PHOTOCHROMIC APPROACH

In response to incident radiation, photochromic materials are able to change between optical states in a reversible way. As discussed above, the use of two-step excitation of fluorescence for voxel generation gives rise voxels that emit light. However, should the voxel generation subsystem employ photochromism, voxel visibility is entirely dependent on the external illumination of the image space. In principle, this creates opportunities for the development of volumetric displays able to satisfy the depth cue of occlusion (see Section 2.3.1) and perhaps even the formation of natural shading.

A photochromic material in optical state A can, under the influence of suitable radiation (of wavelength λ_1), be switched into an optical state (B). Typically, although the material will subsequently revert to state A over time, a more rapidly reversal can be achieved through the application of radiation of wavelength λ_2 [Petty et al., 1995]. Thus,

$$A \underset{\lambda_2}{\overset{\lambda_1}{\rightleftarrows}} B$$

Unfortunately, photochromic materials that are continually switched between optical states may undergo gradual fatigue resulting in longer switching times and loss of coloration, and so refreshing of the material may be necessary.

Observation of photochromic behavior is by no means new and dates back at least as far as the mid-nineteenth century [Fritzche, 1867], while in recent years the study of photochromic materials has attracted great attention. The first proposal for the application of photochromic materials for use in the implementation of volumetric display systems appears to have been made by researchers at the Battelle Development Corporation and is discussed in two patents filed in 1968 [US Patent Numbers 3,609,706 and 3,609,707].[32] The author knows of no recent or ongoing research in connection with photochromic-based displays, which is most unfortunate given the potential of this approach. In the text that follows, some of the proposals made by Arthur Adamson and Jordan Lewis in the two patents cited above are briefly reviewed.

Figure 5.15 provides a diagram of the apparatus discussed by Adamson and Lewis. Here, the image space (21) contains a photochromic material that is assumed to be in a transparent state (state A), and a collimated (and directed) nonvisible beam (17) is used to promote a change to state B (which is colored). However, as the beam enters the image space, coloration will occur and the beam strength will be rapidly attenuated, making it impossible to effect a change of state deep within the image space. To overcome this problem and enable voxels to be formed at any location within the image space, a second beam (produced by source 25) is used. This beam is able to promote the return of the photochromic material from state B to state A and acts as an "eraser" enabling the first beam to propagate

---

[32] An interesting article in *Physics Today* [Kiss, 1970] also suggests (in general terms) the potential application of photochromic materials to 3-D display systems.

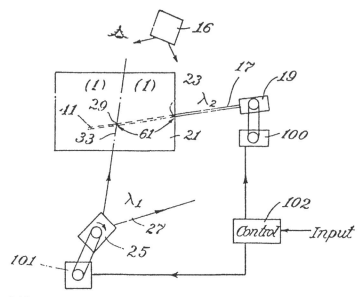

Figure 5.15 The form of apparatus employed by Arthur Adamson and Jordan Lewis. Two directed and nonvisible beams are employed to address an image space (21) comprising a photochromic material. Beam (17) is responsible for the production of the nontransparent state, and its passage through the image space is made possible by an "erasing" beam generated by source (25). (Reproduced from US Patent Number 3,609,707.)

into the image space up to the point at which the visible voxel is to be formed. Unfortunately, in this case, the time needed to activate a voxel is dependent upon its depth within the image space. Furthermore, as the number of voxels comprising an image frame grows, the order in which voxels are activated becomes increasingly important.[33]

The researchers suggest that 1',3',3'-trimethyl-6-nitrospiro(2H-1-benzopyran-2,2'-indoline)[34] would be a suitable photochromic material (see Figure 5.16).[35] They indicate the following:

This photochromic material is preferably dissolved at a rate of 10 milligrams per litre of 95 percent ethanol in water. To reduce convection currents, this resulting solution should be gelled, for example by adding approximately 4 percent by weight of polyvinyl acetate. [US Patent Number 3,609,707]

[33] Failure to activate voxels in the appropriate order may lead to the problem of conditional voxel activation (which we have already discussed in connection with swept-volume displays).

[34] See discussion in Berman et al. [1959].

[35] Lanthenides (rare earth elements) doped into calcium fluoride were mentioned in the previous section as a means of affecting voxel production by the two-step excitation of fluorescence. They also exhibit photochromic properties: "*Four rare-earth elements, lanthanum, gadolinium, cerium and terbium, when treated under reducing conditions, show efficient large photochromic color changes at room temperature.*" [Kiss, 1970].

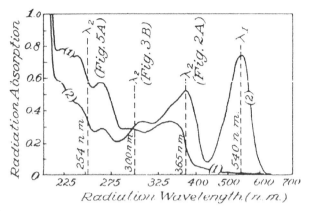

Figure 5.16   Absorption spectra of 1',3',3'-trimethyl-6-nitrospiro(2H-1-benzopyran-2,2'-indoline for optical states (1) and (2). (Reproduced from US Patent Number 3,609,707.)

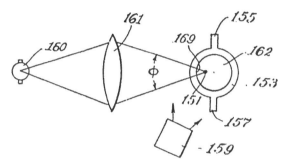

Figure 5.17   In their patents, Adamson and Lewis also discuss the use of thermochromic materials for voxel generation. Here, radiation from source (160) is dynamically focused into an image space (162) and causes a voxel to be formed at point (151). A water jacket (153) with inlet and outlet (155 and 157) prevents overall rises in temperature. (Reproduced from US Patent Number 3,609,707.)

The researchers do not appear to discuss material fatigue and, of course, the formation of a gel would increase the difficulty of refreshing the material.

The patents cited above also provide discussion on the use of thermochromic materials for the implementation of the voxel generation subsystem. The form of the experimental apparatus discussed in relation to this approach is illustrated in Figure 5.17, and the researchers claim to have obtained good results using 1,3-di-4-piperidyl propane. In this context they write:

> *In one specific display system, this preferred thermochromic material is mixed 20 percent by weight with water. To the solution is added 1 percent by weight of polyacrylamide for gelling. If this gelled solution is allowed to sit for one week, it has been observed that the threshold temperature is approximately 25°C and the transition between the two optical states is approximately 0.2°C.*

TABLE 5.4 Some of the General Characteristics that Should Be Considered in the Selection of Photochromic and Thermochromic Materials for Use in the Voxel Generation Subsystem[a]

Photochromic Material	Thermochromic Material
Two readily apparent nonemissive optical states (A and B).	Two clearly apparent nonemissive optical states (A and B).
One optical state (A) is transparent.	One optical state (A) is transparent.
One optical state (B) strongly absorbs certain wavelengths and so exhibits an appropriate color.	One optical state (B) strongly absorbs certain wavelengths and so exhibits an appropriate color.
State transitions may be rapidly induced by means of nonvisible beams of appropriate wavelengths.	State transitions may be rapidly induced by changes in temperature.
Transition from state A to state B may be achieved through the application of radiation of wavelength λ_1.	Transition temperatures should be sharp and well-defined.
Transition from state B to state A may be achieved through the application of radiation of wavelength λ_2 (where $\lambda_1 \neq \lambda_2$).	The change in optical state should exhibit appropriate hysteresis (i.e., the threshold for the change from state A to state B should appropriately differ from that of the converse state change). This impacts on the refresh rate.
Material fatigue should not interfere with display operation.	Transition temperatures should not be excessive and state A should be supported at room temperature.

[a]This table summarizes discussion in a previous work Blundell and Schwarz, 2000.

For convenience, in Table 5.4 a summary is provided of some of the general characteristics that should be considered in the selection of appropriate photochromic or thermochromic materials. This summary is drawn from a previous work Blundell and Schwarz, 2000. Without a doubt, the development of display units able to offer a high voxel activation capacity and that use either photochromic or thermochromic materials for voxel generation is not a trivial undertaking. On the other hand, the benefits that may ultimately ensue from the production of voxels made visible by external illumination should not be underestimated.

5.8 DEAD ZONES

*I was born not knowing
and have had only a little time to change that
here and there.*[36]

In Section 4.7, "dead zones" were introduced in connection with swept-volume displays; in line with a previous work Blundell and Schwarz, 2000, we consider these to be regions in which one or more image space characteristics are compromised to such an extent that image quality falls below an acceptable level. Static-volume displays may also exhibit dead zones; naturally, it is desirable to evaluate their impact prior to display implementation.

Various forms of possible dead zone are summarized below (for more detailed discussion see Blundell and Schwarz [2000] and Schwarz and Blundell [1994a,b]).

1. *Visual Dead Zone:* This form of dead zone was previously introduced in Section 4.7.3 in relation to swept-volume displays and can also occur in static-volume systems—specifically those that employ a nonhomogeneous image space comprising an arrangement of materials and especially when a matrix of elements are employed for voxel generation. In the former case the structure can inhibit the passage of light in certain directions, and in the latter situation the elements may exhibit the type of radiation profile illustrated in Figure 4.25.

2. *Shadowing Dead Zone:* This form of dead zone was previously introduced in Section 4.7.4 and can also exist in static-volume displays whose image space comprises an arrangement of materials and in which one or more directed beams are used for voxel activation. However, the shadowing dead zone is unlikely to occur in displays that employ a homogeneous image space.

3. *Dead Image Space:* This form of dead zone was previously introduced in Section 4.7.4 and may occur in static-volume displays that employ a non-homogeneous image space and also in systems that employ directed beam sources. In this latter case, the beam deflection geometry may prevent the beam sources from reaching portions of an image space (see, for example, Figure 5.20). However, by careful design, dead zones of this type can generally be avoided.

4. *Voxel Placement Dead Zone:* This form of dead zone was previously introduced in Section 4.7.1 and can occur in static-volume display units that employ one or more directed beams for voxel activation. In the case of swept-volume displays, the impact of this type of dead zone is exacerbated when a rotating screen is used in conjunction with one or more directed and stationary beam sources. Because this does not occur in static-volume

---

[36] Attributed to Richard P. Feynman (1918–1988).

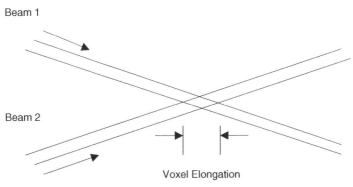

Figure 5.18 A "distortional dead zone" occurring in static-volume displays in which a voxel is formed in the region at which two directed beams intersect.

systems, the voxel placement dead zone can be avoided by ensuring that the digital precision of the deflection apparatus is able to satisfactorily support the necessary minimum inter-voxel spacing throughout the image space.

5. *Distortional (Elongation) Dead Zone:* This form of dead zone was previously introduced in Section 4.7.2 in relation to swept-volume displays and can also occur in static-volume systems in which voxels are activated within the region in which two beams directed intersect (see Figure 5.18). An analysis of the distortional dead zone in static-volume displays employing the beam intersection technique is provided in Blundell and Schwarz [2000], and for our purposes it is sufficient to outline several ways in which we can eliminate this problem:

(a) The dead zone occurs as a consequence of variations in the angles at which the activation beams intersect. Consequently, we can adopt the type of arrangement employed by Korevaar et al. that is discussed in Section 5.6.1. Here, as may be seen from Figure 5.7, the optical arrangement ensures that despite the use of directed beams, the two beams enter the image space such that they always intersect at right angles. Naturally, this prevents the formation of distortional dead zones.

(b) Additional beam sources may be employed, in which case they can be positioned so that the formation of voxels within the image space never requires the intersection of beams whose intersection geometry would give rise to unacceptable voxel elongation. Naturally, this solution requires proper analysis of the beam intersection geometries and care must be taken to ensure that the presence of the sources does not unduly impact on viewing freedom.

(c) Replacement of the directed beams by two 2-D arrays of nondirected beams.

5.9   DISCUSSION

> *To put your life in danger from time to time... breeds a saneness*
> *in dealing with day-to-day trivialities.*[37]

In this chapter we have described various facets of the static-volume technique and several indicative approaches have been introduced. As discussed, the use of a homogeneous image space comprising a solid or liquid leads to boundary refraction and this may impact on the suitability of a display for use in particular applications.[38] Furthermore, the high density of such an image space places restrictions on its maximum practical volume.

The use of materials that support the production of voxels made visible via external lighting provides opportunities for the production of opaque images. As a result, the depth cue of occlusion is supported in a natural manner and many exciting opportunities exist for such displays. In the case of the swept-volume approach, the opportunities for the inclusion of the opacity depth cue are much more limited,[39] although Actuality Systems have devised an approach that builds on the Perspecta display (see Section 8.3.2) and which not only supports image opacity but moreover eradicates the visual dead zone (see footnote 9 in Chapter 12).

In Chapter 9 a range of static-volume display embodiments are introduced. Despite the immense amount of work that has been directed toward the development of such displays, at the time of writing the author is aware of only one commercially available static-volume system: the DepthCube. This display is produced by LightSpace Technologies and is briefly discussed in Section 9.4. It supports the depiction of high-quality images (viewing freedom being limited to a single window onto the digital world).

5.10   INVESTIGATIONS

1. Referring to Figure 5.4. What is the maximum degree of parallelism in voxel activation that this display configuration is able to support?

2. This question relates to discussion in Section 5.4 concerning the incorporation of motion within the voxel generation subsystem. Figure 5.5 depicts the use of two 1-D arrays of nondirected beams. Through the introduction of motion, these are able to exhaustively scan an image space and so permit the display to

---

[37] Nevil Shute (Norway) "Slide Rule," House of Stratus [2000]. A biography, and fascinating account of the development of the R100 and R101 airships. Nevil Shute (1899–1960).

[38] This can lead to image distortion and hamper cursor navigation. Furthermore, in the case that a pointer-based interaction tool is employed, boundary refraction may bend the pointer beam as it enters the image space.

[39] Unless the location of the observer relative to the image space is tracked—in which case standard hidden line removal techniques may be employed (this assumes a single observer).

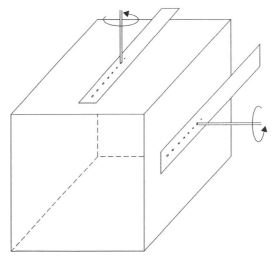

Figure 5.19 Here, we seek to exhaustively scan an image space by means of two 1-D arrays of nondirected beam sources. These two arrays rotate as shown. We assume that the length of each array is equal to the diagonal length of the faces of the cubic image space. (Diagram © P. J. Blundell 2006.)

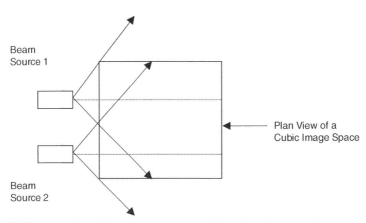

Figure 5.20 Two directed beam sources are used for the activation of voxels in a cubic image space. Here, we assume that voxel activation occurs in the region of beam intersection. The maximum deflection range for each beam is as indicated and in this configuration would give rise to "dead image space." See Question 4 in connection with this diagram.

exhibit a 100% fill factor. In Figure 5.19 a further configuration is illustrated. Here, the arrays move with rotational motion (previously translational motion was employed). Determine whether this approach would allow exhaustive scanning of the image space and, if so, also determine the relative frequencies of motion of the two arrays.

3. Continuing from Question 2, consider that one array rotates while the other moves with translational motion. Would this approach allow exhaustive scanning of the image space? If so, how would the frequencies of motion of the two arrays be related?

4. Consider the "distortional dead zone" (see Section 5.8) that may occur in static-volume displays, in which voxel production occurs in the region in which two directed beams intersect. Assume that the two directed beam sources (each with a beam diameter d) lie normal to one face of a cubic image space (see Figure 5.20), set some criteria to the maximum voxel elongation that you feel may be appropriate (together with any other necessary parameters), and determine the shape of the dead zone within the plane of the beam sources. Extend your analysis to the image space above and below this plane. Also consider the impact of changing the placement of the sources relative to the image space.

5. Obtain copies of the patents cited in Section 5.7 in relation to the Photochromic and Thermochromic approaches (US Patent Numbers 3,609,706 and 3,609,707). These patents are largely the same, although there are some important technical differences. Using these patents as a basis, discuss the implementation of both photochromic- and thermochromic-based displays. Particular attention should be given to the algorithms needed to depict an image data set.

6. Obtain a copy of the patent referred to in Section 5.6.2 (footnote 28) in relation to the two-photon absorption technique (US Patent Number 3,541,542). Discuss the strengths and weaknesses of this approach.

6 Swept-Volume Systems: Limited Viewing Freedom

My lord, eat also, tho' the fair is course,
And only meet for mowers; then set down
His basket, and dismounting on the sward
They let the horses graze, and ate
themselves.

6.1 INTRODUCTION

In this and the next two chapters we discuss the implementation of swept-volume display units. In a previous work [Blundell and Schwarz, 2000], display unit implementations were described within the context of the history of volumetric display system evolution; in the main, systems were introduced in chronological order. In retrospect, it would appear that this was perhaps not the most optimal approach because it may imply that these systems are largely only of historical interest, having little significance to current and future development. This is far from the reality of the situation since many of the techniques used (and reused) in the past may

Enhanced Visualization: Making Space for 3-D Images. By Barry G. Blundell
Copyright © 2007 John Wiley & Sons, Inc.

continue to stand in their own right or be significantly advanced through the incorporation of new technologies and techniques. Furthermore, the extensive number of patents that have been filed in a belief that this is the best way to protect the interests of the inventors and/or owners of volumetric technologies has previously made it difficult to justify continued development of systems by third parties. Many of these patents have now lapsed, and approaches have returned to the public domain. This opens the way for many exciting opportunities.

In this book we prefer to emphasize that numerous volumetric techniques previously proposed retain their relevance, so our discussion is generally structured around the technical aspects of displays rather than their chronological place within an evolutionary process.

The displays discussed in this chapter share a number of characteristics; as indicated in Figure 6.1, these include limited freedom in viewing position (typically, this is restricted to a single 'window' onto the image space). This contrasts with

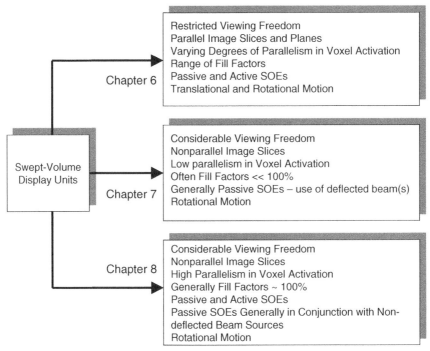

Figure 6.1 A 'road map' to this and the next two chapters. It is convenient to remember that approaches discussed here restrict viewing freedom, generally providing only a single "window" onto the image scene. This is in contrast to the swept-volume systems discussed in the next two chapters that support considerable viewing freedom. In Chapter 7, the display units generally offer a somewhat limited fill factor while for those introduced in Chapter 8 the fill factor is much greater. Although we mainly follow this structuring, occasionally and to maintain continuity, display units are placed according to other criteria. (Diagram © Q. S. Blundell 2006.)

those described in the next two chapters that permit (at least in principle) much greater viewing freedom. In fact, viewing freedom is an important characteristic and strongly impacts on the suitability of a display for use in particular applications. In the case of some applications, viewing freedom restrictions are beneficial, and therefore displays that support only limited viewing freedom should not be considered as inferior.

In the next section, we consider "image slices" and "image planes." The former term will be used when referring to our division of an image space into a series of zones. The voxel data set is preordered, and each voxel is mapped into the most appropriate zone. Thus as the screen passes through a particular zone (image slice), a certain amount of time is available for the activation of all voxels therein. In the case that a display unit exhibits a low degree of parallelism in voxel activation, it is possible that not all voxels can be output in the available time, in which case voxels may be culled (or other techniques may be used such as moving voxels to adjacent image slices, although this may introduce unacceptable placement errors).

In this book we will adopt the term "image plane" when referring to the structured physical positioning of voxels within the image space. Many display units support the positioning of voxels within a series of parallel planes that are stacked together. For example, in the case of a system employing the rotational motion of a planar screen equipped with an active surface of emission (SOE)—comprising a rectangular array of light-emitting devices—a series of parallel image planes are formed, these being stacked *along* the axis of rotation.

In short, image slices relate to the temporal flow of voxel data to the display, and the number and form of these slices may contribute to error in voxel positioning. On the other hand, the formation of image planes influences the homogeneity and isotropy of the image space with respect to voxel positioning, and in the case of systems that support a high degree of parallelism in voxel activation, these planes may impact on image quality, especially in the case of certain static-volume systems.[1]

As indicated above, our discussion of swept-volume implementations is not structured to directly reflect an evolutionary process and we prefer to employ a structure that highlights technical characteristics. There is, however, one exception: the largely unknown account of what would appear to be the first description of a swept-volume volumetric display. This dates back to a British patent that was filed early in 1931 by John Logie Baird. In Section 6.3, we review this patent and a further patent filed in 1942 by the same remarkable individual.

In Section 6.4 we discuss various exemplar display units that permit the formation of a stack of image planes arranged parallel to each other by means of the translational motion of a surface of emission (SOE). In Section 6.5 we describe display embodiments that achieve the same result through the use of rotational motion.

An Appendix to this book provides a tabulated summary of some aspects of the display units introduced in this and the next two chapters. Here we do not

---

[1] Here, for example, a number of voxels may be simultaneously activated and, from a particular viewing position, may lie one behind the other. This can result in the formation of image bright spots.

attempt to provide a critical comparison but rather a brief overview via which the reader can readily appreciate various general characteristics. For each entry in the table, we indicate the section(s) where the display is discussed. To avoid possible confusion when more than a single display unit is referred to in a section, we also assign to each display a reference number.

6.2   IMAGE SLICES AND IMAGE PLANES

> *The best research is not very amenable to organization...*
> *The best researchers are best because of their utter absorption...*[2]

When translational motion is used to generate a series of image slices, each individual slice is of uniform thickness (although thickness may vary between slices) and the slices are stacked in line with the screen's motion. The activation of voxels within each slice occurs during the short period of time that it takes for the screen to sweep through the slice. From the perspective of the graphics pipeline, the voxel data set is appropriately ordered to group voxels according to the slice within which they are to be located in the image space (see Section 11.3). Voxels within each group are output at the appropriate time, either simultaneously or, if this is not possible (due to restrictions in the degree of parallelism supported by the voxel generation and activation subsystems), as quickly as possible. Thus the slices reflect the temporal characteristics of the data flow from the graphics engine to the display unit.

Should rotational movement be used for the creation of the image space, the voxel data set is again ordered to group voxels into the most appropriate slice within the image space. The form of these slices varies according to the shape of the screen. Consider the example display architecture (Ref. 8A) outlined in Section 4.2 (also see Section 8.2). This utilizes the rotational motion of a planar screen equipped with an active surface of emission (taking the form of an rectangular array of light-emitting devices). Here the slices into which voxel data are mapped are not stacked in a parallel manner but rather, are angularly displaced around the axis of rotation (i.e., as a series of identical sectors).[3] As a consequence of the use of a rectangular array of light emitting devices for voxel generation, the visible image comprises a series of image planes stacked parallel to the axis of rotation.[4] Thus we need to distinguish between (a) slices that reflect the ordering and flow of image data to the display unit and (b) those arising from the discrete (quantized) nature of the voxel generation subsystem. For clarity we will refer to the former as image slices and the latter as image planes.

---

[2] Reproduced in Whittle F., *Jet: The Story of a Pioneer*, Frederick Muller, Ltd., 1953. Source of quotation not attributed, p. 302.

[3] In length, such sectors follow the form of the screen. Thus if a helical screen is used in conjunction with a directed beam source, the sectors "wind" through the image space.

[4] The production of parallel image planes in association with rotational motion is not limited to an active SOE—see, for example, Sections 6.5 and 8.3.2.

Each voxel within a data set is specified in terms of its position within 3-D space (x, y, z). The host computer uses these coordinates to map the voxel into the most appropriate image slice. One coordinate value may then be discarded (e.g., z) and the voxel is now represented as (x, y, n)—where n is an integer denoting the sector number. When depicted within the image space, the actual location of the visible voxel is (x, y, q) and $|z - q|$ denotes the error in positioning accuracy (we neglect any resulting inaccuracies in x and y). The maximum extent of this error is limited by the width of the image slice. In the case of systems in which image slices are of uniform width, this maximum error is the same for all voxels within the slice. However, in the case of other approaches (such as those employing image slices that are in the form of sectors), the extent of the error also depends upon either x or y (i.e., the coordinate value denoting the distance of the voxel from the axis of rotation).

For our purposes, we generally assume that image planes are of uniform thickness. Thus any error incurred in mapping a voxel into the appropriate plane is independent of the voxels location within the plane.

As indicated above, voxels are output to each image slice over a short period of time. This is typically equal to T/N, where T denotes the period of motion of the screen and N the total number of image space slices.[5] In the case that image slices and image planes are not physically coincident, voxels are generally output to each image plane over the entire cycle of screen motion (T).

6.3   JOHN LOGIE BAIRD MAKES SPACE FOR THE THIRD DIMENSION

I was definitely able to transmit the living image,
and it was the first time it had been done.
But how to convince the sceptical, hide-bound,
select and exclusive scientific world?
Would they admit that a wretched nonentity
working with soap boxes in a garret had done something
which many of them had stated was not possible?[6]

During extensive literature searches the earliest document the author has located in connection with swept-volume volumetric displays is a patent filed in 1931 by John Logie Baird (see Figure 6.2). The work of this prolific inventor has already

---

[5] Here we assume that the screen permits only a single update per screen rotation and that all image slices are of the same temporal duration.

[6] John Logie Baird quoted in Kamm and Baird [2002].

Figure 6.2   John Logie Baird (1888–1946), who in 1926 publicly demonstrated the first "real" television system. Despite a lifetime of ill health and frequent lack of funding, his spirit and achievements are legendary. He successfully tackled and developed color television (this included a 3-D system permitting the user to view images directly without recourse to viewing glasses). Additionally, he pioneered several volumetric displays (see text for details) and may be considered as the father of display systems able to depict electronic data in three dimensions. This picture was taken in 1931—the same year in which he filed his first patent dealing with volumetric systems. (Picture kindly supplied by, and reproduced by permission of his son, Professor Malcolm Baird.)

been mentioned in Section 1.2 in relation to the development of early television and his ill-fated voyage to Trinidad (see footnote 7 in Chapter 1)! In this section we briefly review the systems he proposed his 1931 publication, along with another swept-volume display that he described in a patent filed in 1942.

6.3.1   Perhaps the First Swept-Volume Displays

In his remarkable 1931 patent (British Patent Number 373,196) Baird describes an image capture system and three associated volumetric displays[7] intended for use in television applications. The capture and the display systems were designed for

[7] This patent does not record the name of the inventor; Baird is named as the applicant.

direct interfacing (harmonious cooperation)—see previous discussion concerning the difficulties faced prior to the advent of flexible electronic systems and computer hardware (Section 1.2.2). In introducing the invention, Baird writes:

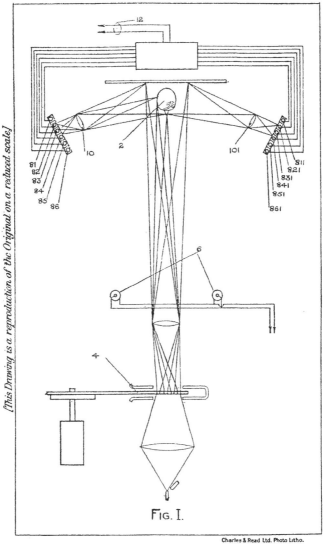

Charles & Read Ltd. Photo Litho.

Figure 6.3   The volumetric data acquisition system described by John Logie Baird in his 1931 patent. Here, a beam of light is repeatedly scanned across the surface of a 3-D object (2). This light is reflected by the object and cast onto photodetectors located in two 1-D arrays (81–86 and 811–861), so enabling the 3-D shape of simple objects to be detected. Photodetectors (6) are also used, these measuring object luminance. (Reproduced from UK patent 373,196.)

> *The present invention ... has for its objective the reproduction of images of scenes or objects in stereoscopic relief, whereby instead of the usual flat representation of an object or scene, an observer at the receiving end of the system sees a representation of the same in three dimensions, giving an impression of the solidity or depth of the object or scene transmitted.*

Two of the volumetric displays described in the patent are swept-volume embodiments (one using translational motion, the other using rotational motion). The third is a static-volume display. We begin by briefly introducing the data capture system and subsequently outline the architecture of the displays.

1. *Data Capture:* The scheme proposed by Baird is illustrated in Figure 6.3. Here, light emanating from a strong source (located at the bottom of the diagram) is passed through a mechanical scanning system (most probably in the form of a Nipkow disc) and subsequently cast onto the 3-D object (2) whose image is to be captured. The relief of the object is acquired by means of two sets of photodetectors (81–86 and 811–861). The incidence of light onto a particular detector is governed by (a) the instantaneous position at which the scanning beam impinges on the object and (b) the object's geometry at that location. Each detector is able to drive a relay that causes a particular level of current to flow. Consequently, the instantaneous level of the signal in the output channel (12) has a value indicating the physical location of the detector within the set of detectors upon which light has fallen. In this respect, Baird writes:

   > *The relays are arranged so that the relay associated with the cell 81 and 811 causes less current to flow than that controlled by the relay associated with the cell 82 and 821, which in turn causes less current to flow than that caused by the relay associated with the cell 83 and 831 and so on.*

   Baird refers to this signal as the "displacement current". Two additional photodetectors (6) are used to detect the intensity of the light reflected by the object as the scan proceeds (one detecting light reflected from the left-hand side of the object and the other from the right). These are shown as being connected in series; this is understandable because the scanning system provides a "flying spot" that moves over the object and cannot illuminate regions on both sides of the image simultaneously. The signal generated by these two detectors is referred to by Baird as the "density current". Thus the system derives (a) the position in space of points on the object by means of the instantaneous position of the Nipkow disc and (b) the position of the photodetector in the two detector arrays upon which the reflected light falls.[8] Additionally, the luminance is measured.

---

[8] Reflected light is cast onto the detector arrays via cylindrical lenses (10 and 101). The adoption of this form of lens would have enabled the use of 1-D arrays of detectors. However, at (or toward) the top and bottom of the object the detector arrays would not have supported data capture.

Unfortunately, much useful information is not included with the patent such as, for example, the scan speed. In fact, in connection with the scanning system, Baird simply writes:

> ... *a spot of intense light is caused to systematically traverse the object 2 by means of the scanning device 4, which may be any of those well-known in the art.*

And in relation to the luminance measuring system he goes on to say:

> ... *and part of the light diffused from the object is received on the photoelectric cells 6, so that these cells generate electric currents that are dependent on the value of the light tones of the object.*

However, despite this lack of detail the description provided within the patent gives the strong impression that its author was writing with the confidence that can only come from practical experience of the technique.[9]

2. *A Swept-Volume Display Employing Rotational Motion (Ref. 6A):* The volumetric display that forms the major thrust of Baird's 1931 patent is illustrated in Figure 6.4. This employs a rotating disc (14) equipped with a number of discharge lights (16). As may be seen from the illustration, these are arranged in a spiral, following the layout of the holes in the Nipkow disc used in the data capture system.[10] The observer's view of the image is limited to a region (32) in which the discharge lamps create an approximately rectangular scan.

The lamps stand out at right angles from the discs' surface and are somewhat unusual in their design. Baird describes them as follows:

> *Each glow lamp has a single wire electrode running down its axis and a series of small electrodes arranged about the electrode, at different distances from the disc. The small electrodes may be outside the glass envelope of the lamp, but in this case high frequency excitation of the glow discharge is necessary. The number of small electrodes corresponds to the number of planes into which the depth of the image is divided.*

Thus in the configuration illustrated in Figure 6.4a a discharge could be generated at four different points along the length of each lamp so enabling the creation of four depth planes. Baird also indicates that this arrangement may be simplified:

> *Instead of the neon tube, the electrodes may themselves revolve in an atmosphere of nitrogen.*

This would therefore have alleviated the need for individual sealed lamps and would have simplified construction and enhanced image visibility. In Figure 6.4a a commutator system is illustrated, this being responsible for

---

[9] Naturally, such a system could only be expected to provide low-resolution depth information in connection with certain shapes of object. Furthermore, the detector arrangement would have precluded data acquisition at (or towards) the top and bottom of the object.

[10] This is not indicated in the patent.

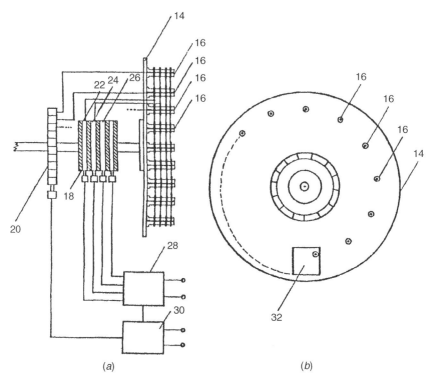

(a)   (b)

Figure 6.4   Probably the first swept-volume display was described in John Logie Baird's 1931 patent. Diagram (a) shows the side view, and (b) the front view of the display apparatus. This employs a rotating disc (14) equipped with a number of discharge lamps (16) arranged as shown. Volumetric images are depicted in a small volume [e.g., region (32) over which the scan produced by the lamps is approximately rectangular]. Each lamp is cylindrical in form and stands out from the disc. Within each lamp a visible discharge can be created at different positions along its length. Thus for example, in the arrangement shown in (a) a discharge could be produced at four different positions along the length of each lamp and so provide an image space with four depth planes. The number of depth planes employed by Baird corresponded to the number of photoreceptors used to generate the displacement current in each of the 1-D arrays within the image capture system. (Reproduced from UK Patent Number 373,196.)

the passage of the density and displacement currents to the revolving neon lamps, and Baird describes in some detail the form of the simple hardware circuits responsible for interfacing between the image capture and display systems.

The display described by Baird exhibits a low sweep efficiency as the actual image space represents only a small portion of the total volume swept out. However, it is important to note that this arose as a consequence of the image capture hardware—had a modern graphics engine been available, a 100% sweep efficiency could have been achieved.

3. *A Swept-Volume Display Employing Translational Motion (Ref. 6B):* Baird briefly outlines an alternative display unit in his 1931 patent. Rather than employing lamps able to create different depth planes, Baird suggests the projection of the image data onto a screen moving with translational motion:

> *The screen may consist of a thin sheet of paper, gelatine or other rigid light diffusing member adapted to move so that the screen is displaced in a direction substantially perpendicular to its plane. Associated with a part of the member on which the screen is mounted ... there may be a ferro-magnetic body ... cooperating with an electromagnet... through the magnetising winding of which is passed a current proportional to, or controlled by, the displacement signals. In this way a displacement of the screen proportional to the displacement signal is produced.*

Baird does not provide important practical details in connection with this approach and it is likely that in order to prevent screen distortion (arising from its motion), it would have been necessary for it to be housed within an evacuated vessel.

4. *A Static-Volume Approach:* Although this chapter concerns swept-volume systems, it is perhaps appropriate to include mention in this section of a static-volume system also referred to by Baird within his 1931 patent. In this embodiment, Baird describes the construction of a lens whose focal length could be varied, and that was used to project image data to different depths within an image space comprising particles able to scatter incident light. In connection with the lens, Baird writes:

> *We may, for example, construct a lens (which may be that which co-operates with the reconstituting device to form the image) of two spherical glass shells, the space between which is filled with say carbon disulphide or nitrobenzene. The displacement signals may be utilised to vary the strength of an electrostatic field in which this lens is situated, thus varying the focal length of the lens. The plane in which any particular portion of the image is reconstituted, will of course, depend upon the position of the conjugate focal plane of the lens, and since this varies in accordance with the incoming displacement signals, an image is seen by the observer as a three dimensional representation within the envelope containing the diffusive medium or suspension.*

The image space into which the lens projects the image data is described as follows:

> *... the screen may consist of an enclosure, the walls of which are pervious to light rays, filled with light diffusing particles held in suspension (for example, air and smoke, or a colloidal sulphur suspension in water or dilute hydrochloric acid, or a fluorescent liquid such as fluorescence or chlorophyll).*[11]

How well such an arrangement could have been made to operate is unclear to the author. However, from the patent one gains the impression that although

---

[11] Here, Baird cites one of his previous patents (UK Patent Number 294,671).

this account appears to have been written in haste, the inventor has practical experience with the implementation.[12] No comments are made on issues such as the impact of the scattering particles on the light propagating out of the image space.

6.3.2   Baird Advances Volumetric Image Depiction (Ref. 6D)

> *Having known real poverty . . . he held avarice in horror.*
> *Once, when we were walking down Fleet Street to the Strand,*
> *he fumbled in his pocket, took out a handful of small change —*
> *and threw it down the drain! . . .*
> *He chuckled, coloured a little and then offered a halting explanation:*
> *"I haven't done that for a long time, Sidney," he said;*
> *"It's just to get some of the Scots 'meanness' out of my system."*[13]

In a patent filed early in 1942 (UK Patent Number 557,837), John Logie Baird describes a further volumetric display unit. This approach is illustrated in Figure 6.5. As may be seen from the diagram, the image space comprises a number of co-rotating discs (16–18) onto areas of which image data is projected via a CRT. A viewing window onto an image space is defined [this is indicated as (23) in the diagram]. Baird writes:

> *Upon sections of these discs are fixed opaque or translucent screens which come into the field of viewing sequence as the discs revolve and receive the projected images, each screen being at a different distance from the observer. Images are projected on the respective screens in sequence.*

These translucent regions are labeled (19–21) in the illustration, and the use of the three discs as indicated in the diagram provides three depth planes. The image space comprises only a small portion of the volume swept out by the discs, and therefore the display would have exhibited low sweep efficiency. In fact, this is an inherent characteristic of the display technique and contrasts with his earlier system (see (2) in the previous subsection) where the sweep efficiency is limited by the image capture hardware to which the display was connected. In his patent, Baird provides some exemplar dimensions: The discs being 20-inch diameter, a 3-inch image space depth, and a square viewing window with sides of 4 inches.[14] This would have provided a sweep efficiency of ~5%. In terms of the rotational frequency, Baird simply indicates (in connection with an a simple approach employing two discs) that *"The discs revolve rapidly so that due to persistence of vision both images are*

---

[12] For example, Baird discusses the organization of the illumination system in which an arrangement of gas discharge lamps were employed—these being operated outside their specified temperature rating.

[13] From the excellent book on Baird by Sydney Moseley [1952].

[14] Naturally, increasing the number of depth planes would erode the dimensions of the viewing window.

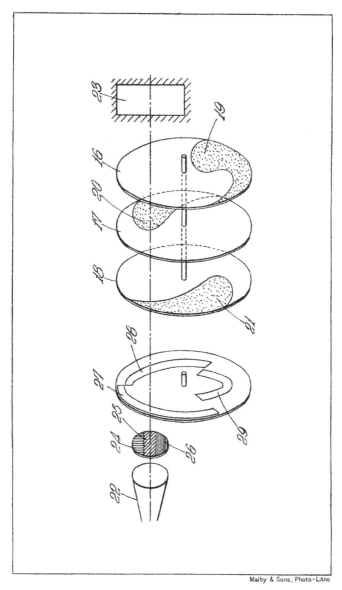

Malby & Sons, Photo-Litho

Figure 6.5   The swept-volume display described by John Logie Baird in his 1942 patent. This employs a series of co-rotating screens and image projection apparatus. Most of the area of each disk is transparent but each has a translucent region. These are arranged so that as one translucent region rotates out of the rectangular viewing window, another moves into it. Image slices are cast in succession onto the translucent regions as they lie below the viewing window. (Reproduced from UK Patent Number 557,837.)

seen simultaneously." With respect to the arrangement used to focus the image data onto the rotating discs, Baird writes:

> *Arranged between the projector and the discs is a lens comprising a plurality of sections each focussed so as respectively to produced a sharp image on one of the discs of a picture on the screen of the projector 22.*

He goes on to say:

> *Arranged between the lens and the discs is a shutter in the form of an opaque disc provided with transparent slots 27, 28 and 29 arranged so that as the shutter is rotated in predetermined synchronism with the discs 17, 18 and 19,[15] the slot 27 exposes the section 24 to the translucent section 19 of the disc 16, the slot 28 exposes the section 25 to the translucent section 20 of the disc 17 and the slot 29 exposes the section 26 to the translucent section 21 of the disc 18.*

The performance of such an arrangement is doubtful and certainly suggests that for each disc only data depicted in a certain region of the display could be cast onto the appropriate disc. However, proffering a simpler and perhaps more practical solution, Baird adds:

> *The division of the projection lens into differently focussed sections is not essential; a single lens having a sufficient depth of focus to produce satisfactory images on each of the screens may be used, the slotted shutter being then omitted.[16]*

The little-known work undertaken by Baird in connection with volumetric displays is paralleled by his research in the early 1940s into the development of a color television system able to support the binocular parallax depth cue (without the need for the viewer to don special viewing glasses).[17] There can be little (if any) doubt that at least two of the volumetric displays described in Baird's 1931 and 1942 patents could have operated successfully, and it is probable that these represent the earliest swept-volume embodiments.[18]

---

[15] These numbers are indicated in the patent but should actually read "16, 17 and 18".

[16] It is surprising that Baird did not refer to the lens with variable focal length that was described in his 1931 patent (see 4 in the previous subsection). This may suggest that the approach was not successful—or perhaps the omission was simply an oversight.

[17] See UK Patent Number 552,582, Wireless World [1942], and also Blundell and Schwarz [2006] (which briefly overviews this interesting approach).

[18] The work of Baird during the 1920s and 1930s in relation to television placed him at the forefront of the field of electronic/electromechanical "flat screen" image depiction. His additional work on color, stereoscopic, and volumetric systems was well ahead of others and on December 13, 1941 the Director of Scientific Research at the Ministry of Supply (Herbert J. Gough) visited Baird's laboratory for a demonstration of the stereoscopic image capture and display system [Kamm and Baird, 2002]. Subsequently, Baird received a letter from the Ministry of Supply: "*Since visiting your laboratory with Major Church on December 13th I have gone most carefully into the question of finding a Service application for the stereoscopic technique you are developing, but I have come to the conclusion that there is nothing that could warrant official support for the continuation of the work, even to the extent of helping you retain the services of technical staff liable for national service. I thank you for an interesting demonstration of your method of stereoscopic presentation which I hope may find its proper piece-time application*" (quoted in Kamm

6.4   PARALLEL IMAGE PLANES USING TRANSLATIONAL MOTION

In Chapter 4, we discussed the creation of an image space by means of either translational or rotational motion. However, although this enables us to broadly distinguish between display embodiments according to the two forms of movement that may be used to create an image space, it does not always reflect upon the geometrical form and distribution of the image slices (see Section 6.2) that comprise the final image. For example, recall from Section 4.3.1 an example embodiment in which an image space is created by means of the rotation of a wheel around the periphery of which a number of small screens are fixed, each being offset from its neighbors (see Figure 4.9). Here, despite the use of rotational motion, the image space is able to support the production of a series of parallel image slices that are stacked perpendicular to the direction of rotation. In this case, the image slices and image planes coincide. This not only facilitates the processing of the image data prior to its depiction but also impacts on the visual characteristics of the image space and on its isotropy and homogeneity.

Consequently, as summarized in Figure 6.6, the use of translational motion will give rise to parallel image slices (and here we note that this does not guarantee that these slices are of the same extent or that they are able to contribute equally

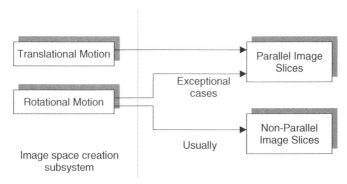

Figure 6.6   Translational motion gives rise to a series of parallel image slices. However, although rotational motion will usually produce image slices that are nonparallel, this is not always the case and it is possible to produce parallel slices. (Diagram © A.R. Blundell 2006.)

and Baird [2002]). However, a significant research activity into the development of 3-D display systems was conducted by the Royal Signals and Radar Establishment and aspects of this work are described in the publication by Parker and Wallis [1948] (see also Section 1.2). Baird was a leading expert (perhaps *the* leading expert) in the field of conventional flat screen displays, and 3-D systems and would have been ideally placed to make a significant contribution to this activity. It is bizarre that he was excluded from such vital wartime work. Kamm and Baird discuss this history but do not allude to Baird's pioneering work with volumetric systems which had direct application to the depiction of radar data. British Patent Number 292,185 filed by Baird in 1926 further demonstrates Baird's ideal suitability for this kind of work.

to the voxel activation capacity). In this case a series of image planes are formed that are stacked in the direction of screen motion. In the case that an active SOE is employed, an image plane(s) may also be formed (stacked at right angles to the direction of screen motion). The use of rotational motion is likely to give rise to nonparallel image slices, but in a small number of cases the image slices may be stacked in a parallel manner. Rotational motion may also give rise to image planes, usually stacked along the axis of rotation. Although these image planes are normally associated with an active surface of emission, they can (in a small number of cases) be created by systems employing a passive SOE. In this section we discuss several display embodiments that employ translational motion for the production of an image space comprising a series of parallel image slices. In Section 6.5, we review some of the techniques that employ the rotational motion of both active and passive SOE's for the creation of parallel image planes.

The earliest work the author has located in literature in connection with a volumetric display employing translational motion dates back to the patent filed by John Logie Baird in 1931 (see Section 6.3.1). Some years later, the Sperry Corporation filed a patent application in relation to various volumetric display embodiments (this was filed in 1943 with the complete specification being published in 1951, see UK Patent Number 652,649). At approximately the same time, similar work was being undertaken by the British Admiralty (see UK Patent Number 592,367). We begin by briefly reviewing aspect of these activities and subsequently summarize various other indicative approaches.

6.4.1 A Reciprocating CRT (Ref. 6E)

This approach is described in the patent referred to above which was filed by The Sperry Corporation (UK Patent Number 652,649). The apparatus is depicted in Figure 6.7.

As may be seen from this illustration, a series of image slices are stored on projection film, these being converted into electronic form before being passed to the oscillating CRT (which is reported as having a frequency of motion in excess of 15 Hz). Despite the simplicity of this volumetric technique and the formation of parallel image slices, the motion of the CRT may well have been problematic, particularly in terms of the vibration of the components comprising the electron gun (this would probably have resulted in image blurring). This is perhaps confirmed by the inclusion of two other embodiments within the patent, neither of which necessitated the motion of the CRT.[19] These are illustrated in Figure 6.8 and are briefly reviewed in the next two subsections.

---

[19] It should be remembered that at the time, CRTs were being developed for use in very harsh environments such as aircraft; consequently, electron guns developed during that period were remarkably rugged. Consequently, the mass of the CRT may have been the most serious drawback to the approach.

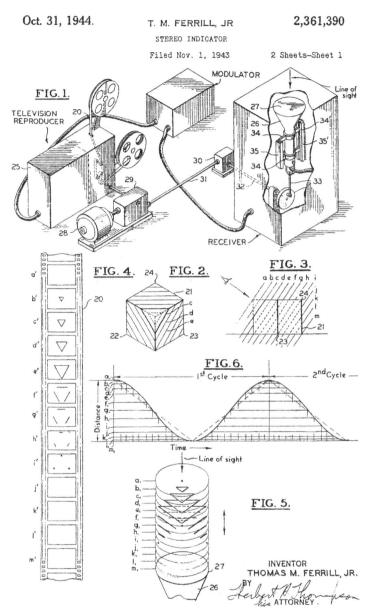

Figure 6.7   An early approach to the implementation of a volumetric display able to produce parallel image slices. The cathode ray tube (26) oscillates vertically with a sinusoidal velocity profile (as shown in Fig. 6). Images stored on projection film (see Fig. 1 and Fig. 4) are output to the CRT as it moves—as indicated in Fig. 5. (Reproduced from US Patent Number 2,361,390.)

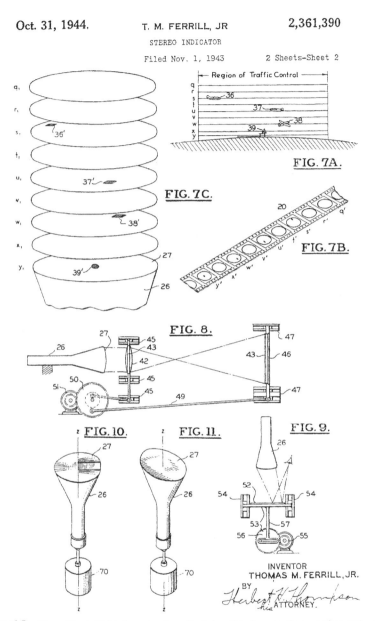

Oct. 31, 1944.   T. M. FERRILL, JR   2,361,390

STEREO INDICATOR

Filed Nov. 1, 1943   2 Sheets–Sheet 2

FIG. 7A.

FIG. 7C.

FIG. 7B.

FIG. 8.

FIG. 10.   FIG. 11.   FIG. 9.

INVENTOR
THOMAS M. FERRILL, JR.
BY
Herbert V. Thompson
his ATTORNEY.

Figure 6.8 Two other embodiments described by the Sperry Corporation (Fig. 8 and Fig. 9). In both cases the CRT is static. Fig. 8 shows a cam driving a lens and screen, and therefore image slices depicted on the CRT may be focused onto the screen as it moves back and forth. Fig. 9 depicts the use of an oscillating plane mirror via which images slices displayed on the CRT are reflected. (Reproduced from US Patent Number 2,361,390.)

6.4.2 Image Slices Focused onto a Moving Screen (Ref. 6F)

Consider the implementation denoted as "Fig. 8" in Figure 6.8 and which uses a bi-convex lens to project the image slices depicted by the CRT onto a screen. As with the previous embodiment, this architecture is described in the patent produced by The Sperry Corporation (UK Patent Number 652,649). Here both the lens and screen undergo translational motion and the amplitude of the screen's movement determines the extent of the image space. Thus each consecutive image slice is brought to focus on the screen and at a certain depth within the image space. Interestingly, for such an approach to operate correctly, the lens and screen must move in opposite directions and have different amplitudes of motion. Let u denote the distance between the CRT and the lens, and v the distance between lens and screen. Then for a lens of focal length f, it is apparent from basic optics that:

$$\frac{1}{u} + \frac{1}{v} = \frac{1}{f}$$

and so,

$$v = \frac{f}{1 - \dfrac{f}{u}}.$$

Several values of v are provided in Table 6.1 for an indicative focal length of 5 cm. Clearly the need to rapidly effect both screen and lens motion coupled with their different amplitudes of movement complicates the mechanical drive.

TABLE 6.1 Here We Assume a Focal Length of 5 cm[a]

CRT-to-Lens Distance (u)	Lens-to-Screen Distance (v)
10 cm	10 cm
15 cm	7.5 cm
20 cm	6.7 cm
25 cm	6.25 cm

[a]In order to maintain focus of the image, the distance between the lens and screen does not remain constant. For example, doubling the CRT-to-lens distance from 10 to 20 cm results in the lens-to-screen distance being reduced by 33%.

6.4.3 Image Slices Reflected by a Mirror: A Sinusoidal Velocity Profile

> *This fellow's wise enough to play the fool,*
> *And to do that well craves a kind of wit.*[20]

Consider the embodiment labeled "Fig 9" in Figure 6.8. In this case, the CRT is stationary and the image slices formed on its screen are reflected in a mirror

---

[20] William Shakespeare, from *Twelfth Night*.

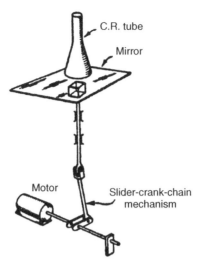

Figure 6.9 An approach employed by Parker and Wallis [1948]. Naturally, due to the presence of the image projection CRT, the observer is forced to view an image from an off-axis location. The use of a mirror enables the creation of an image space whose perceived depth is twice the volume actually swept out. (Reproduced by permission from Parker and Wallis [1948], © 1948 IEE.)

undergoing translational motion (Ref. 6G). An equivalent arrangement is described by Parker and Wallis [1948] in connection with their work at the British Admiralty and is illustrated in Figure 6.9 (Ref. 6H). The patent filed by the Sperry Corporation (UK Patent Number 652,649) reports an amplitude of motion of 1 inch, and Parker and Wallis indicate an amplitude of 1.5 inches.[21] Interestingly, using a mirror in this way increases the perceived depth of the image space; thus, for example, an amplitude of mirror motion of 1.5 inches results in a perceived image space depth of 3 inches. This is illustrated in Figure 6.10 and enables an image space to be created whose perceived depth exceeds the physical volume that is swept out by the moving surface (i.e., a sweep efficiency in excess of 100%).

The use of translational motion can cause mechanical difficulties, and this is confirmed by the author's own experience in this area. However, the systems constructed by the author have employed drive mechanisms built by intuition rather than on the basis of sound mechanical engineering knowledge through which more optimal solutions may be derived. During a presentation of the paper referred to above, before the North-Western Radio Group various discussion questions were put to Parker and Wallis [1949]. These included:

> *Mr. L. N. Vaughan-Jones: I should like to ask whether there are not severe mechanical difficulties attached to the reciprocating-mirror system, since a mirror of at least 6 in*

---

[21] They report the use of a 20-Hz frequency of motion and the projection onto the mirror of a 3-inch-square raster.

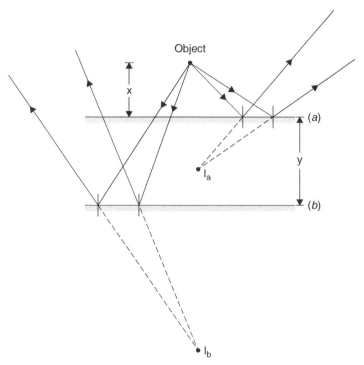

Figure 6.10   When an image space is created by the translational motion of a mirror via which image slices are reflected, the perceived image space depth is twice the physical volume that is swept out. Here, the mirror is shown at the two extremes of its motion (denoted a and b). An object is placed x cm in front of the mirror (when at location a), and the mirror has an amplitude of motion of y cm. Thus when at position a, an image is produced that appears to emanate from point I_a—this being x cm behind the mirror. When at position b, the image appears to be located at position I_b—this being $x + y$ cm behind the mirror. However the mirror is now y cm further away from the observer. Thus the image appears to have changed in position by a distance $2y$. (Diagram © Q. S. Blundell 2006.)

square is required to move at speeds of the order of 20 c/s. It would be expected, at least, to give rise to a great deal of noise. Is this system therefore a practical one, or is it described to indicate a possible approach to the problem?

In response, Parker and Wallis indicated the following:

Mr Vaughan-Jones's doubts about the moving-mirror display are unduly pessimistic, incidentally, as our demonstration equipment includes a 14 in square mirror driven at 20 c/s with little noise or difficulty.

There is no indication as to whether the motion of the mirror was facilitated by placing it within an evacuated vessel and the author has been unable to trace any photographs of the display apparatus. Some further details on this approach may be

(a)

(b)

Figure 6.11   In (a) the first experimental version of the Peritron is illustrated. This comprises an electron gun, motor, crank linkage connecting to the phosphor coated screen (this lies on the right of the photograph), and position sensing solenoid pickup (providing the instantaneous screen position). This assembly is fitted within a vacuum vessel and the screen (and hence the image space) could be observed through a Pyrex window. Figure (b) shows the first experimental implementation of the Peritron based display. Here, the display is mounted vertically (the vacuum vessel is visible in the center of the photograph and is reported as being approximately 30 inches long and 6 inches in diameter). (Reproduced from Withey [1958] (c) 1958 Penton Publishing.)

found in a patent filed by Parker and Wright in 1945 (UK Patent Number 592,367) (see Figure 6.1).

6.4.4   The Peritron (Ref. 6I)

A device referred to as the Peritron appears to have offered a very practical solution to the use of the translational motion of a surface for image space creation [Withey 1958]. This approach is based on CRT technology and mimics the reciprocating CRT technique discussed in Section 6.4.1. The Peritron was mentioned in Section 4.4 (see Figure 4.14) and is further illustrated in Figure 6.11. This approach offers an elegant solution because by placing the screen within a vacuum vessel there is little resistance to its motion. This, in turn, means that the screen and its supporting structure may have a low mass; furthermore, at higher frequencies of motion, acoustic noise would not be problematic.

6.4.5 Image Slices Reflected using a Linearly Moving Mirror (Ref. 6J)

In the late 1980s, workers in Japan reported the development of a prototype display unit developed for the depiction of medical images (particularly in the area of noninvasive angiography [Yamanaka et al., 1988]). The general technique is illustrated in Figure 6.12 and as may be seen from this diagram, images slices depicted on a CRT are reflected by a moving mirror that is oriented at an angle of 45° to the CRT screen. It is reported that the mirror measured 8 cm² and maintained a linear velocity profile over a distance of 8 cm. As discussed in Section 4.2, maintaining a uniform velocity makes it possible to allocate the same time duration to each image slice but does necessitate rapid acceleration and deceleration at each end of the screen's travel. The frequency of reciprocation was rather low—some 12 Hz—and so image flicker is likely to have been problematic. The period of acceleration at either end of the mirrors travel is reported as ~5 ms. We can therefore deduce that during the interval for which the acceleration was zero, the screen speed would have been ~2.5 ms^{-1}. The acceleration at either end of the screen's cycle of motion would have been ~500 ms^{-2}. The mirror is reported to have had a mass of 300 g, and so the force acting on the screen during the period of acceleration (neglecting air resistance) would be on the order of 150 N—which is by no means insignificant.

6.4.6 Image Slices Created Using an Active Surface of Emission (Ref. 6K)

The display units described in the previous subsections employ a passive surface of emission and voxels are activated sequentially [i.e., the parallelism (P) referred to

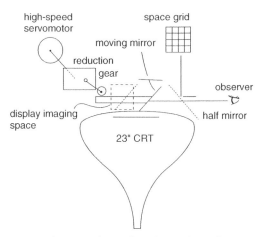

Figure 6.12 A display unit employing a linearly moving mirror to reflect image slices depicted on the CRT screen. The amplitude of mirror movement is reported as being 8 cm with a motion frequency of approximately 12 Hz. (Reproduced with permission from Yamanaka et al. [1988], © 1988 IEEE).

in Eq. (4.9) is unity]. As a result, these systems exhibit a low fill factor. However, an embodiment described by Kameyama et al. [1993] (Ref. 6K) employed an active surface of emission measuring 94 by 30 mm and comprising an array of 48×16 high-brightness light-emitting diodes.[22] The depth of the image space is reported to have measured 50 mm. It enabled the production of 50 image slices and exhibited a refresh rate of 30 Hz.[23]

In a patent filed in 1995, Gregory Brotz also describes the use of an active surface of emission moving with translational motion [see US Patent Number 5,663,740 (Ref. 6L)]. This approach employed the use of a self-reversing screw for the production of constant velocity motion across a large portion of the screen's cycle of movement [as indicated in Figure 6.13, the screw follower (78) is connected to the screen (64)]. The inventor also discusses the use of an array of field emission devices for voxel generation.

6.5 PARALLEL IMAGE PLANES USING ROTATIONAL MOTION

> *If a man writes a book,*
> *let him set down only what he knows.*
> *I have guesses enough of my own.*[24]

As indicated in the previous section, the arrangement of voxels within a series of parallel image slices is a characteristic of systems that employ translational motion. This result can also be achieved through the use of rotational movement. For example, in Section 4.3.1, we discussed the use of a series of small screens attached to the periphery of a rotating wheel. Here, as illustrated in Figure 4.9, each screen is offset from its neighbors and as each of these screens pass through a certain location, an image slice is projected onto them. Thus, the image comprises a series of planes each being offset in depth from the one previously created. This approach parallels the much earlier technique pioneered by John Logie Baird (see Section 6.3.2)[25] In the case of both display techniques a low Sweep Efficiency is achieved and a fairly cumbersome apparatus is needed to produce a relatively small image space.

---

[22] The degree of parallelism supported by such an approach depends on the addressing scheme adopted in the implementation of the voxel activation process.

[23] This display system is especially interesting because it was used in conjunction with a Re-imaging/Projection subsystem (see Section 3.2) to form a "free" image space. This was achieved by means of two concave (converging) mirrors. An image space of this type is able to support the "direct" interaction modality.

[24] Johann Wolfgang von Goethe (1749–1832).

[25] The display proposed in Baird's 1931 patent, which employed the rotational motion of a set of discharge lamps (see Section 6.3.1, Ref. 6A), is somewhat different. Here, the screen motion was intended to reduce the total number of lamps needed within the voxel generation subsystem and played no part in the inclusion of the third dimension.

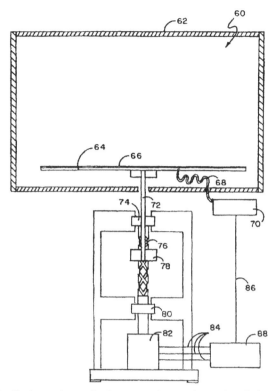

Figure 6.13 A display unit employing an active surface of emission that sweeps out an image space by means of the translational motion of a surface (64). A self-reversing screw is used to achieve constant velocity across a large extent of the screens movement. (Reproduced from US Patent 5,663,740.)

In the following subsections, we introduce other approaches that employ rotational motion for the formation of parallel image planes and use both passive and active SOEs.

6.5.1   Image Planes Formed by Rotors Equipped with an Active SOE (Ref. 6M)

A patent filed by Swapan Chakrabarti in 1995 (see US Patent 5,717,416) describes a volumetric display unit in which the image space is created through the rotation of a series of rotors. As may be seen from Figure 6.14, each of these is angularly displaced from its neighbors and is equipped with a number of light-emitting elements. The rotors turn about a common shaft (a frequency of rotation of 60 Hz is quoted); in doing so, each rotor is responsible for generating a circular image plane. These planes are parallel to each other and are all able to contain the same maximum number of voxels. Naturally, toward the axis of rotation, the presence of the central shaft and the overlap of the rotors will preclude effective voxel formation.

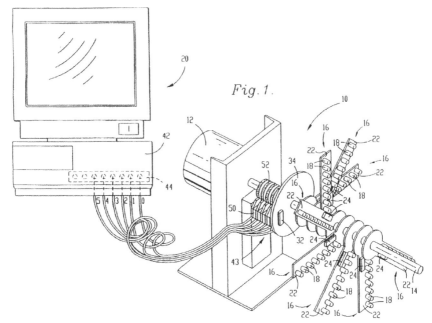

Figure 6.14   A display system outlined by Swapan Chakrabarti who proposes an image space formed by a series of rotors, each being offset from its neighbors. Here, each rotor is equipped with a series of light emitting devices and the apparatus produces a cylindrical image space comprising a series of identical image planes. Signals are passed to the rotors via a commutator constructed using a series of slip rings. The presence of a bulky central shaft will detract from off-axis viewing and give rise to dead image space. (Reproduced from US Patent 5,717,416).

Furthermore, this approach is best suited to viewing from the front (i.e., end-on) because as the image is viewed from more off-axis locations, the presence of the central apparatus is likely to obstruct the passage of light from the far side of the image space.

   In an approach of this kind the number of image planes (coupled with their separation) defines the depth of the image space and, as the number of image planes is increased (by the inclusion of more rotors), the extent of rotor over-lap around the axis of rotation also increases and leads to a greater region of dead image space. Thus this approach is best suited to the production of a small number of image planes and applications in which limited viewing freedom is acceptable.

6.5.2   Image Planes Formed by the Rotation of a Series of Mirrors (Ref. 6N)

This approach is described as an alternative display method in the patent filed by Parker and Wright in 1946 (UK Patent Number 592,367) and was referred to in Section 6.4.3. Figure 6.15 provides an illustration of the apparatus (see the diagram labeled "Fig. 4"). In this embodiment, the rotating component (labeled "Q" in Figure 6.15) turns about shaft "V" and comprises a series of stepped mirrored surfaces onto which the CRT displayed images are projected. Each of these mirrors (or pairs of mirrors) enables an image plane to be created within the cylindrical image space. The inventors comment on the possibility of increasing the number of mirrored "steps" on the rotating component:

> ... there is no limit to the number of steps provided on the surface of the rotor Q and that the resolution of the apparent prism will be increased as the number of steps is increased, it being necessary, however in the extreme case when the number of steps is infinite and the surface of the rotor is therefore smooth to provide a correcting lens to compensate for distortion of the image caused by the fact that the reflecting surface is not parallel to the screen of the cathode ray tube.[26]

In the case of such an approach, the number of image planes formed is equal to the number of levels of mirrored surface fabricated on the rotating screen. When the image space is viewed off-axis, the presence of the steps will create shadows, occluding parts of the image. Increasing the number of steps reduces their height and so the extent of the shadows is also reduced. As we increase the number of image planes, we also place greater demands on the voxel activation subsystem (in this case the CRT). By replacing the CRT with a digital micro-mirror-based projection system, however, we could easily overcome this difficulty.

6.5.3   Image Planes Formed by the Rotation of a Fiber-Optic Bundle

Various interesting and radical approaches are described in a patent filed in 1963 by Rafael Sirkis (US Patent Number 3,300,779). These have features in common with the display unit outlined in the previous subsection and one particular scheme is illustrated in Figure 6.16. As with other patents of the era, the systems were intended for the visualization of aircraft radar data. Two general techniques are summarized below:

1. *A Rotating CRT (Ref. 6O):* In his 1963 patent, Sirkis proposes the use of a rotating CRT (more readily achieved than the translational movement of a CRT; see Section 6.4.1) attached to a co-rotating fiber-optic bundle (labeled 18 in Figure 6.16). This bundle is constructed to form a helical screen, passing the light generated by the CRT directly to the surface of the helix. Thus the volume swept out by the helix forms the image space, and each voxel activated upon it is the result of light passing along a fiber. For such an approach a central drive shaft is unnecessary since the drive mechanism needed to provide the rotational movement can be attached to the periphery of the helical structure. (See Section 6.7: Questions 2 and 3.)

---

[26] Interestingly, the inventors do not specifically propose the use of a helical screen.

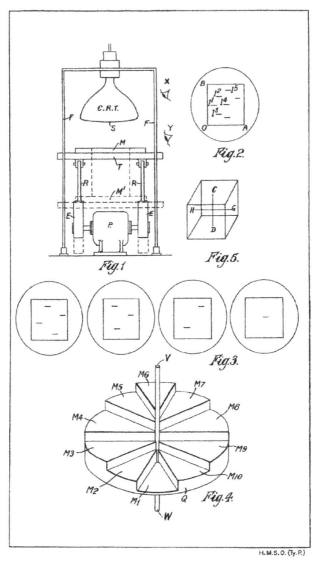

Figure 6.15 The diagram labelled Fig.1 illustrates the use of translational motion for image space creation. Here, image frames depicted on the CRT are reflected by the mirrored surface (N) whose motion is driven by motor (P) via eccentricities (E) and connecting rods (R). The diagram labelled Fig. 4 illustrates an alternative embodiment where a series of mirrored steps are fabricated as indicated. This assembly rotates about a vertical axis (VW) and image slices are projected onto it from a conventional flat screen display. The approach depicted in Fig. 1 employs translational motion for the production of parallel image slices. Using the assembly illustrated in Fig. 4, the same result is obtained (at least in principle) by means of rotational motion. (Reproduced from UK Patent Number 592,367.)

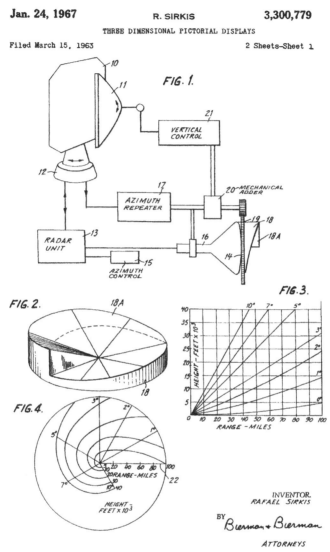

Jan. 24, 1967   R. SIRKIS   3,300,779

THREE DIMENSIONAL PICTORIAL DISPLAYS

Filed March 15, 1963   2 Sheets-Sheet 1

INVENTOR.
RAFAEL SIRKIS

BY Bierman + Bierman

ATTORNEYS

Figure 6.16   A display unit in which a helical screen is employed. This was constructed by means of a fiber optic bundle. Light emitted from a CRT was transmitted to the surface of the helix by these fibers. In the case of such an embodiment, the CRT may be static or may co-rotate with the screen structure. (Reproduced from US Patent Number 3,300,779.)

2. *A Static CRT and Rotating Bundle (Ref. 6P):* The co-rotation of the CRT with the fiber-optic bundle indicated in 1 above, is in fact unnecessary and the same result may be achieved by allowing the CRT to remain static. In this case, the phosphor coating (which constitutes the voxel generation subsystem) cannot be directly deposited onto the inner ends of the optical fibers. However, a standard

short persistence CRT or other form of display may be used, separated by a small distance from the inner surface of the bundle of fibers.[27]

6.5.4   The Archimedes Spiral Approach (Ref. 6Q)

In Section 4.3.1 we briefly discussed a display prototype employing the rotational motion of an Archimedes spiral for the formation of an image space (see Figure 4.11). This was not the first work undertaken in relation to this approach; some years earlier (1967), Roger Lannes De Montebello filed two patents (UK Patent Numbers 1,167,415 and 1,167,416) that describe display embodiments based on this same general technique. These are illustrated in Figures 6.17 and 6.18.

As with the approach referred to in Section 4.3.1, these two systems exhibit a low sweep efficiency and restrict viewing freedom to a single "window". Nonetheless, despite the overall size of the apparatus, the image space that is formed promises to support excellent uniformity. By way of background, the inventor writes (UK Patent Number 1,167,415):

> It is known that, once a series of sections have been obtained from a specimen, for example in biological or anatomical study, researchers often find it difficult when inspecting the sections individually, to visualize in three dimensions the spatial relationship existing among structural details. The researcher in such case is compelled to somehow rearrange the sections in space in their natural order. This may be achieved either in abstract fashion by computation, or concretely by physically or optically "stacking" the sections themselves....
>
> A number of methods have been developed for the physical stacking of enlarged photographs or drawings of the sections, on plastics, glass, or wax sheets, or the like. Such methods are tedious, lengthy (taking from weeks to months) and the results are usually frustrating. The sections are either too few or too numerous; when they are too few, interpolation is difficult and uncertain; when their number is increased, the accumulation of many sections interferes with the direct overall observation, either because of the density of the stack, or because of refraction within the material, which further limits the visibility and distorts the inner structural detail.[28]

6.6   DISCUSSION

> *Have you ever been going somewhere with a crowd*
> *and you're certain it's the wrong road and you tell them,*
> *but they won't listen,*
> *so you just have to plod along in what you know is the wrong direction*
> *till somebody more important gets the same idea?*[29]

In this chapter we have introduced a diverse range of exemplar display units which, in the main, give rise to one or more sets of parallel image slices, each

---

[27] More appropriately, a lens may be used to project the CRT image onto the fiber bundle. Simply leaving a space between the CRT screen and the fiber-optic ends will result in image blurring as light intended for a single fiber may also be able to enter other adjacent fibers.

[28] These latter comments may also be applied to certain static-volume displays in which the refractive index of the image space is significantly greater than the surroundings.

[29] James Hilton, *Random Harvest*, Macmillan & Co. Ltd. (1941).

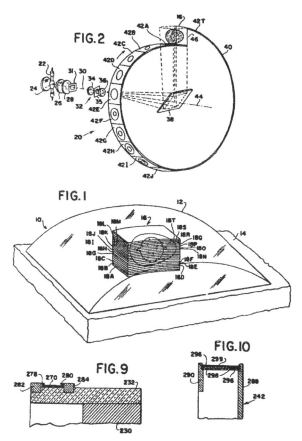

Figure 6.17   The use of a rotating spiral onto which a series of image slices are projected via a stationary mirror (38). Light from source (22) is spatially modulated as it passes through film containing the image sequence to be depicted and is strobed at the appropriate rate. The viewing window is depicted in Fig 2. (Reproduced from UK Patent 1,167,415.)

individual slice being of uniform thickness. The displays discussed here also place restrictions on viewing freedom, generally only providing a single "window" onto the image scene. As previously indicated, such a limitation is not automatically disadvantageous and there are numerous situations in which this is not only satisfactory, but also desirable (from both the perspectives of data visualization and interaction opportunities).

In Section 6.3 we referred to some of the pioneering work undertaken by John Logie Baird. His work in relation to the development of volumetric systems has long since largely faded into history; during the course of extensive literature searches in relation to the volumetric approach, the author has encountered only one publication citing Baird's 1931 patent [and no works that cite his 1942 patent (also relating to volumetric systems)]. This citation appears in a patent filed by Irving Wolff in 1938 (which was not granted until 1958).[30] As a result, many workers in the field have

---

[30] US Patent Number 2,837,735. See Section 7.6 for details of the volumetric display discussed in this comprehensive patent.

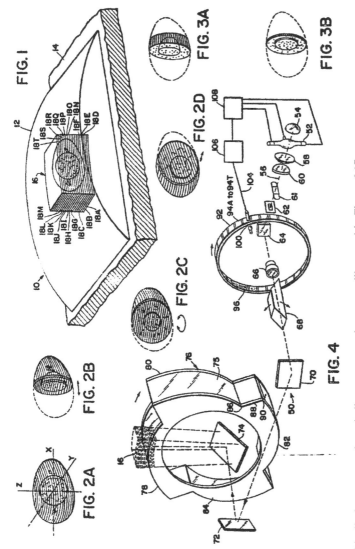

Figure 6.18 This display operates in a similar manner to the system illustrated in Figure 6.17. In the case of this embodiment the image space is refreshed four times for each turn of the rotor. (Reproduced from UK Patent Number 1,167,416.)

218

considered the extensive publication by Parker and Wallis [1948] as representing the origin of discussion in relation to swept-volume systems. Fortunately, it is now possible to correct this omission not only in respect of Baird's work, but also in relation to that of Irving Wolff.

The visit by Herbert J. Gough (Director of Scientific Research at the Ministry of Supply) and Major Church (also at the Ministry of Supply) to Baird's laboratory, and the subsequent decision not to provide official support for the work being undertaken there, may well have considerably impacted on the evolution of 3-D systems. With the passage of time, it is unlikely that we will ever know why such a decision was taken. In relation to this history, Kamm and Baird [2002] write:

> It seems that Baird's concept, which in December 1941 had been stated by the Ministry of Supply to have no military application, had nevertheless been taken on by the Admiralty shortly afterwards. This episode further supports the conclusion that Baird was deliberately excluded from the radar effort during World war II, despite some degree of overlap between his research and the development of radar.

However, their assessment did not include Baird's long forgotten work in the area of volumetric systems. It is interesting to note that Baird's patent in relation to the volumetric display described in Section 6.3.2 was filed on the March 4, 1942, only some 11 weeks after the visit by the Ministry of Supply staff. It is hard to imagine that this display technology would not have been mentioned, perhaps even demonstrated during the visit. We do know that shortly afterwards, volumetric systems (and other approaches including a technique that "... *resembled Baird's anaglyphic system*" [Kamm and Baird, 2002]) were being researched at the Royal Signals and Radar Establishment, for direct military application.

6.7 INVESTIGATIONS

The world is a book,
and those who do not travel
read only one page.[31]

1. Consider the embodiment described in Section 6.5.2 and in which image slices are created by the rotation of a series of stepped mirrors upon which image slices are projected from a conventional flat screen display. Discuss this approach, particularly from the perspective of viewing freedom and the processing and depiction of the image data. In the case that the depth of the image space is increased, how does this impact on viewing freedom?

2. Consider the approach described in Section 6.5.3 (Ref 6O). What is the overall shape of the image space formed by means of the rotating screen? How does this impact on the usefulness of the approach?

---

[31] Attributed to Saint Augustine (354–430).

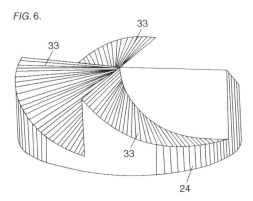

FIG. 6.

Figure 6.19   An alternative form of screen constructed from a fiber optic bundle and employing rotational motion. In principle, this enables an image to be updated four times per rotation of the screen. (Reproduced from US Patent Number 3,300,779.)

3. Consider the screen profile illustrated in Figure 6.19. Any point (x, y, z) on the surface may be specified by

$$x = a \cos\theta, \, y = a \sin\theta, \, z = z_m \frac{\theta}{\pi/2},$$

where a can take any value between zero and the maximum radius of the assembly, z_{max} is the maximum height of the helix, and in the case that four helices are arranged on the surface, θ may take on any value between zero and $\pi/2$. Determine the strengths and weaknesses of this screen shape.

4. Referring to Section 6.5.3 (Ref. 60). What other screen shapes could be employed? What are their relative strengths and weaknesses?

5. In Section 6.3.1, three display units described in John Logie Baird's 1931 patent are outlined. Unfortunately, Baird described only one of these in detail. Consider the static-volume approach and research the feasibility of this method.

6. In this chapter we have described a range of display embodiments in which viewing freedom is restricted. Propose novel ways of interacting with images depicted on such systems. In what way might the degree of parallelism supported by the voxel activation subsystem impact on the implementation of the interaction paradigm?

7. Design a re-imaging/projection system suitable for use with one of the display embodiments outlined in this chapter and that is able to cast a physical image space into "free space". What impact would your optical arrangement have on viewing freedom and on interaction opportunities?

7 Low Parallelism Swept-Volume Systems

7.1 INTRODUCTION

The displays discussed in the previous chapter restrict viewing freedom to a single "window" onto an image space. Distinguishing between volumetric systems according to the viewing freedom they offer is a useful exercise, since the extent of the viewing freedom supported by a display often impacts on its suitability for a particular application. For example, in situations in which a display is to be used by a single operator, limitations in viewing freedom may not only be acceptable, but may even be desirable. Once we limit the viewpoint to a particular "window" onto the image space, we can, for example, be assured that text can be more easily read

Enhanced Visualization: Making Space for 3-D Images. By Barry G. Blundell
Copyright © 2007 John Wiley & Sons, Inc.

and from the operator's perspective, there is no need to physically move around the image space and so the user may be seated before the display. Perhaps even more importantly, the use of a single window onto the image space allows us to manipulate the linear perspective cue and so enhance depth perception.

In other situations it may be desirable for a number of observers to simultaneously look onto the image space from different orientations. In such a scenario, the display becomes a centerpiece with the users looking inward. Placing text within such a display is then made more difficult and although character labels may be slowly rotated (to make them visible to all observers), this limits the speed with which they can be read. Furthermore, the presence of such labels is likely to clutter the image space because, for example, for a significant period of time, each will not be readable from a particular orientation. Supporting all-round viewing freedom also makes it impossible to enhance the perceived depth of the image space through the manipulation of linear perspective. Additionally, when displays support all-round viewing, we have little control of the backdrop against which images are viewed. For example, an observer may view images against the backdrop of the walls of the room where the display is situated. In fact, a second observer located on the opposite side of the image space may provide the backdrop against which images are seen. Changes in the backdrop can impact on the clarity of volumetric images.

Despite difficulties of this nature, there are numerous situations in which all-round viewing freedom is desirable—although it is important to remember that such freedom is not in itself a panacea, and volumetric systems that limit viewing freedom and provide only a single window onto the image space should not be deemed inferior.

Within this chapter, we introduce a number of exemplar volumetric embodiments that support (at least in principle) all-round viewing of the image space. We generally restrict our discussion to approaches that exhibit a low degree of parallelism in the voxel activation subsystem, deferring until the next chapter consideration of systems that permit a large number of voxels to be simultaneously activated. Generally, the display units described in this chapter do not support the exhaustive addressing of the image space (their fill factors are less than 100%), although there are a small number of exceptions, such as the approach outlined in Section 7.2.1. Here, although the display is used in such a way as to support an exhaustive scan, this is not an inherent characteristic of the display unit *per se*, but arises from the implementation of the control hardware.

Although it is possible for systems that employ a passive surface of emission to support varying degrees of parallelism in the voxel activation process, those with an active surface of emission invariably exhibit a high degree of parallelism and a 100% fill factor.[1] Consequently, in this chapter we focus on systems that employ

[1] The Actuality Systems Perspecta display (see Section 8.3.2) provides us with an example of a display that employs a passive SOE but which supports a very high degree of parallelism in the voxel activation process.

a passive surface of emission (in conjunction with directed beam sources) and for which the parallelism in voxel activation is essentially unity.[2]

> *For the purposes of this book, we consider the parallelism in voxel activation to reflect the data flow to the voxel activation mechanism. Thus, for example, consider a display in which image slices depicted on a cathode ray tube (CRT) screen are cast onto some form of moving surface. Here, the flow of data into the voxel activation subsystem (the CRT) is entirely sequential and therefore we consider that such an approach exhibits a parallelism of unity. However, if we were to replace the CRT by a digital micro-mirror based projection system (see Section 8.3.2), then the system could demonstrate a high degree of parallelism.*

In the sections that follow, we group display units according to the form of the screen (planar, helical, and other).

7.2   THE PLANAR SCREEN AND FIXED BEAM SOURCE(S)

The earliest account of a display unit employing the rotational motion of a planar screen (in which the axis of rotation lies in the plane of the screen[3]) that has come to the author's attention is provided in the extensive paper written by Parker and Wallis [1948][4] (Ref. 7A). One of the approaches that they outline is illustrated in Figure 7.1.

Parker and Wallis recognized the problems that occur when the plane of the screen lies at an acute angle to the axis of the projection apparatus. These are discussed in Section 4.7 and for convenience are summarized below:

1. **Voxel Elongation (Distortional Dead Zone):** When, for example, a beam impinges (or is cast) onto a screen, an elongated image is seen. This arises due to the acute angle of incidence.

2. **Voxel Separation (Voxel Placement Dead Zone):** Consider the use of the arrangement illustrated in Figure 7.1, but which uses only a single projection apparatus. If we assume that the beam deflection signals are converted from digital-to-analog form, then the precision of the digital-to-analog converter coupled with the deflection range of the tube and the distance between the tube and rotating screen will determine the minimum attainable separation of

---

[2] Display units discussed in Chapter 8 utilize both passive and active surfaces of emission (SOE's) and are characterized by a high degree of parallelism in voxel activation.

[3] In the case of the earlier systems described by Baird (see Section 6.3), the axis of rotation was normal to the plane of the screen(s).

[4] This paper is also referred to in the previous chapter and in Section 1.2.

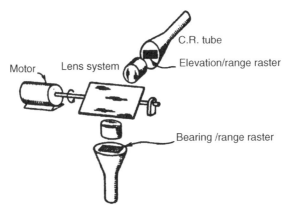

Figure 7.1 This perhaps represents the earliest proposal for a volumetric display unit employing the rotational motion of a planar screen equipped with a passive surface of emission (and in which the axis of rotation lies in the plane of the screen). In this embodiment, CRT images (depicting aircraft radar data) are projected onto a surface able to scatter the incident light and so give rise to a visible image within a cylindrical volume. The CRTs are arranged at right angles to ameliorate various dead zones, (see text for details). (Reproduced by permission from Parker and Wallis [1948], © 1948 IEE.)

two adjacent voxels. This minimum is obtained when the plane of the screen lies at right angles to the axis of projection. As the screen moves away from this position, the minimum adjacent voxel separation will become larger: Distances are magnified by the orientation of the screen relative to the beam projection apparatus.

3. **Dead Image space:** When the plane of the screen is parallel (or closely parallel) to the axis of the projection apparatus, it will be impossible to address the screen.

Thus when the problems indicated above in (1) and/or (2) exceed some threshold, images cannot be satisfactorily cast onto the screen, and it is for this reason that Parker and Wallis introduced a second projection apparatus such that:

- At any time, only one projection apparatus is in use.
- The beam projection apparatus that is in operation at any time is the one with respect to which the screen is most favorably oriented.

In this section we briefly review a number of swept-volume embodiments that employ a planar screen equipped with a passive surface of emission and which use one or more stationary (and directed) beam sources for voxel activation. In contrast, the display units discussed in the next section employ one or more beam sources that co-rotate with the screen, and therefore the geometrical location of the voxel activation beam(s) with respect to each image slice does not vary. Consequently, should the same data set be written to all image slices within the display volume, the spatial arrangement of the voxels and their shape will (in principle) not vary.[5]

7.2.1 The Planar Screen and Stationary Electron Gun(s)

Although simple in terms of its general architecture, the approach described by Parker and Wallis (see Figure 7.1) necessitates the use of a projection apparatus able to maintain image focus across the range of distances existing between each beam source and the screen. The presence of such a projection apparatus increases the overall size of the display and is likely to introduce image distortion. Richard Ketchpel overcame these difficulties by enabling electron beam(s) to directly impinge upon a rotating planar screen equipped with a phosphor coating. The basic system he proposed is described in a patent filed in 1960 (US Patent Number 3,140,415) and is illustrated in Figure 7.2 (Ref. 7B). The display takes the form of a modified CRT that has an approximately spherical envelope, and within this is a rotating screen. The screen is reported as being constructed from a metallic frame supporting a wire mesh onto which the phosphor particles are bonded.

Clearly, the use of a single beam source gives rise to the addressing problems indicated above; in an alternative embodiment, Ketchpel describes the use of two electron guns arranged as shown in Figure 7.3 (Ref. 7C). This is equivalent to the use of the two projection sources described by Parker and Wallis.

The scanning technique used by Ketchpel is of particular relevance to our discussions. Here, he sought to exhaustively scan the image space using a raster scan (with the scan lines parallel to the axis of rotation. Thus in the embodiment illustrated in Figure 7.2, the scan takes the form of a series of vertical lines). In this context he reports the use of:

1. A variable gain amplifier enabling the production of scan lines of variable length, thus approximately fitting the lines to the form of the circular screen. Consequently, the length of lines gradually diminishes with their radial distance from the rotational axis.

2. A variable gain amplifier enabling the distance between the lines of the raster scan to be reduced as the angle between the plane of the screen and the axis of the beam source becomes more acute. This addresses the minimum voxel separation issue (voxel placement dead zone) referred to at the beginning of this section (also see Section 4.7). The use of a variable gain amplifier would therefore allow all image slices to contain approximately the same number of scan lines (although as mentioned above, when the plane of the screen becomes closely parallel to the axis of the beam, it cannot be properly addressed).

---

[5] However, the optical characteristics of the image space and containing vessel may impact on the visible image. Therefore, even though there is no difference between the form and spatial distribution of voxels in each slice, differences may still be perceived by the observer.

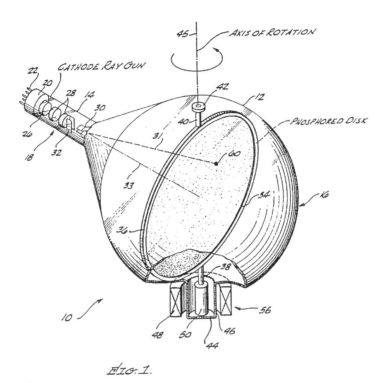

Figure 7.2 A display unit implemented by Richard Ketchpel. In this embodiment, a single electron gun activates voxels on a rotating planar screen. Naturally, addressing the screen becomes increasingly difficult as the angle between the plane of the screen and the axis of the beam source becomes smaller. This gives rise to a dead zone. (Reproduced from US Patent Number 3,140,415.)

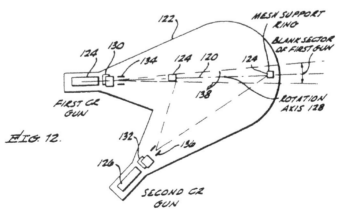

Figure 7.3 In an alternative embodiment Ketchpel describes the use of two electron beam sources to circumvent the problems indicated in Figure 7.2, which occur as a result of the continually varying beam source/screen geometry. Here, each beam source is responsible for voxel generation across one half on the image space volume. (Reproduced from US Patent Number 3,140,415.)

Ketchpel indicates a typical screen rotation frequency of 15 Hz. This would have been quite satisfactory as the symmetrical nature of the screen permits two image refreshes during a single screen rotation. Consequently, despite a 15-Hz rotation, the actual refresh frequency could have been 30 Hz. He reports the use of 128 image slices, each comprising 128 raster lines.[6] The time spent in each sector is therefore ~0.52 ms. In his patent, Ketchpel does not appear to indicate the diameter of the screen used. However, if we assume an indicative radius of 9 cm, then we can readily calculate the approximate total distance moved by the beam as it creates the raster scan within each image slice.[7] Assuming the use of 64 lines per image slice, we obtain a total distance traveled of approximately 9.6 m (per image slice). Thus, in this scenario, the speed at which the beam must move across the surface of the screen[8] is ~18 km · s^{-1}! Let us digress for a moment and consider aspects of the electrostatic deflection process employed in the display reported by Ketchpel and other similar systems [such as the cathode ray sphere (CRS); see, for example, Sections 1.6.1 and 4.6]. Consider an electron (whose charge is denoted by e) that is accelerated by a voltage V_{acc} to a speed v. The energy gained by the electron is eV_{acc} and thus

$$eV_{acc} = \frac{1}{2} mv^2. \tag{7.1}$$

The velocity imparted to an electron (or stream of electrons) may be expressed as

$$v = \sqrt{\frac{2 eV_{acc}}{m}}. \tag{7.2}$$

The force (F) on an electron when it passes through the electric field (E) produced by the two parallel deflection plates[9] illustrated in Figure 7.4 is given by

$$F = ma = eE. \tag{7.3}$$

where the acceleration (a) of the electron is in the direction of the electric field. The electron experiences the force whilst between the two plates—i.e. for a time t. Assuming that they are of length L, then this time is given by $t = L/v$. The acceleration of the electron is[10]

$$a = \frac{2s}{t^2},$$

---

[6] These are distributed across the surface of the screen as a whole—on either side of the axis of rotation.

[7] Here, we need to take into account the different lengths of each of the vertical scan lines. We assume that these form a set of parallel cords across the circular screen. The calculation is facilitated by assuming that $(1 + x)^{1/2} \approx 1 + nx$ and recalling that $1 + 2^2 + 3^2 + \cdots + n^2 = \frac{1}{6}n(n + 1)(2n + 1)$.

[8] This assumes that all lines are drawn at the same speed.

[9] We assume that the electric field is at right angles to the axis of the beam source.

[10] Here we use the standard equation of motion $s = ut + \frac{1}{2}at^2$, and the initial velocity (u) in the direction of the electric field is zero.

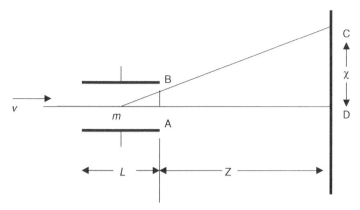

Figure 7.4   An electron beam travelling with a speed v passes between two parallel plates between which a voltage V_{def} exists. The beam experiences a force in the direction of the electric field and is deflected. Note that whilst between the plates, the deflected beam follows a parabolic path. However, when the path of the beam (after it has emerged from between the plates) is traced back, it appears to emanate from a point m that lies centrally within the deflection plates. This point therefore provides a convenient reference for measurements. (Diagram © A. R. Blundell 2006.)

where s denotes the distance traveled in the direction of the field. We now eliminate t and substitute the expression into Eq. (7.3) for a. Thus,

$$s = \frac{eEL^2}{2mv^2}.$$

The deflection (χ) of the electron (or electron beam) at a distance Z from the deflection plates may then be found from the similar triangles indicated in Figure 7.4. And so

$$\chi = \frac{eEL}{mv^2}\left(Z + \frac{L}{2}\right).$$

It is convenient to eliminate mv^2 by means of Eq. (7.1); furthermore, the electric field E may be expressed in terms of the differential voltage applied to the deflection plates (V_{def}) and their separation (d) using the relation $E = V_{def}/d$. Thus,

$$\chi = \frac{V_{def}L}{2V_{acc}d}\left(Z + \frac{L}{2}\right). \tag{7.4}$$

It is instructive to substitute some values into this expression. Let us assume that the deflection plates are 20 mm in length, are separated by 8 mm, and lie some 200 mm from the target (screen). Given a maximum differential deflection voltage of 300 V and an electron beam that has been accelerated using an anode potential of 2000 V, we obtain a value for χ of ~4 cm (leading to a deflection range of ~8 cm).

As may be seen from Eq. (7.4), the basic electrostatic deflection technique is limited in various ways:

1. Reducing the separation of the deflection plates may enhance the deflection sensitivity. However, they must be sufficiently set apart in order that the deflected electron beam does not impinge on them.

2. Increasing the acceleration voltage of the beam to increase image intensity results in a reduction in the deflection sensitivity.

3. Increasing the length of the deflection plates increases deflection sensitivity— but as may be seen from Figure 7.4 (and as with decreasing the plate separation), this restricts the maximum deflection angle that may be achieved. This may also impact on the frequency response of the deflection apparatus.

4. Increasing the distance between the deflection plates and the screen increases the deflection sensitivity but results in a more cumbersome display apparatus.

Consequently, the design of the deflection apparatus is based on a number of compromises, and the basic electrostatic deflection technique is only suitable for use in systems that employ a low electron beam accelerating voltage. Furthermore, unless one is prepared to significantly increase the distance between the deflection apparatus and the screen, the maximum dimensions of the screen (and hence the image space) are somewhat limited. However, these difficulties may be overcome through the use of electron guns equipped with "post-deflection acceleration" (PDA) apparatus. This issue is discussed in Section 12.3, and for the moment it is sufficient to note that guns of this kind enable the electrostatic deflection of a low-energy beam which is *subsequently* accelerated through a high potential. Additionally, they are able to magnify the beam deflection caused by the electrostatic deflection plates. In this way, small deflection voltages are able to operate effectively within a system that gives rise to high-energy beams. This opens up opportunities for the development of high-performance low-cost volumetric systems.

In an article that appeared in 1962 describing Ketchpel's display [Ketchpel, 1962], it is suggested that the use of a 21-inch screen is "*mechanically feasible*"- since the screen rotates within an evacuated vessel, this is certainly the case. Interestingly, in his patent, Ketchpel suggests a way of avoiding the "dead image space" associated with the display unit employing a single electron gun (and which occurs when the plane of the screen is in line with the axis of the beam source (or nearly so)). The approach proposed is illustrated in Figure 7.5 and employs additional pairs of deflection plates that offset the beam to one side enabling it to impinge on the screen, even when the plane of the screen is in line with the axis of the beam source. However, unless the amount of offset is considerable, the angle of incidence between the beam and screen would be highly acute and so the voxel elongation and voxel placement issues referred to previously are likely to limit the usefulness of this technique.

Further useful details of this display paradigm are provided by Ketchpel [1963]. In the mid-1980s, the author commenced research on a display technique that built on the pioneering work conducted by Richard Ketchpel some 20 years earlier.

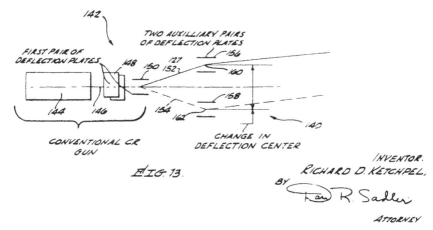

Figure 7.5   A proposal made by Ketchpel for use with the display embodiment illustrated in Figure 7.2. This is intended to overcome the difficulty of addressing the screen when its plane is aligned with the axis of the beam source. Here, additional deflection plates are employed to offset the beam. (Reproduced from US Patent Number 3,140,415.)

This has led to a number of prototype "cathode ray sphere" (CRS) systems (see, for example, Sections 1.6.1 and 4.6—also Section 12.3). For our current purposes it is sufficient to note that unlike the displays researched by Ketchpel employing an exhaustive scanning technique, the CRS prototypes have used a dot graphics approach. This enables the speed of beam deflection to be decoupled from the dimensions of the image space.

7.2.2   The Video Drive Frequency with Exhaustive Scanning

In the previous subsection we estimated the speed at which an electron beam must be deflected so as to achieve an exhaustive scan of an image space. Although this estimation was based on the display paradigm described by Richard Ketchel, it is applicable to other embodiments using one, or a small number, of beam sources for voxel activation. This denotes only one aspect of the demands placed on the voxel activation mechanism, and of equal importance is the frequency response that must be supported by beam modulation hardware (i.e., the video drive frequency).

Let us continue to use the values employed in the previous subsection—namely, the use of 128 image slices, 64 scan lines per image slice, and a rotational frequency of 15 Hz. We assume that there are two image updates per screen rotation. For simplicity we will assume the use of a square screen (so that all scan lines are of the same length) and that for each scan line it is possible to create up to 128 voxels. This implies a beam modulation frequency on the order of 32 MHz.[11] Should we

---

[11] For a screen with dimensions of 18 cm, this would lead to voxels in the central region of approximately 1.5 mm in length.

attempt to increase the refresh rate, the resolution of the scan or the dimensions of the image space then this will directly impact on the beam modulation frequency.[12]

7.3   THE PLANAR SCREEN AND CONSTANT BEAM SOURCE GEOMETRY

Creativity is inventing, experimenting, growing, taking risks, breaking rules, making mistakes, and having fun.[13]

In the case of the display units introduced in the previous section, the orientation of the voxel activation mechanisms with respect to the screen continually varies. Consequently, the accuracy with which voxels can be placed within the image space, and the actual shape of voxels is affected by the instantaneous location of the screen with respect to the beam sources. Furthermore, as we have seen, when the plane of the screen is closely aligned to the axis of the beam source, it becomes impossible to activate voxels on its surface. This leads to a region of dead image space within which voxels cannot be satisfactorily placed. One approach to solving these difficulties is to provide a second beam source arranged so that each source is responsible for voxel activation across one-half of the image space. However, the inclusion of a second beam source increases the complexity of the display unit and interface hardware (here it is important to bear in mind that the coordinate systems of the deflection apparatus associated with each beam source must be appropriately mapped onto a single coordinate system assigned to the image space).

Other strategies may be adopted. For example:

1. We may use a beam source (and deflection apparatus) that co-rotates with the screen.
2. We may use a stationary beam source (and deflection apparatus) and a beam projection apparatus that co-rotates with the screen. This apparatus would ensure that a constant geometry is maintained between the voxel activation subsystem and each image slice within the display volume.

In this section we briefly introduce various approaches that highlight these options.

7.3.1   The Planar Screen and Co-Rotating Electron Guns

Consider the display unit illustrated in Figure 7.6 (Ref. 7D), which is described in a comprehensive patent filed by Max Hirsch in 1958 (US Patent Number 2,967,905). In this embodiment, co-rotating the beam sources (electron guns and deflection

---

[12] In the case of the 3-D Rotation introduced in Section 7.3.2, a video drive frequency of ~300 MHz is reported as being used to support a high-resolution raster scan.

[13] Mary Lou Cook (1918–)

apparatus) with the screen enables a fixed geometry to be maintained between the beam sources and each image slice. The use of two electron guns enables the creation of two-color images [the surfaces of emission (denoted 120A and 120B in Figure 7.6) are each coated with phosphors that generate a different color].

This straightforward approach to the preservation of constant geometry is not without problems—namely, the rotation of the entire vacuum vessel and the passage of signals to and from the rotating components. However, both of these can be readily solved (especially as in the latter case, optical links may now be employed; see, for example, Section 11.5). In an alternative embodiment, Hirsch describes the implementation of a display unit using an axially rotating CRT the output from

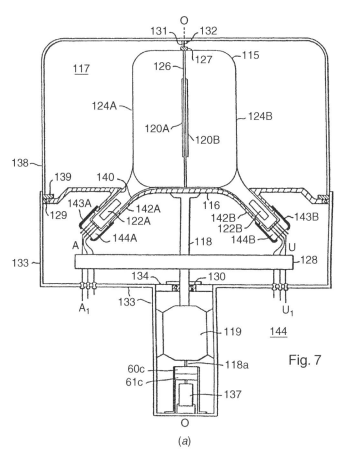

(a)

Figure 7.6 (a) Overview of a display unit developed by Max Hirsch. The screen, two electron guns, the beam deflection apparatus, and the vacuum vessel co-rotate. This ensures that a fixed geometry is maintained between the electron guns and each image slice. Two electron guns are employed so as to enable the production of color images. (b) Plan view, provided together with an illustration showing the axis of rotation relative to the electron guns. (Reproduced from US Patent Number 2,967,905.)

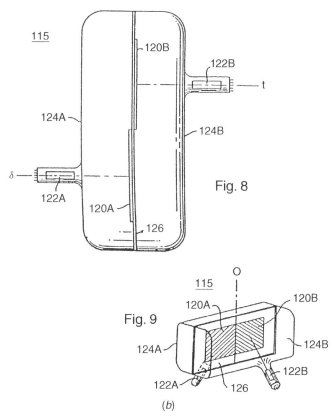

Figure 7.6 *(Continued).*

which is projected (via an appropriate optical arrangement) onto a co-rotating pla-nar screen (Ref. 7E). In the patent, this device is referred to as the Generescope and is illustrated in Figure 7.7.

The presence of the optical components—especially (54) and (55) together with the supporting structure (79)—as indicated in Figure 7.7 would have impacted on viewing freedom. Since these co-rotated with the screen, this configuration is equivalent to the use of a nontransparent screen for image space creation and limits the extent of the image space that can be seen by an observer from any one viewing location. In fact, Hirsch used this advantageously by defining two "viewing zones" at the "front" and "rear" of the display. Each of these occupied approximately one-half of the image space, and to each a complete image is out-put.[14] The comprehensive patent filed by Hirsch retains much of its relevance and

---

[14] This general technique where an image space is divided into two through the use of a nontrans-parent screen (or due to the presence of other components within the image space) could have applications in training and video games.

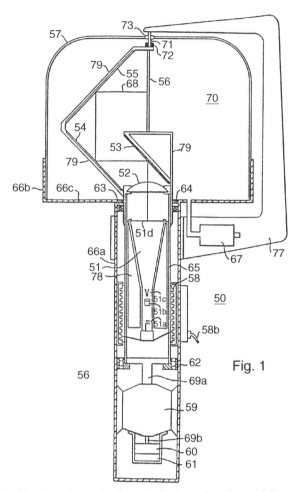

Figure 7.7 In this alternative embodiment, Hirsch employed an axially rotating CRT, the output from which is projected onto a co-rotating screen (56) via reflecting surfaces 53, 54, and 55. These co-rotate with the CRT and screen. Due to the presence of these components, light emitted from the screen can only be seen from within a restricted range of viewing positions. Additionally, the image is portrayed against a nontransparent background, and this may have improved image clarity. (Reproduced from US Patent Number 2,967,905.)

includes discussion on issues relating to interaction with volumetric images (see Section 11.6).

The use of co-rotating electron beam sources is not limited to the work of Max Hirsch, and a brief letter originating from CBS Laboratories [Goldberg, 1962] outlines a similar technique (Ref. 7F). This is illustrated in Figure 7.8. Here, an electron gun located below the viewing region impinges on a co-rotating phosphor-coated plate. As with other embodiments of that period, the purpose of the display was for the depiction of aircraft radar data; interestingly, the inventors employed a

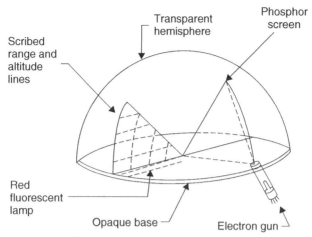

Fig. 1 – Monochrome 3-D display.

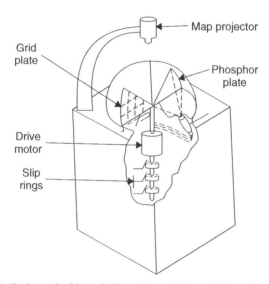

Figure 7.8 A display unit able to depict volumetric data within an image space containing a physically generated graticule and floor map. Mixing the volumetric image with other forms of imagery offers to augment the visualization experience. This system was reported in 1962 and, as with other approaches of the period, was intended for use in the visualization of aircraft radar data. (Reproduced from Goldberg [1962] © 1962 IEEE.)

screen for voxel formation located on only one side of the rotational axis. On the other side of this axis, they positioned a glass plate with etched markings—this being "*edge lighted by a red light from beneath*". This formed a graticule able to supply reference markings. Furthermore, Goldberg indicates the projection of a terrain map of the floor of the image space. Rather than pass the high voltages required by the electron gun via a commutator. Goldberg indicates that these were produced by co-rotating circuitry.[15] An image refresh period of 30 Hz is indicated.

7.3.2 The Planar Screen and Nonevasive Projection Techniques

> *Every human being has a finite number of heartbeats available to him,*
> *and I don't intend to waste any of mine*
> *running around doing exercises.*[16]

As indicated in the previous subsection, the Generescope employed optical components and an associated supporting structure located *within* the image space. These would have obstructed the propagation of light to the observer and hence restricted viewing freedom. Since the late 1950s when the Generescope was first described, researchers have sought to employ similar projection techniques [and so ensure constant geometry between each image space slice and the beam (image) source(s)], but with the optical components arranged to avoid them impacting on the visible image. Below we briefly outline three approaches:

1. **CRT Images Projected onto a Planar Screen (Ref. 7G).** ITT Laboratories' Aviation Lab researched the display illustrated in Figure 7.9 during the late 1950s. As may be seen from the illustration, it employs a planar screen onto which image slices depicted by a CRT are projected [*Aviation Week*, 1960]. The projection apparatus comprises lenses attached to the face of the static CRT and two mirrors that co-rotate with the screen.

In embodiments of this type, the optical apparatus is located below the image space and consequently its presence does not impact on viewing freedom. The extent to which this display unit was developed is unclear as it was stated that:

> *The model displayed here, using a cylinder measuring approximately 12 inches in diameter and six inches high, employed small lamps instead of a CRT .... Company is now anxious to find an interested customer in order to build a fully operable model ....*[17]

2. **A Scanned Beam Projected onto a Planar Screen (Ref 7H).** In 1990 Robert Batchko filed a patent concerning various aspects of a volumetric display unit architecture (US Patent Number 5,148,310). In one embodiment, Batchko

---

[15] The difficulty of implementing display units where electronic circuits co-rotate with the screen should not be underestimated. A component with mass 20 g that is located 20 cm from the axis of rotation, and which rotates at a frequency of 20 Hz will experience a force of some 63 N. When the frequency of rotation is 60 Hz, the force approaches 600 N! The author recalls a display prototype in which a considerable amount of circuitry co-rotated with the screen. When in operation at a rotation frequency of 30 Hz, this circuitry decided to follow its own instincts by traveling in a straight line. As no protective surround was used, the results were spectacular, both on the surrounding walls and the author's face ....

[16] Attributed to Neil Armstrong. Quoted in Breuer, W. B., *Race to the Moon*, Praeger (1993).

[17] Plus ça change ....

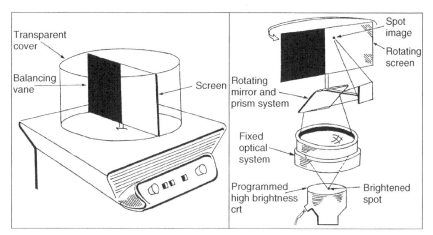

Figure 7.9   A simple optical arrangement enabling image data depicted on a CRT to be projected onto a rotating planar screen. The co-rotating optical components lie beneath the image space and therefore do not impact on viewing freedom. As can be seen from the diagram, image slices are projected onto a screen located on only one side of the axis of rotation. This would have facilitated the processing of the image data. (Reproduced, with permission from Aviation Week [1960].)

describes the use of a scannable laser—the output from this being directed into the image space in a manner akin to the method used in approach 1 above. The arrangement that he describes is illustrated in Figure 7.10. Here, it may be seen that the scanned beam source is directed to the screen via two reflectors (labeled 35 and 38); these reflectors co-rotate with the screen (44). By locating the optical components below the image space, Batchko ensured that they would not adversely impact on image visibility. For further discussion see *Laser Focus World* [1993] and Batchko [1994].

3. **The 3-D Rotation (Ref. 7I).**   The two display units introduced above employ two mirrors to project the image data onto a co-rotating screen. In both cases, one of these mirrors is offset from the axis of rotation and is therefore subjected to a significant force resulting from the rotational motion. For example, if we assume a rotational frequency of 30 Hz, and estimate that the mirror is some 30 cm from the axis of rotation, then a mirror of mass 50 g will experience a force of ~500 N.

In the early 1990s, workers at the Sony Corporation developed a display unit employing a projection method which removed the need for a nonaxial rotating mirror Shimada, 1993. This publication begins as follows: *"This system will be the first system in history to display a practical, dynamic 3-D full-colour image that can be seen at any angle without using 3-D glasses."* Given the rich history of volumetric display system development prior to the early 1990s, such a claim is clearly unfounded! However, within the publication, Shimada describes a very interesting approach, and the basic principle of operation is illustrated in Figure 7.11. In this system, three CRTs are used (reported as having 7-inch screens), and these

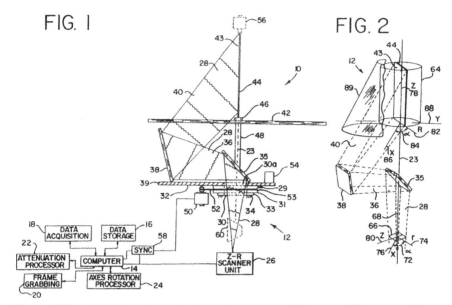

Figure 7.10   A display unit employing a planar screen (44) onto which a scanned beam is projected. The projection system makes use of two mirrors (35) and (38) which co-rotate with the screen and so uniform geometry may be maintained between the projection source and the image slices. Since the projection apparatus is located below the image space, it does not interfere with viewing freedom. (Reproduced from US Patent Number 5,148,310.)

provide the source of the RGB image data that are projected upward toward the image space. A mirror (D) co-rotates with the screen (A) and reflects these images to a fixed spherical mirror (reported as being deposited around the equator of the inner surface of an enclosing container). The spherical mirror projects the image data depicted by the CRTs onto the rotating screen and so replaces the co-rotating nonaxial mirror used in the embodiments described in approaches 1 and 2 above.

Interestingly, Shimada adopted the use of a raster scan and he discusses some of the issues that occur when this exhaustive scanning method is used. For the raster scan employed, a video drive frequency of approximately 300 MHz (per CRT) is considered to be appropriate; as indicated by Shimada, this is on a par with the drive frequency employed in a 20×20-inch high-resolution monitor manufactured at that time. Clearly, this demonstrates that even a display unit that exhibits no parallelism in the voxel activation process can, when properly developed, achieve high performance.

The image space is reported as being 30 cm in diameter and 15 cm in height. Increasing these measurements would necessitate a reduction in scan resolution or an increase in both the scan speed and video drive frequency.

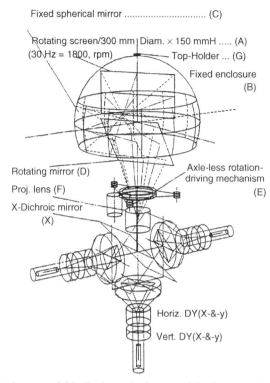

Fixed spherical mirror .... (C)

Rotating screen/300 mm Diam. × 150 mmH ..... (A)
(30 Hz = 1800, rpm) — Top-Holder ... (G)

Fixed enclosure
(B)

Rotating mirror (D)
Proj. lens (F)
X-Dichroic mirror
(X)

Axle-less rotation-
driving mechanism
(E)

Horiz. DY(X-&-y)
Vert. DY(X-&-y)

Figure 7.11 In the case of this display unit, the nonaxial mirrors employed in the systems illustrated in Figures 7.9 and 7.10 are replaced by a fixed spherical mirror deposited on a part of the inside surface of the display enclosure. The "rotating mirror" reflects image data onto this spherical mirror. Since the latter circumscribes the lower part of the image space, it is able to cast the image data reflected by the rotating mirror into each image slice (and maintain uniform geometry between each image slices and the CRT display screens). (Reproduced from Shimada [1993]. © 1993 Society for Information Display.)

7.4 A HELICAL SCREEN AND PASSIVE SOE

In 1976 Professor Rüdiger Hartwig at IBM's Heidelberg Scientific Center filed a patent describing the creation of an image space by means of a thin helical surface and the activation of voxels by means of a directed laser beam(s) (German Patent Number DE 26 22 802 C2).[18] The configuration described in this patent is illustrated in Figure 7.12.

The use of a surface of this form offers a number of significant advantages:

1. Due to its shape, the helical screen possesses greater rigidity than a planar screen formed from materials of the same thickness. Thus the helix offers to support the creation of larger volume image spaces.

---

[18] See also Brinkmann, 1983.

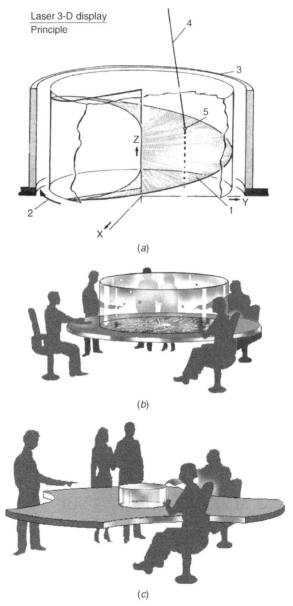

Figure 7.12   In (a) the original display paradigm employing a single bladed rotating heli-cal screen on the surface of which voxels may be illuminated by means of a scanned laser beam. In (b) and (c) impressions of the helix based display designed for use in applications such as air-traffic control. This approach is intended to increase the image space volume (and so improve spatial clarity) without the need to support large amplitude deflection of the laser beams used for voxel activation. (Images kindly supplied by Professor Rüdiger Hartwig.)

2. The use of a helical screen permits considerable freedom in viewing orientation.

3. In the case that the helix is equipped with a passive SOE, the beam source(s) are best located in line with the axis of rotation (usually this axis is arranged vertically) and so the beam sources may be located either above or below the image space. This leaves the curved surface of the cylindrical image space free from any obstructions that may otherwise be caused by the presence of any beam projection apparatus.

In 1978–1979, the Hartwig system was prototyped using a semitransparent single bladed helix rotating at 20 Hz (Ref. 7J). The cylindrical image space swept out measured 60 cm in diameter and 40 cm in height. This pioneering activity has formed the basis for a considerable amount of subsequent research. In this section we briefly review aspects of this work, confining ourselves to display units in which a passive SOE is employed and that exhibit a low degree of parallelism in the voxel activation subsystem. Details of a display unit architecture employing a helical screen and active surface of emission parallelism are presented in Section 8.4.

7.4.1 A Helix within a CRT (Ref. 7K)

A patent filed in 1987 (Japanese Patent Number JP63254647) describes the incorporation of a transparent rotating helical screen within a CRT, as illustrated in Figure 7.13. Here, the surface of the helix is coated with a short persistence phosphor, and voxels are activated by means of an electron beam.

7.4.2 HL3D-Based Systems (Ref. 7L)

The work undertaken by Rüdiger Hartwig in the late 1970s has provided the basis for a considerable amount of research activity relating to the use of the helical screen with one or more laser beams being employed for voxel activation. Display units of this type are commonly referred to using the acronym HL3D [Helix-Laser 3-D (display)].

In the 1980s and early 1990s, work was undertaken at Texas Instruments [Williams and Garcia, 1988] into the development of such systems. This encompassed the creation of multi-color images (achieved by mixing light from three modulated laser sources) in large volume image spaces. During this period a number of 'OmniView™' display systems were developed and an interesting overview of this work is provided by Clifton and Wefer [1993]. Other displays have been developed in an extensive research effort conducted for the US Navy by key researchers such as Parviz Soltan and Mark Lasher.

Soltan et al. [1992] report two display prototypes systems. The first employed a double bladed aluminium helix 13 inches in diameter and 10-inches in height (the rotation frequency being 10 Hz with the double bladed configuration enabling two image updates per cycle of rotation). This publication also describes a second version of screen in development. Again this was double-bladed but measured

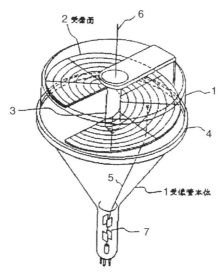

Figure 7.13 A helical screen placed within a CRT. In this embodiment, the electron beam is able to activate voxels through the use of a phosphor coating. Naturally, the accommodation of the motor drive within the vacuum vessel increases the difficulty of construction and may have exacerbated the extent of the dead image space that occurs around the axis of rotation of a helix. (Reproduced from Japanese Patent Office Publication Number 63254647A.)

36 inches in diameter and 18 inches in height and was fabricated using injection-molded polystyrene plastic.[19] Both systems used acousto-optic (AO) scanners for the deflection of the laser beams. By using four scanners, a voxel activation capacity of 40,000 is reported with a 20-Hz refresh frequency Soltan et al., 1994.[20] Additional discussion is provided in Soltan et al. [1995; Lasher et al., 1996; US Patent Number 5,854,613]. See also Hanson [1997], who provides interesting discussion concerning the application of volumetric display techniques to the field of air traffic control. In connection with the use of volumetric systems as a training medium, he writes:

> *Horizontal manoeuvres, vertical separation, and the adroit use of time to manage anticipated proximity are all attributes of the visual and kinaesthetic learning enhanced by a real time, three dimensional volumetric display.... The dynamic relevance of the*

---

[19] With the overall helix being formed "...*from 18 one inch tall segments, vertically stacked and bonded together. It has a uniform thickness of 2 mm, except for a half inch diameter cylinder concentric with its vertical axis that houses a centre pin .... The upper surface of the helix is treated with an opaque white finish to enhance reflectivity and light diffusion. The helix and pin weigh 5.0 lbs. The helix is fully enclosed in a transparent cylindrical housing that rotates with it ... The housing also rotates the volume of entrained air, alleviating the helix of any drag load*" [Soltan et al. 1994].

[20] See also Soltan et al. [1995].

*display to the real world allows people to "get" the relationship of the symbols on the
screen to an aircraft full of people much more quickly.*

In recent patents (German Patent Number DE 100 47 695 and US Patent Number
6,958,837 B2), Rüdiger Hartwig describes a helix-based display that is specifically
designed for use in areas such as Air Traffic Control. In correspondence with the
author, he writes:

> ... *a key objective of the new patents is to make the HL3D image space larger and
> more reasonable in price. The high-speed deflection systems that are normally used
> are replaced by (quasi-static) systems. This approach represents 3D images as "point
> groups" comparable to "symbols" in space. Additional mechano-optical devices pro-
> vide the air traffic controller with pictorial information about flight direction and
> speed.*
>
> *The new approach can be employed in applications with relatively few picture
> objects e.g. 128 aeroplanes in the 3D cylindrical image space (for the depiction of
> "macro images," as they are used in air-traffic control or CAD) and offers support
> for a large image space volume. For example, in the case of air traffic control, this
> approach could support an image space some 120 cm in diameter and 60 cm in height.*

The architecture is therefore intended to increase the image space volume (and
so improve spatial clarity) without the need to support large amplitude deflection
of the laser beams used for voxel activation (which is generally characterized by
bulky deflection apparatus and/or high cost). See Figures 7.12b and 7.12c.

For further reading in relation to the use of helix-based systems, see the patent
filed by Neil Acantilado (US Patent Number 5,945,966) in which aspects of the
software system are discussed, and the brief patent filed by Eric Whitesell (US
Patent Number 6,177,913B1) that focuses on the helical screen. Additional background details are given in the paper by Belfatto [1998].[21] Also see publications
by Knut Langhans and co-workers, who describe exciting and ongoing research in
this general area Langhans et al., 2002, 2003, and 2005.

7.4.3   Projection onto a Helical Screen (Ref. 7M)

A patent filed in 1989 by Roger Morton and assigned to the Eastman Kodak
Company (US Patent Number 4,922,336) describes the projection of image data
depicted by a CRT onto a rotating helix. The configuration discussed in this patent
is illustrated in Figure 7.14.

Here, as may be seen, image data depicted on a CRT is projected onto the helix
via a convex lens and an anamorphic lens. This latter component co-rotates with the
helix and is required because points on the surface of the helix vary in distance from
the CRT screen and convex lens. Consequently, in the absence of the anamorphic
lens, image data projected by the convex lens onto the helical screen would not be

---

[21] At the time of writing (April 2006), the author understands that the work carried out by Parviz
Soltan and Mark Lasher is, for the moment, on hold. This is most regrettable as the technologies
that have been developed and applications that have been studied are well advanced.

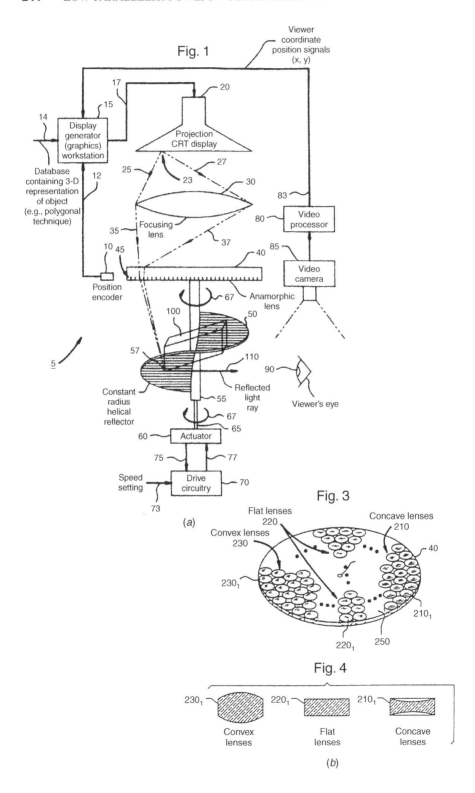

Fig. 1

Viewer coordinate position signals (x, y)

14 — Database containing 3-D representation of object (e.g., polygonal technique)

15 — Display generator (graphics) workstation

17

20 — Projection CRT display

25 23 27 30

83 — Video processor

80

35 — Focusing lens

37

85 — Video camera

10 45 40

Position encoder

67 — Anamorphic lens

50

100

110 — Reflected light ray

57

90 — Viewer's eye

Constant radius helical reflector

55

67

65

60 — Actuator

75 77

Speed setting

73

Drive circuitry — 70

5

(a)

Fig. 3

Flat lenses 220

Concave lenses 210

Convex lenses 230

230₁

40

230₁

210

220₁ 250

210₁

Fig. 4

230₁ Convex lenses   220₁ Flat lenses   210₁ Concave lenses

(b)

uniformly focused and furthermore image distortion would occur. The form of the anamorphic lens is illustrated in Figure 7.14b. As may be seen, it consists of an array of lenslets that vary in shape. As indicated in this illustration, those lenses on the left are convex (converging) while those on the right are concave (diverging). Those lenslets lying in between these two extremes have less curvature. Thus the lenslets compensate for variations in distance between the primary convex lens and the helical surface. Naturally, for this approach to operate correctly, the anamorphic lens must co-rotate with the screen.

In this informative patent, the author also discusses the provision of a tracking system able to sense changes in the location of the observer relative to the image space. In principle, this permits the inclusion of hidden line removal techniques and so provides a sense of image opacity. However, this would only work correctly for a single observer and, in the case of more complex images, is likely to introduce an undesirable latency between observer motion and image update.

7.5   ALTERNATIVE CONFIGURATIONS

When demonstrating swept-volume display units employing the rotational motion of a planar screen or helix, the author has found that one of the questions asked most frequently by audience members concerns the viability of adopting some alternative form of screen or screen configuration. During the discussions that follow, suggestions for a different screen shape and/or a possible change in the location of the rotational axis are commonly made. Suggested approaches are generally flawed, and the author has found that without recourse to a physical model, it is difficult to quickly describe weaknesses that may occur when some form of screen sweeps through a 3-D space.

That is not to say, however, that the helix (with its central axis of rotation) and the planar screen (with the axis of rotation in the plane of the screen) represent the only possible configurations—there are indeed others. For example, in Section,4.3.1,[22] we refer to the use of the Archimedes spiral and also to an embodiment employing a series of screens set along the periphery of a rotating disc. However, both of these approaches demonstrate very low sweep efficiencies and therefore do not necessarily represent highly practical solutions. Furthermore, in

---

[22] See also Section 6.5.4.

Figure 7.14   (a) Display unit in which image data depicted on a CRT screen (20) is projected onto a rotating helical screen. Convex lens (30) and anamorphic lens (40) ensure that the projected data points are properly focused onto the surface of the helix. (b) The anamorphic lens) co-rotates with the helical screen and compensates for variations in distance between points on the helical screen and the principle convex lens. (Reproduced from US Patent Number 4,922,336.)

both cases, viewing freedom is limited. In the case that we wish to provide considerable viewing freedom, opportunities for alternative geometries and changes in the orientation of the rotational axis with respect to the screen are somewhat limited. In this section we briefly introduce some exemplar embodiments that highlight the difficulty of identifying solutions that provide overall performance superior to the more standard screen configurations encountered previously in this chapter (which support considerable viewing freedom).

7.5.1   A Tilted Planar Screen (Ref. 7N)

A patent filed in 1990 (US Patent Number 5,042,909) and two European patents (European Patent Numbers 0 310 928 A2 and 0 491 284 A1), filed by Felix Garcia and Rodney Williams, discuss swept-volume techniques in which an image space is formed by the rotational motion of a planar screen. Unusually, as illustrated in Figure 7.15a, the axis of rotation lies at an angle of 45° to the screen's surface. Although this may be advantageous as far as the voxel generation and activation subsystems are concerned, it gives rise to an image space that is no longer cylindrical (as may be seen in Figure 7.15b, the screen fails to sweep out cones 25 and 27). The usefulness of such an image space is therefore limited. This point is recognized in a further patent filed by Garcia and Williams[23] [European Patent Number 0 418 583 A2] in which they write:

> *It is readily apparent that two conical areas extending upwardly and downwardly from the axis of rotation of the screen are incapable of receiving a portion of the display.*

A solution proposed by the researchers to this problem is outlined in Section 7.5.3.

7.5.2   An Alternative Screen Shape (Ref. 7O)

> *The reasonable man adapts himself to the world:*
> *The unreasonable one persists in trying to adapt the world to himself.*
> *Therefore all progress depends on the unreasonable man.[24]*

A patent filed in 1962 (US Patent Number 3,204,238) by Albert Skellett describes a display unit (intended for the visualization of aircraft radar data) that employs a rotating phosphor coated screen addressed by a single electron beam. The approach is illustrated in Figure 7.16 and as can be seen from this diagram, the screen shape is somewhat unusual. Skellett describes the screen as follows:

> *... the screen tilts upwards at a constant rate with change in position around the axis of the tube, or axis of rotation, going from perpendicular to the axis of rotation to parallel with the axis of rotation in 324° around the axis. That is, in every 36 degrees around the axis of the face of the screen will increase its tilt by 10° so that along*

---

[23] The U.S. patent was assigned to Texas Instruments, noted as the applicant on the three European filings.
[24] Attributed to Robert Anson Heinlein (1907–1988).

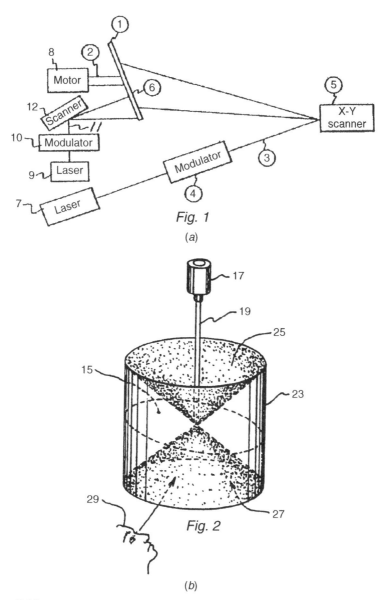

Fig. 1

(a)

Fig. 2

(b)

Figure 7.15   (a) Image space formed by the rotational motion of a planar screen (1). Here, the axis of rotation lies at an angle of 45° to the screen's surface. Unfortunately, as may be seen from (b), the screen fails to sweep through a solid cylinder—cones (25) and (27) are not part of the image space. (Reproduced from European Patents 0 310 928 A2 and 0 491 284 A1.)

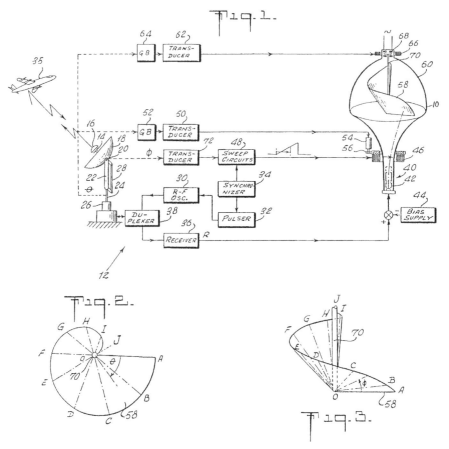

Figure 7.16 A display unit described by Albert Skellett which employs an unusual screen shape. An electron beam is used to activate voxels on the surface of the screen (which is phosphor-coated and is therefore likely to be only semitransparent). (Reproduced from US Patent Number 3,204,238.)

line OA the screen will be perpendicular to the axis, along line OB, displaced 36° clockwise from OA, the screen will be inclined 80° to the axis of the tube and so on until along line OJ, displaced 324° clockwise from OA, the screen will be parallel to the axis of the tube.[25]

The reader is left to consider the strengths and weaknesses of this screen configuration (see investigation 4 in Section 7.8).

---

[25] See Figure 7.16 for details of references to OA, OB, etc.

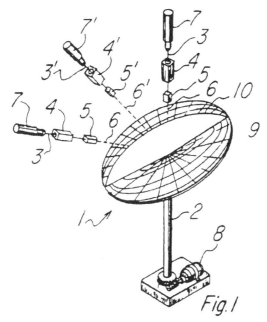

Figure 7.17   A proposal to extend the display paradigm discussed in Section 7.5.1 The addition of a surface (10) lying at right angles to circular surface (1) enables the upper cone [labelled (25) in Figure 7.15(b)] to be swept out and therefore form a part of the image space. This is likely to create problems for the voxel activation subsystem since, when in certain positions, parts of the screen obstruct the propagation of the activation beam (the shadowing dead zone introduced in Section 4.7.4). Furthermore, the presence of the additional screen will hamper the propagation of light through the image space. (Reproduced from European Patent Number 0 418 583 A2.)

7.5.3   Augmenting the Planar Screen (Ref. 7P)

The approach summarized in Section 7.5.1 is further developed in additional patents filed by Felix Garcia and Rodney Williams (US Patent Number 5,172,266 and European Patent Number 0 418 583 A2).[26] Here, as illustrated in Figure 7.17, a circular planar screen is employed, with the axis of rotation lying at an angle of ~45° to the plane of the screen. As may be seen from the diagram, an additional screen surface is used (this component is located at right angles to the surface of the circular screen). The objective of the researchers was clearly to provide a method of "filling in" the upper conical region referred to in Section 7.5.1, and indeed this arrangement would have met this goal. On the other hand, the configuration would cause addressing problems for a beam-based voxel activation mechanism (as a result of shadowing dead zones) and furthermore would negatively impact on the propagation of light through the image space.

---

[26] This patent contains a number of interesting embodiments and is well worth perusal.

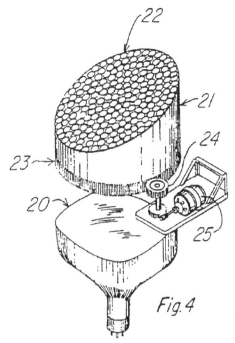

Figure 7.18 Here, a bundle of optical fibers rotate and project image data depicted by a CRT into an image space. As with the embodiment illustrated in Figure 7.15, a conical region centered on the axis of rotation is not swept out. This severely impacts on the usefulness of this approach. (Reproduced from European Patent Number 0 418 583 A2.)

7.5.4 A Sliced Fiber Bundle (Ref. 7Q)

In the patent referred to in the previous subsection (European Patent Number 0 418 583 A2), Felix Garcia and Rodney Williams outline various other embodiments, such as the one illustrated in Figure 7.18. This technique restricts viewing freedom to a single "window," and therefore it would have been appropriate to include this display paradigm within the previous chapter. However, it is has been included at this point to provide a further example of a cylindrical image space exhibiting a conical "depression." Naturally, this is likely to restrict the usefulness of the approach. Additionally, it is probable that points of light illuminated on the CRT would not only enter the intended fibers but also pass along adjacent fibers. This would result in a loss of image sharpness. It is interesting to compare this technique with the embodiments introduced in Section 6.5.3.

7.5.5 Two Degrees of Freedom (Ref. 7R)

In the patent referred to in the previous two subsections (European Patent Number 0 418 583 A2), Garcia and Williams also propose the arrangement illustrated in Figure 7.19. Here, the screen is housed within a transparent sphere and its motion

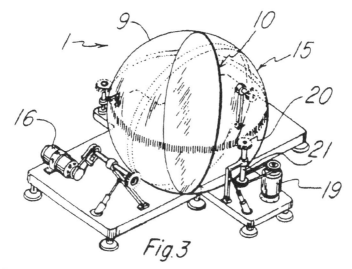

Figure 7.19   In this embodiment it is suggested that a planar screen (or the screen illustrated in Figure 7.17) be fixed within a spherical transparent housing and driven by two motors (16) and (19). Thus two degrees of freedom are supported and so the screen may be driven in any direction. Furthermore, sequences of screen movement may be employed. (Reproduced from European Patent Number 0 418 583 A2.)

is defined using *two* motor drives arranged orthogonally. Two degrees of freedom are therefore supported in screen rotation, and sequences of screen movement may be accommodated. Given a sufficient rate of movement, this opens up several exciting opportunities but is likely to introduce interesting challenges as far as voxel activation is concerned.

7.6   AN EARLY VOLUMETRIC RADAR DISPLAY (REF. 7S)

> *Now he has departed from this strange world a little ahead of me.*
> *That means nothing.*
> *People like us, who believe in physics,*
> *know that the distinction between past, present, and future*
> *is only a stubbornly persistent illusion.*[27]

In 1938, Irving Wolff filed a patent in connection with a radar system ("radio vision") (US Patent Number 2,837,735).[28] This patent begins:

---

[27] Attributed to Albert Einstein (1875–1955).

[28] Interestingly, this patent was not granted until 1958, possibly as a consequence of its military potential.

My invention relates to radio vision, the term "radio vision" being applied to pictures in two coordinates and to three-dimensional space pictures which are built up from signals derived from reflected radio waves.[29]

The apparatus discussed by Wolff is illustrated in Figure 7.20 and from our current point of view, the method of data depiction is of particular importance. In the diagram labeled "Fig. 1," a standard means of representing the radar echo is depicted. Wolff writes:

The distance coordinate may be represented by the vertical movements of a cathode ray trace and the horizontal direction or coordinate by the horizontal trace. The distance and horizontal coordinates for a point or object A are illustrated in Fig. 1 where the spot A' appearing on the cathode ray tube screen is a representation or image of the object A . . . . If the scene is to be reproduced in the vertical plane, the coordinates are preferably interchanged. It should be understood that the cathode ray is moved in one direction in synchronism with the angular movements of the radio beam.

This technique fails to bring together within a single framework the horizontal direction, elevation, and distance information. However, Wolff recognized the value of integrating this information within a single perspective image, and he designed a system able to achieve this goal (indeed a remarkable achievement in 1938!). To this end, a hinged and oscillating mirror (denoted 29 in "Fig 3.") was used to form an image space. The operator (41) viewed the reflection of data depicted on the CRT screen (27) indirectly, and the mirror motion made space for the third dimension. Wolff writes:

The cathode ray tube is arranged with its screen 27 in a horizontal plane. A plane mirror 29 is hinged adjacent the screen, and arranged so that the mirror may be oscillated through the angles of approximately 45° to slightly less than 90° from the plane of the screen. The mirror movement or scanning is effected by mechanically coupling 31 the mirror, through a reduction gear 33, to a motor 35 which actuates the array for vertical scanning. When the radio beam is horizontally directed, the mirror is in the 90° − K° position. When the radio beam vertically directed, the mirror is in the 45° position. The reduction gear 35 provides the necessary ratio of movement. A screen 37, including a suitable aperture 39, is arranged between the cathode ray screen and the eyes 41 of the observer.

It is useful to place this technique in context by recalling previous discussion in Section 1.2.2 concerning the difficulties that arise when only simple electronic systems are available for the implementation of the interface between the data acquisition system and the display. In this respect, Wolff did not have the opportunity to employ digital technologies and was not able to buffer the radar returns. Consequently, the motion of the mirror and the vertical scanning of the radar dish

[29] As mentioned in Section 6.6, in his patent, Wolff references Baird's 1931 patent (see Section 6.3.1). This is the only document in the author's possession to do so. It is ironic that despite the comments made by the Director of Scientific Research at the Ministry of Supply during WWII concerning the irrelevance of Baird's work to the war effort, Baird's work had already been recognized within a patent relating to radar image depiction. This patent was, however, filed in the United States. . . .

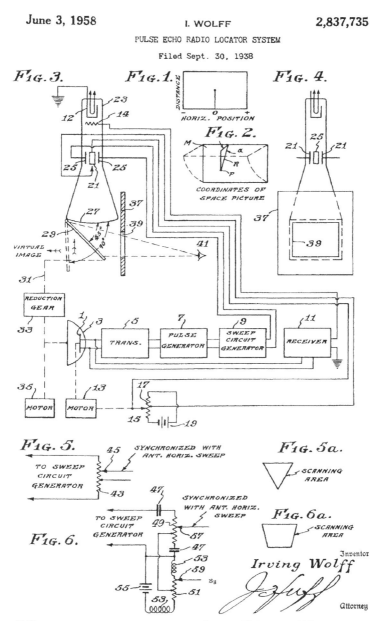

June 3, 1958   I. WOLFF   2,837,735

PULSE ECHO RADIO LOCATOR SYSTEM

Filed Sept. 30, 1938

Figure 7.20 The apparatus described by Irving Wolff in his 1938 patent. The image depiction technique enables the integration of horizontal direction, elevation and distance data within a single 3-D perspective view (a visualization paradigm that even today is still not generally available to radar operators). In this embodiment, the data depicted on the CRT is reflected by an oscillating and hinged mirror (28) whose motion is synchronized to the vertical scan of the radar apparatus. See text for details. (Reproduced from US Patent Number 2,837,735.).

were synchronized. This would have impacted on the maximum rate at which the mirror was able to oscillate and hence the perceived level of image flicker. In this context, Wolff writes:

> *The resulting image produces a three-dimensional space picture. It should be understood that the images may be formed at a rate which produces a persistent picture, or the images may be formed more slowly whereby the scene is analysed rather than reproduced as a whole.*

Unfortunately, the frequency of oscillation of the mirror is not quoted, but given the need for synchronized movement (and as may be seen from the extract below the mirror's frequency of oscillation was in fact half of the vertical scan frequency of the radar beam), it is likely that the image would have exhibited considerable flicker (see Section 7.8, investigation 6). Wolff discusses image formation as follows:

> *The space occupied by one form of such picture is represented in perspective in Fig. 2.[30] The image of a point P is represented in cylindrical coordinates in Fig. 2 which corresponds to the space or volume occupied by the successive images of the screen of the cathode ray tube as formed by the mirror. The coordinates are as follows: (a) The distance coordinate is represented by the length R of the line between the axis M and the point P; (b) the vertical angular position of the point P is indicated by the angle α; and (c) the horizontal angular position is indicated by the position of the point with respect to the zero O of the reference axis. The foregoing coordinates are obtained (a) by making the "fore and aft" position of the spot on the cathode ray screen correspond to the distance of the reflecting object, as previously explained; (b) by synchronizing the angular position of the mirror so that it moves with half the vertical angular velocity of the radio beam scanning; and (c) by synchronizing the horizontal position of the spot on the cathode ray tube with the horizontal angular position of the radio beam.*
>
> *Consideration of the nature of the foregoing system of coordinates and image shows that a space picture having satisfactory perspective will be obtained. It follows that there are many uses of the device . . . .*

And the operation of the system is summarized in the following way:

> *Thus the invention has been described as a radio vision device. The scene to be reproduced is scanned vertically and horizontally by a beam of radio pulses. In synchronism with the radio scanning a cathode ray is scanned across the fluorescent screen of a cathode ray tube. The depth position of the indication on the screen is synchronized as a function of the distance travelled by the radio pulses. A mirror, which is suitably positioned with respect to the screen which is in a horizontal plane, scans the radio beam vertical scanning.*

Although filed in 1938, Wolff's patent was not granted until 1958 and was assigned to RCA.[31] The patent is certainly worth perusal because it provides an interesting

---

[30] See Figure 7.20.
[31] Radio Corporation of America.

insight into the development of a volumetric system for the depiction of radar data.[32]

7.7 DISCUSSION

In this chapter we have introduced a range of techniques that may be brought to bear in the implementation of swept-volume systems. Generally, the displays described here give rise to systems that exhibit a relatively low voxel activation capacity (perhaps on the order of 100,000) and a fill factor that is considerably less than 1%. However, both Ketchpel [Section 7.2.1 (Ref. 7C)] and Shimada [Section 7.3.2 (Ref. 7I)] have demonstrated that even in the case of display units exhibiting a parallelism in voxel activation of unity, an exhaustive scan (providing a satisfactory and useful resolution) can be achieved.

We have also seen some of the difficulties that can arise when there is a continually varying geometry between the beam source deflection apparatus and the screen. Max Hirsch working in the late 1950s (see Section 7.3.1) pioneered two solutions to this problem. One of these techniques [the Generescope (Ref. 7E)] was the precursor to other embodiments that also sought to eliminate the variable geometry problem. Additionally, researchers have developed optical arrangements such that the projection apparatus does not interfere with viewing freedom (see Section 7.3.2).

Several of the systems introduced in this chapter have employed a helical screen for image formation. As we have discussed, generally the characteristics offered by the planar and helical screen geometries tend to be superior to other configurations. However, this does not necessarily indicate that other forms of screen cannot be used—although one must be cautious in identifying possible weaknesses.

Finally, the patent filed by Irving Wolff in 1938 represents a landmark in merging a volumetric display technique with a radar system. Consequently, this patent has been discussed in some detail. The fact that this and other subsequent (and perhaps more practical) systems have not been widely adopted for applications of this type does not detract from the importance of the original pioneering research effort.

---

[32] Digital programmable hardware greatly facilitates the production of graphics within either a volumetric image space or on a conventional flat screen display. As discussed in Chapter 1, before the widespread proliferation of computer technologies this was a difficult undertaking. In this context it is interesting to quote once again from the Wolff patent: *"In some installations, for example in aircraft, it may be helpful to reproduce a space picture which has sight lines between angular representation and perspective. One suitable modification for this type of picture is shown in Fig. 6. The potentials from the sweep circuit generator are applied through capacitors 47 to a potentiometer 49. A second potentiometer 51 is connected through choke coils 53 to a battery 55. The two potentiometers 49, 51 are connected together. The scanning voltages are obtained by connections to the variable contacts 57, 59 which are moved in synchronism with the antenna horizontal sweep. The resulting cathode ray scanning pattern covers a trapezoidal pattern..."* Simple graphics could certainly be produced, but the design of necessary analog circuits required great ingenuity!

7.8   INVESTIGATIONS

1. Consider the display unit (Ref. 7C) described in Section 7.2.1 employing an exhaustive scanning technique. Here, the length of each line of the raster scan within an image slice is adjusted so as to approximately equal the length of the cord across the screen at the point at which the line is formed. Thus scan lines drawn close to the axis of rotation are longer than those drawn further away. This is reported as having been achieved by means of a variable gain amplifier. Does the use of a variable gain amplifier for this purpose represent an optimal solution and what (if any) would be the impact on image intensity? Are you able to suggest a better solution?

2. Consider an electron beam accelerated via an anode potential of 5000 volts. Calculate the speed of electrons within this beam. Assuming the use of a pair of electrostatic deflection plates of length 20 mm, calculate the time an electron within the beam would take to pass between these plates. What impact (if any) would this have on the high-frequency response of the deflection apparatus?

3. As mentioned in Section 7.2.1, Richard Ketchpel suggested the feasibility of employing a screen some 21 inches in diameter [Ketchpel, 1962]. Assuming the use of the exhaustive scan described in Section 7.2.1 comprising 64 lines per image slice, 128 image slices per screen rotation, and a rotational frequency of 15 Hz (with two refreshes per rotation), calculate the speed at which an electron beam must sweep across the screens surface. Compare this sweep speed to that of an electron beam employed within (a) an average CRT-based TV display and (b) a typical CRT-based high-resolution monitor. Does the scan speed needed to exhaustively sweep out the image space (when a 21-inch-diameter screen is used) appear to be practical?

4. Consider the screen shape employed by Albert Skellett and which is briefly described in Section 7.5.2. Identify key strengths and weaknesses of this approach. You should especially focus on the ability of the electron beam to effectively activate voxels on the surface of the screen and on any impact that the screen (semi-transparent) may have on the propagation of light to the observer.

5. Consider the display embodiment illustrated in Figure 7.19. Setting aside implementation issues and assuming the use of a planar screen, how could support for two degrees of freedom in screen motion be employed so as to largely eliminate voxel activation difficulties that occur close to the axis of rotation when only motion around a fixed axis is employed?

6. In relation to the system described by Irving Wolff in his 1938 patent and that is outlined in Section 7.6 consider the issue of image flicker. Could equipping the CRT with a longer persistence phosphor reduce flicker?

8 Highly Parallel Swept-Volume Systems

And sport and tilts and pleasure (for the time
Was maytime, and as yet no sin was dream'd,)
Rode under groves that look'd a paradise
Of blossom, over sheets of hyacinth
That seem'd the heavens upbreaking thro' the earth.

8.1 INTRODUCTION

In this, the last of the three chapters dealing with swept-volume display unit embodiments, we turn our attention to systems that employ rotational motion and exhibit a high degree of parallelism in the voxel activation subsystem. Such displays generally exhibit a 100% fill factor and may employ either passive or active voxel generation techniques. In the case that a passive surface of emission is adopted, the voxel generation beams are usually nondirected (i.e., not angularly deflected

Enhanced Visualization: Making Space for 3-D Images. By Barry G. Blundell
Copyright © 2007 John Wiley & Sons, Inc.

between voxel locations) and the use of conventional forms of beam deflection apparatus is therefore avoided.

Systems discussed here and in the previous chapter differ most significantly in terms of the degree of parallelism supported by the voxel activation subsystem. Although distinguishing between systems in this way is convenient, the results can be somewhat misleading—especially in the case of display embodiments that employ one or more CRTs from which images are projected into an image space (e.g., Refs. 7G, 7I, 7M). Although we consider that these approaches support sequential voxel activation, they could readily be adapted to support highly parallel voxel activation through the use of digital micromirror devices (DMDs) (see Section 8.3.2). Consequently, although we have chosen to distinguish between display units by reference to specific embodiments, it is important to remember that these may be advanced through the incorporation of other technologies, and the resulting systems may exhibit somewhat different characteristics. An example of this is provided in Section 8.5, where we refer to a patent filed in 1991 describing the incorporation of the DMD techniques into a display unit previously patented by Garcia and Williams. As a result, a system exhibiting a parallelism in voxel activation of approximately unity was readily advanced into a display possessing a high degree of parallelism in voxel activation.

In Section 8.2 we begin by considering display units that employ a planar screen and active surface of emission. In the case of such displays, the actual degree of parallelism that is demonstrated is usually determined by the addressing scheme used in the activation of the voxel generation elements. In this respect the designer has considerable freedom in the development of the interface between the graphics engine and display unit. Subsequently, in Section 8.3 we introduce exemplar display units that use a planar passive surface of emission addressed by a plurality of beam sources. Our discussion includes a brief overview of the Perspecta display system manufactured by Actuality Systems. Here, the use of DMDs supports a high degree of parallelism in voxel activation and therefore a very high voxel activation capacity (and 100% fill factor).

Having discussed planar screen embodiments, in Sections 8.4 and 8.5 we focus on systems that employ a helical form of screen (with both active and passive surfaces of emission). This leads on to discussion in Section 8.6 of an approach in which a helical screen is used in conjunction with a set of nondirected beam sources for voxel activation. As will be seen, by rotating both the screen and set of beam sources at different rates, we are able to reduce the number of beam sources needed to exhaustively address the image space.

Finally, in Section 8.7 we briefly consider the formation of volumetric images by means of a rapidly spinning lens.

8.2 THE PLANAR SCREEN AND ACTIVE SURFACE OF EMISSION

The implementation of display units that employ the rotational motion of an active surface of emission (SOE) introduces a number of interesting design challenges. For example:

1. The passage of the voxel activation signals to the rotating screen.

2. The fabrication of the screen, and particularly the occlusion of light that may be caused by voxel generation elements interposed between an active voxel location and the observer—that is, the minimization of the extent of the visual dead zone (see Section 4.7.3).

3. Minimization of screen mass.

4. The fabrication of any voxel addressing hardware that must co-rotate with the screen.

The first of the exemplar systems described in Section 4.2 employed the rotational motion of a planar screen equipped with an active surface of emission. Edwin Berlin (US Patent Number 4,160,973) adopted this approach (Ref. 8A); a diagram of the display unit described in his patent is reproduced in Figure 8.1. Here, the screen (1020B) employs either an array of LEDs or gas plasma display elements [in this latter case, Berlin describes the use of 256×128 elements and 128 image slices (sectors) per rotation (30 Hz)]. Thus, in principle, $\sim$4.2 million voxels may be activated during each image update period. If we assume that each voxel is represented by 4 bits per voxels (as indicated by Berlin), then this yields a maximum data rate of approximately 503 Mbits $\cdot$ s^{-1} (however, in reality, only a small number of available voxel locations would be activated during each image refresh). If the rectangular array of voxel generation elements are located at intervals of 1 mm, and assuming that the entire array is located on one side of the rotational axis (as indicated in Figure 8.1), then the resulting image space would be approximately 13 cm in radius and 26 cm in height.

As may be seen from Figure 8.1, the screen and co-rotating electronics (1007B) are driven by a motor (1006B) located below the image space. Power is passed to the rotating electronics (which includes approximately 2 Mbytes of image memory) via a conventional slipring commutator (1011B and 1011B$'$) and data via an infrared link.[1] Here, the transmitter and receiver (1009B and 1008B, respectively) are located centrally and pass the data along the axis of rotation. It is indicated that this provides a throughput of 1 MHz, thereby enabling the image data to be uploaded to the image memory in approximately 15 seconds (this assumes that every memory location is sequentially addressed—various opportunities exist for reducing this time).

The position of the rotating screen is determined by means of an optoelectronic sensor (1014B) attached to the base of the rotating hardware. A static element (1013B) interrupts the passage of light between the transmitter and receiver once per revolution; from this, the necessary timing information may be derived. Interestingly, Berlin did not return this position information to the host computer (the data transfer link being unidirectional).[2]

---

[1] See Section 11.5 for discussion on an alternative form of optical link.

[2] Naturally, the implementation of a bidirectional link would assist in debugging the rotating hardware system and, more importantly, would facilitate interaction opportunities.

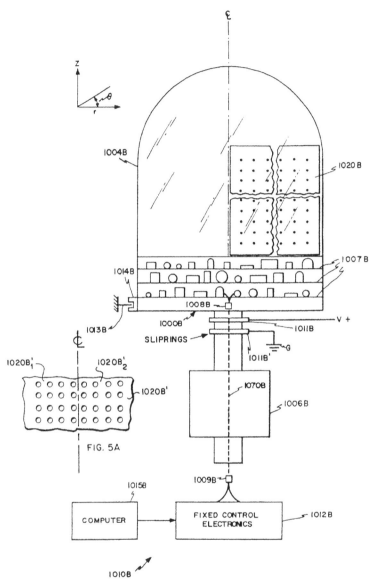

Figure 8.1   The display unit developed by Edwin P. Berlin and described in a patent filed in 1977. Here a rotating matrix of voxel generation elements are employed on the screen (1020B). Electronic circuitry (1007B) (including the image memory), co-rotates with the screen. Data are passed to this circuitry via a unidirectional IR link that is arranged along the axis of rotation (the transmitter is denoted as 1009B and the receiver as 1008B). The screen is described as being either located on a single side of the rotational axis or as symmetrically spanning this axis. (Reproduced from US Patent Number 4,160,973.)

A further embodiment employing the rotational motion of an active surface of emission is described by Coddington and Schipper [1962] (Ref. 8B). Here, an electroluminescent panel is employed to which voxel activation signals are passed via a commutator comprising 100 sliprings!

8.3 THE PLANAR SCREEN AND PASSIVE SURFACE OF EMISSION

I have not failed.
I've just found 10,000 ways that don't work.[3]

In the previous chapter, we considered display units that exhibit a low degree of parallelism in the voxel activation subsystem (typically unity). As we have discussed, such systems frequently employ one (or a small number) of directed beam sources for voxel activation. In the case that we wish to significantly increase the parallelism in voxel activation, the use of individually directed beam sources becomes impractical and it is preferable to employ either an array of nondirected beams or alternatively simultaneously deflect groups of beams. In this section we briefly consider several exemplar embodiments.

8.3.1 A Plurality of Scanned Beam Sources (Ref. 8C)

A patent filed in 1999 by LoRe, Favalora, and Glovinco (US Patent Number 5,936,767) describes a display unit that employs a linear array of light sources which are projected onto a rotating screen equipped with a passive surface of emission. As illustrated in Figure 8.2, these sources are simultaneously scanned at high speed across the image space.

In one embodiment, the inventors propose the use of some 32 laser diodes (denoted as elements 20 in Figure 8.2), the output from which are simultaneously scanned by reflection from an octagonal mirror (24) that rotates at high speed.[4] Images are created by suitably controlling the relative rotational rates of the screen and the multifaceted mirror, while at the same time modulating the light output from each of the laser diodes.[5] In the case that an octagonal mirror is used, then the maximum scan angle is $90°$. This is demonstrated in Figure 8.3. Here an octagonal mirror is illustrated in Figure 8.3a. Each face is able to reflect the beam as it moves through an angle of $45°$. In Figure 8.3b we illustrate a ray of light reflected from a

---

[3] Attributed to Thomas Alva Edison (1847–1931).

[4] In US Patent Number 5,936,767, it is indicated that as each set of scan lines are created, the screen moves less than $3°$. In the case where an octagonal mirror is used, this indicates that the mirror is rotating some 15 times faster than the screen. If 32 lines are drawn simultaneously, then the total number of scan lines created during each rotation of the screen (neglecting voxel placement and voxel elongation dead zones) would be ~3840.

[5] The author understands that one prototype was able to depict $64 \times 64 \times 64$ voxels on a Plexiglas screen equipped with a vellum layer. Screen dimensions being $\sim6 \times 4$ inches.

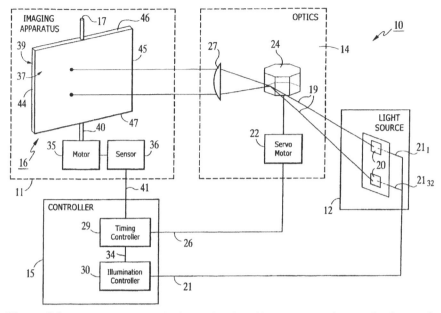

Figure 8.2 A display unit employing a plurality of beam sources that are simultaneously scanned and cast onto the rotating screen (46). Scanning is achieved through the use of a rotating multifaceted mirror (24). Naturally, the mirror must rotate more rapidly than the screen. See text for further details. (Reproduced from US Patent Number 6,183,008 B1.)

horizontally placed mirror (position 1). The angle of incidence of this ray (relative to the normal) is θ. The mirror is then rotated by an angle of 45° (position 2), and the incident ray now makes an angle of $\theta - 45$ with the normal of the newly positioned mirror. From the angles shown in the illustration, it is apparent that the angle Δ between the two reflected rays (denoted B and C) is 90°. More generally, for an n sided mirror the maximum scan angle is given by $720/n$. Although increasing the number of mirrored faces enables a greater number of scan lines to be formed per cycle of mirror rotation, it also has the adverse effect of reducing the extent of each scanned line.[6] As the screen rotates, its horizontal cross-section as measured from a single static viewpoint will continuously change and therefore the use of a scan of constant length will result in a varying proportion of each scan actually impinging on the screen. Furthermore, as the angle between the surface of the screen and the scanning device becomes more acute, voxel placement and elongation difficulties are likely to occur. As in the case of other display embodiments, the addition of an appropriately located second set of beam sources and scanner provides one solution to this problem.

---

[6] In the patent cited above, the inventors also discuss the use of two sets of scanned beam sources for voxel activation within a static-volume display.

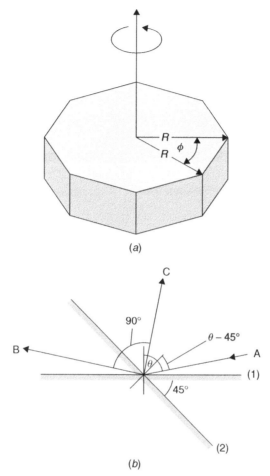

(a)

(b)

Figure 8.3   In (a) an octagonally shaped rotating mirror is illustrated. Each face of this mirror is able to scan the incident beam as the mirror moves through an angle of 45°. In (b), to readily determine the maximum beam deflection that may be produced by an octagonal mirror, we illustrate two mirrors. The first is shown located horizontally [position (1)] and the second tilted by 45° [position (2)]. These two mirrors correspond to a single face of the octagonal mirror illustrated in (a) as it moves through 45°. The incident ray is denoted as (A) and is reflected from the mirror when in position (1) along path (B). However, when the mirror is in position (2), the reflected ray follows path (C). If the angle of incidence with the mirror [in position (1)] is θ, then when the mirror is in position (2), the incident ray impinges on the mirror at an angle of θ-45 (relative to its normal). From the angles provided, it follows that the angle (Δ) between rays (B) and (C) equals 90°. (Figure (a) reproduced by permission from O'Shea [1985] © 1985 John Wiley & Sons.)

In another patent (US Patent Number 6,183,088 B1) the inventors use the above display paradigm as an exemplar embodiment and discuss a number of screen shapes intended to reduce the impact of the visual dead zone (see Section 4.7.3).

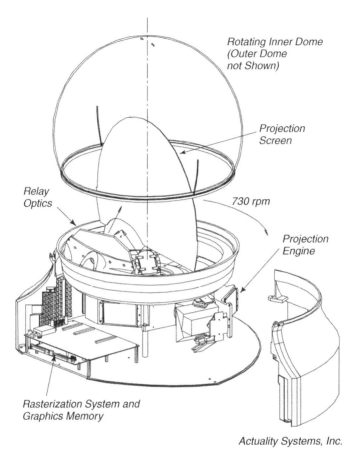

Actuality Systems, Inc.

Figure 8.4 The Perspecta display employing the rotational motion of a planar screen onto which image slices depicted by three DMDs are output. The spatially modulated beams are projected upwards onto optical components that co-rotate with the screen. (Reproduced by kind permission of Gregg Favalora, Actuality Systems Inc.).

8.3.2   The Perspecta Display (Ref. 8D)

Actuality Systems Inc. (USA) manufacture a swept-volume display called the Perspecta®. The general architecture of this display is illustrated in Figure 8.4. Three spatial light modulators (SLMs) (in the form of digital micromirror devices (DMDs) each comprising 1024×768 mirror elements[7]) are used for voxel activation. These generate spatially modulated RGB beams that are cast onto a planar rotating screen.[8]

---

[7] In fact, not all of these elements are used in the creation of image slices Favalora et al., 2002, each image slice being limited to 768×768 elements.

[8] The spatial modulation of a projected beam can be achieved in numerous ways and here DMDs provide a particularly elegant solution. Texas instruments initiated a research program in this area

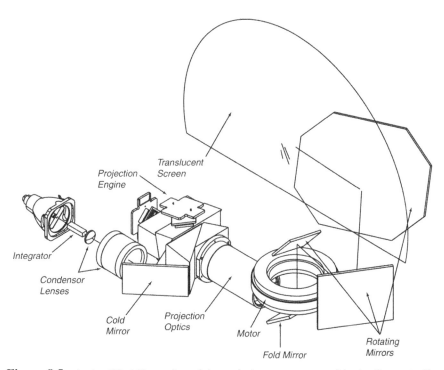

Figure 8.5   A simplified illustration of the optical components used in the Perspecta display. A high-pressure mercury arc lamp is employed as the light source, and three DMDs provide individual red, green and blue channels. The spatially modulated beams pass upward (axially) and are then projected onto the screen by co-rotating optical components (c.f. approaches reported in Section 7.3). Thus constant geometry is maintained between the spatially modulated beams and each image slice. (Reproduced by kind permission of Gregg Favalora, Actuality Systems Inc.)

In Figure 8.5 a diagram is provided showing a simplified layout of the optical system. Here, it may be seen that the light source (a 150-W ultra-high-pressure mercury arc lamp), SLMs, and various optical components are located below the image space and project the spatially modulated RGB beams axially onto a mirror

in the 1970s and by 1987 had developed the DMD. Over the coming years this was refined and was commercialized in 1996 in the form of Digital Light Processing™ technology [Dudley et al., 2003]. The basic principle of operation of a DMD is simple. The device comprises a planar 2-D array of tiny, closely spaced, square mirrors (sides ~ 16 μm), each of which can be individually addressed and made to tilt between two angular positions (e.g., $+12°$ and $-12°$). These mirrors are fabricated over a standard SRAM (static random access memory) chip and the mirrors can be latched into either of the two positions according the binary state of the SRAM cell located beneath each mirror. The movement of the mirrors is caused by the electric field existing between each mirror and the cell. A typical DMD may comprise 1024×768 mirrors and the application of such devices to volumetric systems makes it possible to achieve very high voxel activation capacities.

system that co-rotates with the screen (the rotating optical components follow the general basic approach described previously in Section 7.3 and maintain constant geometry between the projection apparatus an each image slice).

To ensure that viewing freedom of the image space is preserved, both the screen motor drive and optical components reside below the display volume. As may be seen from the illustration, an "open frame" motor is employed, enabling the light to pass upward through its center. The screen rotates at 24 Hz and is some 10 inches in diameter. The resulting image space is divided into 198 sectors, where each slice may contain 768×768 voxels. Thus the voxel activation capacity is approximately 116 million. This is made possible by the very high degree of parallelism supported by SLMs, which, in the case of the Perspecta, need only exhibit a frame rate of $24 \times 198 \sim 5$ kHz. The display unit is supported by a custom-built graphics engine (see Section 11.4) and associated software. More detailed discussion may be found in Favalora et al. [2001] and Favalora et al. [2002].[9]

8.3.3   Images Cast onto Rotating Mirrors

> *As a propaganda poster put it:*
> *"Dein Körper gehört dem Führer"...*
> *The president of Jena University...*
> *banned smoking on the campus*
> *and was known for snatching cigarettes*
> *from students' mouths.*[10]

The use of a rotating plane mirror is discussed in a patent filed in 1997 by Toshiyuki Sudo (US Patent Number 5,815,314) (Ref. 8E). In terms of the definition of the volumetric display paradigm used in this book, this does not truly represent a volumetric technique. However, it is included here because it is an interesting embodiment and may at first sight appear to represent a volumetric rather than a stereoscopic approach. The basic embodiment discussed in the patent employs a back-light LCD display on which image frames are depicted. These are projected onto, and reflected by, a rotating mirror (see Figure 8.6). A viewing window (7) defines the users view onto the rotating mirror (3). Figure 8.7 shows the basic light path in plan view. In this illustration, the instantaneous location of the mirror is at an angle of $45°$ to the optical axis of the projection apparatus. The projection apparatus (2) casts an image (22), and the reflection by the mirror (3) gives rise to an image that is brought to focus at (23). The technique operates by arranging the projection system in such a way as to ensure that views on an image are directed to the appropriate eye, as illustrated in Figure 8.8. Here, in (a), the instantaneous position of the mirror relative to the observer is such that the image is visible only to the left eye (42); at some short time later, the mirror lies at a position such that the

---

[9] Also see the Actuality Systems website (www.actuality-systems.com).

[10] Taken from Cornwell J., *Hitler's Scientists*, Penguin Books [2004]. Translation of the German: "Your body belongs to the Führer."

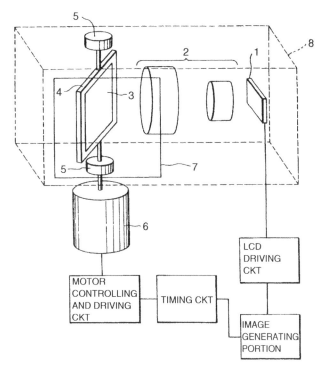

Figure 8.6   A display described by Toshiyuki Sudo in which images depicted on a back-light LCD display are cast onto a rotating mirror. The view of the LCD screen is restricted so that as the mirror rotates each eye is presented with a separate view (see Figure 8.8). (Reproduced from US Patent Number 5,815,314.)

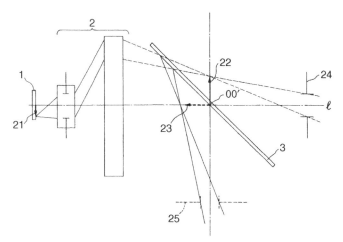

Figure 8.7   A plan view of the optical arrangement described by Toshiyuki Sudo. The image depicted on the LCD panel (21) is projected onto the rotating mirror (3). In this diagram, the mirror is shown at an angle of 45° to the optical axis of the projection system and image (23) is formed. (Reproduced from US Patent Number US Patent Number 5,815,314.)

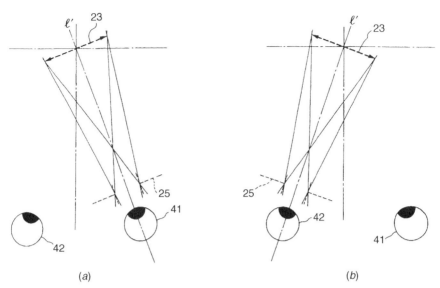

(a)   (b)

Figure 8.8 The image formation process ensures that each eye receives a different view onto the image scene. Thus in (a), the instantaneous position of the mirror relative to the observer's visual system is such that image (23) is visible only to the left eye. A short time later, the mirror has moved so that the image is now only visible to the right eye. Consequently, this represents a stereoscopic rather than a volumetric approach. (Reproduced from US Patent Number 5,815,314.)

image is visible only to the right eye (41), as indicated in diagram (b). Naturally, this approach will operate only if the extent of the viewing window is restricted. This display paradigm bears some similarities to two volumetric embodiments developed in the late 1960s and mid-1970s by Professor William [Simon, 1969; Simon and Walters, 1977]. Although both of these systems restrict viewing freedom and support only sequential voxel activation, they are included here so that they may be readily compared with the technique discussed above. The approach outlined in the earlier of these two publications (Ref. 8F) is illustrated in Figure 8.9.

As may be seen from this diagram, when the mirror lies at exemplar positions A, B, and C, the reflection of the face of the CRT (and image data depicted on it), will appear to originate from the three indicated locations. A virtual image space may therefore be defined. As a consequence of the continually varying geometry between mirror and CRT screen, this approach exhibits a sweep efficiency that is considerably less than 100%. Simon indicates the use of a PDP-8 for monitoring mirror position and outputting image data to the CRT, the use of a two-sided brass mirror and suggests the possible adoption of a multi-sided mirror as a means of reducing image flicker for a given rate of rotation. The system was used to depict vector electrocardiograms.

Simon recognized the difficulty of photographing volumetric images (see Section 1.6.1) and in this context writes:

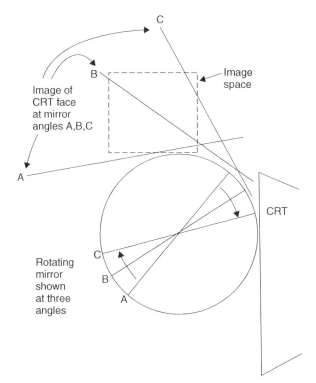

Figure 8.9   The spinning mirror technique developed by Professor William Simon. Here, a rotating mirror reflects image slices depicted via a CRT. The mirror provides an image space whose volume is less than that swept out by the rotating mirror. (Reproduced by permission from Simon [1969] © 1969 The Psychonomic Society.)

It must be realised that the image produced by this method is truly three-dimensional. Thus it cannot be photographed in the usual sense without losing its three-dimensional quality. An illustrative stereo-pair can be photographed....

The approach outlined above was significantly refined and is described in a subsequent publication Simon and Walters, 1977 (Ref. 8G). Here, as indicated in Figure 8.10, a mirror is mounted on the end of a diagonally sliced rotating cylinder.

Rotation is around the axis of the cylinder and the principal direction of observation is along the axis (a wide variety of others are possible) so that the edge of the mirror is never within the field of view. The axial view produces a three-dimensional image which is visible over a much wider range of observer positions than was the case with the previous design. [Simon and Walters, 1977]

Additionally, unlike the previous approach, the observer's own reflection does not become visible as the mirror rotates. In connection with one embodiment, the researchers indicate the use of an aluminum cylinder 6 inches in diameter and a rotation frequency of 10 Hz. Naturally, the mirror cannot reflect images during its

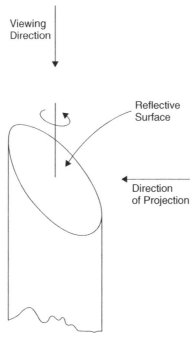

Figure 8.10 The display paradigm discussed by Simon and Walters [1977]. Here, a mirrored surface is mounted on the end of a diagonally sliced cylinder. Image data depicted on a conventional flat screen display are reflected by the rotating mirrored surface leading to images appearing to originate from an image space formed below the mirror.

entire rotational cycle; in fact, image data can be output for only ~20 ms during each rotation. The sweep efficiency is therefore somewhat restricted. However, the researchers indicate a voxel activation capacity of ~1000. The display unit was evaluated using both a PDP-9 computer driving a HP1300A display and a Z-80[11] microprocessor system linked to an oscilloscope display operating in XY mode.

In their conclusion and in relation to the volumetric approach, the researchers write:

> *It is difficult to describe the subjective effect of viewing a true three-dimensional computer display. Most people feel initially that it must be a psychophysical trick. Except for persistence of vision, it is not. The display really is three-dimensional. It provides a large field of view as well as a large depth of field, and provides the appearance of displayed points "hanging" in space. It has, however, one serious drawback, which is that only transparent structures can be displayed. In some cases, such as the display of molecules, this is desirable. . . . Fortunately, there are many such transparent structures of interest as computer outputs.*

---

[11] The Z-80 is an 8-bit microprocessor that became very popular in the 1970s and was used for many control applications.

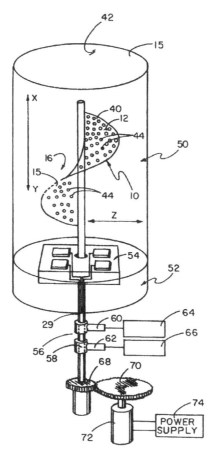

Figure 8.11   A display unit employing a helical screen equipped with an array of light emitting components such as LED's or field emission devices. (Reproduced from US Patent Number 6,115,006.)

8.4   THE HELICAL SCREEN AND ACTIVE SURFACE OF EMISSION (REF. 8H)

A patent filed in 1997 by Gregory Brotz (US Patent Number 6,115,006) briefly outlines a proposal for a display unit employing the rotational motion of a helical screen equipped with an array of voxel generation elements. The use of both LEDs and field emission devices is discussed.[12] A diagram of the display unit is reproduced in Figure 8.11. As may be seen, control hardware (54) co-rotates with the screen, with signals and power being passed via brushes (60) and (62) to slip

[12] Relatively little work has been undertaken in investigating the opportunities that may be derived from the use of field emission devices in the implementation of the voxel generation subsystem. This is an area in which interesting opportunities exist.

rings (56) and (58); the use of an optical link(s) for signal transfer does not appear to be considered. The patent tends to discuss general issues and practical implementation details are not provided. Consequently, it is difficult to confidently assess the screen's complexity, mass and the level of obstruction that it may impose on the passage of light through the image space.

8.5 THE HELICAL SCREEN AND PASSIVE SURFACE OF EMISSION

In a patent filed in 1998 (US Patent Number 6,064,423) several approaches to the implementation of volumetric display units that employ a helical form of screen addressed by a large number of nondeflected beam sources are outlined (Ref. 8I). As with some other patents filed in relatively recent times in connection with volumetric display system architectures, it is difficult to accurately assess the extent to which the patent reports on concepts that have already been implemented by the inventor, as opposed to a collection of ideas whose viability has at the time of filing still to be determined.[13]

In the first embodiment, a light source is passed through several optical components before being reflected by a spatial light modulator (SLM) as illustrated in Figure 8.12a. As may be seen from the diagram, the light from source (1) is cast onto the SLM via a beam splitter (4) and the SLM serves to spatially modulate the beam. Subsequently, this beam is projected [via lens system (7)] onto a rotating helical screen. To create meaningful images, the signals passed to the SLM must be synchronized with the instantaneous location of the helix. This embodiment is referred to by the inventor as a "front projection system" since "...*images are projected onto the rotating helix surface from the same side as viewers view the 3D images.*" In a further embodiment, the use of a large array of vertical cavity surface emitting lasers (VCSELs) is proposed (see Figure 8.12b). In this configuration, rather than achieving the spatial modulation of a beam by reflection from an SLM, the spatial modulation is directly provided by an array of light sources (40). In this illustration (41) represents a micro-lens array used to project the beam onto the surface of the helix.

Both embodiments provide (at least in principle) a method of achieving exhaustive addressing of an image space without the need to scan the voxel activation beams. Without more details of the projection systems [(7) and (41)] it is difficult to determine the extent to which voxels generated within the image space will remain evenly focused.

---

[13] For example, in connection with a discussion on the use of a 2-D array of vertical cavity surface emitting lasers (VCSELs), the inventor writes "*A 8 × 8 VCSEL array has been introduced to the market .... Large arrays on the order of 512 × 512 can be envisioned.... Since the VCSELs can be grown in high density on semiconductor chips, the VCSEL/Helix design has the potential of producing a very high spatial resolution for volumetric 3D display.*" Although such comments are useful, the extent to which the inventor has actually incorporated VCSELs into a volumetric display is unclear.

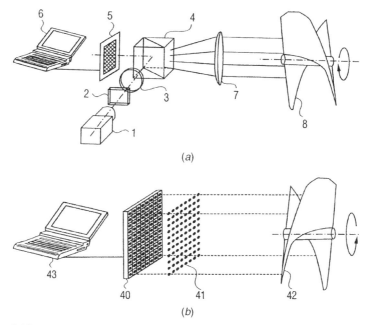

Figure 8.12   Diagram (a) illustrates a display unit in which a light source is projected onto an SLM (5). The reflected (spatially modulated) light is cast [via optical system (7)] onto a rotating helical screen. In principle such an arrangement enables exhaustive addressing and so a 100% fill factor—without the need for beam deflection. In diagram (b) we illustrate a suggested embodiment in which a spatially modulated beam is created directly via an array of light source elements [vertical cavity surface emitting lasers (VCSELs) are suggested by the inventor for this purpose.] (Reproduced from US Patent Number 6,064,423.)

In an earlier patent (filed in 1991) by Earle Thompson and Thomas DeMond, assigned to Texas Instruments Incorporated (US Patent Number 5,162,787), the use of SLMs for the production of both flat screen and volumetric images is described in some detail. In the case of the volumetric embodiment (Ref. 8J), the spatially modulated beam is cast onto a rotating helical screen[14] (cf. the Perspecta system that is outlined in Section 8.3.2 and that employs the use of DMDs in conjunction with a rotating planar screen). A diagram showing a projection arrangement for use in conjunction with a static planar screen is provided in Figure 8.13. Here, the light from source (10) is collimated and cast onto an SLM employing a DMD. This selectively redirects portions of the incident light along path (6). This beam passes through an enlarger lens (5) before arriving at the screen (2). As the inventors indicate, this general arrangement is suitable for use not only in conjunction with a static planar screen (so supporting a conventional display tableau) but also with a rotating helical screen, thereby allowing the production of volumetric images.

---

[14] Of the type that was previously discussed by Garcia and Williams in their HL3D system (US Patent Number 5,042,909), see Section 7.4.

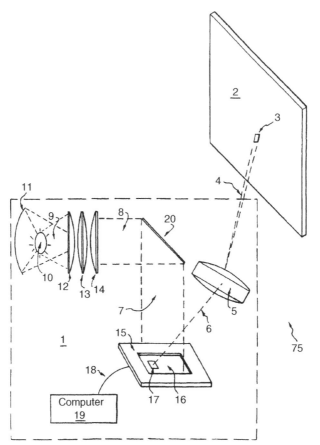

Figure 8.13 Illustrating an optical arrangement in which collimated light from source (10) is cast onto a DMD type SLM, (15). The micro-mirrors selectively reflect light along path (6). This spatially modulated beam is projected onto a static planar screen (2) by enlarging lens (5) so giving rise to a conventional 2-D tableau. (Reproduced from US Patent Number 5,162,787.)

8.6 THE RELATIVE ROTATIONS OF A SCREEN AND AN ARRAY OF LIGHT SOURCES

In Section 7.4 we discussed display units that employ a helical screen equipped with a passive surface of emission and that use one or more directed beam sources for voxel activation. In this section we briefly refer to a technique used by the author that enables the helical screen to be employed in conjunction with a plurality of nondirected beams, and in which the number of beam sources may be minimized.[15]

---

[15] Also see discussion in Blundell and Schwarz [2000].

Consider the configuration illustrated in Figure 8.14a in which a plurality of nondirected beam sources[16] (arranged in a series of concentric circles) are located below a helical screen (Ref. 8K). It is readily apparent that, for a given display resolution, the number of sources needed to address the helix approximately increases in proportion to the square of the radius of the helical screen. Thus, increasing the radius by a factor of 3 will increase the number of elements in the array by a factor of ~9. Consequently, to reduce the number of elements, it is desirable to restrict the radius of the screen. Unfortunately, the helix is particularly suited to the creation of image spaces whose height is significantly less than the diameter. Thus if we restrict the radius of the image space so as to limit the number of elements within the voxel activation subsystem, we also restrict the image space height. One solution to this difficulty is to introduce rotational motion to the voxel activation array such that the helix and array rotate at different rates. The relative motion of these two components enables a reduction in the number of voxel activation sources without compromising minimum inter-voxel spacing. For example, let us assume that the helix rotates at an angular velocity of ω and the array of voxel activation sources with an angular velocity of 2ω. Then, in principle (assuming that the light-emitting elements offer sufficient bandwidth), we could now replace the series of concentric circular arrangements of sources with the single linear array indicated in Figure 8.14b. In practice, such a reduction may place unrealistic demands on the light sources responsible for the creation of voxels toward the outer circumference of the helix. For example, consider the use of a helical screen with a radius of 30 cm rotating at 30 Hz. Assuming that the minimum spacing of voxels along each circular track is 1 mm, then the outermost light-emitting element would be responsible for the production of ~1880 voxels. Since we have assumed that the array of light-emitting elements rotate at twice the angular velocity of the screen, then it follows that these voxels must be output in 1/60th second—providing a time of less than 9 μs for the production of each voxel. Naturally, as the image space diameter is increased, additional voxel activation elements would be required in the outer tracks. The practical implementation of such an approach may be facilitated by causing the screen and array to rotate at the same rate—but in opposite directions.[17] (See US patent Application Number US 2002/0140631 A1 for general discussion.)

The relative motion of an array of light-emitting elements may be further extended by increasing the speed of rotation of the array and offsetting the two axes of rotation. In this way, the number of concentric rings of light-emitting elements may, in principle, be reduced.[18]

---

[16] These may take the form of, for example, laser diodes or be derived via an SLM.

[17] The author has prototyped a basic display unit to evaluate this general approach. For details of a suitable high bandwidth optical data transfer link, see Section 11.5.

[18] The author has not evaluated this approach.

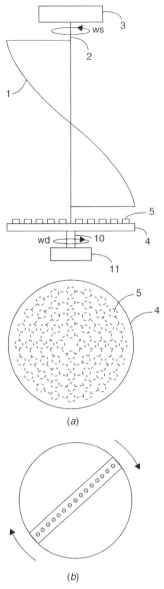

(a)

(b)

Figure 8.14 In (a) we illustrate a helical screen below which a set of light emitting elements are arranged in a series of concentric circles. The output from each of these elements is projected onto the surface of the screen and so by appropriately controlling the output from each element, voxels may be formed within the cylindrical image space. By rotating the array at a different angular velocity to that of the screen, the number of elements in each of the concentric circles may be reduced (without compromising minimum voxel separation). Figure (b) shows the limiting case in which the voxel activation subsystem comprises a linear array of rotating elements. [Diagram (a) reproduced from US Patent Application Number US 2002/0140631 A1.]

8.7   THE SPINNING LENS APPROACH

In this and the previous two chapters, we have encountered swept-volume systems utilizing the translational motion of a planar screen, the rotational motion of planar, helical, and other screen shapes, systems that exploit the benefits that may be derived through the relative motion of both the screen and the voxel activation mechanisms, and even an embodiment in which the screen is able to move with two degrees of freedom. Without a doubt, great ingenuity has been applied to the development of these displays, and it is appropriate to end this discussion of swept-volume embodiments by referring to a particularly interesting and elegant technique in which a rotating lens is used to create volumetric images in "free space".

This approach is described in a patent filed by Bernard Ciongoli in 1985 (US Patent Number 4,692,878) and is further discussed in various brief articles such as *Electronics* [1985], *IEEE Spectrum* [1987], and Fajans [1992].

Central to this technique is a converging lens that rapidly rotates about an axis which lies normal to the lens' principal axis (see Figure 8.15). Image data points are depicted on a 2-D screen (such as a CRT or back-light LCD panel)[19] and are projected by the lens into an image space that appears to be located between the spinning lens and observer. Consequently, the location of a voxel within the image space is determined by the position of the corresponding point of light depicted on the planar screen and the instantaneous angular position of the lens. Ciongoli writes:

> *The relationship between 3-D dixel locations and the 2-D pixel locations and the corresponding Δt (flash time) for each pixel can be easily and accurately approximated empirically by measuring the extreme location at which dixels appear in 3-D space with respect to maximum/minimum x, y pixel locations at maximum/minimum viewable Δt's and interpolating the remaining pixel locations $(x\text{-}y)$, and flash time (Δt), versus the corresponding dixel location $(X,Y$ and Z or depth). Only the 8 extreme pixel and corresponding dixel point locations need be measured. The remaining tens of thousand of pixel/dixel relationships can be interpolated by a calibration procedure or computer program.*[20]

In his patent Ciongoli provides the equations that enable, for a given angular position of the lens, points (x,y) depicted on the 2-D screen to be mapped into corresponding points (X,Y,Z) within the image space. In connection with image quality Fajans [1992] writes:

> *Displays are bright and not only tolerate ambient illumination, but are actually enhanced by it. Sperical aberration does not affect display sharpness, because the eye accepts only a small bundle of light rays. However, sperical aberration does cause distortion if the observer moves far off axis. Displays with 10^4 3-D pixels have been generated.*

---

[19] Alternatively, a DMD could be used.

[20] For "dixel read voxel."

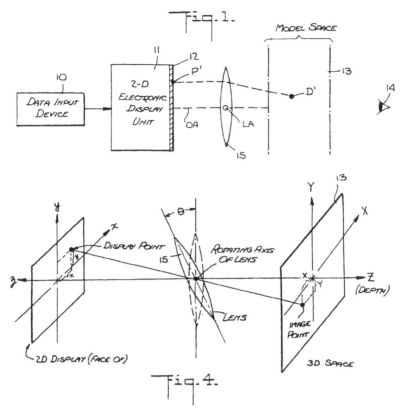

Figure 8.15 In (a), an overview of the apparatus employed in the rotating lens technique is provided. This approach enables data points depicted on a 2-D screen (12) to be projected into a "free-space" display volume (13). In (b) a data point displayed on the 2-D screen is projected to a corresponding point within the image space. The location of a point illuminated on the 2-D display coupled with the instantaneous angular location of the lens determines the position of the corresponding point within the image space. (Reproduced from US Patent Number 4,692,878.)

8.8 DISCUSSION

> *No! let me taste the whole of it, fare like my peers,*
> *The heroes of old,*
> *Bear the brunt, in a minute pay glad life's arrears*
> *Of pain, darkness and cold.*
> *For sudden the worst turns the best to the brave.*[21]

The exemplar display units that we have briefly considered here and in the previous two chapters highlight the rich diversity of techniques and great ingenuity that has been applied to the implementation of swept-volume systems. As we have seen,

[21] Robert Browning (1812–1889), "Prospice".

since the pioneering work of John Logie Baird some 75 years ago, every decade has given rise to new techniques and to the re-examination/re-invention of earlier systems. Despite such major efforts, practically all of these systems have failed to evolve from laboratory prototype to commercial product. This does not reflect inherent weaknesses of the swept-volume paradigm, although it is important to acknowledge that no system is without fault—the "perfect" swept-volume display does not exist! However, many of the systems that have been prototyped could significantly advance the human–computer interface, particularly in situations where there is great need for techniques able to facilitate the visualization and interaction processes.

In assessing the strengths and weakness of a display technique, it is important that careful reference be made to the intended application or range of applications. Consequently, for example, the displays described in this chapter that generally support a very high degree of parallelism in voxel activation are not necessarily superior to those discussed in the previous chapter for which voxel activation equals (or is close to) unity. For example, in the case of some applications, image space dimensions and display cost may be more important criteria than voxel activation capacity. Similarly, the display systems discussed in Chapter 6 which restrict viewing freedom are not necessarily inferior—as we have already discussed, support for essentially unrestricted viewing freedom imposes various constraints on display usage and therefore is not necessarily a panacea.

In the next chapter, we outline a number of exemplar static-volume display units. As will be apparent, the ingenuity and effort that has been applied to the implementation of swept-volume systems is paralleled by that which has been applied to systems that place no reliance on motion for the formation of an image space.

8.9 INVESTIGATIONS

1. In the case of the display paradigms developed by Simon [1969] and Simon and Walters [1977] and that are outlined in Section 8.3.3, discuss issues that restrict viewing freedom.

2. The display embodiments described in Section 8.3.3 (Refs. 8F and 8G) employ very simple hardware and can be prototyped with minimal cost. Assemble one of these displays and use it to gain a better insight into the volumetric approach. (An analysis of the relationship between the location of a data point on the display screen, the instantaneous position of the mirrored surface, and the apparent location of the point in the image space may be found in Simon and Walters [1977].)

3. The swept-volume embodiments introduced in Chapter 7 exhibit a low degree of parallelism in the voxel activation process ($P \sim 1$). Select two of these systems and identify techniques that may be used so as to enable them to support a very high degree of parallelism in voxel activation.

4. Discuss the issues that determine the extent of the image space generated by means of the "spinning lens" technique that is briefly outlined in Section 8.7.

.

9 Static-Volume Systems: Example Implementations

He left the barren-beaten thoroughfare,
Chose the green path that show'd the
rarer foot,
And here among the solitary downs,
Full often lost in fancy, lost his way.

9.1 INTRODUCTION

Here, we build on discussion presented in Chapter 5 and outline various exemplar static-volume display embodiments which, as we have seen, place no reliance on mechanical motion for image space formation. As with our discussion of swept-volume systems, these displays are not introduced according to their chronological place within an evolutionary process but are grouped according to certain technical considerations relating to the techniques used in the implementation of the subsystems that comprise each display. In this way, we bring together technologies

Enhanced Visualization: Making Space for 3-D Images. By Barry G. Blundell
Copyright © 2007 John Wiley & Sons, Inc.

that share broadly similar technical attributes, and seek to emphasize that many of the older systems do not necessarily represent mere historical curios.

The earliest static-volume system that the author has located is discussed in a patent that was filed in 1912 (see Section 9.5). Despite extensive researches, the author has been unable to locate any other discussion of this display modality prior to the description contained in the patent filed in 1931 by John Logie Baird (see Section 6.3.1). It was not until the late 1950s and early 1960s that research into static-volume systems began to be undertaken on a significant scale; since then, display embodiments have been researched, invented, and re-invented on a fairly regular basis. The displays previously introduced in Chapter 5 and those discussed here have been selected to best highlight aspects of this display technique—by no means does this account purport to provide a comprehensive discussion of all approaches that have been developed to date.

In the next section we consider systems that employ an active matrix of voxel generation elements and re-emphasize the difficulties that are associated with this seemingly straightforward approach. Subsequently, in Section 9.3 we provide two examples of static-volume embodiments in which voxel activation can be achieved by means of one or more nonintersecting beam sources. Here, we encounter a particularly ingenious solution in which a cloud of moving dust particles are used for voxel generation. In Section 9.4, we briefly outline the principle of operation of the DepthCube™ (this is a commercially available static-volume display system manufactured by LightSpace Technologies).

The activation of voxels by means of two intersecting beams was previously discussed in Section 5.6, and in Section 9.5 we provide additional examples of displays that employ this general approach. Finally, in Section 9.6 we briefly discuss two systems able to generate a series of parallel image planes (depth planes) by means of a plurality of 2-D display screens and beam splitters.

9.2 THE USE OF AN ACTIVE MATRIX OF VOXEL GENERATION ELEMENTS

In this section we briefly introduce several display unit architectures that employ a 3-D array of active voxel generation elements. As discussed in Chapter 5, there are four basic problems associated with the implementation of display units of this type. In summary, these are:

1. Accommodating the rapid growth of voxel generation elements that occurs as the image space dimensions are increased (without compromising the minimum inter-voxel spacing, and hence the resolution supported by the display).

2. The incorporation within the image space of a large number of voxel generation elements (and associated connections) in such a way that they do not interfere with the passage of light (especially in terms of anisotropic attenuation and/or refraction).

3. The fabrication of an image space comprising a very large number of voxel generation elements and associated connections. This would usually necessitate the use of automated production techniques, which would probably only be financially feasible if a display embodiment were to be produced in large numbers.

4. Fabricating the connections between the large number of voxel generation elements and the graphics engine.

In the subsections that follow, we review four indicative embodiments. Further details of displays of this type can be found in Blundell and Schwarz [2000], or in the references cited in relation to specific approaches.

9.2.1   From Bulbs to Gas Discharge

In Section 5.2 we referred to a proposal made by Nithiyanandam in his 1975 publication for the implementation of an image space comprising a 3-D matrix of light emitting elements. In fact, the use of a 3-D array of small lamps forms a central theme to a patent filed in 1969 (US Patent Number 3,636,551), and a very similar scheme was proposed some years earlier by Martin Ruderfer (US Patent Number 2,749,480, filed in 1952). In this latter patent the inventor begins by suggesting the use of a 3-D matrix of bulbs. However, he recognized the negative impact that their presence would have on the visible image and writes "... *using lamps ... which would cause distortion of the light from lamps furthest from the observer when there are many lamps ...*". Consequently, the use of a matrix of bulb filaments contained within an image space filled with an inert gas is proposed. Finally, the inventor suggests a more practical scheme involving the use of gas discharge elements. Here, as illustrated in Figure 9.1, two sets of orthogonally positioned wires pass through an image space filled with, for example, neon gas.[1] The application of a potential between two appropriate wires will then cause a discharge to occur within the region at which they pass with closest proximity. Given the use of wires of minimal thickness, this provides a workable scheme.[2] For a cubic image space comprising n^3 voxel generation elements, $2n^2$ connections are required and will, support a parallelism in voxel activation of at least n.

9.2.2   A Gas Discharge Display

Approximately two years after Ruderfer filed his patent, Robert Fryklund described the use of a similar technique (US Patent Number 2,762,031) in which (as illustrated

---

[1] As discussed in Section 6.3.1, Baird had suggested the use of a similar scheme based on gas discharge nearly 30 years earlier. However, unlike Ruderfer, Baird incorporated motion into the image space subsystem so ensuring that the number of voxel generation elements needed did not increase with the cube of the image space dimensions.

[2] This provides an image space that would give rise to only minor refraction (at its boundary). However, the maintenance of constant tension on the conductors would be an important consideration otherwise it would be necessary to incorporate supporting structures within the image space.

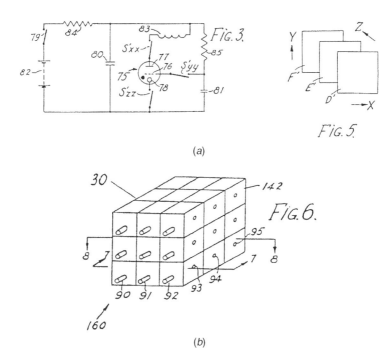

(a)

(b)

Figure 9.1 Two approaches proposed by Martin Ruderfer. In (a) the addressing of an image space comprising a set of small gas discharge lamps is illustrated. In (b) discharges are produced by the application of appropriate voltages to two sets of orthogonally located conductors (labelled 90, 91, 92 and 93, 94, and 95 in the illustration). The image space is filled with an appropriate gas at low pressure (e.g., neon). This removes the need to employ separate lamps and therefore improves image visibility. (Reproduced from US Patent Number 2,749,480.)

in Figure 9.2) a set of conducting rods (27) pass through holes within a series of planar screens [approximating to coarse wire meshes (31)].[3] Here, the display volume is to be viewed from a single face (28) and is filled with a low-pressure gas such as neon. The application of a suitable potential between a rod and planar screen results in a visible gas discharge in the region at which the rod passes through the screen.

Interestingly, as may be seen from the illustration, the size of the screens is gradually reduced with distance from the viewing window and hence the rods lie in closer proximity. Fryklund writes *"The screens are shown diminishing in size as they proceed to the right. This is to give the effect of perspective due to beam convergence."* and provides us with a sound example of our ability to exaggerate

---

[3] See also Balasubramonian et al. [1981] for interesting discussion on another display unit employing gas discharge for voxel generation.

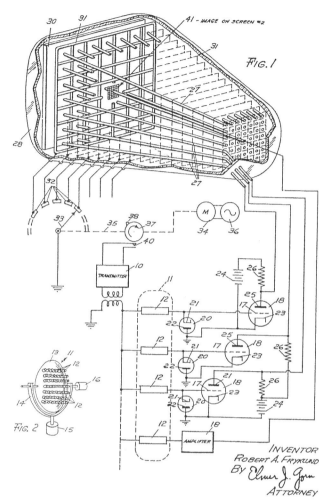

Figure 9.2 A display unit employing gas discharge for voxel generation. The application of a voltage between an appropriate conductor (27) and coarse mesh screen (31) gives rise to a visible gas discharge in the region at which the rod and screen are in closest proximity. The screens become smaller (and the rods are more closely spaced) with distance from the viewing window so as to exaggerate the linear perspective cue. (Reproduced from US Patent Number 2,762,031.)

the linear perspective cue (see Section 2.3.1) when we confine the viewer to a single window into the image space.

9.2.3 An Optical Fiber Technique

Rather than route electronic voxel activation signals into an image space, Duncan MacFarlane describes a novel technique involving the use of a large number optical fibers [MacFarlane, 1994; MacFarlane and Schultz, 1994]. Here, each fiber is able to give rise to a single voxel, and the activation of each voxel is achieved by passing light (e.g., ultraviolet) down an appropriate fiber. This impinges on a fluorescent material located at the fiber ending which fluoresces, thereby producing the visible voxel. Naturally, the presence of a large number of optical fibers within the image space can be potentially problematic in respect of the propagation of light. In relation to this MacFarlane writes:

> *To eliminate stray Fresnel reflections off the different glass to air surfaces which may distort an image, we fill the voids between the voxels with an index matching medium. Our prototypes built thus far have relied on liquid index (or more generally "impedance") matching solutions. In particular, we have eliminated multiple reflections by using either a custom blend of Dow–Corning Silicone oils or a commercial product (Cargille Immersion liquid).*

Further details of this are provided in MacFarlane [1994].[4] The controlled passage of light into the fiber-optic bundle is achieved using a spatial light modulator in the form of a rear-light LCD display panel. Naturally, as with other static-volume display units employing a matrix of active voxel generation elements, the production of large image space volumes able to depict high-resolution images is dependent on the use of automated assembly techniques; this, in turn, requires significant initial investment. In Section 12.6 we refer to a derivative technique which aims to reduce the number of fibers within an image space (without compromising the voxel activation capacity) and simplifies the voxel activation process.

9.2.4   A Stack of LCD Panels Illuminated with Polarized Light

An interesting approach to the implementation of a static-volume display unit is outlined in a patent filed by Martin Leung in 1995 (US Patent Number 5,745,197). The technique is illustrated in Figure 9.3, where it may be seen that the image space is formed using a stack of LCD panels (10a–10d), through which polarized light is projected. Each element within each panel may be individually addressed, and addressing one or more elements within a panel will result in a change in the polarization of the transmitted light. Such changes are made visible through the use of a second polarizing filter (14a) via which the observer views the volumetric image (i.e., the display provides a single "window" onto the image space). Unfortunately, the patent does not appear to provide details of the refresh rate or of the voxel activation capacity (although the use of LCD panels able to depict 640×480 elements is mentioned as an example in connection with the addressing scheme).[5]

---

[4] Also see Blundell and Schwarz [2000] for summary discussion.

[5] Also, the patent does not appear to quantify the number of panels used or the approximate image space depth.

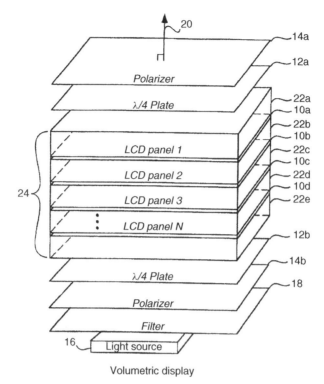

Volumetric display

Figure 9.3 In this embodiment, a stack of LCD panels are used to form an image space—these being sandwiched between two polarizing filters. Light entering the image space passes through a polarizing filter (14b). Addressing elements within an LCD panel will result in a change of the polarization of light transmitted through the panel in the addressed regions and, due to the presence of polarizer (14a) this will cause a change in the intensity of light emerging from the image space. (Reproduced from US Patent Number 5,745,197.)

9.3 VOXEL ACTIVATION USING DIRECTED BEAM SOURCE(S)

> *There are three classes of people: Those who see.*
> *Those who see when they are shown.*
> *Those who do not see.*[6]

Many beam addressed static-volume display units achieve voxel activation at the intersection of two directed beams (see Sections 5.6 and 9.5). However, a small number of embodiments achieve voxel activation through the use of a single directed beam (or small number of beams) that are individually able to stimulate voxel production. Here, we provide two examples of displays of this sort.

---

[6] Attributed to Leonardo Da Vinci.

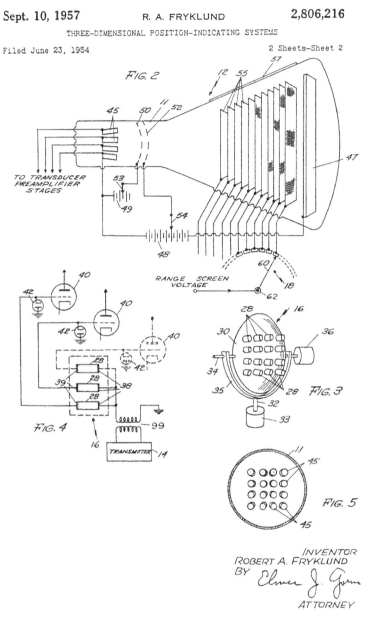

Sept. 10, 1957   R. A. FRYKLUND   2,806,216

THREE-DIMENSIONAL POSITION-INDICATING SYSTEMS

Filed June 23, 1954   2 Sheets–Sheet 2

Figure 9.4   A display unit designed for use in an echo based position-indicating system. Here, a plurality of electron beams are used. These pass through a number of phosphor coated mesh screens on the route to anode (47). By applying a positive potential to a particular screen and gating all but one of the beams, a voxel may be activated at a particular location within the image space. Naturally the presence of the screens would have been likely to negatively impact on image visibility. Furthermore, some beam current would be lost to each of the screens. Consequently, voxels activated further to the right hand side may have been less intense. (Reproduced from US Patent Number 2,806,216.)

9.3.1 Electron Beams and a Series of Screen Meshes

A patent filed in 1954 by Robert Fryklund[7] describes a novel approach to the implementation of a static-volume display for use as part of an echo based position-indicating system (US Patent Number 2,806,216). The display unit discussed in the patent is illustrated in Figure 9.4 and employs a plurality of electron beam sources (45), the beam currents of which can be individually controlled.[8] These beams are accelerated toward an anode (47) and pass through a number of phosphor coated screen meshes. Through the application of a positive potential to a particular mesh, the electron beam will impinge more strongly on a region of the mesh and thereby cause the phosphor coating to emit light.

The image space is viewed from the side, but despite this viewing restriction, it is likely that the presence of the meshes would have caused some visual obstruction. The number of electron beams used in this system corresponds to the number of transducers employed in the position-indicating array, and so the use of beam deflection apparatus may be avoided. In relation to previous discussion concerning the difficulties of interfacing image capture and display systems prior to the proliferation computer-based and electronic technologies (see Section 1.2.2), this provides us with a further example of the need to match the output characteristics of the data capture system with those of the display unit.

9.3.2 An Image Space Comprising Dust Particles

A patent filed in 2003 by Kenneth Perlin and Jefferson Han (US Patent Application Number US 2004/0218148 A1) describes and ingenious approach to the implementation of a static-volume display. The apparatus discussed in this patent is illustrated in Figure 9.5. The image space is formed from dust particles (8) moving in air—in relation to which the inventors write:

> ... the "display volume" in which the object appears contains a concentration of moving dust particles 8. The dust particles 8 can be relatively large, on the order of 0.5–1.0 millimeter in length.... In practice, good visual results have been achieved using lint particles.... The cloud of particles 8 can be relatively sparse so that the individual particles 8 are not visible to the unaided eye under normal lighting conditions.

The dust particles are in constant motion as they pass through the image space, and the use of "air curtain" technology confines the particles within the image space region. A voxel may be activated when a scanning (visible) laser beam (the laser is denoted as 2 in Figure 9.5, and 5 denotes the scanning apparatus) impinges on individual particles. For image formation to be possible, the graphics engine must be able to determine the instantaneous positions of each of the continually moving particles. This is achieved by means of a second, nonvisible (infrared) laser beam [derived from source (1)] that also scans the image space (the visible and nonvisible beams are

---

[7] See also Section 9.2.2.

[8] In this embodiment, the use of multiple beams is intended to avoid the need for beam deflection apparatus. This would have simplified the complexity of the interface between the display and the data capture hardware.

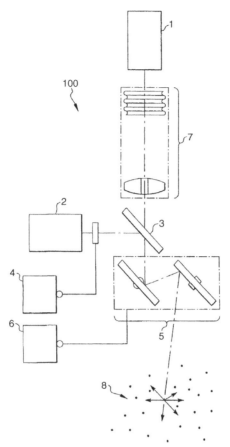

Figure 9.5 A display embodiment in which the image space is formed by dust particles (8) moving in air. Two laser sources are used (1) and (2)—the beams from which are combined by optical element (3) and scanned in 2-D by scanners (5). One of the laser sources (1) provides a nonvisible beam and is used to determine the instantaneous depth of each dust particle within the image space (see text for details). During the scan, as the instantaneous location of each particle is determined, the second (visible) laser is turned on for a brief period and a visible voxel is seen as a result of the scattering of the laser light by the dust particle. (Reproduced from US Patent Application Number US 2004/0218148 A1.)

brought together by optical element (3) such that their optical axes are coincident). Thus the two beams can move through the image space in unison and operate as follows:

1. Assume the visible beam is turned off. When the IR beam encounters a dust particle, light scattering occurs and a portion of the scattered light returns through the optical system to a distance detector (7).

2. One embodiment of the distance detector described by the inventors is illustrated in Figure 9.6 and is described in the following way:

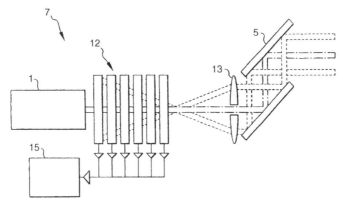

Figure 9.6 A technique used for the determination of the depth of a dust particle within the image space illustrated in Figure 9.5. Here, some of the nonvisible radiation scattered by a dust particle is returned via the scanning system and passes through a convex lens (13). A series of ring shaped photodetectors (12) are placed beyond the lens' focal point. The degree to which the radiation impinges on individual photodetector rings is determined by the depth of the dust particle within the image space. In this embodiment (1) represents the source of the IR radiation and (5) the scanning apparatus. In their patent, the inventors also suggest an alternative arrangement for the photodetectors. (Reproduced from US Patent Application Number US 2004/0218148 A1.)

> ...the beam from laser 1 travels unimpeded through a set of successive ring-shaped photodetectors 12, and then passes unimpeded through a hole in the middle of a convex lens 13 of focal length f. The beam is then deflected by a time-varying optical beam steering mechanism 5. Returning light, which has now been scattered by a particle of dust, travels back though the optical steering mechanism 5, and is focused by convex lens 13. After converging at a point at a distance somewhat greater than f from the lens, the light spreads out again and hits the set of ring-shaped photo-detectors 12, whose respective distances from the lens vary monotonically from 2f to $f + \varepsilon$. When the dust particle is very far away, a greater portion of the returning light will impinge on the detectors which are closest to the lens ...

In this way, the location of each dust particle encountered during a scan can be measured and rapidly, the voxel attributes at this location in space can be extracted from the volumetric data set. The source of visible laser[9] radiation may then be used to activate the voxel by addressing the dust particle.

Of particular importance with this approach, is its ability (in principle) to support "free space" image production[10] and permit the hand (or interaction tool) to "touch" the image).[11] Interestingly, the order in which voxels are activated during each image refresh period cannot be predefined. In this sense, the inventors write:

---

[9] Light from lasers able to emit red, green, and blue radiation may be combined so as to support the creation of multiple color images.

[10] For discussion on the "free space" image see Section 11.6.

[11] Furthermore, the depth efficiency (χ) equals 100%.

As the rapidly moving dust particles 8 intersect the sweeping beam at random intervals of time, and at random places along the beam, a volume of induced brightness is stochastically swept out within the air. An observer will see a glowing object floating in this volume.

In their patent, the inventors indicate a sweep frequency of at least 50 Hz, but do not appear to specify either the image space dimensions or the accuracy in positioning of voxels in the third dimension. Illustrations show images comprising 1070, 3400, and 10,600 voxels; without a doubt, this approach demonstrates tremendous ingenuity.

9.4   THE DEPTHCUBE™

In Section 9.2.4 we considered a display system in which a stack of LCD panels (each comprising a 2-D array of individually addressable elements) are used to modify the angle of polarization of light passing through an image space. A commercially available static-volume display known as the DepthCube™ also employs a stack of LCD panels; however, in this case each panel is addressed as a single entity (i.e., the state of the entire panel is changed as a whole: It does not comprise an array of individually addressable elements). In this case, addressing a panel causes it to change from a transparent state to one that strongly scatters incident light.

The general architecture of the DepthCube is illustrated in Figure 9.7. As may be seen from this diagram, a high-speed projector (employing DMDs) is used to

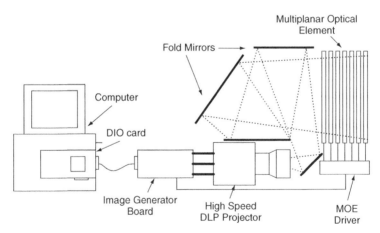

Figure 9.7   The DepthCube™ display unit. A high-speed projector casts a spatially modulated beam (comprising a series of image slices) into an image space. This is formed from some 20 LCD panels, each of which can be switched between transparent and scattering states. Note that each panel is switched as a whole—the panels do not comprise a set of individually addressable elements. As each image slice is cast into the image space, a corresponding panel scatters the light (all other panels being in a transparent state); thus, to an observer the image slice appears to emanate from a certain depth within the image space. A more recent version of this system employs a GigE interface and alternative mirror arrangement (Image reproduced with the kind permission of Alan Sullivan, President and CEO of LightSpace Technologies Inc.)

cast image slices into the image space via a series of fold mirrors. As each of these slices is projected into the image space, an appropriate LCD panel is switched into a scattering state and so the image slice appears to the viewer to originate from a certain depth. In essence, this approach represents the "all electronic" equivalent of the display units introduced in Chapter 6 that employed the translational motion of a passive surface of emission.

Viewing freedom is restricted to a single window onto the image space that measures some $15.6 \times 11.8 \times 4.1$ inches [Sullivan, 2004]; this supports a field of view of $\pm 45°$, both horizontally and vertically. Consequently, both vertical and horizontal parallax are supported across a satisfactory range of viewing position. The DepthCube employs 20 liquid crystal panels,[12] these being arranged parallel to each other and separated by an air gap. The response profile of the LCD panels used in this system is illustrated in Figure 9.8.

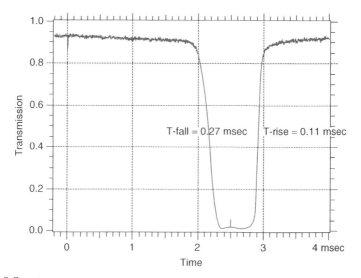

Figure 9.8   The temporal response of the LCD panels used in the DepthCube display. As may be seen, the material switches from the transparent to scattering state in 0.27 ms and from scattering to transparent states in 0.11 ms. A brief delay is introduced between the output of image slices, thereby enabling one panel to change from scattering to transparent and the next panel from transparent to scattering states. The small signal spike that may be seen at 2.5 ms is not an optical effect but electrical noise picked up by the measuring system when the electric field is reapplied to the cell. Switching speed is influenced by temperature, and therefore the DepthCube circulates air in the spaces between panels and so maintains a high temperature uniformity between cells. Additionally, a temperature transducer is used by the control hardware to monitor temperature changes and adjust the timing of the drive signals accordingly. (Image kindly supplied by Alan Sullivan, President and CEO of LightSpace Technologies Inc.)

---

[12] Based on polymer stabilized cholesteric texture material (see Yang et al. [1992]).

LightSpace Technologies indicate that the projector outputs 1500 image slices per second and that each of the 20 panels are able to display up to 1024×748 voxels [LightSpace Technologies White Paper]. The actual voxel activation capacity is therefore $\sim$15.3 million. Additional information on this approach can be found in Sullivan [2003] and in the related patent (US Patent Number 6,100,862).[13] The DepthCube is one of very few commercially available volumetric display systems and is described on the LightSpace Technologies website.[14]

9.5   THE BEAM INTERSECTION APPROACH

> *More and more I come to value charity and love*
> *of one's fellow being above all else...*
> *All our lauded technological progress —*
> *our very civilization —*
> *is like the axe in the hand of a pathological criminal.*[15]

It would appear that the first static-volume display employing a beam intersection technique was first researched nearly 100 years ago.[16] A patent filed in 1912 by Émile Luzy and Charles Dupuis (French Patent Number 461,600) describes a system utilizing the spatial modulation of two beams. These were projected into an image space comprising selenium chloride. The presence of portions of these beams within the image space is said to have produced an optical change, within the region of their intersection. The beams are reported as having wavelengths of 380 and approximately 700 nm (i.e., one beam operating in the UV and the other in the near IR regions of the electromagnetic spectrum). Their spatial modulation is reported as being achieved by passing each through a suitably prepared photographic plate. The apparatus described in the patent is illustrated in Figure 9.9. As discussed in Blundell and Schwarz [2000], this approach gives rise to spurious or "ghost" image elements, a problem which is exacerbated as the depth of the image space is increased.

In Section 5.6 we briefly considered the beam intersection technique and initiated discussed by reference to the work undertaken by Isaac Kim, Eric Korevaar, Harel Hakakha, and Brett Spivey in connection with the stepwise excitation of rubidium vapor. In the case that rubidium is used, the practical implementation of the display is slightly complicated due to the need to maintain the display volume at a temperature of $\sim$100°C. Furthermore, these workers had to employ a mechanical beam scanning system that restricted scan speeds and therefore limited the voxel activation capacity. The use of acousto-optic scanners and a larger volume image space (both suggested by Kim et al. [1996]) would have significantly advanced this

---

[13] This patent also briefly discusses the projection of the DepthCube image into "free space".

[14] http://www.lightspacetech.com (visited December 2005).

[15] Attributed to Albert Einstein (1875–1955).

[16] This may well represent the first proposal for a volumetric display of any kind.

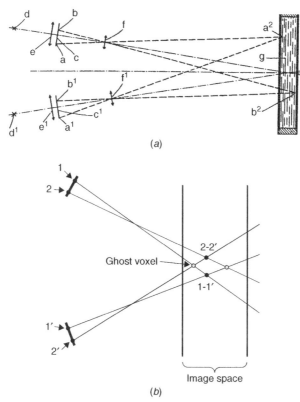

Figure 9.9 (a) General form of the apparatus described by Luzy and Dupuis in their 1912 patent. Two nonvisible spatially modulated beams intersect in an image space comprising selenium chloride, and their combined presence is said to give rise to a visible change in this material. Due to the spatial modulation technique employed within the "voxel" activation subsystem, spurious "ghost voxels" can occur—as illustrated in (b). Here $1 - 1'$ and $2 - 2'$ represent desired voxel locations. However, in addition, two ghost voxels are formed. (Diagram (a) reproduced from French Patent Number 461,600; diagram (b) reproduced from Blundell and Schwarz 2000.)

promising technology. From the perspective of the optical arrangement employed, the use of curved mirrors to ensure that the activation beams intersected with constant geometry is of particular note. This ensures that voxels maintain the same shape throughout the image space, and it may also lead to uniform voxel placement (see Section 5.8 for a summary of distortional and voxel placement dead zones).

In the subsections that follow, we briefly describe some exemplar embodiments and so build upon previous discussion.

9.5.1 The Stepwise Excitation of Mercury Vapor

In Section 5.6.1 we briefly referred to a comprehensive patent filed in 1961 by Jack Fajans (US Patent Number 3,123,711). This publication can be broadly divided into two parts. In the first of these, Fajans deals with the stepwise upconversion process in various vapors, and in the second the photostimulation and photoquenching of phosphor particles dispersed within a transparent solid medium. In this section we focus on the former, details concerning the latter may be found in Section 9.5.4. It appears that Fajans may well have been the first to research in detail the potential of using the two-step excitation of fluorescence of a vapor for the production of visible voxels. The apparatus used is illustrated in Figure 9.10. Here, a vessel equipped with transparent windows contains a vapor (such as the mercury isotope 198 ($_{80}Hg^{198}$)[17] at a pressure of no greater than 0.1 mm, Hg.[18] When used in conjunction with mercury, the first beam source used has the same wavelength as that subsequently employed by Zito and Schraeder [1963] (2537 Å), whereas the second beam source provides excitation to the 7^3S_1 level (the wavelength of this beam is reported as 4358 Å (in comparison to 4047 Å used by Zito and Schraeder[19]). Fajans arranged the beam projection apparatus to produce both a collimated beam and a beam spread out to form a planar sheet of radiation (with the plane lying at right angles to the surface of the page in Figure 9.10). Beam deflection to different parts of the image space was then achieved via a drive system that simply moved the location of the beam source apparatus relative to the image space!

In Table 9.1, other materials that Fajans suggests for use in place of mercury are indicated. It is important to note that this list was primarily determined by the availability of suitable excitation sources at the time of Fajans work. Today there are far greater opportunities!

9.5.2 Erbium-Doped Calcium Fluoride

Although the publication by Lewis et al. [1971] primarily focuses on the use of the stepwise excitation of fluorescence of erbium-doped calcium fluoride crystals (see Section 5.6.2), the authors of this paper highlight a number of issues of relevance to a wide range of static-volume display paradigms. The experiments conducted provided the "proof of concept," and voxels were activated in a 2-cm cube of CaF_2 doped with approximately 0.1% Er^{3+}. Xenon lamps with appropriate filters (rather than lasers) were used to produce two beams with wavelengths 1.54 μm and 0.83 μm (with powers of approximately 50 mW and 30 mW, respectively). In this particular experiment, the researchers report the production of a green voxel (with a diameter of less than 2 mm) and an output of 2×10^{-8} W radiated isotropically.[20]

---

[17] Fajans reports increased voxel intensity when this isotope is used. Natural abundance is 10.1% [Weast, 1988]. A small amount of nitrogen was also present.

[18] The display operated at room temperature.

[19] Therefore, in this scheme the transition to the metastable 6^3P_0 state was not a requirement.

[20] The theoretical output (F_{31}) from a voxel in the limit of nonsaturating beam powers and assuming a simple two-step excitation model as illustrated in Figure 5.6a is given by

$$F_{31} = \frac{nB_{12}B_{23}I_{12}I_{23}\eta_{31}}{M^2R} \text{photons} \cdot \text{cm}^{-2}\text{s}^{-1}$$

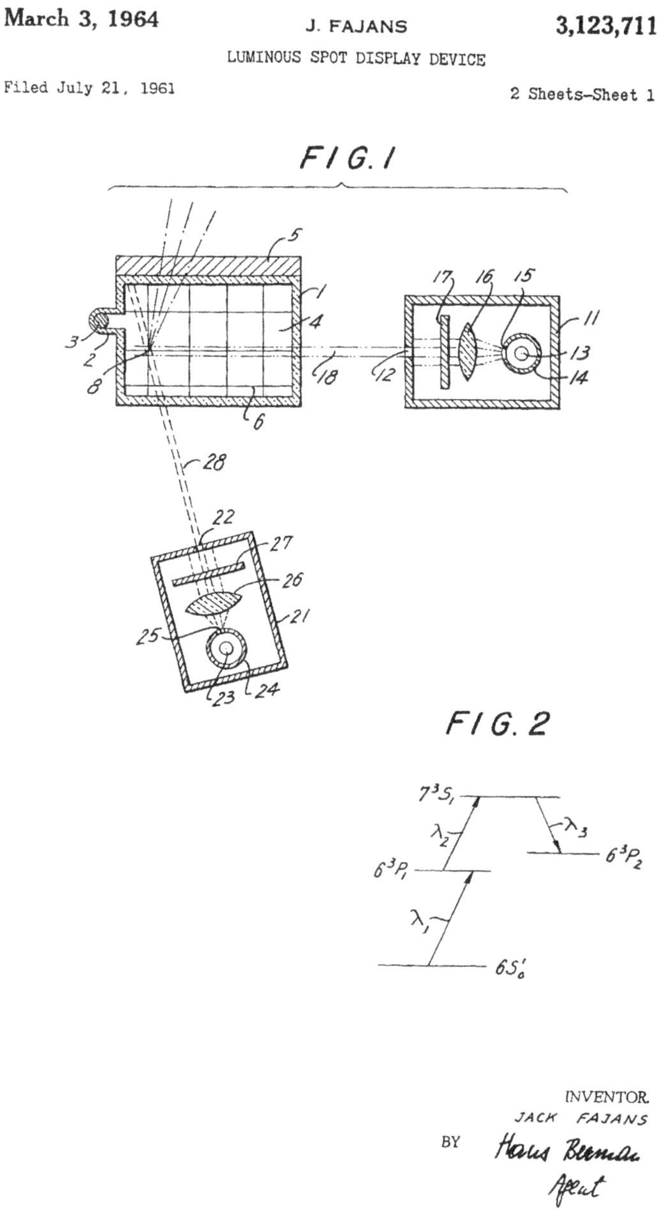

March 3, 1964   J. FAJANS   **3,123,711**
                    LUMINOUS SPOT DISPLAY DEVICE
Filed July 21, 1961   2 Sheets—Sheet 1

F I G. I

F I G. 2

INVENTOR
JACK FAJANS
BY   *Hans Berman*
          Agent

Figure 9.10   The apparatus employed by Jack Fajans, which is described in the remarkable patent that he filed in 1961. Here, two arc lamps are used as beam sources and are used to activate voxels within an image space comprising a vapor such as mercury. As with the subsequent work undertaken by Zito and Schraeder, it is likely that greatly improved results could have been achieved had appropriate laser sources and beam deflection apparatus been available. In fact, Fajans directed the beams by controlling and shifting the positions of the light source apparatus (in its entirety)! (Reproduced from US Patent Number 3,123,711.)

TABLE 9.1 Elements Suggested by Fajans for Use in the Production of a Gaseous Volumetric Image Space

Vapor	First Beam (λ)	Second Beam (λ)	Suggested Temperature ($^{\circ}$C)	Emission (λ)
Zinc	3076	4722	250–450	4811
Cadmium	3261	4799	150–400	5086
Potassium	7665	5360	80–175	5360
Cesium	8521	6217	100–250	6217

[a]Wavelengths are quoted in angstrom units (Å).
Source: US Patent Number 3,123,711.

Lewis et al. also consider the use of a gaseous material and recognize the impact of refraction as light emerges from the image space. In this context they write:

> *A corollary benefit of gases is the lack of foreshortening distortion present in solid or even a liquid display volumes due to refraction.*

They also discuss the importance of ensuring that the lifetime of the first excited state is such that it does not result in the production of spurious voxels[21]:

> *... the ground state pump will produce a line of excitation along its entire path through the display volume. If the lifetime of the first excited state τ_2 is long compared to the time interval between the generation of successive spots[22] in the display, intersection of the excited state pump with this line will produce undesirable spots ("ghost" images).*

Further valuable discussion on this work is provided in a patent filed by Lewis and co-workers in 1971, which was assigned to the Battelle Development Corporation (US Patent Number 3,829,838). Here, brief proposals are made for the use of various materials and processes via which visible voxels may be formed. For example:

> *Alternatively, the display medium may be liquid or solid and have finely ground phosphors distributed throughout. In this case, excitation to produce photoluminescence is achieved with one wavelength, and quenching with another wavelength. In addition and as still another alternative, the display medium may be characterized as being photochromic or thermochromic; and instead of a luminescent display, an opaque display is produced.*

The excellent research carried out by Lewis et al. is frequently cited in literature. Similar work carried out by Michael Brown and Geoffrey Waters, which was the

---

where B_{12} and B_{23} are the absorption cross sections for the two transitions, I_{12} and I_{23} are the power densities of the two beams (measured in photons $\cdot$ cm^{-2}s^{-1}), n represents the density of fluorescent centers, η_{31} represents the probability that once excited by the two beams a radiative decay will occur with the emission of a photon with wavelength λ_{31} [Lewis et al., 1971]. Here it is assumed that a total of M voxels are activated in a time $1/R$, and hence the beams dwell for a time MR on each voxel (other time components relating to the activation process are neglected).

[21] This is also discussed by Miyazaki et al. [2005].

[22] Voxels.

subject of earlier patents filed in 1964 and 1965, is often overlooked (British Patent Number 1,103,861 and US Patent Number 3,474,248). In this patent, the two-step excitation of fluorescence is used in conjunction with various materials. Initially, the patents discuss the use of an image space formed using "... *1.0 atomic percent of erbium providing impurity ions in a triply ionised state in a host lattice of strontium fluoride*". In this case, the two beam sources may operate in the infrared at wavelengths of 1.5 μm and 1.15 μm. Subsequently, other transparent host materials are proposed (lanthanum fluoride, calcium fluoride, strontium fluoride, and barium fluoride) along with other fluorescent centers (thulium, holmium, and erbium). A diagram showing the form of the apparatus used by these workers is reproduced in Figure 9.11. Interestingly, the light sources were formed in a manner similar to that described by Fajans (see Section 9.5.1) inasmuch as one acted as a planar sheet of radiation which was scanned vertically through the image space, while the other was a collimated beam. The arrangement ensured that both sources entered the image space at right angles to its surface, thus maintaining a constant intersection geometry between the two beams. The scanning arrangement would have severely restricted the refresh rate because, as can be seen from Figure 9.11, both beam sources were moved by mechanical systems—beam deflection apparatus not

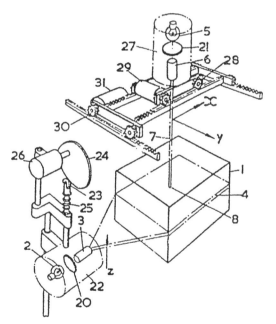

Figure 9.11 The stepwise excitation of fluorescence using rare earth elements as fluorescent centres, and a transparent host material such as lanthanum or calcium fluoride. In this prototype embodiment, scanning is achieved by physically moving the light sources (and associated optical systems). Light from one source takes the form of a collimated beam, and that from the other takes the form of a sheet spanning the width of the image space. (Reproduced from US Patent Number 3,474,248.)

being used. The vertically positioned scanner moved in a 2-D plane, whereas the horizontal positioned scanner moved only in a single plane.

9.5.3 Rare Earth-Doped ZBLAN

In Section 5.6.2 we briefly considered work carried out in the development of a wholly "solid-state" volumetric display and in which rare earth lanthanides [for example, praseodymium (Pr^{3+}), erbium (Er^{3+}) and thulium (Tm^{3+})] are incorporated within a heavy metal fluoride glass such as ZBLAN. The use of radiation beams of appropriate wavelengths gives rise to the stepwise excitation of fluorescence and the emission of visible light. For example, in the case of praseodymium the emission of red light can be effected through the application of two infrared beams (1014 nm and 840 nm). Similarly, erbium and thulium can be used to generate green light and blue light, respectively. Armed with a voxel generation subsystem comprising these three types of fluorescent center, it is in principle possible to create (by color mixing) full color images. The most obvious (and perhaps the most elegant) way of achieving this goal would be to incorporate these three materials within the same transparent host. This appears to be problematic, and in this context Downing et al. [1996] write:

> Higher concentrations of the dopants lead to decreased upconversion efficiency because of cross relaxations between the ions, which depletes the populations of the intermediate levels. This decreased upconversion has, unfortunately, prevented co-doping of all three ions into a single monolithic bulk material to obtain wavelength-addressable colour. The problem is compounded by the pump wavelengths used to induce TSTF[23] upconversion in one ion inducing single-frequency upconversion in another ion ... Single-frequency upconversion in other than the target ion causes the IR pump wavelengths to show up as visible lines in the display ....

Downing et al. [1996] therefore propose an alternative approach in which the image space is formed by a series of thin slices bonded together with an index matching adhesive material, in which each slice is doped with a single type of fluorescent center. It is suggested that each slice would be some 100–500 μm in thickness and that two linear arrays of voxel activation beams be used such that a pair of beams (one from each array) would be directed into each slice—from the slice edge as indicated in Figure 9.12. This scenario leads to varying beam intersection geometry and therefore the possibility of distortional dead zones (see Section 5.8). Furthermore, in the case of larger image spaces, refraction of the beams as they enter the image space may cause visible image distortion.[24] Hesselink et al. [1995] suggest a strategy in which voxel activation is achieved using two 2-D arrays of VCSELs. In this scenario, by arranging the arrays so that they are orthogonal,

---

[23] TSTF: Two Step Two Frequency.

[24] In the case of display units offering great freedom in viewing direction, distortion that may occur at the image space boundary as light *emerges* cannot be corrected by the host computer. On the other hand, the host computer may be used to compensate for the refraction of the voxel activation beams as they *enter* the image space with continually changing trajectories.

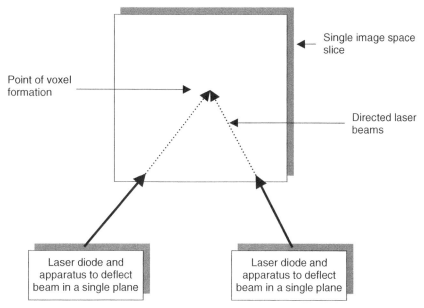

Figure 9.12 Voxel activation technique suggested by Downing et al. [1996] for the production of full color images. The image space is formed by stacking together appropriately doped ZBLAN slices to form RGB layers. For each slice a pair of lasers would be used for voxel activation (these being deflected in a single plane).

voxels may be activated in the region at which a pair of beams intersect. The need for beam deflection is avoided, and the beam intersection geometry is constant throughout the image space.[25]

9.5.4 The Use of Phosphor Particles Dispersed in a 3-D Medium

The patent filed by Jack Fajans in 1961 (US Patent Number 3,123,711), previously discussed in Section 9.5.1 (in connection with the stepwise excitation of gaseous media), also describes the use of phosphor particles dispersed within a solid transparent host material. In this case, he describes the formation of an image space as follows:

The apparatus... consists of two radiation sources and a carrier body in which a phosphor is dispersed. The carrier body consists of a material which is substantially transparent to the electromagnetic waves employed. In the specific embodiment illustrated, the carrier body consists essentially of polymethyl methacrylate in which a phosphor is dispersed.

---

[25] In the case where a display is to create images of only a single color, various approaches may be adopted in the implementation of the voxel activation subsystem (see, for example, Soltan and Lasher [1996]).

Fajans suggests the use of phosphor particles approximately five microns in size and a concentration in the polymethyl methacrylate of approximately 10 milligrams per cubic inch. He goes on to say that the image space is prepared as follows:

> ... *by grinding the phosphor until it has the desired particle size distribution, and by mixing the powder obtained with monomeric methyl methacrylate in the indicated ratio. Upon block polymerisation of the monomer there is obtained a body at least a portion of which is close to the desired composition. The block is trimmed and cut into sections... Each section is polished and tested.*[26]

Examples of possible phosphors are provided in Table 9.2. Fajans describes two methods of voxel activation. The first involves voxel creation at the intersection of two directed beams (of appropriate wavelength), thereby causing stepwise excitation and the emission of photons within the visible region of the electromagnetic spectrum (photostimulation). Alternatively, a single beam may, in its own right, cause excitation such that visible light is emitted along the entire length of its passage through the media. A second beam is then used to inhibit light output and so restrict its production to the region in which the voxel is to be illuminated (photoquenching). As discussed in a previous work [Blundell and Schwarz, 2000], because the majority of any image space is void, the use of such an erasure technique is likely to be less efficient than the direct voxel activation method (also see Section 5.7).

9.5.5   Beam Intersection in a Phosphor Cloud

While Jack Fajans sought to disperse phosphor particles in a solid media, William Rowe describes in a patent filed nearly 15 years later the production of a phosphor cloud within an evacuated vessel (US Patent Number 4,063,233), alleviating the need for a host material. The form of this display is illustrated in Figure 9.13; as may be seen from this diagram, voxels are activated at the region of intersection of two electron beams. The inventor indicates:

> *Each individual beam's current is maintained at less than the threshold luminescence of the particles but the combined currents may be caused to exceed that threshold by a controlled amount thereby producing light spots of variable brightness at the beam intersection point....*

Since the beams do not represent coherent sources, the "threshold" referred to must relate to electron density rather than beam energy.[27] As with the display unit referred to in the next subsection, if this system was ever in fact prototyped, it is likely that beam registration would have been problematic. This and other detailed (but important) implementation issues are unfortunately not discussed, leaving the impression that the patent describes a concept, rather than a physical reality. This is reinforced by discussion concerning the agitation of the phosphor

---

[26] Fajans does not indicate the dimensions of the sections that were successfully fabricated using this approach, and the author has to date been unable to locate this researcher.

[27] For useful practical discussion on light output from phosphor materials, see Poole [1966].

TABLE 9.2 Exemplar Phosphor Materials that Can Be Used for Voxel Generation within a Static-Volume Image Space[a]

Composition	First Beam (λ)	Second Beam (λ)	Emission (λ)	Process
Cub.-Sr (S:Se):[flux]:Sm:Eu	4,600	9,300	5,700	Photostimulation
Cub.-CaS:[flux]:Sm:Eu	4,800	11,700	6,600	Photostimulation
Cub.-SrS:[flux]:Sm:Ce	2,900	10,200	4,800	Photostimulation
Hex.-ZnS:Cu:Pb[SO$_4$]:[NaCl(2)]	3,700	7,500 or 13,200	4,880	Photostimulation
Hex.-9ZnS:1CdS:Cu(0.0073)	~4,200	7,200	—	Photoquenching
ZnS(Cu)	<4,200	~7,000	—	Photoquenching

[a]Wavelengths are quoted in angstrom units (Å). See text and source for details.
Source: Reproduced from US Patent Number 3,123,711.

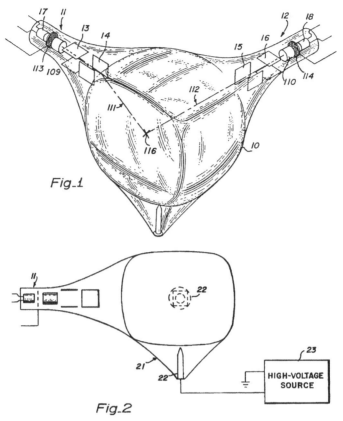

Figure 9.13   Voxel generation by means of a continually agitated cloud of phosphor coated particles. The voxel activation subsystem takes the form of two directed electron beams. The inventor claims voxel activation within the region of intersection. An electrostatic field is said to have been used for the continual agitation of the particle cloud, but this would impact on electron beam trajectories. (Reproduced from US Patent Number 4,063,233.)

cloud, indicated as being achieved by means of an electric field generated within the image space. This field is reported as having been produced by the application of a high voltage to the metallic spike located at the bottom of the display vessel (labeled 22 in Figure 9.13). Although this approach may have been effective in producing a continual agitation of the phosphor coated particles, it would have impacted on the electron beam trajectories and made their cross registration even more difficult. In this respect the inventor writes:

> It is desirable in any application of the high-gradient pump to employ screening electrodes to minimize the effect of the field of the pump on the trajectory of the electron beams.

In practice, this could have proved a difficult undertaking, since the presence of screening materials would probably have impacted on image visibility. . . .

9.5.6   The Intersection of Particle Beams in a Gas

A patent filed in 1945 by Fred S. Howell describes the activation of voxels by means of two electron beams using nitrogen gas as the voxel generation medium (US Patent Number 2,604,607). The display apparatus described in the patent is illustrated in Figure 9.14. Two electron beams are scanned so that (at least in principle) they continually intersect. The inventor claims that the energy of either beam is insufficient to cause visible excitation of the gas, and further that even in the region of intersection no visible output occurs unless the beam intensity is increased by a change in the grid voltages, as a consequence of an input signal from the radar system to which the display is connected. Unfortunately, the two electron beams do not represent two coherent sources, and so (as with the display unit outlined in the previous subsection) the region of their intersection corresponds to an area in which only the beam current is modified. Changing the

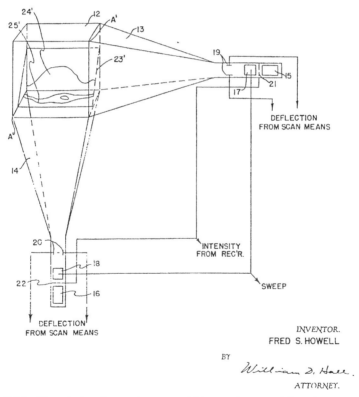

Figure 9.14   Two electron beams intersect within a region containing nitrogen gas at low pressure. The inventor claims that a visible voxel could be generated at the region of their intersection by increasing the beam currents. However, it is likely that some light would have been emitted along the entire extent of each beam's path through the gas. (Reproduced from US Patent Number 2,604,607.)

grid voltage of either electron gun will further influence the beam current, and so any threshold that gives rise to visible voxels must be as a consequence of a change in beam current, rather than a change in beam energy. It would therefore appear that the emission of some light would have been caused by both individual beams as they propagated through the gas. Perhaps this was significantly less intense than that generated in the region of their intersection. As with the approach referred to in Section 9.5.5, beam registration is likely to have been problematic.

9.6   STACKING IMAGE SLICES

Information is not knowledge.[28]

Two display embodiments are briefly discussed in this section. These provide a series of parallel image slices (depth planes) and employ a plurality of 2-D display screens and beam splitters (which enable the image slices to be assembled). Interestingly, this approach finds its roots in a theatrical illusion that gained great popularity during the nineteenth century and that was known as Pepper's Ghost.[29] For a brief overview of this simple but highly effective theatrical illusion, see Blundell and Schwarz [2006].

9.6.1   The Use of Beam Splitters: Basic Configuration

In an interesting publication [Tamura and Tanaka, 1982], a display technique is discussed that employs a plurality of conventional 2-D display screens; the images depicted on these are overlayed at different depths within an image space. An arrangement of this type able to create three image planes is illustrated in Figure 9.15. Central to this approach is the use of semi-silvered plane mirrors which, from a side elevation viewpoint, form an "X" arrangement. Let us suppose that the three CRTs (or LCD panels) denoted CRT 1, 2, and 3, respectively, lie at distances d, $2d$, and $3d$ (as measured from, for example, the location at which the mirrors cross). Then the image of CRT 1 will lie at a distance d behind the mirror within which its image is reflected. Similarly, the image of CRT 3 will be at a distance of $3d$ and since CRT 2 is directly viewed through the mirrors, it provides an image at a distance $2d$ below the mirrors. Thus the observer is presented with three parallel image planes. Tamura and Tanaka also describe other mirror/screen configurations that provide additional image planes (e.g., nine planes) and discuss the use of this display technique for the depiction of medical images.

---

[28] Attributed to Albert Einstein (1875–1955).

[29] Although attributed to Professor John Henry Pepper, the technique seems to have been invented by a little-known engineer, Henry Dircks. See also reference to the Phantasmagoria in Blundell and Schwarz [2006]. This was an earlier theatrical "special effects" technique and loosely resembles the display paradigm outlined in Section 9.3.2, which uses an image space comprising dust particles.

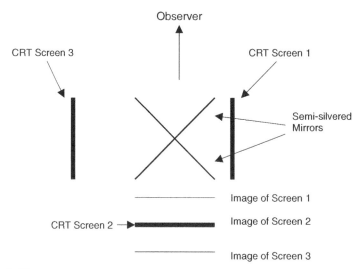

Figure 9.15   Three CRTs (or rear light LCD panels) each project an image slice onto two semi-silvered mirrors. The observer looks downwards onto the mirrors and sees the images formed by reflection. CRT screen 1 lies closer to the mirror and its image is the highest of the three. CRT screen 2 is directly viewed through the mirrors and its screen corresponds to the image location. CRT screen 3 is the furthest from the mirrors and its image is the most distant from the observer.

Describing problems encountered in relation to the implementation of the display, they write:

> *... the five-layer 3-D images are rather degraded because of (1) thickness of the half-mirrors and resulting join gaps, (2) misalignment of the half-mirrors, and (3) mosaic brightness caused by a different number of passages through the half-mirrors. The principle reason for degradation is (1). Therefore, the five-layer 3-D image will be improved by using thin half-mirrors or a prism-type beam splitter.*

9.6.2   The Use of Beam Splitters: With Additional Optical Components

> *There is a story that a visitor once met the beau's valet*
> *carrying a basketful of crumpled neckcloths,*
> *and upon the visitor inquiring as to what they were, the valet replied:*
> *" These, sir, are our failures!"*[30]

A patent filed by Dennis Ricks in 1977 (US Patent Number 4,190,856) describes the stacking of image slices by means of a series of beam splitters in a manner analogous to the subsequent approach adopted by Tamura and Tanaka and which was outlined in the previous subsection. In this document the inventor also pays

[30] George Bryan Brummell, Source: Wild L., *The Story of Beau Brummell* (circa 1900).

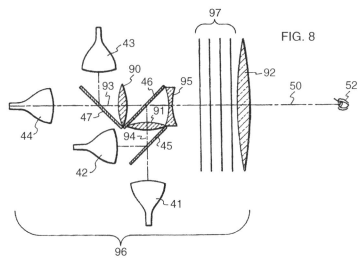

Figure 9.16 An image space in which the image slices depicted by four CRTs are stacked. In this approach, a number of lenses are used to shorten the optical paths and magnify/reposition the image so that it appears to lie closer to the observer. Here the image is viewed from the right hand side via lens (92). The image planes appear to be located at (97). (Reproduced from US Patent Number 4,190,856.)

attention to issues such as reducing the length of the optical paths within the display unit (so reducing its physical size), increasing the size of the visible image, placing this image in a position so that it appears to lie closer to the observer, and achieving apparent opacity of the image planes. A basic scheme discussed in this patent which is able to integrate the four image planes depicted by CRTs (41–44) is illustrated in Figure 9.16. The operation of the basic optical arrangement of lenses may be described by reference to Figure 9.17. Here, the purpose of lens (86) is to reposition the image slices in such a way that they appear to lie closer to the observer. Ricks recognizes that a display of this type, in which a number

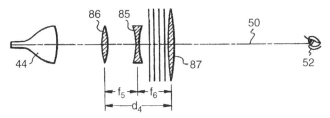

Figure 9.17 The operation of the lens arrangement illustrated in Figure 9.16 may be readily understood by considering its application to the image slices generated by a single display. See text for details. (Reproduced from US Patent Number 4,190,856.)

of display screens and beam splitter are employed, results in the formation of an image that

> *... would be at the far end of an optical tunnel formed by the beam splitters, which for home television, is unacceptable.*

Consequently, given that the space between the lens and display screen (u) is greater than the focal length of the lens (f_1), an image is formed at a distance (v) from the lens on its right-hand side (i.e., closer to the observer) such that

$$v = \frac{f_1 u}{u - f_1}.$$

Lens (87) has a focal length f_2 and serves two purposes. Firstly, although lens (86) repositions the image, it also impacts on image magnification such that the image planes will appear to be of different sizes.[31] Lens (87) ameliorates this problem and, further, provides overall image magnification. The distance between the lenses is arranged to be equal to the sum of their focal lengths ($f_1 + f_2$) where $f_1 < f_2$. Finally, the inclusion of the concave (diverging) lens (85) permits a reduction in the focal lengths of the other two lens' (f_1 and f_2), thereby allowing the use of a more compact optical system.

Ricks' patent includes valuable discussion on various facets of this technique (including the support for image opacity) and is recommended to the interested reader.

9.7 DISCUSSION

The static-volume display units introduced in this chapter (along with those referred to in Chapter 5) have been selected to highlight the diversity of approaches used in the implementation of displays of this type. These systems provide a clear insight into the coupling that exists between the subsystems that comprise a display because, as we have seen, the definition of one particular subsystem will generally influence (and may even define) the techniques that may be employed in the implementation of the others. The classification of volumetric displays employed in this book is able to encompass the great majority of approaches; however, there are some exceptions. For example, consider the swept and static-volume classification. Recall from Chapter 4 that we have assumed that all swept-volume systems "*employ a mechanical system that causes a surface (or 3-D structure) to rapidly and repeatedly sweep through a physical volume*"; in contrast, as indicated in Chapter 5, static-volume systems "*place no reliance on mechanical motion for image space creation.*" However, consider for a moment the display introduced in Section 9.3.2 that uses a cloud of dust particles as voxel generation centers. This display technique requires *continuous motion* of the dust particles, and therefore it

---

[31] Magnification $= |v/u|$.

does not quite fit into our static-volume classification.[32] On the other hand, it operates in quite a different way to the swept-volume systems discussed in Chapters 6, 7, and 8 and so does not readily stand along side other swept-volume embodiments. Refining our definitions to encompass (without exception) all volumetric systems proposed to date would be an unproductive exercise and would simply lead to undue complication. Consequently, to retain simplicity in dealing with the majority, it is perhaps better to tolerate a degree of ambiguity and accept that because of the great diversity of approaches that may be adopted in the implementation of volumetric display systems, some systems are best treated in their own right.

In the next chapter, we turn our attention to varifocal display techniques and consider some exemplar embodiments.

9.8   INVESTIGATIONS

1. Discuss the display technique outlined in Section 9.3.2 that uses a cloud of dust particles as scattering centers. Identify alternative techniques that may be used to determine the instantaneous depth of the dust particles within the image space.

2. Again with reference to the display outlined in Section 9.3.2, consider the motion of the dust particles. Is there an optimum speed at which they should move through the image space?

3. Consider the following sentence encountered by the author in a recent publication: "*Swept volume displays can produce good results but suffer from the drawback of using large moving parts that makes them difficult to scale in size.*" Discuss restrictions that may be placed on image space dimensions through the use of both swept and static-volume systems. Is either paradigm generally better suited to the formation of the large volume image space?

4. For the optical arrangement illustrated in Figure 9.17 [and ignoring the diverging lens (85)], calculate the overall magnification (assume that the distance between the lenses equals the sum of their focal lengths).

---

[32] The need for motion could be overcome by distributing passive voxel generation centers throughout a transparent solid. However, in this case the positioning of these centers would be critical because this will impact not only on the ability of the activation beam(s) to reach each desired center, but also on changes in image brightness with viewing angle.

10 Varifocal Mirror Techniques

Arthur came, and labouring up the pass
All in a misty moonshine, unawares
Had trodden the crown'd skeleton, and
the skull
Brake from the nape, and from the skull
the crown.

10.1 INTRODUCTION

The varifocal display technique has attracted research interest for some 40 years. The basic principle of operation of this approach was previously introduced in Section 1.6.3, so in this chapter we consider aspects of these systems in more detail. We begin by discussing some of the basic optical characteristics of the spherical mirror. Here, we briefly derive the well-known "mirror equation" and examine the impact of changes in mirror curvature on the location of the reflected image. In Section 10.3 we consider spherical aberration and briefly contrast spherical and parabolic forms of mirror. Discussion in Section 10.4.1 concerns the issue of the image update rate, and here we review two conflicting requirements: (a) the need to update sufficiently frequently to avoid image flicker and (b) the desirability of minimizing audible noise that may arise from the motion of the mirror.

Unlike volumetric systems, the varifocal approach does not lend itself to such a diverse range of implementation techniques. However, it is instructive to consider the manner in which researchers have sought to develop such systems, and so in Section 10.5, having laid various ground work, we review some of the research that has been undertaken in this area. This discussion enables us to more easily identify some of the strengths and weaknesses of this simple, but highly effective, display paradigm.

Okoshi [1976] provides a brief summary of the varifocal technique, and excellent coverage may be found in the chapter written by Lawrence Sher in McAllister [1993]. An interesting review of various 3-D displays paradigms (including the varifocal approach) is provided by Owczarczyk and Owczarczyk [1990].

10.2   THE GEOMETRY OF THE CURVED MIRROR

Here wait the dumb, whose voices rule the earth;
Here rest the dead, whose life is quick and free.
Hush, living lips, before their solemn mirth;
Life, learn of them the true vitality.[1]

The operation of the varifocal mirror display is underpinned by the optical properties of a curved mirror, for which only a small change in curvature is needed to produce a considerable shift in the position at which an image is brought to focus. In this section, we begin by deriving the "mirror equation" with which image, object, and radius of curvature of a curved mirror are related. Subsequently, we consider the impact that changes in a mirror's curvature have on the location of the focused image.

1. The Mirror Formula: For simplicity we confine ourselves to the concave (converging) mirror, although as indicated below, through the use of an appropriate sign convention, the result that we obtain can be applied to both concave and convex forms of spherical mirror. Referring to Figure 10.1, we assume that a ray of light emanating from a point O (which lies on the principal axis) impinges on the mirror at point A and subsequently crosses the principle axis at I. Furthermore, point C denotes the mirror's center of curvature (the radius of curvature being R).

The line CA forms the normal to the mirror at the point that the ray strikes the mirror's surface, and given the elementary law of reflection which indicates

---

[1] Katharine Aldrich in *Munsey's Magazine*, date not known. Quoted by E. Priestley, *The Story of a Lifetime* (In a Library), Trench Trübner and Co., Ltd. (1908).

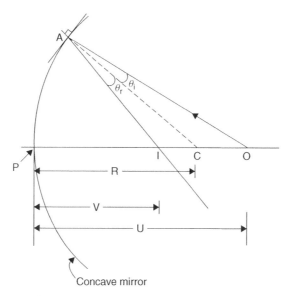

Figure 10.1 A ray from a point O is reflected by a concave (converging) mirror. The point C denotes the radius of curvature and angles θ_i and θ_r are equal. See text for discussion.

that the angles of incidence and reflection are equal, it follows that $\theta_i = \theta_r$. Therefore,

$$\frac{\overline{OC}}{\overline{OA}} = \frac{\overline{IC}}{\overline{IA}}. \tag{10.1}$$

However, $\overline{OC} = u - R$ and $\overline{IC} = R - V$ and in the case where the ray OA has a small angle relative to the principal axis (the paraxial approximation [O'Shea, 1985]), $\overline{OA} \approx u$ and $\overline{IA} \approx V$. Thus Eq. (10.1) can be rewritten

$$\frac{u - R}{u} = \frac{R - V}{V},$$

and therefore within the paraxial region we have

$$\frac{1}{u} + \frac{1}{v} = \frac{2}{R}. \tag{10.2}$$

The primary (object focus) is defined as

$$\lim_{v \to \infty} u = f_o,$$

and the secondary (image focus) is expressed as

$$\lim_{u \to \infty} v = f_i.$$

Therefore, from Eq. (10.2) it follows that

$$\frac{1}{f_o} + \frac{1}{\infty} = \frac{1}{\infty} + \frac{1}{f_i} = \frac{2}{R}$$

and so $f_o = f_i = R/2$. If we simply denote the focal length of the lens as f, then the mirror formula is given by the well-known expression

$$\frac{1}{u} + \frac{1}{v} = \frac{1}{f}. \tag{10.3}$$

It is important to remember that this assumes that the rays incident on the mirror lie at a small angle to the principal axis (see Section 10.3). Furthermore, although we have derived this formula in relation to the concave mirror, it is equally applicable to the convex mirror (in which case we would assign to R a value of the opposite sign). In this way, f is deemed to be positive for concave mirrors and negative for convex mirrors.

2. Varying the Curvature of the Mirror: Consider a point object located at a distance u from a varifocal mirror that has a continually changing radius of curvature $R(t)$. The image will be formed at a distance v from the mirror, where v is also a function of t. Thus Eq. (10.2) may be written

$$\frac{1}{u} + \frac{1}{v(t)} = \frac{2}{R(t)}. \tag{10.4}$$

Referring now to Figure 10.2, it will be apparent that

$$(R(t) - h(t))^2 = \frac{d^2}{4} + R(t)^2,$$

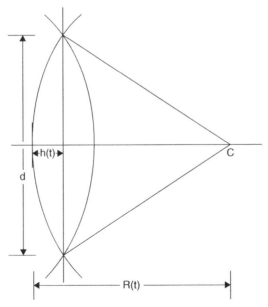

Figure 10.2   Here, a mirrored surface moves between two extremes and so, throughout each cycle of motion forms both concave and convex reflectors. Distance d denotes the diameter of the mirror. See text for discussion.

and so

$$R(t) = \frac{-1}{2h(t)} \left[\frac{d^2}{4} - h(t)^2 \right].$$

Assuming that the maximum mirror displacement is very much less than d, then this expression may be approximated to[2]

$$R(t) \sim \frac{-d^2}{8h(t)}.$$

Substituting into Eq. (10.4), we obtain

$$v(t) \sim \frac{-d^2 u}{16uh(t) + d^2}.$$

If we assume a sinusoidal motion such that $h(t) = |h_{max}| \sin \omega t$, then

$$v(t) \sim \frac{-d^2 u}{16u|h_{max}| \sin \omega t + d^2}.$$

It is instructive to consider a numerical example. Let us therefore assume a maximum peak-to-peak amplitude of motion of 4 mm, a mirror diameter (d) of 40 cm, and a point object lying some 80 cm from the pole. At the two extremes of movement, the image will be located at distances of $\sim$95 and $\sim$69 cm. Thus although the mirror only moves through a maximum displacement of 4 mm, the image has been repositioned across a distance of $\sim$26 cm! Under these conditions we could therefore expect (at least in principle) to create an image space of this depth.

Unfortunately, as the curvature of the mirror changes during each cycle of motion, so does the magnification provided by the system. In this context, Sher [1988] writes:

> The net inescapable price one pays is a display volume whose shape is the frustum of a rectangular pyramid.

However, the variations in magnification can be readily calculated and an appropriate scaling factor applied to each image slice prior to its output to the display. For a detailed development of the varifocal mirror imaging equations, see Rawson [1968].

10.3   SPHERICAL ABERRATION

The mirror equation developed in the previous section applies most accurately in the paraxial region (i.e., close to the principal axis), and as the aperture of a spherical mirror is increased, so too is the degree of "spherical aberration" (leading to the gradual degradation of image quality). Ideally, therefore, we would most probably

---

[2] In the analysis that follows, we draw on discussion by Lawrence Sher in McAllister [1993].

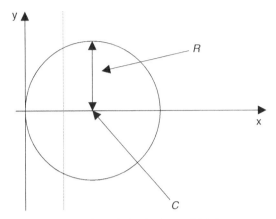

Figure 10.3 The cross-section of a spherical mirror which has a center at C and a radius of curvature R. We consider the case that $x < R$.

choose to employ a mirror with a parabolic shape (paraboloid of revolution). In relation to the parabolic reflector, Smith [1957] writes:

The parabola is a curve possessing the following remarkable property: the normal at any point on it makes equal angles with a line through that point parallel to the axis and with the line joining it to the focus.

It is instructive to consider how the spherical mirror differs from that of its parabolic counterpart.[3]

Consider the sphere of radius R that is illustrated in cross section in Figure 10.3 and that is centered on a point C. The cross section of this sphere in the $x-y$ plane is given by

$$y^2 + (x - R)^2 = R^2,$$

and so

$$x^2 - 2Rx + y^2 = 0.$$

Solving for x gives

$$x = R \pm \sqrt{R^2 - y^2}$$

Referring to Figure 10.3. To discuss a concave mirror, we confine ourselves to the case that $x < R$ and so can neglect the sum in the above expression. If we now

---

[3] Here we follow texts such as Hecht and Zajac [1974].

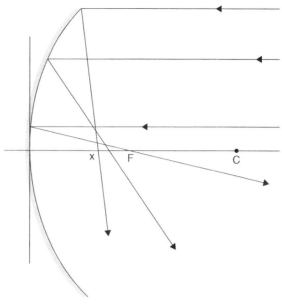

Figure 10.4   Three rays that travel parallel to the principle axis. As may be seen, rays that lie at a greater distance from the principle axis (nonparaxial rays), do not converge on the focus. The outermost of these rays (which impinges on the periphery of the mirror) crosses the principle axis at point x. The distance between x and the focal point may be used as a measure of the spherical aberration of the mirror.

use the binomial expansion, we obtain

$$x = \frac{y^2}{2R} + \frac{y^4}{8R^3} + \frac{y^6}{16R^5} + \cdots. \tag{10.5}$$

The first term in this expression matches the equation for a parabola possessing symmetry about the x axis and with a focus (f) such that

$$x = \frac{y^2}{4f}.$$

In this case, $R = 2f$ and therefore the additional terms in Eq. (10.5) may be considered as representing deviations from the parabolic form of mirror, and it is these terms that contribute to the spherical aberration outside the paraxial region. Their impact becomes significant when y is relatively large when compared to the radius of curvature.

As indicated in Figure 10.4, in the case of a ray that lies close to, and travels parallel to, the principal axis, it will be reflected through the focal point (f). However, for rays that travel parallel to the principal axis but which are more distant to it, upon reflection, they no longer pass through the focal point. In this context, Smith [1957] writes:

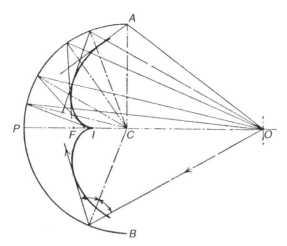

Figure 10.5 Caustic curves that indicate the astigmatic behavior when nonparaxial rays are reflected by a spherical mirror.

As the distance ... of any ray in the incident beam from the principle axis increases so does the reflected ray cross the axis at a point which gets closer to the mirror. The envelope of all rays in the plane of the diagram is the caustic curve and if we imagine the diagram to be rotated about the axis PC the caustic curve traces out a caustic surface.

The form of the caustic curve is illustrated in Figure 10.5.

In the case of the paraboloidal form of mirror, incoming rays that are parallel to the principle axis are reflected so as to converge at the focal point—irrespective of their distance from the principal axis. However, for off-axis objects, both the spherical and parabolic mirrors give rise to aberration. In this context, Smith and Thomson [1975] write:

A paraboloid of revolution does not, however form a perfect image for objects off the axis, and if it is intended to use an extended field of view in an optical telescope it will be necessary to consider off-axis aberrations, which grow more rapidly with angle for a paraboloid than for a spherical reflector.[4]

10.4 TECHNICAL CONSIDERATIONS

In this section, we briefly review some of the issues that need to be considered in the design of a varifocal display unit. This discussion is intended to illustrate various technical considerations, and for further details the interested reader is referred to the chapter concerning varifocal systems written by Lawrence Sher in McAllister [1993].

[4] For discussion of off-axis aberrations see, for example, Smith and Thomson [1975].

10.4.1 Image Update and Acoustic Noise

You don't have to burn books to destroy a culture.
Just get people to stop reading them.[5]

As with the volumetric systems described in previous chapters, it is desirable to ensure that image refresh takes place at a frequency of no less than 30 Hz. Although this frequency may be reduced (a little), any perceived image flicker (and possibly subliminal flicker) is likely to cause strain to the visual system and so make it difficult to use a display continuously for long periods of time.

In Section 4.2 we introduced various exemplar volumetric systems, the second of which employed translational motion for image space creation. Here, we discussed the issue of performing two image refreshes during each cycle of the screen's motion, and we noted that only voxels lying centrally to the screen's extremes of motion would be updated at equal intervals. As a result, in the case of the translational motion of a screen, we cannot employ two image updates during each cycle of a screen's movement to either reduce the frequency of screen motion or reduce image flicker. This also applies to the varifocal technique.

> Although two image updates may be performed during each cycle of the mirror's movement, with the exception of voxels located midway in the mirror's range of motion, these updates will not occur at equal time intervals. This approach cannot therefore be used to uniformly reduce image flicker throughout the image space.

Consequently, a varifocal mirror needs to operate at a frequency of approximately 30 Hz. On the other hand, the lower bound to the human sense of hearing lies in the range of 16–32 Hz (although 30 Hz is a value that is most frequently quoted). Therefore, as we increase the frequency of vibration of the mirror to satisfy our quest for a flicker free image, we also increase the amount of audible noise emanating from the display (a problem that is exacerbated when we employ larger sizes of mirror).

Naturally, we do not wish to compromise otherwise high-quality images by accepting perceptible image flicker, and one possible solution is to devise a system in which the vibrating mirror can be housed within a transparent vacuum vessel. Alternatively, a noise cancellation technique might be employed; although this is unlikely to be fully effective, it may lead to a significant decrease in noise output (see, for example, Section 10.5.3).

> Audible noise is not an inherent problem associated with the varifocal approach. With judicious design, the level of such noise can be greatly reduced or even eliminated.

---

[5] Attributed to Ray Douglas Bradbury (1920–).

10.4.2 Mirror Motion

In Section 10.2 we considered a mirror employing a sinusoidal motion profile. As with the volumetric systems discussed in Chapter 6 and that employ the translational motion of a screen for image space formation, if the mirror moves with sinusoidal motion, the graphics engine will need to output image slices in such a way as to ensure their even spacing within the image space. Consequently, slices lying closer to the mid-point of mirror movement will have to be output over shorter time intervals than those that lie toward the extremes of mirror displacement.

An alternative strategy is to adopt a motion profile that imposes linear velocity over the largest possible range of mirror movement (cf. discussion in Section 4.2). This technique was studied by Eric Rawson (see Section 10.5.2), and it is important to note that the location of the reflected image does not vary linearly with mirror displacement. Consequently, to enable the graphics engine to output image slices at uniform intervals and support their uniform depiction within the image space, the mirror displacement signal is not the sawtooth waveform that one might initially anticipate.

10.5 VARIFOCAL DISPLAY SYSTEM DEVELOPMENT

In this section we review a number of varifocal systems reported in literature. As with our discussion of volumetric embodiments, we do not provide exhaustive discussion on this fascinating history, but rather focus on the activities of a number of researchers whose achievements provide us with an insight into the technical progress made to date.

10.5.1 The Work of Alan Traub

From the literature available to the author, it appears that Alan Traub was the first to develop varifocal display systems for use as computer displays.[6] He describes aspects of this work in a patent filed early in 1966 (US Patent Number 3,493,290) and in a subsequent paper [Traub, 1967].

In his comprehensive patent, Traub provides background discussion in relation to the need for display systems able to support the depiction of 3-D images and writes:

> *The world in which we live is a three-dimensional world; but the retina of the eye, being a two-dimensional sensitive surface, can receive only a two-dimensional image. Hence our perceptions of distance and depth of field are inferences which we draw, immediately and unconsciously, from the several clues with which nature has provided us; namely, perspective, parallax, obscuration, shadowing and, in the narrow sense implying binocular vision, stereopsis. But it is quite otherwise when the object field from which the two-dimensional retinal image is derived is itself two-dimensional—e.g., a photograph, a painting, a diagram, a chart, a lantern slide, or the like. With a single such "flat" object field, several of the clues fail. While the observer can still infer that the photographer, the painter, or the draftsman intended to represent a three-dimensional object field, and may conclude that he succeeded or that he failed, such*

---

[6] However, the varifocal membrane mirror had been discussed several years earlier (see Muirhead [1961]). Mirrors were constructed using a Mylar membrane with diameters of up to ~3.6 m.

inferences are of the second order and are not of the same compelling and immediate character as the inferences drawn from the missing clues. Moreover, these second order inferences are dependent on the observer's familiarity with objects of the class depicted. Thus, for example, he knows that a horse is bigger than a dog; and if he sees a picture showing a horse and a dog with like sizes, he infers that the horse was further away from the camera or from the painter's easel than was the dog. Evidently, even the drawing of such second order inferences fails in the case of representations of objects with which the observer has no acquaintance. Yet it is frequently in this very situation that the immediate perceptions of distance and depth are of greatest importance.

As we have seen, during the 1940s through until the 1970s, research activity relating to the development of volumetric displays was generally intended to provide advanced visualization systems better able to depict radar returns from aircraft. This was also the thrust of the work undertaken by Traub, and in Figure 10.6 we reproduce from his 1967 publication a stereoscopic photograph of a varifocal system depicting simulated air traffic control data.

He reports the use of mirrors 20 cm and 38 cm in diameter. These were implemented using an aluminized Mylar membrane (thicknesses ranging from 6 μm to 25 μm) attached to a loudspeaker. In relation to the formation of the mirror, Traub writes:

The frame is a pair of concentric aluminium rings with tapered mating surfaces, like an embroidery hoop, and with bolted flanges to ensure that the rings will grip the material

Figure 10.6 A stereoscopic pair illustrating the use of Traub's varifocal mirror display for the depiction of simulated air traffic control data. Within either of the two images, the CRT-based display is on the left and the varifocal mirror is to the right. By viewing this pair of images with a stereoscope (or by viewing the pair directly and "fusing" the images (this can take a little practice)), the 3-D nature of the image depicted by the mirror is readily apparent (the image space lies "behind" the mirror). The images may be fused by slightly "crossing" the eyes. (Reproduced from Traub [1967], by kind permission and copyright of the Optical Society of America.)

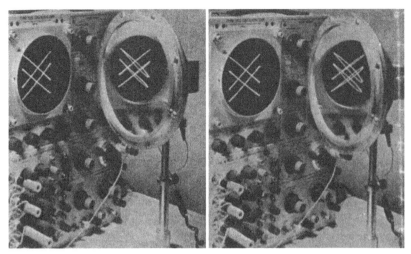

Figure 10.7 A 3-D Lissajous figure depicted on Traubs varifocal display. Here the image is depicted on an oscilloscope screen (seen on the left-hand side of the photo) and is reflected by the varifocal mirror (which is to the right). The mirror motion is achieved by means of a loudspeaker, a part of which may be seen at the far right of each photograph. As with the previous figure, by viewing these images with a stereoscope (or by simply "fusing" them), the image depicted in the mirror becomes 3-D. (Reproduced by permission from Rawson [1969], with permission of IEEE.)

and stretch it tightly. A subsequent heat treatment removes tiny residual wrinkles in the membrane and yields a mirror of better quality than one might expect.

A further photograph of the display is provided in Figure 10.7. He reports the amplitude of motion as being *"typically less than a few millimeters"* and the use of a range of drive frequencies. As one would expect, he confirms that below ~20 Hz, image flicker becomes problematic.

In an alternative approach and to better support the implementation of large wall-mounted mirror systems, Traub reports on experiments carried out in relation to the implementation of an electrostatic drive system. Here, the membrane forms one plate of a capacitor, and behind this a metallic sheet is placed—this being the second capacitor plate. The two are separated and through the application of a high voltage (~10 kV) across the pair, the Mylar is distorted (due to the electrostatic field). This arrangement is reported to have provided satisfactory performance for a 38-cm mirror.[7]

Naturally, when the mirror is convex (diverging), a virtual image is formed (i.e., the image appears to lie behind the mirror). A real ("free") image may be formed (i.e., one that is brought to focus between the mirror and the observer) by

---

[7] The rigid metallic plate is reported as being coated with silicone rubber compound to discourage electrical breakdown. This was not fully effective.

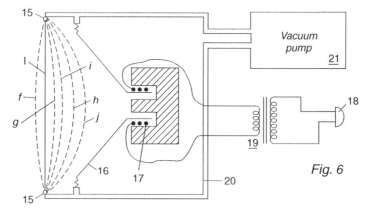

Figure 10.8 To provide better support for the production of a real image (i.e. one that is brought to focus between the mirror and observer(s)—the "free space" image), Traub describes the biasing of the membranes curvature so that it only moves between planar and concave states. This is achieved by slightly reducing the pressure within chamber (20) thereby predistorting the membrane. (Reproduced from US Patent Number 3,493,290.)

only making use of a relatively small portion of the mirror's range of motion.[8] In his patent, Traub proposes an alternative arrangement which is illustrated in Figure 10.8. Here, the membrane mirror forms the front wall of a chamber (20) and within this vessel (a loudspeaker ((16)/(17)) is used to cause motion of the mirror. A vacuum pump is then used to *slightly* reduce the pressure within the chamber, thereby producing a pressure difference across the membrane. This results in the mirror being pre-distorted to a concave state; thus when driven by the loudspeaker, its motion is biased and the convex state can be avoided. Traub also suggests the creation of a system in which the varifocal mirror is replaced by a convex lens of variable focus. In this way, Traub sought to support image production such that *"the image be viewed by light transmitted through the varifocal element instead of reflected from it."* The proposed lens arrangement is illustrated in Figure 10.9. In this scenario, the lens is formed from a liquid contained within a flexible and transparent envelope. By modulating the pressure of the liquid, the lens may be made to vary in thickness, and so corresponding changes in its focal length will ensue.

Finally, in relation to Traub's interests in applying varifocal technologies to the visualization of aircraft radar data, he suggests the production of a display able to take input from various sources and amalgamate these within an image space. The proposed technique is illustrated in Figure 10.10. In brief, various forms of imagery (e.g., depicted on CRTs (41 and 42) or produced as a physical terrain model (38)) are brought together using partially reflecting mirrors (50–53) so that the images are projected along a common axis. If viewed directly, an observer would then see

---

[8] To create real ("free space") images, even when in the concave state, only a limited portion of the mirror's motion can be used. This is restricted to positions in which the mirror's focal length is less than the object distance.

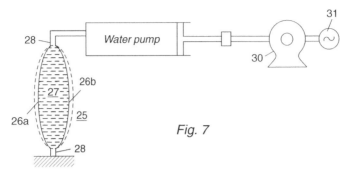

Fig. 7

Figure 10.9 To support an optical arrangement in which the image is projected onto the varifocal component from the rear, Traub discusses the use of a varifocal lens. Here, the lens comprises a transparent deformable envelope containing a liquid (27). By rapidly modulating the pressure of the liquid, variations in lens thickness can be achieved. This parallels the approach suggested by Baird in his 1931 patent in which the refractive index of the lens material was (in principle) varied by the application of an electric field, (see Section 6.3.1). (Reproduced from US Patent Number 3,493,290.)

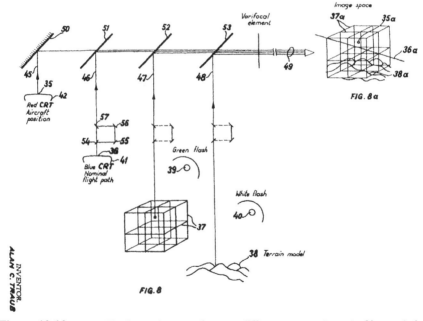

Figure 10.10 Here, Traub sought to amalgamate different sources (types) of image (relating to the visualization of aircraft radar data) within a single image space. Each image source is made visible (illuminated) momentarily as the varifocal element exhibits the focal length needed to cast the image data into the appropriate image space location (depth). (Reproduced from US Patent Number 3,493,290.)

these image sources as emanating from different depths. However, Traub describes an arrangement in which each of these image sources is only made visible for brief periods of time and employs a varifocal element. In this way, by illuminating each image source at the appropriate time (corresponding to the varifocal element exhibiting a particular focal length), the image sources can be positioned at any required depth within a common image space. This arrangement does not compensate for changes in magnification that occur as the varifocal element moves through each cycle of motion.

10.5.2   The Work of Eric Rawson

In the late 1960s Eric Rawson working at Bell Telephone Laboratories conducted research into the varifocal technique. As with Alan Traub, Rawson demonstrates a very clear perception of the need to advance the human–machine interface, and in one of his publications [Rawson, 1969] which appeared at the time of the first manned Moon expeditions, he begins:

> *A miniature television camera held by an astronaut made the beauty of the moon and earth vivid for millions of viewers. This same camera, when focused on instruments and controls within the Apollo 10 cabin, testified to the complexity of man–machine interactions.*
>
> *Much of the data involved in these interactions are three-dimensional in nature; and technologists have continually stressed the need for a good three-dimensional man-machine interface. The lack of such a device has forced us into unnatural compromises for data handling. For example, the three-dimensional positions of aircraft in the vicinity of an airport are presented on a two-dimensional interface—a cathode ray tube (CRT). If the aircrafts' altitude are shown, they are represented by numbers painted besides the radar echo marks. Like the air traffic controller, the submarine commander who operates in a three-dimensional environment would probably be happier if he could replace his two-dimensional CRT sonar display with an equivalent three-dimensional man–machine interface. . . .*

In this publication, Rawson describes the implementation of a varifocal system used for the depiction of computer-generated films. The technique used for this application is illustrated in Figure 10.11. A specially prepared 16-mm film contains a series of image slices—a set of 15 of which are output to the mirror as it moves toward the observer. Subsequently, 15 opaque frames are output during the period that it returns to its most distant point. The projector is reported as operating at 450 frames per second (indicating a vibrational frequency of 15 Hz).

In another publication [Rawson, 1968], Rawson provides an interesting analysis of mirror motion and particularly considers the form of the mirror drive waveform that is needed to permit the graphics engine to output image slices at equal time intervals, and support their equidistant depiction within the image space.[9] In this context Rawson identifies two problems, one of which is analytical and the other mechanical. In relation to the former, Rawson writes:

---

[9] He sought to achieve this linearity across 90% of the mirror's range of displacement.

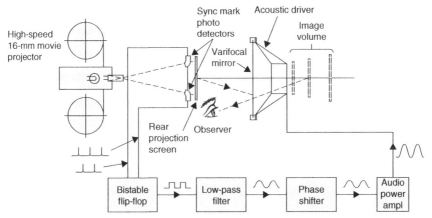

Figure 10.11 The apparatus described by Rawson for the depiction of 3-D "movies." Here, specially prepared film sequences (computer generated) are output in synchronism with the motion of a varifocal mirror. As the mirror moves towards the observer, 15 frames are output at a rate of 450 images per second. (Reproduced by permission from Rawson [1969], © 1969 IEEE.)

> *...the image distance is a nonlinear function of the mirror pole displacement. Hence a sawtooth image motion requires a more complicated mirror displacement waveform. The problem is to determine what mirror displacement waveform will yield the desired sawtooth image motion.*

The mechanical problem investigated by Rawson concerns the motion of the mirror when driven by a waveform containing higher-frequency Fourier harmonics. In Figure 10.12, fine granules of salt scattered onto a horizontally placed varifocal mirror gather at nodal regions and so reveal the pattern of vibration. Rawson indicates that a 20-cm-diameter configuration will oscillate in the zero-order mode up to a frequency of ~150 Hz, after which higher-order modes of oscillation are excited [Rawson, 1969].[10]

Mirror motion is analyzed in more detail in [Rawson, 1968]. Apparatus used to measure the displacement of a point on the mirror's surface over time is indicated in Figure 10.13. Here, a spot of dust on the mirror's surface is illuminated using a laser source and the scattered light projected onto a moving strip of photographic film.

Rawson [1969] also refers to the issue of "anomalous perspective" previously reported by Alan Traub. As illustrated in Figure 10.14, the magnification of the mirror varies with its curvature. As a result, image slices that appear to lie closer to the observer are diminished in size; conversely, image slices that appear more distant may subtend a larger angle at the eye. This is contrary to natural real-world perspective (see Section 2.3.1). The problem may be overcome by scaling the image slices prior to their being output to the display. In this way, all slices

---

[10] Rawson therefore employed an arrangement in which the displacement waveform was filtered to strongly attenuate frequency components beyond 150 Hz. Unfortunately, he does not discuss the issue of acoustic noise.

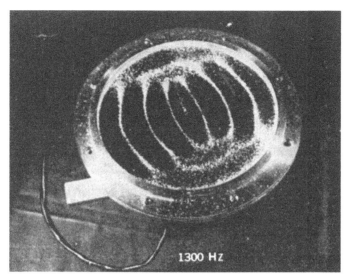

Figure 10.12 When the mirror is driven at higher frequencies by means of a loud speaker, different modes of vibration occur. In this image, vibrations are made visible by means of fine salt granules that have been scattered on a horizontal varifocal mirror. These particles gather in nodal regions and so reveal the vibration pattern. (Reproduced from Rawson [1969] with permission from IEEE.)

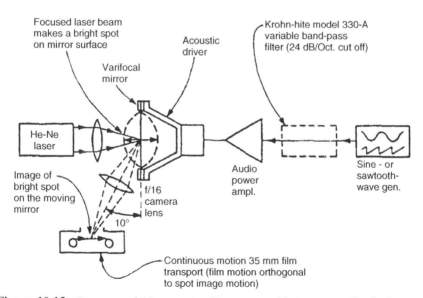

Figure 10.13 By means of this apparatus, Rawson was able to measure the displacement of a point on the mirror over time. The laser light is scattered by a dust particle on the screen. Some of the scattered light is projected onto a moving strip of photographic film, so capturing mirror motion. (Reproduced by permission from Rawson [1968], © 1968 Optical Society of America.)

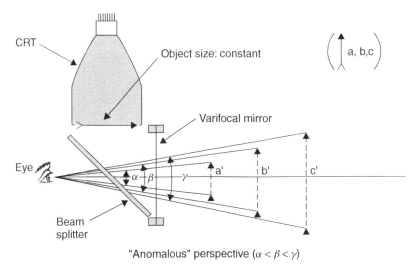

Figure 10.14 The issue of anomalous perspective. The magnification of the varifocal mirror varies according to its curvature. Consequently, image slices that appear to lie closer to the observer subtend a smaller visual angle than those that are more distant. This difficulty may be overcome by scaling the image slices prior to their being output to the display. (Reproduced with permission from Rawson [1969] © 1969 IEEE.)

may have the same spatial extent and therefore their perspective may be perceived naturally.[11]

10.5.3   The Work of Lawrence Sher

The two approaches described above make use of a flexible membrane mirror, and in a patent filed by Lawrence Sher in 1977 (US Patent Number 4,130,832) an alternative varifocal mirror design is described. Although the membrane mirror is simple and easily implemented, Sher highlights some of its weaknesses. For example:

1. The level of acoustic noise created when the mirror is vibrated at frequencies of ~30 Hz. This increases with the size of the mirror.

2. The onset of higher modes of vibration. These impact on both acoustic noise and image distortion.

3. The displacement of the mirror is strongly influenced by the shape of the displacement waveform and the characteristics of the loudspeaker. This impacts on the achievement of high instantaneous displacement accuracy and is problematic because the velocity profile of the mirror in the forward and reverse

---

[11] Additionally, since the varifocal technique provides only a single "window" onto the image space, the image slices may be scaled, thus increasing the perceived image space depth.

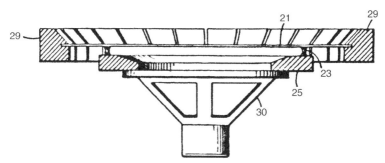

Figure 10.15   A cross-section of the varifocal assembly described by Lawrence Sher. This employs a structure that resonates at the displacement frequency and the use of a membrane mirror is therefore avoided. See text for details. (Reproduced from US Patent Number 4,130,832.)

directions is unlikely to be identical. This is likely to cause problems when we attempt to output image slices over both half-cycles of mirror motion.[12]

Sher therefore sought a solution that would address these weaknesses. In essence, the technique that he describes employs a structure that resonates at the displacement frequency. A cross section of the varifocal mirror assembly is reproduced in Figure 10.15. The lower part of this diagram shows the loudspeaker (30), which is attached to a solid metallic support ring (25). The mirror is formed using a stiff material (such as an acrylic plastic sheet) that is silvered (21).[13] This sheet extends beyond the diameter of the loudspeaker and support ring and is separated from the latter by a flexible ring (23) of, for example, Buna-N-rubber, which exhibits a high degree of compliance. An adhesive is used to bond this ring to both the supporting ring and the acrylic mirrored plate. Finally, around the rim of the mirrored plate, weights are added. In one embodiment these take the form of a number of segments which are individually bonded to the acrylic plate, a small gap being left between each segment.[14] These weights stress the panel (see Figure 10.16) and provide a structure with the appropriate resonant frequency. Sher writes:

> *The design of the plate, therefore, including its stiffness, its edge weighting, its diameter, and its support, must be such that its resonant frequency is the desired frequency of oscillation, which is typically 30 Hz.*

He goes on to say:

> *The flexing mode in which the plate/weighting means system operates is one in which the movement of the rim is out-of-phase with the motion of the central portion of the*

---

[12] Recall that in the system described in Section 10.5.2 and that was used for the depiction of 3-D movies, Rawson output image slices only during the period that the mirror was moving in a single direction.

[13] In one embodiment Sher indicates a diameter of 16 inches and a thickness of 0.12 inches.

[14] In connection with the embodiment referred to in the previous footnote, Sher indicates the use of 50 segments each of mass 21 g and a gap between the segments of ~0.02 inches.

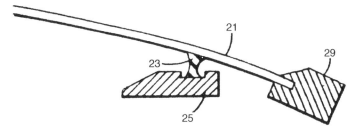

Figure 10.16 A cross-section showing the loading of the stiff mirrored plate (21) by a series of weights (29) that are attached to its periphery. In this diagram Sher exaggerates, for clarity, the bending of the plate. The solid ring (25) is attached to the rim of the loudspeaker (this is not shown but would lie below this assembly) and (23) denotes a flexible rubber ring which is bonded to both the mirrored plate and to the solid metallic ring. (Reproduced from US Patent Number 4,130,832.)

> *plate 21, there being a circular node spaced somewhat inside the rim of the plate. The location of the support ring is chosen to produce a most desirable curvature distribution across the face of the mirror from the point of view of the desired optical characteristics.*

Commenting on the level of audible noise generated by the mirror assembly, Sher indicates that it is markedly less than that generated by a membrane mirror of the same diameter. In this context he writes:

> *...the rim and the central portion of the plate undergo movement in opposite axial directions.... In essence, the high pressure zone generated on a forward moving central portion of the plate is discharged into the low-pressure zone created by the oppositely moving rim rather than being radiated into the surrounding space.*

In this way, a degree of noise cancellation is achieved. Additionally, Sher indicates that the assembly permits image slices to be output to the display throughout the entire cycle of mirror motion.[15]

The general architecture of the graphics engine described by Sher in the patent that he filed in 1977 is illustrated in Figure 10.17. As may be seen, image frames are depicted on a CRT (these then being reflected by the varifocal mirror). Here it is important to note that the 2-D display must support very short image persistence.[16] Additional details of the work undertaken by Sher in this area and specifically the SpaceGraph display system (a table-top varifocal display able to interface to a standard PC) may be found in Sher [1988].

---

[15] However, in the case of the membrane mirror, it is possible that the mirror's instantaneous position could be continuously measured (or at least calibration measurements made of its motion profile). In this way, support for image slice depiction throughout the mirror's cycle of motion might be achieved.

[16] In the chapter written by Sher that appears in the book edited by McAllister [1993], he indicates that P46 (KG) phosphor provided satisfactory performance. After removal of the excitation stimulus, light output falls to the 10% level in 160 ns. This contrasts with the characteristics of both P4 (WW) and P31 (GH) phosphors which respectively decay to the same level in 150 µs and 35 µs. Not surprisingly, neither of these two phosphors was found by Sher to be satisfactory. (Data source: EIA [1987].)

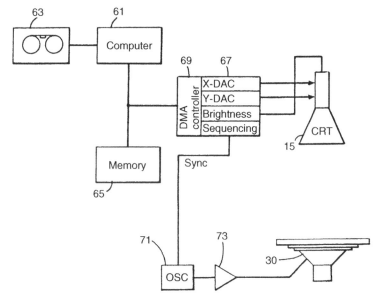

Figure 10.17   The graphics engine discussed by Sher. Here, the image slices are depicted on a conventional 2-D screen (supporting electrostatic beam deflection and exhibiting short persistence). These are reflected by the varifocal mirror which is viewed from an off-axis location. (Reproduced from US Patent Number 4,130,832.)

10.5.4   The Application of the Varifocal Mirror to Medical Imaging

In 1981 Genisco, operating under license from Bolt Beranek and Newman (BBN), brought to market a varifocal display system—sadly, the venture did not succeed. Subsequently, Lawrence Sher [whose 1977 patent (discussed in the previous subsection) was assigned to BBN] developed a small and inexpensive system (Sher writing in McAllister [1993]). In 1987 David Kennedy and Alan Nelson applied a BBN SpaceGraph varifocal mirror to medical imaging and in an ensuing publication [Kennedy and Nelson, 1987] discuss its use in brain anatomy and the analysis of bifurcation of the carotid artery as revealed using magnetic resonance techniques. In their introduction, the researchers write:

> *The inherent three-dimensionality of tomographic images is impaired when viewed conventionally as a series of two dimensional images.*

Consequently, their research sought to determine the usefulness of the varifocal approach; certainly, even 2-D photographs of the 3-D varifocal images that they obtained are impressive (see, for example, Figure 10.18). Parallel research was conducted by Harris et al. [1986], again with the intention of evaluating the benefits that could be derived by depicting a set of tomographic image slices within a 3-D space. The first two paragraphs of their publication are particularly relevant

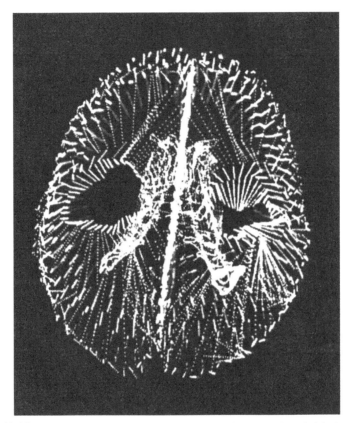

Figure 10.18   The depiction of the human brain including the left and right hemispheres and ventricles using a varifocal system. (Reproduced from Kennedy and Nelson [1987], copyright © 1987 IEEE.)

to readers who may have limited knowledge of this type of application. These are therefore quoted in full:

> *Three-dimensional display of stacks of tomographic images, utilizing a varifocal mirror display system, addresses the fundamental dilemma that while tomographic images contain no superposition, they also contain no three-dimensional information even though comprehending three-dimensional shapes and/or spatial relationships is often desirable, if not vital. For example, an image of an oblique section may, on one hand, provide an unambiguous view of a slice through an organ but still be completely useless if the viewer does not understand the orientation of the slice with respect to structures of interest. The fact of this fundamental limitation of tomography is reinforced by the observation that even in magnetic resonance imaging, where the orientation of the scanning plane is not constrained by a physical gantry, only the relatively few "standard" image orientations are generally utilized.*
>
> *When insight such as appreciating 3-D spatial relationships or shape is required, 2-D display of tomographic images is one dimension short. Generally, this shortcoming is*

(a)   (b)

Figure 10.19 The varifocal display employed by Harris et al. A CRT-based display (which can be seen at the top of each photograph) projects image slices downward onto the angled varifocal mirror. In (b) the reflection of the CRT screen in the mirror may be seen. (Reproduced from Harris et al. [1986], with permission from IEEE.).

overcome by generating multiple parallel tomographic images which span the anatomic extent of the organ(s) of interest. The required insights are gained by mentally assembling the organ shape while viewing the multiple images one after another or arranging the images in a "multiformat" 2-D array.

Photographs of the varifocal display employed in this study is reproduced in Figure 10.19. In their publication the workers present images comprising, for example, 27 depth planes—each permitting the activation of 128×128 voxels (leading to a voxel activation capacity of ~440,000).[17] For additional interesting discussion relating to the use of the varifocal technique for the depiction of tomographic images, see, for example, Udupa [1983].

10.5.5 The Work of King and Berry

Workers at Bell Telephone Laboratories developed an interesting and novel video imaging system in which two varifocal mirrors were employed [King and Berry, 1970]. As illustrated in Figure 10.20, the first of these mirrors is used for data

[17] For more discussion concerning advanced interaction with medical images depicted on a flat screen display see, for example, Hinckley et al. [1998] and summary discussion in Blundell and Schwarz [2006].

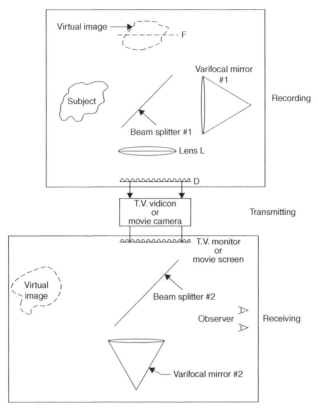

Figure 10.20 Here, two 38 cm varifocal mirrors are used — one for data acquisition and the other for data depiction. The two mirrors oscillate at the same frequency, but are 180° out of phase. See text for details. (Reproduced by permission from King and Berry [1970], © 1970 Optical Society of America.)

acquisition while the second one is used for data display. As may be seen from this illustration, light scattered from a 3-D object passes through a beam splitter and is reflected by a varifocal mirror. An observer looking into the beam splitter (from below) would therefore see a virtual image at the indicated location. A lens (L) with large aperture and low f-number is located so that its focal plane is centered on the virtual image. Such a lens has a small depth of focus, and therefore only the part of the image that is close to the focal plane will be brought to focus on the screen (D). As the varifocal mirror sweeps through each half-cycle of motion, the virtual image sweeps back and forth through the plane (F), and therefore a series of image planes are depicted on the projection screen (D). These may be captured using video camera and transmitted to the display apparatus. The varifocal mirror used for image depiction vibrates at the same frequency as that used for data capture, and the operation of the display follows the standard approach. King and Berry provide an excellent analysis of the distortion of the image resulting from the optical systems used for data capture and display, and they show that a distortion free image may be readily obtained. The workers highlight several shortcomings of the technique and propose possible solutions. For example, they write:

> *The primary shortcoming of the system is the noise from the out-of-focus images, which significantly degrades the quality of the reconstruction. However, the noise is predominantly of low spatial frequency, and could be filtered out by optical or electronic means.*

Additionally:

> *At the monitor end of the system additional optics would be necessary to give the observer a greater feeling of involvement with the reconstructed image. At present the viewer observes a virtual three-dimensional image located a few feet behind the face of the second varifocal mirror. This hinders the three-dimensional effect since the image appears to be located at the end of a long hollow tube. This shortcoming could be overcome by imaging the reconstruction to the front of the varifocal mirror by leans of a large conical mirror.*[18]

10.6   DISCUSSION

> *The thought of working with Barnes Wallis angered Mitchell so much that he could scarcely bring himself to speak to him. If Barnes Wallis came into the office at one door, he marched out through the other. Unable to stand the situation, Mitchell absented himself from Supermarine, and nobody had any idea where he was...*
> *it was unwise and undiscerning of Sir Robert to expect two men of such stature and individual personalities to work together....*[19]

In this chapter we have briefly outlined aspects of the varifocal display technique and have provided an overview of aspects of the research that has been carried out in this area. As with other creative 3-D display paradigms, the varifocal approach is not without weaknesses—but opportunities exist to overcome or at least ameliorate these and so produce an effective, low-cost display solution. Unfortunately, all too often, the varifocal technique is dismissed on the basis of the acoustic noise that is generated by the moving surface. This is not an inherent weakness of the approach, and with judicious design a noise-free varifocal display could be developed.

In Section 12.2 we again refer to this form of display and suggest areas in which additional refinements could and should be investigated.

---

[18] For related discussion on the use of a varifocal mirror for 3-D imaging see Ishii [2003].

[19] Barnes Wallis—a brilliant creative engineer: designer of the R100 Airship, the WWII Wellington Bomber, the "bouncing bomb," and the 'earthquake bomb' and a leading expert on supersonic flight. R. J. Mitchell was an equally brilliant and creative figure—the designer of the high-speed aircraft that competed for the British for the Schneider Trophy (and which won the Schneider Trophy outright for Britain) and of course, the Supermarine Spitfire. Without either of these figures, WWII may well have had a quite different outcome. Such remarkable individuals are seldom team players...! Quotation from Mitchell G. (ed.), *R. J. Mitchell Schooldays to Spitfire*, Nelson and Saunders [1986].

10.7 INVESTIGATIONS

1. Consider the varifocal lens proposed by Alan Traub, illustrated in Figure 10.9. Determine an equation that relates the curvature of the lens surfaces with the focal length of the lens. To form a useful image space, estimate the dimensions of the lens that would be needed and the necessary variation in lens thickness.

2. Discuss the possibility of employing a DMD as an image source for use with a varifocal mirror.

3. Discuss difficulties that may occur when we seek to produce a real ("free space") image (i.e., one that is brought to focus between the observer and the varifocal mirror).

4. In the case of most 3-D display paradigms, the convergence and accommodation cues are not correctly satisfied. Does the varifocal technique satisfy these cues in a natural manner?

5. The two varifocal mirrors employed in the system outlined in Section 10.5.5 oscillate at the same frequency but with a phase difference of 180°. Explain the reason for this phase difference.

11 The Graphics Pipeline and Interaction Issues

And when at last he came to Camelot,
A wreath of airy dancers hand-in-hand
Swung round the lighted lantern of the hall;
And in the hall itself was such a feast
As never man had dream'd; for every knight
Had whatsoever meat he long'd for served...
While the wine ran: so glad were the spirits and men.

11.1 INTRODUCTION

In the first part of this chapter we briefly consider issues relating o the characteristics of graphics engines needed to support the operation of volumetric and varifocal systems. The detailed architecture of the hardware and software systems that comprise the graphics engine is influenced by a number of factors. These include the characteristics of the image data set, the nature of the application, the display unit architecture, and the form of the interaction techniques that are to be supported. Consequently, we avoid detailed hardware descriptions and focus our discussion on general issues relating to the overall operation of the graphics engine and to its development for use in different situations.

We open our discussion by considering facets of the image data set that forms the primary data input to the graphics engine and the output (that takes the form of a series of appropriate voxel descriptor attributes) and which are passed to the voxel activation mechanisms in synchronism with any temporal demands imposed by the display. We identify a number of display characteristics that must be considered in developing the lower-level stages of the graphics engine. This leads on to discussion in Section 11.3 concerning the general architecture of a graphics engine suitable for use with display systems that support a parallelism of unity in voxel activation. In Section 11.4 we briefly consider display units in which highly parallel voxel activation can be supported (here we build discussion upon that presented in a previous work [Blundell and Schwarz, 2000]) and in which general proposals were made for a highly parallel graphics engine architecture.

In the case of swept-volume display systems that employ an active surface of emission, there is often the need to support the passage of voxel descriptors to electronic systems that co-rotate with the screen. Consequently, in Section 11.5 we describe an optical link that can be scaled to support parallel data transfer.

Although the primary function of the graphics engine is to effectively process the input data stream and support the visual characteristics of the display, the display itself cannot be considered in isolation but must be viewed as part of an integrated interaction environment. Consequently, advances in the interaction process and support of haptic feedback, impact upon the hardware and software systems that form the graphics engine. In Section 11.6 we turn our attention to the interaction process; however, we largely confine our discussion to issues relating to the characteristics of the display and their influence on interaction opportunities.[1] In this context we consider the "physical," "virtual," and "free" image space modalities previously introduced in Sections 1.5 and 3.2, and we also consider their suitability for use with the "direct," "transferred," and "pointer-based" interaction techniques. We pay particular attention to the formation of the "free space" image, and here we identify two general techniques that may be used for the formation of image spaces of this type. We refer to these as the "Re-imaging/Projection"-based and "Directly Generated" approaches.

11.2 GRAPHICS ENGINE: INPUT AND OUTPUT

The graphics engine takes its primary input from various sources such as data acquisition hardware and/or a data repository and provides output matching the data format requirements and temporal demands of the display system to which it interfaces. Additionally, the graphics engine takes input from secondary sources—particularly

---

[1] Although support for advanced interaction techniques impacts upon the architecture of the graphics engine, it is the display itself that ultimately determines the interaction techniques that can be supported. Given that a display unit is suited for use with a particular interaction modality, any necessary developments of the graphics engine can usually be readily achieved.

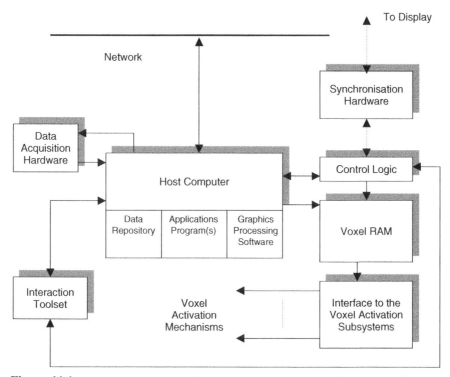

Figure 11.1 Basic components within a simple exemplar graphics engine. Here, we assume that the volumetric display forms a computer peripheral and that the processing of the image data is performed by the host computer (which acts as a key part of the graphics engine). This data may be derived from numerous sources and the graphics engine is responsible for its processing and outputs the results of the computational process in such a way as to meet the both the data format requirements and temporal characteristics of the display. In this model, the voxel RAM is assumed to comprise two RAM banks—one of which is updated by the host computer while the other is output to the display. In this way, image animation can be supported. The graphics engine must also make provision for interaction activities. (Diagram © Q. S. Blundell 2006.)

interaction tools used by the operator to control the display and manipulate the visible image.

As discussed, volumetric and varifocal displays are particularly suited to the depiction of point form volumetric (voluminous) data, and in Figure 11.1 we illustrate key elements that comprise an exemplar graphics engine suitable for use with a display system for which the parallelism in voxel activation is unity. As may be seen from this diagram, we assume that the host computer to which the display is connected is responsible for the processing of the image data set. Data may be obtained in numerous ways. For example, it may be gained in real time from data acquisition hardware such as a radar or sonar system, it may exist within a data repository (located within the host computer or be accessed remotely via a network connection), or it may be generated via some applications program. In fact, the data to be depicted on the display are likely to have been amalgamated from a plurality of sources, and for our present purposes it is sufficient to simply distinguish between data that are obtained and depicted in real time and those that are not:

1. *Real-Time Depiction:* In this scenario an incoming data stream is processed in real time and passed to the display for immediate depiction. Such data may, for example, portray the spatial separation and motion of aircraft. In this case, although the operator may, as part of the normal interaction process, wish to rotate the image scene and perhaps zoom into features that are of particular interest, the necessity of continually relocating the image to avoid, for example, regions of dead image space is highly undesirable! Certainly, unless a volumetric image space is able to exhibit isotropy and homogeneity in voxel placement, is without dead image space, and properly supports the propagation of light through the image space, it is unlikely that we can be confident of complete image fidelity. In this case, we would, for example, run the risk that aircraft could momentarily disappear—not as a result of a physical catastrophe but due to the aircraft icon briefly passing through a region of dead image space, or because of conditional voxel activation issues.

2. *Non-Real-Time Depiction:* In the case that an image data set is stored within the host computer, it is possible to be a little more tolerant of adverse image space characteristics. In this situation, the operator may interact with the data set to scale and reposition an image so that it may be portrayed to best advantage. However, this becomes more difficult when animated image scenes are to be shown.[2] Furthermore, the ability of an operator to make best use of an image space which exhibits undesirable characteristics presupposes that the operator has a technical knowledge of the display hardware, and this limits the usefulness of a display for general-purpose applications.

For all applications, it is desirable that an image space should provide a uniform and predictable tableau—with respect to both voxel placement and light propagation. Although for non-real-time applications it is possible for an operator to scale and position an image so that it is shown to best advantage, this becomes more difficult in the case of dynamic image sequences. For real-time applications, the need for such repositioning cannot be tolerated: Image space uniformity and predictability are of paramount importance.

---

[2] In this case, although it may be possible to locate the initial image so that it is presented most advantageously, subsequent motion (which may be difficult to predetermine) may cause parts of the image scene to pass through regions of an image space in which adverse image depiction or light propagation characteristics exist.

Returning to Figure 11.1, irrespective of the source(s) of the input data, the graphics engine must process the data in such a way as to generate a unified output which matches the requirements of the display. In the illustration, the output from the host computer is shown as being passed to "voxel RAM" (which stores each image frame and is able to support image animation) and to control logic (responsible for various tasks—particularly meeting the temporal requirements of the display).

Below we briefly review some important characteristics of a display unit that directly impact on the form of output that must be generated by the graphics engine.

1. *Specification of Voxel Location:* The primary input to the graphics engine may comprise volumetric (voluminous) data that take the form of "... *a set of scalar values defining one or more properties at discrete 'points' within a 3-D space.... In the case of volumetric data corresponding to a physical measurement, each member of the data set has associated attributes indicating quantities such as material density, temperature, or intensity of electromagnetic radiation at a particular location in a 3-D space*" [Blundell and Schwarz, 2006]. Alternatively, the data may be in the form of a set of high-level graphics primitives such as 3-D splines and NURBS[3] surfaces. In this case, the graphics engine must at some point decompose these primitives into discrete points within a 3-D space (voxels).

   Each voxel comprises a set of attributes: some of these can be manipulated by the graphics engine, while others are defined by the display. Those attributes that can be controlled by the graphics engine will be referred to as comprising the "voxel descriptor". Key voxel attributes are indicated in Figure 11.2. For each voxel, its location $\{u, v, w\}$ is specified[4] and additional information such as color, grayscale, and perhaps even opacity is included. As far as specifying the locations at which voxels are to be activated within the image space, different volumetric display architectures have different requirements. Below we briefly consider three indicative examples:

EXAMPLE 1

   Consider a swept-volume display that employs the translational motion of a planar surface of emission moving with constant velocity and that utilizes a single directed beam for voxel activation (exemplar System 2 in Section 4.2). In this case, and assuming the use of a dot graphics display technique, coordinates $\{u, v, w\}$ must be mapped to $\{\theta x_1, \theta y_1, t\}$ where $\theta x_1, \theta y_1$ represent the horizontal and vertical beam

---

[3] NURBS: nonuniform rational B-spline.

[4] Naturally we are not restricted to the use of a rectangular coordinate system, and both cylindrical and spherical coordinate systems can be used. The choice of coordinate system is influenced by issues such as the physical shape of the image space, the technique used for image space creation, and the geometry of the voxel activation subsystem relative to the image space. Furthermore, as discussed below, in mapping the voxel descriptor into a form suitable for the requirements of the display, $\{u, v, w\}$ will be used to derive other positional information.

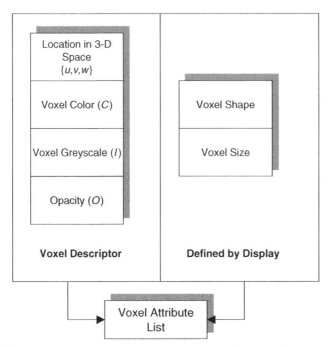

Figure 11.2 A voxel descriptor comprises a set of attributes such as those indicated on the left-hand side of this diagram. The graphics engine can manipulate these attributes and convert them into a form that meets the data format requirements of the display unit. Additionally, various attributes are defined by the characteristics of the display (such as those indicated on the right-hand side) and cannot be controlled by the graphics engine. Together, the voxel descriptor and display defined attributes are said to form the "voxel attribute list." (Diagram © M.C.E. Blundell 2006.)

deflection angles and t the time (within the screen's cycle of motion) at which the screen will be passing through the appropriate location within the image space. In turn, we use this information to derive $\{\theta_x, \theta_y, n\}$ where n denotes the identifier of the image slice into which the voxel will be placed. For convenience, the order in which voxel descriptors are stored in RAM addresses usually corresponds to the order with which they are to be output to the display (thus the RAM holds a sequential list of voxels to be output to the display). In this case, n is simply used by the host computer/control logic to correctly place the other voxel descriptor attributes into the appropriate image slice page (see Figure 11.3) and may subsequently be discarded.

EXAMPLE 2

Consider the case of a static-volume display in which voxel generation is achieved via the stepwise excitation of fluorescence and in which two directed beams are used for voxel activation (again we assume the use of a dot graphics display technique).

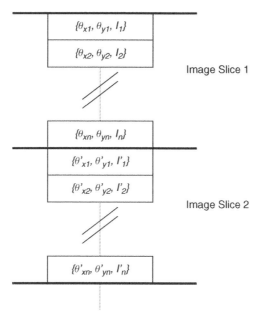

Figure 11.3 A simple approach to the storage of voxel descriptors in voxel RAM and which facilitates their output to a swept-volume display employing the translational motion of a planar screen addressed by a single directed beam source (see Example 1). Here the memory space is divided into a series of identical pages each of which relates to a corresponding image space slice. A counter synchronized to the motion of the screen is used to address sequential memory locations, each of which contains beam deflection angles and a beam intensity value (for simplicity we neglect color image generation). Measurement of the screen speed yields the maximum number of voxels that we can output into each image slice. Once this number is reached, the counter is loaded with the starting address of the voxel descriptor list for the next slice and the process repeats. Despite its simplicity, this scheme has several weaknesses. For example, equal memory space is allocated to all image space slices, irrespective of their voxel population. Also if the counter is clocked at a constant rate (corresponding to the worst-case voxel activation time), shorter move times are not taken into account. (Diagram © Q. S. Blundell 2006.)

Unlike Example 1, the time at which a voxel is activated does not determine its position within the image space and therefore temporal constrains are not introduced.[5] Beam deflection angles must be calculated and for this architectural arrangement we require the generation of two pairs of angles. Thus $\{u, v, w\}$ is mapped to $\{\theta_1, \theta_2\}$ and $\{\theta_3, \theta_4\}$ where the former pair represent the horizontal and vertical beam deflection angles for beam 1 and the latter provide the corresponding information for beam 2.

---

[5] To maximize the voxel activation capacity of the display, we may seek to undertake an approximate ordering of the data set, thereby minimizing the total distance traversed by the beams during each image refresh period. In such a situation, temporal considerations are in fact introduced.

EXAMPLE 3

> Consider the case of a varifocal mirror-based display employing a dot graphics approach and in which images are projected onto the mirror via a CRT. In this case, the mapping typically follows that used in Example 1.

2. *The Use of Several Voxel Activation Sources:* As we have seen in Chapter 7, in the case that we employ a static directed beam source for voxel activation in conjunction with a rotating screen, the continually varying geometry between beam and screen leads to distortional and voxel placement dead zones. One solution is to employ two or more beam sources that are positioned so that each is responsible for voxel activation throughout a portion of the image space. In this way, a beam is used only when the geometry between the beam source and screen is favorable and the display continues to exhibit a parallelism of unity in voxel activation.

   If we adopt this approach in the implementation of a display unit, then it is necessary to ensure that voxel descriptors are directed to the appropriate beam source. Here, we may adopt two simple strategies. Firstly, we may include within each voxel descriptor a code (of one or two bits) that defines the beam source to be used for the activation of the voxel. This code is then interpreted by the interface to the voxel activation subsystems (see Figure 11.1), and the remainder of the descriptor is routed accordingly. In a second scenario, we avoid the need to insert such codes by simply determining the voxel activation mechanism to which a voxel descriptor is to be passed from the descriptors location in the voxel RAM. Thus the image slice number (or the address at which the voxel descriptor is stored) is used to provide the routing information.

3. *Parallelism in Voxel Activation:* The ability of a display to support parallel voxel activation has a significant impact on the design of the graphics engine. This is briefly discussed in Section 11.4.

4. *Synchronization:* As we have seen, in the case of swept-volume (and varifocal) systems, the output of voxel descriptors to the display unit must be synchronized to the continually varying location of the screen. This means that the display needs to be equipped with hardware able to sense the location of the screen, and this information is fed back to the graphics engine. Two approaches may be adopted: The first of which involves the use of a sensor system that provides a "start of motion cycle" signal (i.e., indicates that the screen has just entered image slice zero), and an additional signal is generated each time the screen enters a new slice.[6] Such an arrangement was employed by the first cathode ray sphere prototype developed by the author (see Figure 11.4). Here, a disc (which co-rotates with the screen) is used in conjunction with two photodetectors. The disc is equipped with a "start of

---

[6] This type of approach was used in the implementation of the position sensing system employed in some early floppy disk drives during the 1970s.

revolution mark" and additionally a series of holes that denote movement between image slices.

Alternatively, if we assume constant screen speed throughout each cycle of motion (as is generally the case for systems employing rotational motion), we may employ an approach in which only the "start of motion cycle" is provided.[7] In this case, when the signal is received by the graphics engine, a counter is enabled. This continues to count clock pulses until the receipt of the next "start of motion cycle" at which point the value held in the counter is passed to a register; the counter then resets to zero and the counting process recommences. The value stored in the register is then divided by the number of image space slices and so provides us with a measure of the time available for the output of voxel descriptors within each image slice (and hence the maximum number of descriptors that may be output in each slice).[8] Here we are using the speed of the previous cycle of motion to indicate the speed of the current cycle.[9]

5. *Voxel Descriptor Throughput:* The maximum rate at which voxel descriptors are passed from the graphics engine to the display via the voxel activation pathways is determined by the voxel activation time (see Section 4.4).

6. *The Registration of Directed Beam Sources:* In the case where a display unit employs one or more directed beam sources for voxel activation, it is necessary to map between the coordinate system ascribed to the image space and that associated with each set of beam deflection apparatus. Such a mapping may be readily achieved through the use of homogeneous transformations[10]; here, both hardware and software support is needed to determine elements within the transformation matrix. Ideally, an automatic calibration system should be implemented.[11] Details of a manual beam source calibration procedure are presented in Blundell and Schwarz [2000].

---

[7] For displays employing the rotational motion of a screen, the screen acts as a flywheel, thereby helping to support constant angular velocity throughout each cycle of motion. Naturally, the situation is further improved if the screen moves within an evacuated vessel or, alternatively, if air turbulence is avoided.

[8] In performing the division of the value held in the counter by the number of image slices (m), care must be exercised. The division operation may be achieved by, for example, right shifting the counter value q places (where $q = \log_2 m$). However, to avoid the introduction of unacceptable error we need to arrange that the screen speed counter (C_1) and the counter responsible for cycling through memory locations (C_2) are clocked at different rates. Here, the clock used for C_1 would be of a higher frequency than that used by (C_2)—with both clocks being derived from the same source.

[9] The use of a phase locked loop also provides a convenient means of obtaining synchronization.

[10] See, for example, Boff et al. [1986] or standard computer graphics texts.

[11] Naturally, it is preferable to develop an approach that does not require the precise mechanical alignment of beam source deflection apparatus relative the image space. Furthermore, even if at the time of manufacture sufficient mechanical precision was achieved, during the lifetime of the display, it is likely that this would be eroded due to, for example, changes in the characteristics of associated electronic components. An automated system enabling the initial calibration of display hardware and periodic recalibration would therefore be advantageous. See Section 12.3.

(b)

(a)

Figure 11.4 The first of the cathode ray sphere (CRS) prototypes developed by the author (also see Sections 1.6.1, 4.6, and 12.3). In (a) the display is illustrated. Three windows provide views of the image space and these are interspersed by three electron guns. Despite the use of three electron beams, this system supported only sequential voxel activation. The pumping system may be seen—located below the display vessel. The screen motor drive is located well above the display chamber (the considerable separation of the motor drive and display chamber was intended to ensure that stray magnetic field produced by the drive did interfere with electron beam trajectory—in fact, this was an unnecessary precaution). Illustration (b) shows the display under construction. This was the only CRS prototype to use a screen position sensing disc that employed a sensing system providing both a "start of cycle of motion" signal (i.e., entry into sector zero) and an additional signal corresponding to the screens entry into each subsequent sector. Although this general technique provides accurate timing information and is simple to implement, sector timing can also be derived from a single "start of cycle of motion" detector (provided that we are able to assume constant angular velocity throughout each cycle of motion). This is a reasonable assumption since the screen acts as a flywheel and therefore evens out small fluctuations in screen motion during each rotation. (Original images © 2006 B.G. Blundell.)

11.3 THE GRAPHICS ENGINE: SEQUENTIAL VOXEL ACTIVATION

The ultimate result of shielding men from the effects of folly,
is to fill the world with fools.[12]

In the previous section, we introduced a simple architectural model of a graphics engine (suitable for use with display units exhibiting a parallelism of unity in voxel activation). This provided a basis for discussion concerning primary data input to the graphics engine and various display unit characteristics that define the output that must be generated. In this section, we turn our attention to the passage of image data through the graphics engine and as with previous discussion we confine ourselves to issues that highlight general principles of operation.

In Figure 11.5, various stages within a graphics pipeline are illustrated. Although some of these stages (particularly those at the higher level) are applicable to most volumetric and varifocal paradigms, others vary according the display architecture. In this diagram, we have assumed the use of a swept-volume display employing one or more directed beams for sequential voxel activation. On the left-hand side of this diagram, we indicate two exemplar sources of primary input, and these are passed to the pre-processing stage. Here, various tasks are performed. For example, in areas such as medical imaging, volumetric data sets tend to be enormous and therefore the pre-processing of such data prior to depiction will involve tasks such as feature extraction and the filtering/amalgamation of data. Ultimately, images that are to be displayed must match the pixel or voxel activation capacity of the display upon which they are to be depicted. In the case of a conventional display, we have the opportunity to display images comprised of $\sim 10^6$ pixels [although for many applications only a subset of these pixels (and hence a portion of screen area) will actually be used for the depiction of the image data]. As we have discussed, volumetric systems that support sequential voxel activation are typically limited to a voxel activation capacity (N_a) of less than 10^5 voxels and exhibit a low fill factor. Other volumetric systems that offer considerable parallelism in voxel activation may support a 100% fill factor, and N_a may be on the order of 10^8. It may therefore appear that at the low end, volumetric systems are inferior to the conventional 2-D screen in terms of their display bandwidth and at the high end outperform the conventional display. However, in reality, such a comparison is misleading and although volumetric systems that support highly parallel voxel activation can indeed outperform the pixel capacity of the conventional 2-D screen, in practical terms, volumetric displays are at their best when used for the depicting sparse data sets.

---

[12] Attributed to Herbert Spencer (1820–1903).

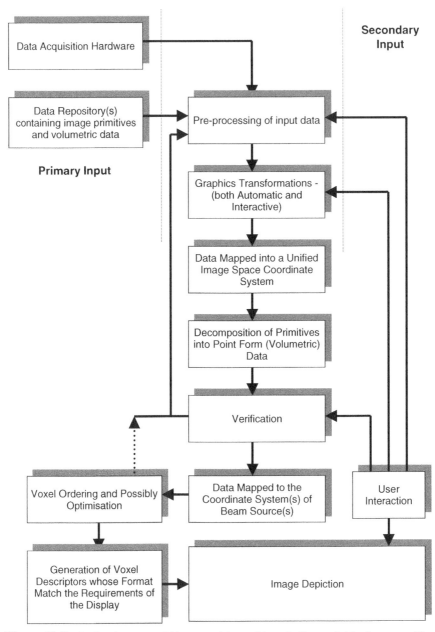

Figure 11.5 Basic elements within a model graphics pipeline suitable for use with a swept-volume display employing one or more directed beams and in which voxel activation is sequential. (Diagram © A.R. Blundell 2006.)

The depiction of data sets comprising large numbers of voxels may:

- *Clutter the image space and make it more difficult to discern spatial relationships.*
- *Result in undesirable superposition (although this problem is ameliorated by the translucent nature of most volumetric images).*
- *Increase the difficulty of achieving effective interaction with the image.*
- *Decrease the speed of the interaction process as a consequence of the extent of the data that must be processed.*

In relation to superposition, Harris et al. [1986] write:

Display of a stack of tomographic images utilizing the varifocal system means that superposition, the elimination of which is a primary objective of tomography, returns. Fortunately, the undesirable effects of superposition can effectively be overcome by allowing the user to interact with the image data, e.g., to non-destructively cut or peel away overlying image regions to more clearly visualize the image regions of interest.

Support for appropriate interaction modalities can therefore ameliorate problems caused by superposition, however, as the extent of the data set increases, so too does the time taken to process it in response to operator interaction. A balance must therefore be maintained between the type of interactive techniques to be supported, the number of voxels that comprise an image frame, and the cost of the graphics engine hardware. Reducing the number of voxels within the displayed image may not in itself reduce interaction latency. It is important to remember that the primary input data supplied to the graphics engine may well have been considerably reduced prior to its depiction. In this case we must consider whether the scope of interactive operations is to be limited to the computation of the displayed data, or is to involve more extensive computation that includes all or a large part of the primary source data set. In the former case, reducing the number of voxels per image frame will also reduce interaction overheads; in the latter situation, this may not be the case.

Recall: It is not appropriate to compare the pixel capacity offered by a conventional 2-D screen with the voxel activation capacity of a volumetric display: any such comparison overlooks the enhanced information content that can be derived by making proper provision for the third dimension. In this sense, the volumetric display does not necessarily present simultaneously to the viewer a greater number of data elements, but enhances the information content associated with each element that is displayed.

> When assessing a displays output "bandwidth," we should not only consider the number of elements which comprise the depicted image, but should also take into account the information content provided by each individual element, and by the elements when viewed collectively.

Returning to Figure 11.5, once the primary sources of input data have undergone suitable processing and we have defined "what we want to depict," the next task in the simple exemplar pipeline is to bring image data together within a unified image space coordinate system. For example, image entities may be scaled, rotated, and positioned; in this way we define the general layout of the image scene—that is, "how we want the scene depicted". To reduce the computational cost, it is better to carry out (whenever possible) such operations on graphics primitives rather than on their decomposed "point form" representations. However, once we have unified the coordinate systems and "defined the image scene," decomposition must be undertaken as we next need to be assured that the display is able to faithfully depict the image data set without, for example, data loss due to issues such as homogeneity and conditional voxel activation. In Figure 11.5, this is referred to as the "verification" stage. Although some aspects of the verification process can be handled automatically, in the case of a display unit that exhibits poor image space characteristics, operator intervention is likely to be necessary. Should the verification procedure identify problems, the operator will certainly need to take an active role in their resolution. As indicated previously in this chapter, verification becomes much more problematic when we are dealing with dynamic image sequences, and the best way of facilitating this process is to ensure that unfavorable image space characteristics are eliminated from the display unit architecture or are, at the very least, minimized.

Once the verification process has been satisfactorily accomplished, then in the case of, for example, a swept-volume display employing one or more directed beam sources, each voxel should be mapped into the most appropriate image space slice and beam deflection angles calculated. Additionally, we may wish to maximize the voxel activation capacity by reducing the total distance through which the activation beam moves within each slice. This involves computing the order that voxels will be output within each slice (see Section 4.4.2, Blundell and Schwarz [2000], and Schwarz and Blundell [1997]). Unfortunately, the gains that can be made by manipulating the order in which voxels are output within each slice depend on the spatial distribution of the voxels and therefore cannot be predicted in advance. Consequently, if an ordering procedure is implemented and the ensuing reduction in the average voxel activation time enables an increase in the number of voxels that may be contained in one or more image slices, it is necessary to pass once more through the higher levels of the pipeline.[13]

---

[13] In practice, the benefits of ordering are offset by the computational cost required to achieve even a relatively small advantage. If an application requires a voxel activation capacity that pushes

Finally, attributes within each voxel descriptor may need to be modified to meet the requirement of the display (specifically the voxel activation subsystem). Voxel descriptors can then be loaded into the voxel RAM ready for output to the display.

11.4 THE GRAPHICS ENGINE: PARALLEL VOXEL ACTIVATION

As discussed, display units that exhibit a high degree of parallelism in voxel activation are able to support a voxel activation capacity well in excess of the "pixel capacity" of a conventional 2-D display and may provide a 100% fill factor. To effectively utilize the potential of such a display, it is vital that we ensure that the performance it offers is not inhibited as a consequence of graphics engine limitations. In this respect, many issues must be considered—three examples are summarized below:

1. *Voxel RAM:* Suppose that a display unit is able to offer a voxel activation capacity of 10^8 and a 100% fill factor. If we were to activate all these voxels (or a large portion of them) during a single image update period, we would simply create a major source of light! Consequently, only a fraction of these voxels will be activated at any time, perhaps a maximum of $\sim$10% (more typically, less than 1%). This impacts on the extent of the voxel RAM that we need to employ. Since the maximum number of voxels that we are likely to activate within a frame defines the maximum number of voxel descriptors that we need accommodate within voxel RAM, we do not *necessarily* need to make provision for the actual voxel activation capacity. In such circumstances, the number of voxels descriptors that we need to store for output in a single image update period is given by $\psi_{max} N_a$.

2. *Voxel Throughput:* The output stages of the graphics pipeline should be able to support the maximum voxel bandwidth offered by the display unit. Continuing with the numerical values used in (1) above, and assuming a 30-Hz refresh frequency, the output stage of the graphics engine should be able to support a maximum voxel throughput of 3×10^9 voxels $\cdot$ s^{-1} (even though as indicated above we are most unlikely to ever activate more than 10% of the available voxels during each image refresh period). Failure to meet this requirement is likely to compromise image space predictability.

the limits of a display technology, then the application and display are not well-suited: Ordering is unlikely to reconcile the two! Furthermore, the cost associated with even an approximate optimization process will add to interaction latency.

> Recall: Support for a 100% fill factor enables us to activate vox-
> els at some, or all, of the available voxel locations. This enhances
> predictability. Support for smaller fill factor values does not neces-
> sarily detract from image space predictability—provided that when
> selecting a set of N_a voxels that we wish to activate from the set of
> possible voxel locations, no restrictions are placed upon the selection
> process.

3. *Processing of the Input Data:* As indicated in the previous section, support
   for the depiction of more extensive data sets may negatively impact on the
   interaction process. For the majority of applications, the processing capabilities offered by the graphics engine should be able to support real time
   interaction. Ultimately, this may necessitate the use of a parallel processing
   architecture.

Lowell Harris provides an interesting account of a graphics engine developed for
use with a varifocal mirror based display [Harris, 1988]. The display system was
able to operate in raster mode and was developed for the depiction of tomographic
images. The provision of effective support for real-time user interaction was a primary consideration (and despite the architecture of the graphics engine becoming
somewhat outdated, the author's emphasis on interaction ensures the publication's
continued relevance). The general architecture of the graphics engine is illustrated
in Figure 11.6. Image-processing hardware (contained within the upper right-hand
rectangle) performs high-speed computation and the varifocal mirror display interfaces via the "3-D controller." An internal bus operating at 200 Mbyte·s^{-1} supports
data flow within the image processor (IP). Provision is made for the operator to
interact with the varifocal images by means of a display (providing a 512×512
pixel resolution) equipped with a keyboard and trackball.

In the context of interactive operations supported by the system, Harris writes:

> *The first class of manipulations is the basis of dynamic pan, zoom and image rotation.*
> *The extraction of a $128 \times 128 \times 30$ subvolume from the $256 \times 256 \times n$ raw data file*
> *requires 0.1 seconds, i.e. to the operator it "feels" like he can move through the volume*
> *in "real time".*

And he concludes:

> *The IP based varifocal mirror display system facilitates a fully interactive image anal-*
> *ysis system. Operations such as rotation, pan, zoom, numerical dissection, numerical*
> *dissolution, and pointing are all available in "real time".*

Favalora et al. [2000] outline a high-performance graphics engine architecture
developed for use with the Perspecta display (see Section 8.3.2). A "raster engine"
is used to convert the incoming data transferred from the users PC (comprising 3-D primitives and volumetric data) into "*a series of projector illumination*

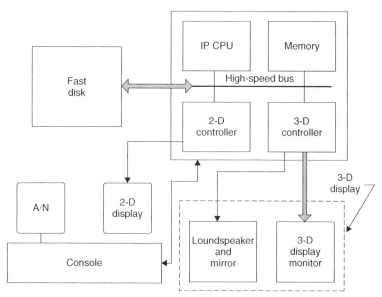

Figure 11.6   The graphics engine developed by Lowell Harris for use with a varifocal mirror display. This operates in raster mode and supports the depiction of 128x128x30 voxels. Harris placed particular emphasis on the importance of supporting real-time interaction. (Reproduced by permission from Harris [1988], © 1988 SPIE.)

patterns which are routed into 6 Gbits of DDR SDRAM".[14] The system provides three output channels each offering 800 Mbyte·s^{-1}. A more recent graphics engine architecture that is now used with the Perspecta system is illustrated in Figure 11.7. In correspondence with the author, Gregg Favalora writes:

The present "core rendering electronics" architecture was designed to suit customer requirements and act as a general computational module for a variety of our display technologies. For example, a doctor planning time-varying radiation cancer therapy planning may need to see an animated loop of a patient CT scan, overlaid with treatment data, of breathing lungs showing the tumor location. This corresponds to 100s of MBytes of input data which are processed for a 3-D display, a pipeline that includes 3-D cursor overlay, transformation to a new coordinate system, color mapping, and segmentation. Furthermore, Actuality's 3-D displays consume significant opto-electronic bandwidth—our multiplanar and quasi-holographic systems are driven by three MEMS-based spatial light modulators, such as those found in Texas Instruments, Inc.'s Digital Light Processing technology. For example, three

---

[14] The RAM is reported as being organized as 1 Gbit per color (3 colors) and two RAM banks for animation (i.e., double-buffering). DDR SDRAM: Double Data Rate Synchronous Dynamic Random Access Memory. SDRAM chips operate in a programmable "burst" mode. *"In the burst mode, accesses are started at a given location and continue for a programmable number of locations, typically 2, 4 or 8, in a programmable sequence. SDRAM chips are characterized by their clock speed and initial access latency.... DDR SDRAM doubles the data rate by providing data values at both rising and falling clock edges"* [Heuring and Jordan, 2004].

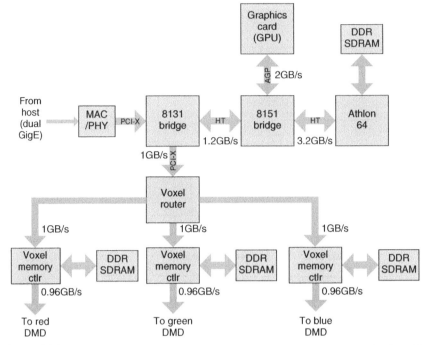

Figure 11.7 A graphics engine providing a "core rendering architecture" developed by Actuality Systems Inc. for use with displays such as the Perspecta. See text for details. (Reproduced by kind permission of Gregg Favalora, Actuality Systems Inc.)

XGA-resolution SLMs running at 6,000 Hz require 1.8 GByte/s of control data. Finally, the 3-D image data are double-buffered for flicker-free animation, requiring on-board RAM, and that RAM must be synchronized to time-varying elements of the display, such as the phase of a rotating screen.

We therefore designed the Perspecta Core Rendering Electronics for easy input, fast processing, and links to fast SLMs. We started with a 64-bit x86 architecture using the AMD Athlon-64 chipset running a modified version of Linux. The CRE is a network device, with two gigabit Ethernet jacks as input—our technical staff can "telnet" to it if needed. Today's graphics processing units (GPUs) are extraordinarily versatile processors, so we use an NVIDIA GPU as a coprocessor that outputs results over AGP read (rather than its video output). The processed voxel data are shuttled through two bridges and a custom "Voxel Router," implemented in an FPGA, that routes them to any of three color-specific local banks of SDRAM. Up to three SLMs (TI digital mirror devices) can be controlled, each at a bandwidth of nearly 1 GByte/s.

This architecture is very fast. We have demonstrated the ability to magnify or pan around a 512 × 512 × 512 medical data set several times per second. Previously, this operation took 45 minutes!

The interested reader is also referred to work being conducted by Actuality Systems into the development of a hardware/software platform via which a common interface (SpatialGL) to a range of creative 3-D display technologies may be obtained [Chun et al., 2005]. This could open up many interesting opportunities for the coexistence and meaningful evaluation of different creative display techniques.[15]

11.4.1   A Parallel Architecture

In this subsection we briefly review discussion provided in a previous work [Blundell and Schwarz, 2000] and focus our attention on issues relating to the development of a scalable graphics engines able to satisfy the needs of display units in which a high degree of parallelism in voxel activation is supported. In this context we refer to the use of "voxel activation pathways"—these represent the signal paths along which voxel descriptors pass and that link the graphics engine to the voxel activation mechanisms. For our purposes the number of voxel activation pathways will usually be assumed to correspond to the parallelism in voxel activation supported by a display unit [16]

Three simple examples are provided below:

1. Consider the cathode ray sphere (CRS) display illustrated in Figure 4.18. This employs two directed beam sources for voxel activation. Each source is responsible for voxel activation over 50% of the image space volume, and in this way the impact of distortional and voxel placement dead zones is ameliorated. The two sources do not operate simultaneously and so may be connected to the graphics engine via a single voxel activation pathway. In this scenario, an additional bit within each voxel descriptor may be used to identify the descriptors designated voxel activation mechanism. Thus we have a display exhibiting a parallelism of unity in voxel activation, and a single voxel activation pathway connects to two voxel activation mechanisms.

2. Consider a static-volume image space employing a 3-D array of voxel generation centers. In the extreme case that each of these elements can be individually addressed (and assuming that a voxel activation pathway cannot simultaneously address more that a single element), then the number of voxel activation pathways would equal the voxel activation capacity of the display.

3. Consider a varifocal mirror display in which images are cast onto the mirror via a CRT. In this case the CRT is connected to the graphics engine via a single voxel activation pathway and despite 2-D images slices being projected onto the mirror, the parallelism in voxel activation is unity.

---

[15] See Favalora [2005] for related discussion.

[16] Although this is a useful assumption, caution must be exercised particularly when an activation pathway (which supports the rapid sequential flow of voxel descriptors) links to hardware able to convert this to parallel form prior to its passage to voxel activation mechanisms. If the voxel activation pathway has sufficient bandwidth, it will be able to support a plurality of voxel activation mechanisms such that they are able to act in parallel. By way of an example, consider displays employing one or more DMD for voxel activation. Here, it would be more appropriate for each "voxel activation pathway" to relate to the signal flow to each individual micro-mirror.

The voxel activation subsystem comprises one or more voxel activation mechanisms, and each of these is responsible for the production of visible voxels across
all or part of the image space volume. It is convenient to view an image space as
comprising one or more "subspaces":

A subspace is defined as the physical region over which a voxel activation
mechanism participates in voxel production.

In the simplest case (for example, System 2 in Section 4.2), an image space is
represented by a single subspace. For the majority of volumetric embodiments the
image space comprises a plurality of subspaces; these may be spatially disjoint or
may overlap. The first of the exemplar systems introduced in Section 4.2 provides
us with a convenient example of the former, and in this embodiment the image
space comprises a set of circular subspaces (see Blundell and Schwarz [2000] for
more detailed discussion).

Consider for a moment the cathode ray sphere illustrated in Figure 4.18. Typically, each of the two beam sources is responsible for voxel activation across
one-half of the image space volume, and in this case the two subspaces do not
overlap. However, we could (in principle) relax our dead zone criteria and allow
the two sources to each address perhaps two-thirds of the image space volume. This
would lead to two partially overlapping subspaces, and in the region of overlap a

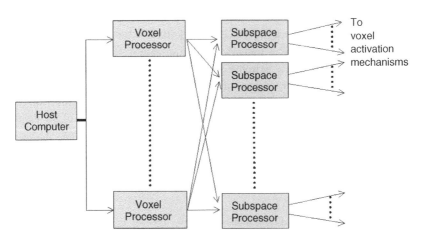

Figure 11.8 A simple architectural model of a scalable graphics engine able to support
parallel throughput of voxel descriptors. The voxel processors perform computation upon
the image data set and direct suitably processed voxel descriptor attributes to the most
appropriate subspace processor. In the simplest scenario, the subspace processors take the
form of memory units (and associated control logic) by means of which image data can be
output to the display (i.e., they do not necessarily include processing capability).

higher voxel density could be achieved.[17] In this case, the subspaces would partially overlap in both the spatial and temporal domains.

In Figure 11.8, a simple architectural model of a scalable graphics engine is illustrated. The graphics engine is assumed to comprise two sets of elements: voxel processors and subspace processors. The functionality of these elements is briefly summarized below:

1. *Voxel Processors:* The primary image data set is transferred from the host computer to the "voxel processors". The way in which it is distributed between these elements will be influenced by the nature of the application; however, we assume an equitable distribution. The host computer in association with the voxel processors performs computation on the image data set and produces the set of voxel descriptors to be displayed. The voxel processors direct each of these descriptors to the most appropriate subspace processor.

2. *Subspace Processors:* The subspace processors need only be concerned with the voxels to be depicted within the region(s) of the image space for which they are responsible, and their output characteristics must match the peak throughput requirements of the voxel activation mechanism(s) to which they are connected.[18] In the simplest case, the subspace processors take the form of memory space and associated control logic and therefore need not necessarily have any processing capability. Alternatively, so as to better support the depiction of animated image sequences and real-time user interaction, these elements may be equipped with processing hardware and have the ability to relocate voxel descriptors into other subspace regions (necessitating the passage of voxel descriptors to other subspace processors).

More detailed discussion on this parallel architecture may be found in Blundell and Schwarz [2000]. For our purposes, it is sufficient to note that when dealing with very large image data sets, a graphics engine that supports the sequential processing of image data and is able to match the peak bandwidth requirements of the display to which it is connected may not necessarily be able to cope with computational issues arising as a consequence of real-time interaction. Ultimately, parallel-processing techniques are likely to be needed, and this opens up many exciting challenges and opportunities

11.5   PARALLEL DATA TRANSFER

As we have seen, a number of swept-volume display units employ the rotational motion of a screen equipped with an array of active voxel generation centers (see,

---

[17] However, this would reduce overall image space predictability.

[18] Each subspace processor may be connected to a single voxel activation mechanism or may be able to support the needs of a plurality of activation mechanisms.

for example, System 1 in Section 4.2), or employ one or more directed beams such that the beam deflection apparatus co-rotates with the screen (see, for example, Section 7.3.1, Ref. 7D). In such cases, provision must be made for the rapid transfer of voxel descriptor attributes from external (stationary) components to rotating electronic hardware. With this in mind, in a previous work [Blundell and Schwarz, 2000] the author proposed a scalable optical data transfer link enabling a plurality of transmission channels to operate in parallel.

The approach used to implement a single optical link is illustrated in Figure 11.9. A stationary cylinder is shown and is equipped with four optical transmitters (e.g., LEDs) that point inward. A second cylinder that co-rotates with the screen (and other hardware) is located within the stationary cylinder and is equipped with

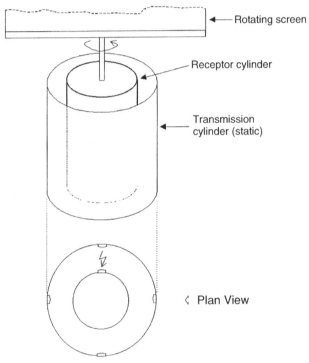

Figure 11.9 Here, the operation of a single data transfer link is illustrated. The outer cylinder is stationary and the inner cylinder co-rotates with the screen. In this scenario, four light-emitting components point inwardly from the outer cylinder and a single photoreceptor is attached to the inner cylinder (this points outwardly). The transmitters are connected in parallel. The diameters of the two cylinders are such that given the directional characteristics of the optical components, the receiver is always able to "see" a transmitter. Data transmission can therefore occur throughout the course of each rotation. See Figure 11.10 for a photograph of a prototype implementation in which a number of independent data transfer channels are provided.

a single photoreceptor (that points outward). Both cylinders are centered on the screen's axis of rotation.

The transmitters are connected in parallel and the diameters of the two cylinders are arranged so that, based upon the directional characteristics of the optoelectronic devices, the receiver is always able to "see" one of the transmitters. Thus from the receiver's perspective, as one transmitter falls toward the horizon, another rises from the opposite horizon—there is no nighttime!

A photograph of a prototype bi-directional data transfer link developed by the author is provided in Figure 11.10. In this embodiment "daytime" is preserved by

Figure 11.10   A parallel data transfer link prototyped by the author. Here, a number of independent data transfer channels are able transmit data to electronic hardware that co-rotates with the screen. Each channel operates in the manner illustrated in Figure 11.9, and in this implementation some 14 independent channels are stacked vertically along the axis of rotation. Although in the previous figure, four phototransmitters were employed for a single channel, in this embodiment only three are needed. The motor drive is located at the bottom of the photograph. (Original image © B.G. Blundell.)

means of only three transmitters—and a single receiver is used. Furthermore, as may be seen from the photograph, a set of such transmission channels are stacked vertically and are able to operate independently. Thus the data transfer system can readily be scaled to support the displays transmission requirements.

11.6   CONCERNING INTERACTION

> *All men dream, but not equally. Those who dream by night*
> *in the dusty recesses of their minds wake in the day to find that it was all vanity:*
> *but the dreamers of the day are dangerous men,*
> *for they may act their dreams with open eyes, to make it possible.*[19]

Volumetric, varifocal, and other creative 3-D display systems offer to advance the visualization process. These displays also offer to facilitate our interaction with the digital world, and the synergy that exists (or should exist) between the display and the interaction modalities should not be underestimated.

The provision of a display tableau able to "make space" for the depiction of 3-D images provides opportunities for the development of new interaction modalities.[20] These may include new forms of interaction tool and may augment the benefits that may be derived from the support for haptic feedback. In turn, the 3-D display and the interaction modalities that it is able to support will naturally impact on the ways in which we interact with the digital world, and so new ways of working will evolve.[21] Consequently, we should not attempt to anticipate and impose interaction techniques upon end users, but rather should, in the first instance, develop flexible interfaces to creative displays that enable intuitive interaction techniques to evolve. Interesting work has been carried out in this area. For example, Cutler and co-workers performed trials in connection with a creative 3-D display system known as the Responsive Workbench[22] bibCutler et al., 1997. Users were able to interact bi-manually via a set of tools such as Fakespace PINCH gloves and/or a Polhemus stylus[23]. In their publication Cutler et al. write:

---

[19] Attributed to T. E. Lawrence (1888–1935).

[20] Over the years, various interaction devices have been proposed and prototyped but have generally failed to gain widespread acceptance. Sometimes these have proved unsuitable for use with the conventional flat screen display or did not enter into common usage simply because, at the time that they were developed, our interaction requirements had not sufficiently evolved to warrant their general adoption. When considering new interaction tools, we should carefully examine devices that have previously been proposed and consider their potential for use with creative display systems and their ability to meet current (and future) interaction requirements.

[21] In this context we should consider both uni-manual and bi-manual interaction (see Blundell and Schwarz [2006].)

[22] This is a high-performance display system able to create 3-D images which appear to "sit" upon a tabletop. The stereoscopic images are presented by means of temporal coding techniques.

[23] **PINCH gloves:** Each equipped with six-degrees-of-freedom (DOF) position sensors and can detect the 'pinching' together of different fingers. **Polhemus stylus:** This is a pen-like interaction tool that employs a six DOF position tracking system. It is equipped with a single selection button.

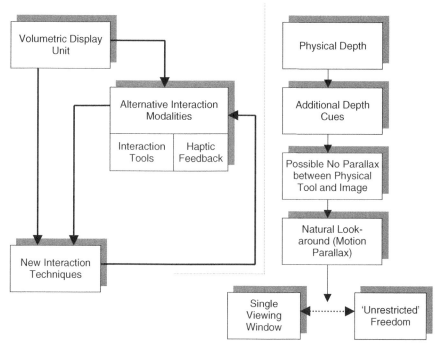

Figure 11.11   A volumetric display system offers to support alternative interaction modalities. These, together with the visual characteristics of the display, impact on the techniques by which we undertake interaction activities: the ways in which human skills are best directed towards interaction with the digital world. In turn, as these new approaches evolve, this is likely to lead to a refinement of the interaction tools. On the right-hand side, we illustrate some of the characteristics of the volumetric display which are likely to promote natural and intuitive interaction. The left-hand diagram is not limited to the volumetric approach and can be applied to any creative display—however, the characteristics shown on the right-hand side vary according to the specific creative display under discussion. (Diagram © M.G.K. Blundell 2006.)

When beginning this work we thought that all the two-handed input techniques would need to be explicitly designed and programmed. However, when using the system we found that perhaps the most interesting tasks emerged when the user combined two otherwise independent uni-manual tools.

Consequently:

It is generally not possible to decide in advance the manner in which users will choose to perform tasks, and best experience is derived through the provision of flexible interaction opportunities and observation (gained visually or by recording user activities via the underlying software systems). [Blundell and Schwarz, 2006]

Referring to Figure 11.11, on the right-hand side of the diagram, we list several volumetric display characteristics that directly impact on the interaction process.

Although this list is self-explanatory, it is perhaps useful to spend a moment discussing the importance (as far as the interaction process is concerned) of the natural "look-around" capability offered by the volumetric approach. Consider a conventional flat screen display able to support the depiction of stereoscopic images using temporal or spatial coding techniques (see Section 3.3). Through the support of the binocular parallax depth cue images *appear* to occupy a physical depth and so in order to effectively interact with them, we need to be able to navigate the cursor in three dimensions.

In this situation, determining that a condition of "no-parallax" exists between the cursor and a particular image component is difficult because of our inability to move the head from side to side and view the image scene from slightly different orientations. In short, the absence of support for the motion parallax cue may seriously hamper the interaction process.[24] In the case of the stereoscopic approach, the obvious solution is to add support for head-tracking (although this is often limited to motion in the horizontal direction). However, as image complexity increases, latency may occur such that the operator perceives a lag between head motion and image update.

The ability of all volumetric and varifocal systems to provide natural support for the motion parallax cue should not be undervalued. This plays a vital role in our visualization and interpretation of the 3-D image and is a key requirement for the development of intuitive interaction techniques.

In Section 1.5, five general forms of image space that are associated with a range of display paradigms were identified.[25] From the perspective of our discussion concerning volumetric and varifocal systems, we need only consider three of these: "physical," "free," and "virtual" image spaces. Additionally, we introduced three interaction modalities: "direct," "transferred," and "pointer based" techniques. Below, we briefly consider interaction with the physical and virtual forms of image space and in Section 11.6.1 turn our attention to the "free" image space.

1. *Interacting with a Physical Image space:* In Figure 11.12 we indicate several issues that relate to our interaction with a physical image space. We define this type of image space as being bounded by a physical container, or as comprising static and/or moving components that preclude the entry of physical interaction tools into the image space volume. Consequently, it is not possible to employ direct interaction techniques; however, both transferred and

---

[24] In this situation, we may find, for example, that aligning the cursor requires not only cursor navigation but also image rotation(s).

[25] Also see Section 3.2.

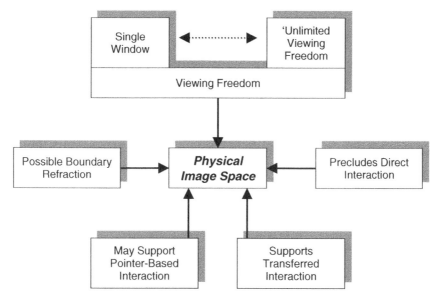

Figure 11.12   Here, several issues that impact on our interaction with a 'physical' image space are indicated. See text for discussion. (Diagram © A.R. Blundell 2006.)

pointer-based interaction modalities are supported. Interestingly, in the case of the latter, Max Hirsch provides us with an early example of a pointer-based interaction device for use with a swept volume system; the Generescope (see Section 7.3.1, Ref. 7E). In his 1958 patent (US Patent Number 2,967,905), Hirsch describes the use of one or more gas discharge light sources placed around the image space. The beams from these lamps (see Figure 11.13) may be adjusted to cross the image space along any desired track. As a result of the rotational motion of the screen (which provides a scattering surface), the trajectory of the beam(s) within the image space is made visible. This mimics the current use of laser pointers, which are especially useful when several people are viewing volumetric images and provide an ideal means of "pointing" to features of interest.[26]

Hirsch further developed this approach by linking the control hardware (graphics engine) to the lamps in such a way that by means of a control (102f in Figure 11.13), the user could adjust the time relative to the start of a rotational cycle at which the lamp was briefly activated. In this way, the trajectory of the beam across the image space could be made invisible

---

[26] The laser pointer is particularly suitable for use with swept-volume displays as the motion of the screen makes the laser beam visible across the extent of the images space. This technique may also be satisfactorily employed with a limited number of static-volume architectures.

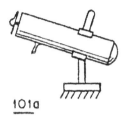

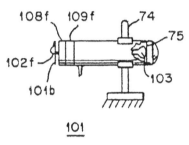

Figure 11.13 A pointer based interaction technique is discussed in the patent filed by Max Hirsch in 1958 for use with the Generescope. Here, a plurality of lamps are used. The location and orientation of these relative to the image space may be adjusted. A control knob on each lamp (102f) enables the operator to adjust the time at which the lamp is briefly turned on by the control hardware relative to the start of each rotational cycle of the screen. This enables the depth at which a cursor appears (relative to the lamp to be adjusted). Hirsch used this scheme to create cursors (such as arrows) within the image space. The general technique parallels todays use of laser pointers to "point to" regions of a volumetric image—a method which is particularly suited for use with swept-volume system. (Reproduced from US Patent Number 2,967,905.)

and a cursor created whose depth within the image space (relative to the lamp) could be adjusted. Returning to Figure 11.12, displays that give rise to a physical image space may restrict viewing freedom to a single "window," or at the other extreme may provide essentially unrestricted viewing freedom. The extent of the viewing freedom supported by a display impacts on both interaction modalities and interaction techniques. In this respect, it is important to note that when viewing freedom is restricted to a single "window," the observer's orientation and working position relative to the image space is defined. On the other hand, in the case of displays that impose little restriction on viewing freedom, the orientation of the observer(s) is no longer defined and this has the potential to lead to disorientation. By way of example, consider the air-traffic controller able to move around the display volume. While the display will greatly assist in facilitating the visualization of the spatial position of aircraft, instructions provided by the operator must map between the operator's current frame of reference and that of each pilot.

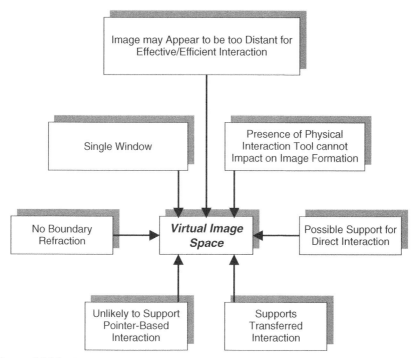

Figure 11.14   Summary of several issues that impact on our interaction with a "virtual" image space. See text for discussion. (Diagram © Q. S. Blundell 2006.)

This has the potential for error and is akin to operating a remote-controlled plane (e.g., rudder reversal as the plane flies toward, rather than away from, the "pilot").[27]

Finally, as discussed previously, boundary refraction occurring as light emerges from the "physical" image space can result in image distortion. In turn, in the case of the transferred interaction technique, this may lead to cursor positioning inaccuracies and/or make cursor navigation more difficult.

2. *Interacting with a Virtual Image Space:* Several issues relating to interaction with a virtual image space are summarized in Figure 11.14. In the case of the direct interaction modality, we require that the image and interaction spaces are coincident (and in the case of the "physical" image space, we have seen that the presence of physical materials within or surrounding the image space preclude this condition). A second and obvious condition requires the image and interaction spaces to be simultaneously visible to the user. In the

---

[27] Admittedly, this problem is also associated with a display that provides only a single window onto the scene as the operator may rotate the image so as to obtain a different viewpoint. However, we are well adapted to the single "window" scenario and have much to learn as far as effectively working with an unrestricted display volume.

case that we employ the varifocal mirror technique for the production of a virtual image space, although we can meet the first condition, the second condition is not achievable. In this situation, the image space appears to emanate from a location behind the varifocal mirror. By reaching around the apparatus, it is possible to position the interaction device so that it lies within this virtual image space. However, since the mirror and drive assembly are nontransparent, we cannot view both the image and interaction spaces simultaneously.

Although the basic varifocal technique precludes direct interaction with virtual images, it is possible to create an optical system whereby this interaction modality is supported. Such a scheme is illustrated in Figure 11.15 (for discussion on aspects of this approach, see, for example, Schmandt [1983] and Mulder et al. [2003]).

As discussed in the next subsection, the insertion of a physical interaction tool into a "free" image space may disrupt image formation. In the case that a virtual image space is able to support this interaction modality, the presence of the interaction tool *cannot* impact on image formation.

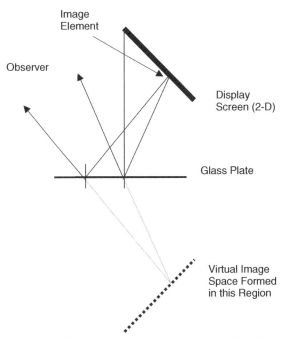

Figure 11.15 A simple and effective method of creating coincident image and interaction spaces and enabling the two to be simultaneously observed. Here, temporally multiplexed stereopairs are depicted on the 2-D screen and are reflected by the glass plate—leading to a virtual image space that appears to be located at the position indicated. By reaching around the glass plate, the operator can insert a physical interaction tool "into" the virtual image space. A similar approach may be used in conjunction with a varifocal mirror.

Returning to Figure 11.14, a single "window" is provided onto a virtual image space and boundary refraction is not an issue. However, the virtual image may appear to emanate from a location that is somewhat distant from the observer, and this may hamper the interaction process.

11.6.1 The "Free Space" Image

The "free" image space enables the formation of 3-D images that appear to be suspended in space: The images are clearly visible but are without substance.[28] Techniques able to give rise to this form of image space must be considered with great care, and here it is instructive to quote from Michael Halle's excellent review article in which he introduces the "Projection Constraint" as follows:

> *A display medium or element must always lie along a line of sight between the viewer and all parts of a spatial image.*

He writes:

> *Photons must originate in, or be redirected by some material. The material can be behind, in front of, or within the space of the image, but it must be present. All claims to the contrary violate what we understand of the world... Technologies lavished with claims of mid-air projection should always be scrutinized with regard to the fundamental laws of physics.*

Summarizing from a previous work [Blundell and Schwarz, 2006]:

> *In short, and disregarding relativistic phenomena, light travels in a rectilinear manner unless influenced to do otherwise as a consequence of the presence of some material.*

The volumetric display discussed in Section 9.3.2 provides us with an excellent example of an approach able to give rise to a "free" image space, here the dust particles act as scattering centers able to redirect incident light in an omnidirectional manner.[29] More generally, display systems able to produce a "free" image space employ optical components such as mirrors and lenses.[30] In order to see images created in this way, the observer must look toward the optical component that provides the light output.

Two interesting publications [McKay et al., 1999 a, b] discuss the formation of "free" space images by means of large diameter (up to 120 cm) membrane mirrors.[31] Here, adjusting the air pressure across a mirrored membrane sets the

---

[28] Assuming that a haptic feedback device is not employed when "touching" the image.

[29] For displays employing this technique, the presence of the scattering centers may not be readily detected. For example, in the case of the Phantasmagoria (a precursor to the "Pepper's Ghost" theatrical illusion), images were projected into a cloud of smoke particles. A subsequent refinement employed fine barium oxide powder: "An ultraviolet image cast into this fine dust caused it to glow and shimmer. However, under normal lighting conditions, the presence of the powder was less noticeable." [Blundell and Schwarz, 2006].

[30] In the case of the latter, see, for example, Section 8.7.

[31] The second of these publications [McKay et al., 1999b] focuses on the implementation of a stereoscopic display architecture that uses a mirror of this type.

radius of curvature and so enables low-cost production of lightweight, flexible high-quality mirrors. In relation to the construction of the mirror, McKay et al. write:

> *A SMM [Stretchable Membrane Mirror] uses a thin sheet of aluminised polyester film which is stretched over a specially shaped frame, forming an airtight cavity behind the membrane. Removal of air from that cavity causes the resulting air pressure difference to force the membrane back into concave shape. Controlling the pressure difference acting over the membrane now controls the curvature or f/No. of the mirror.*[32]

Details do not appear to be given concerning dealing with variations in mirror curvature caused as a result of changes in atmospheric pressure. However, the development of a system able to automatically measure changes in mirror curvature and use this information to adjust the air pressure within the chamber would appear to be a fairly straightforward undertaking.

In principle, images depicted in a "physical" image space may be projected to reside in either "free" or "virtual" image spaces. Furthermore, we can project between both "free" and "virtual" image spaces. Many optical arrangements may be devised for such purposes, and over the years numerous techniques have been proposed and employed. For example, in a patent filed in 1910 (US Patent Number 995,607), Hans Kempinski describes the simple projection arrangement illustrated in Figure 11.16.[33] By means of a concave mirror, a physical object (A) is projected and forms a "free" space image (A′). This technique was intended for use in shop windows such that:

> *The mirror B produces a magnified image A′ of the bottle in upright position.... This image will be seen by the outside spectator when his eyes are in the path of the light beams reflected by the mirror B.... When the spectator moves on the street toward or from the window pane... the image of the bottle will disappear.*[34]

An interesting projection arrangement is described in a patent filed in 1922 by Harry Roach (US Patent Number 1,552,451). The optical system is illustrated in Figure 11.17. Roach identifies an essential weakness of the type of approach proposed by Kempinski and writes:

> *It has been attempted in the past, to produce an image of an object by means of a reflecting element, but in order to produce a true image with a single reflector, it is necessary to place the object on the axis of the reflector, the result of which is that the*

---

[32] The f-number of a lens corresponds to its focal length divided by its aperture (diameter). Thus a lens with a 2.5-cm aperture and a 5-cm focal length has an f-number of 2 (usually expressed $f/2$). McKay et al. report the use of membrane mirrors able to achieve f-numbers down to $f/1$.

[33] This patent opens as follows: "*Be it known that I, Hans Kempinski, a subject of the King of Prussia, residing at Berlin, in the Kingdom of Prussia and German Empire, have invented a new and useful Improvement in Window-Displays....*" Sadly, today's patents open in a far more mundane manner!

[34] The physical bottle is masked by an opaque sheet (F). However, the presence of the physical bottle disrupts image formation (see Section 11.8, Question 3) in the same way that the insertion of a physical interaction tool into a "free" image space can obstruct the formation of parts of an image that lie between the tool and the observer.

H. KEMPINSKI.
WINDOW DISPLAY.
APPLICATION FILED OCT. 6, 1910.

995,607.

Patented June 20, 1911.

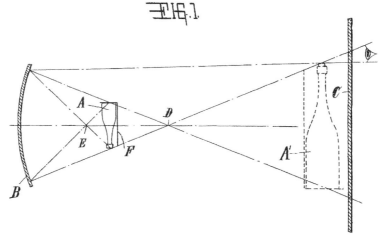

Figure 11.16 A simple projection arrangement described in Kempinski's 1910 patent. A physical object (A) is projected so as to create a "free space" image that can be seen from certain locations. (Reproduced from US patent 995,607.)

image will be formed in a plane substantially at right angles to the same axis; hence the presence of the object or other element or elements of optics will interfere with the passage of the reflected light rays, and in this way, a very serious practical difficulty arises.

The obvious solution is therefore to place the object "off-axis". In this context he writes:

If it is attempted to utilise a reflecting element to reflect light rays from an object placed off of the axis of the reflecting element, the light rays from the object will be reflected and may be used to form an image, but such an image will not be a true image....

The degree to which the physical object and reflected image differ need not concern us here. A patent filed in 1951 by Robert Oetjen (US Patent Number 2,628,533) provides yet another example of a projection apparatus. As may be seen from Figure 11.18, two concave mirrors are employed in conjunction with reflector (8)—this being silvered on both its front and rear surfaces.

Indeed, there would seem to be no end to the arrangements that have been devised, and for our current purposes there is one other technique that we should definitely not overlook. A patent filed in 1970 by Virgil Elings and Caliste Landry (US Patent Number 3,647,284) describes a remarkably effective and simple projection technique that employs two concave mirrors. The inventors write:

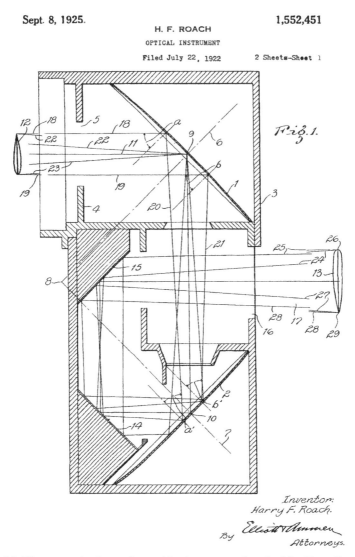

Sept. 8, 1925.

H. F. ROACH

OPTICAL INSTRUMENT

Filed July 22, 1922

1,552,451

2 Sheets—Sheet 1

Figure 11.17 The projection and magnification system described by Harry Roach in his 1922 patent. Two concave (converging) mirrors are employed (1) and (2) together with two plane mirrors (14) and (15). The object is denoted (12) and the image (13). (Reproduced from US Patent Number 1,552,451.)

A pair of concave mirrors are placed with their concave sides toward each other and one is optically apertured, either with a hole in the mirror or by an unsilvered portion in a mirror of transparent material. An object placed on the mirror that is not apertured will project a real image at the region of the aperture if the curvature and spacings of the mirrors are correct. The image may be left-right reversed or may have the same orientation as the object depending upon the reflective paths of rays from the object.

Feb. 17, 1953   R. A. OETJEN   2,628,533
IMAGE FORMING OPTICAL REFLECTING
AND CONVERGING MIRROR DEVICE
Filed Oct. 17, 1951

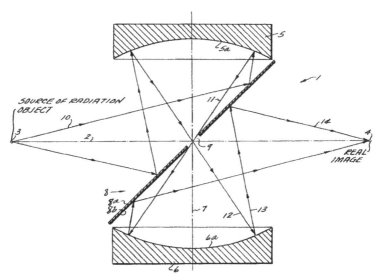

Figure 11.18 An optical projection system described by Robert Oetjen. This employs two concave mirrors and a plane mirror (8) which is silvered on both its front and rear surfaces. This mirror is also equipped with a central hole (9) (Reproduced from US Patent Number 2,628,533.)

This approach may be readily understood by reference to Figure 11.19. In the upper diagram, the two mirrors are shown in cross section and a physical object (12) is placed on the lower mirror (11). The upper mirror (10) is equipped with a hole (16). This can be seen in the middle diagram, which provides the plan view. In this scenario, the construction rays are shown as being reflected once by either mirror before emerging and forming the image. In Figure 11.20, a projection system of this type is illustrated.

The lower diagram in Figure 11.19 depicts the use of two mirrors of greater curvature. By comparing the ray paths followed in the top and bottom diagrams, it is apparent that in the case of the former, left-right reversal occurs, whereas for the latter this will be avoided.

In their patent, Elings and Landry discuss an alternative embodiment in which, rather than employing two mirrors that form a complete volume of revolution about their principal axes, the mirrors are restricted in their extent to two sectors as indicated in Figure 11.21. The inventors write:

> *A full image could be produced if the sectors were rotated about their optical axis A.*
> *If the sectors are rotated at a frequency which is less than the critical flicker frequency*

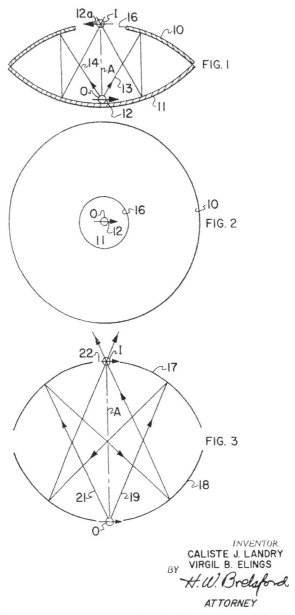

Figure 11.19 The projection apparatus described by Elings and Landry. Two concave mirrors are used. The upper mirror is equipped with an aperture and an object (12) placed on the lower mirror is projected to form an image (12a). The upper diagram shows the mirrors in cross section and this ray path gives rise to an image which is left-right reversed. The middle diagram provides a plane view. In the lower diagram, the curvature of the mirrors is increased and the ray path indicated gives rise to an image whose orientation corresponds to that of the object. (Reproduced from US Patent Number 3,647,284.)

Figure 11.20   The optical projection technique described by Elings and Landry. Here a small plastic pig placed on the lower mirror appears to exist just above the aperture. Although the viewing angle is restricted, the image is very realistic. This arrangement may be adapted to provide magnification. The possibility of projecting volumetric images by means of such an arrangement is intriguing. Unfortunately, large mirrors would needed; although these could perhaps be located below the floor level and if properly implemented, the results could be spectacular. (Image © 2005 A. R. Blundell.)

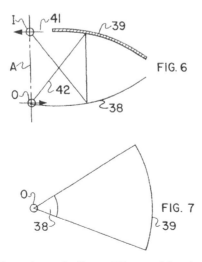

Figure 11.21   In an alternative embodiment Elings and Landry propose the use of two concave mirrors each of which is limited in extent to a sector (as indicated in the lower illustration that provides a plan view). By rapidly rotating the two mirrors about their principle axes the arrangement is able to give rise to complete images (i.e., mimics the action of two mirrors which form a complete volume of revolution about their optical axes). (Reproduced from US Patent Number 3,647,284.)

of the human eye, the image will flicker.... If the sectors are rotated at a frequency greater than the critical flicker frequency, the image will not flicker.[35]

11.6.2 "Free" Image Space: Directly Generated and Projection Techniques

Finally in relation to our discussion of the "free" image space, it is useful to summarize those aspects of this form of image space which impact on interaction opportunities. In fact, as we have seen, two essentially different approaches may be adopted for the formation of the image space:

1. The image may be directly formed by means of, for example, particles able to scatter incident radiation (by way of example, see Section 9.3.2).
2. A Re-Imaging/Projection technique may be employed, and in this case the image space occupies a region that is located between the observer and the final optical output element employed by the Re-Imaging/Projection subsystem.

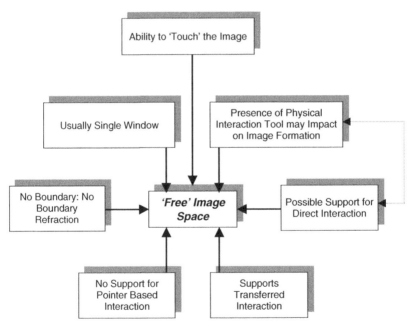

Figure 11.22 Here, we summarize several issues that impact on interaction with a free image space formed by means of a re-imaging/projection subsystem. As can be seen, some of these opportunities differ to those indicated in Figure 11.23 (which assumes the use of a direct image formation approach). (Diagram © Q. S. Blundell 2006.)

[35] See Section 11.8, Question 5.

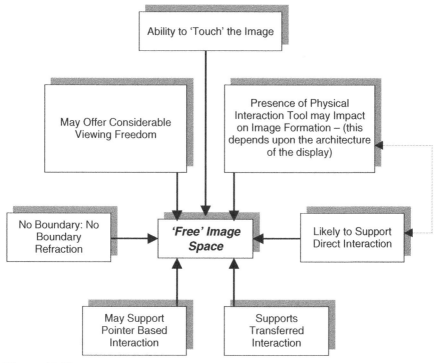

Figure 11.23 Summary of several issues that impact on interaction with a free image space formed by means of a direct image creation technique. As can be seen, some of these opportunities differ to those indicated in Figure 11.22 (that assumes a re-imaging/projection subsystem is used). (Diagram © A. R. Blundell 2006.)

As is evident from Figures 11.22 and 11.23, these two general approaches give rise to image spaces that differ in a number of respects. For example, the first technique supports (at least in principle) greater viewing freedom (as in the case of the projection technique the observer must be looking *into* the optical output element).

A 'free' image space may be formed by means of a Re-Imaging/Projection subsystem, or may employ a volume (containing, for example, scattering centers 'floating' in air) within which voxels may be directly activated. These two approaches give rise to image spaces that differ in certain important respects. We refer to these approaches as "the Re-Imaging/Projection based 'free' image space" and the "Directly Generated 'free' image space."

11.7 DISCUSSION

What is life?
It is the flash of a firefly in the night.
It is the breath of a buffalo in the wintertime.
It is the little shadow which runs across the grass
and loses itself in the sunset.[36]

In the first part of this chapter, we briefly focused on issues relating to the graphics engine that is responsible for the processing of the image data set and for the passage of appropriate voxel descriptor attributes to the display in such a way as to satisfy the display's data format and temporal requirements. As we have seen, different forms of volumetric display have widely differing voxel activation capacities, and although for certain applications benefits can be derived through the presentation to the human visual system of images comprising a vast number of voxels, this may detract from real-time interaction opportunities (in which the graphics engine plays a pivotal role). Thus we must carefully balance the number of voxels activated per frame with the demands that will be placed on the graphics engine when we interact with the displayed image.[37] Ultimately, if we are to accommodate real-time interaction with large data sets, it is likely that we will need to support parallel processing and data throughput within the graphics engine. With this in mind, we have briefly examined greatly simplified sequential and parallel architectures together with an optical link able to support parallel data transfer to swept-volume displays equipped with an active surface of emission.

In Section 11.6 we turned our attention to the interaction process and have summarized issues that should be considered when we seek to interact with the "physical," "virtual," and "free" forms of image space via the "direct," "transferred," and "pointer-based" interaction modalities. Images depicted in "free space" offer many exciting opportunities, and therefore we have paid particular attention to this technique. We attempted to address misconceptions often associated with this display paradigm and have identified two general approaches that may be employed in the production of the "free space" image (the Re-Imaging/Projection and Direct Generation methods). Without a doubt, the "free" image space has great potential, especially when coupled with haptic interaction. On the other hand, it is important to remember that this modality is no panacea and is not without inherent limitations.

---

[36] Crowfoot, Blackfoot Indian (1821–1890).

[37] The data depicted on a display may represent only a small portion of a far more extensive data set. Although some forms of interaction (such as the rotation of an image depicted on a volumetric display which supports "unrestricted" viewing freedom) may be performed on the displayed data set without reference to the parent data, other interaction requirement will involve the data set as a whole. *Thus, restricting the number of voxels depicted within each image frame does not automatically reduce computational overheads.*

11.8   INVESTIGATIONS

1. With reference to Figure 11.3, consider alternative ways in which we may choose to arrange voxel descriptors within RAM and effect their output to a swept-volume display employing (a) the translational motion (constant velocity) of a planar screen and (b) a single directed beam source for voxel activation.

2. In terms of the varifocal mirror technique, what criterion has to be met in order that a "free" image space is produced?

3. Consider Figure 11.16. To what extent would the presence of the physical wine bottle (A) obstruct image formation?

4. A cube with sides of length 2 cm is placed 30 cm from a concave (converging) mirror whose focal length is 20 cm, as indicated in Figure 11.24. Determine the location, shape, and degree of distortion of the resulting image. In the case where the object is generated as a result of an imaging system, how would you correct for such distortion?

5. Toward the end of Section 11.6.1, reference is made to an embodiment of the projection technique described by Elings and Landry, in which the two concave mirrors are of limited extent and rotate about their principle axes. Consider the practicalities of using this approach as a means of projecting images depicted by a swept-volume display equipped with a planar screen. Could the mirrors simply co-rotate with the screen, or should they rotate more rapidly?

6. Using Ray-Tracing techniques, develop software able to simulate the projection system developed Elings and Landry [it is recommended that you access their original patent (US Patent Number 3,647,284)]. Your program

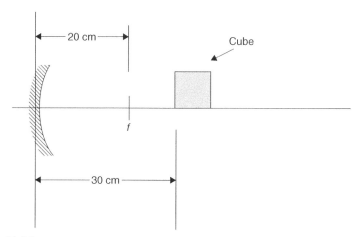

Figure 11.24   A cube is placed 30 cm from a concave mirror which has a focal length of 20 cm. See Investigations Question 4.

should enable the user to interactively vary the curvature and diameter of the mirrors together with their separation. Use your program to investigate the magnification opportunities offered by this approach and determine the feasibility of using this method for the "free" space projection of volumetric images depicted within a "physical" image space.

12 General Discussion: Suggestions du Jour

The twain together well might change the world.
And even in the middle of his song
He falter'd and his hand fell from the harp,
And pale he turn'd and reel'd and would have fall'n,
. . . nor would he tell
His vision; but what doubt that he foresaw.

12.1 INTRODUCTION

In this brief and final chapter, we focus primarily on a number of display paradigms that do not appear to be the subject of current research, but which seem to the author to warrant further investigation. Two key issues underpin the relevance of such a selection. Firstly, our visualization and interaction needs have rapidly evolved, and therefore a highly practical volumetric or varifocal display solution proposed some decades ago might, at that time, have had little relevance. In the light of

Enhanced Visualization: Making Space for 3-D Images. By Barry G. Blundell
Copyright © 2007 John Wiley & Sons, Inc.

current needs, this situation may have changed considerably. Secondly, remarkable advances have been made in mechanical, optical, and electronic technologies, and opportunities therefore exist to apply such advancements to older display embodiments.

In selecting display architectures for discussion in this chapter, the author has considered a number of issues including the need to provide examples of systems that can be implemented at low cost without access to extensive workshop facilities. The prototyping of such systems offers opportunities for students at all levels to gain multidisciplinary experience, and also an insight into the paradigm shift needed to effectively work with a 3-D image space. Experience of this sort can play a critical role in the educational process.

In proposing display techniques for further consideration, it is impossible to completely set to one side one's own personal experience and outlook. It is therefore important that the reader should not discount other approaches not mentioned here.[1] Furthermore, to avoid promoting—or, more importantly, running the risk of overlooking—any particular recent or ongoing activities, discussion is, where possible, of a general nature or is confined to embodiments that, to the author's knowledge, are not the subject of ongoing research activity. Consequently, for example, in the main body of the chapter, displays that utilize the remarkable DMD approach are not included.

In the next section, we briefly comment on the varifocal approach and then turn our attention to questioning the ongoing usefulness of electron beams as a means of effecting voxel activation. Subsequently, reference is made to the use of the gas discharge process and to the two-step excitation of fluorescence. Finally, in Section 12.6 we refer to other volumetric display architectures and associated areas of activity that may be particularly fruitful. In summary, this chapter simply contains some of the author's "Suggestions du Jour!"

12.2   THE VARIFOCAL TECHNIQUE

> *All paths lead nowhere,*
> *follow the path with heart.*[2]

The varifocal mirror technique offers a very effective single "window" view onto a "virtual" image space. Given the simplicity of this approach and its potential to augment the visualization process as a desktop computer peripheral, coupled with the low manufacturing costs (and the minimal resources needed to produce such displays), it is surprising that this display paradigm is not in widespread use.[3]

---

[1] The author has included a small number of "favorites"—display techniques whose implementation would be challenging and whose display characteristics are intriguing.

[2] Attributed to Carlos Castaneda (1931–).

[3] Particularly when we consider the opportunities that could arise by making available simple low-cost 3-D displays for Internet-based applications.

Unfortunately, in literature the varifocal technique is often dismissed on the basis of the acoustic noise generated by the vibrating mirror. As we have discussed, this is not an *inherent* weakness and this potential problem may be readily overcome by judicious design. Furthermore, it is possible to use a Re-imaging/Projection subsystem to form a "free" image space. As for the shape of the image space, this may be modified and improved by suitable manipulation of the image slices prior to their depiction.

The author is not aware of any ongoing research in this area, and with the passage of time it would be appropriate to re-examine this display paradigm and investigate the opportunities for its advancement through the inclusion of more recent technical developments (such as thin panel and DMD-based displays for the production of the 2-D image slices). Some relevant issues are summarized in Figure 12.1.

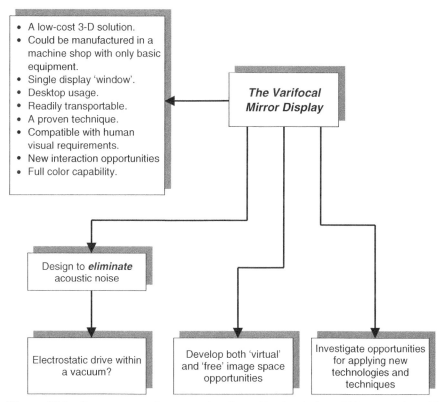

Figure 12.1 Summary remarks concerning the varifocal technique. This approach could rapidly fulfil some of our current 3-D visualization needs, provide a basis for student project work, and assist in the development of tools and techniques needed to efficiently interact with a 3-D image space. Here is a proven technology from which we could immediately derive considerable benefit—particularly for Internet based applications. (Diagram © M. R. B. Blundell 2006.)

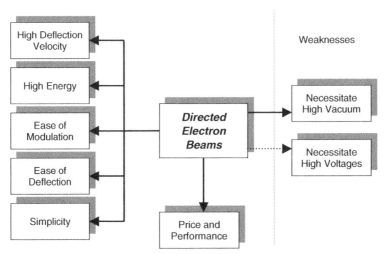

Figure 12.2   Author's summation of key strengths and weaknesses associated with the use of directed electron beams for voxel activation. The requirement for high voltages is not a significant weakness and is easily dealt with. See text for general discussion. (Diagram © M. R. B. Blundell 2006.)

12.3   DO ELECTRON BEAMS HAVE A FUTURE ROLE IN VOXEL ACTIVATION?

For some decades, the CRT has dominated the conventional electronic display system market. Thin panel displays (together with DMD-based systems) are now increasingly challenging this traditional technology and there can be little doubt that in time conventional flat screen CRT-based display systems will be superseded. This does not necessarily mean that electron beam based technologies have no future role to play in the implementation of volumetric systems. As summarized in Figure 12.2, directed electron beams have several advantageous characteristics and in terms of both price and performance, the use of directed electron beams for voxel activation remains a valid design decision.

For display architectures in which voxel activation is to be achieved by means of an array of nondirected beams, Field Emission Devices (FEDs) have great potential. In the case of an FED, the electron emission does not necessitate the use of a heated, oxide coated cathode, but may occur via a suitably shaped "cold cathode". The approximate local current density (J) may generally be expressed by the Fowler–Nordheim equation [MacDonald and Lowe, 1997]:

$$J = A \left[\frac{E^2}{\phi} \right] \exp \left[-B \frac{\phi^{1.5}}{E} \right],$$

where E represents the local electric field, ϕ is the work function of the cathode material, and A and B are constants. Naturally, to maximize the beam current, it is essential to minimize the work function and maximize the local electric field. In the case of the latter, this can be significantly increased (for a given anode–cathode potential) by employing cathode structures in the form of a sharp edges or "needle points" (microtips). MacDonald and Lowe [1997] provide an interesting overview of this approach.

Returning to the use of deflected electron beams, as discussed in Section 7.2.1 for a conventional electron gun employing the electrostatic deflection technique, the deflection voltage needed to produce a given angular deflection of the electron beam is coupled to the potential used for beam acceleration. Thus as the beam energy is increased (so as to increase voxel intensity), it is necessary to also increase the beam deflection voltages. In the case that a "dot graphics" approach is adopted, the bandwidth of the deflection voltage amplifiers is likely to set the ultimate limit on the voxel activation capacity. By use of more advanced electron guns equipped with post-deflection acceleration (PDA) apparatus, we are able to essentially decouple the beam deflection voltage from the final beam energy. An illustration of an electron gun that employs PDA is provided in Figure 12.3. In summary, electron beams continue to provide a low-cost high-performance solution to the implementation of the voxel activation subsystems, and much work remains to be carried out in this area.[4] The author's choice of three exemplar electron-beam-based systems that warrant further research are indicated below:

1. **The Hirsch Display (Ref. 7D):** This display dates back to the 1950s and was briefly discussed in Section 7.3.1. In the case of this approach, two directed electron beam sources co-rotate with a planar phosphor coated screen. In this way, the inventor sought to avoid the problems associated with continually varying screen-beam geometry. Additionally, this approach is able to support two-color image depiction (and could be adapted for full color). In short, although mechanical complications occur as a result of electron gun rotation, this approach offers a fairly uniform image space, gives rise to minimal boundary refraction, and may be implemented at low cost. Additionally, it has the potential to support an exhaustive image space scan and thereby offer a 100% fill factor.

Although a traditional commutator is required for the transmission of static potentials to the rotating components, an optical link of the form outlined in Section 11.5 would provide a convenient method for the transmission of deflection and beam blanking signals. Naturally, the rotating vacuum vessel would need careful design and an additional protective enclosure (perhaps constructed from polycarbonate) would be needed to provide protection in the case of an implosion. However, this approach could open up some interesting interaction opportunities and has the potential to support the production of high-intensity, high-quality images—a must for all those with an inventive mind and a love for "*spinny-wacky*" electromechanical systems!

---

[4] For example, the author is unaware of any volumetric display that has been implemented using electron guns equipped with PDA apparatus. This is an area that the author is currently investigating through the development of a prototype display.

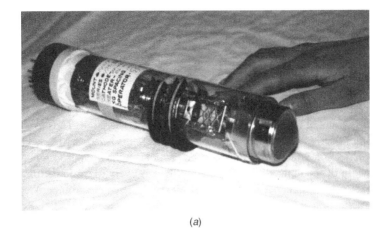

(a)

(b)

Figure 12.3 In (a) an Electron gun employing electrostatic deflection and PDA is shown. Here, the electrons emerge from the gun through a fine domed metallic mesh. A high potential is maintained between this mesh and the target screen which results in the electron beam being further accelerated after it emerges from the electron gun. In this way, a relatively small accelerating voltage is employed within the electron gun and so only small deflection voltages are required. Additionally, a PDA arrangement may be used to magnify the beam deflection produced by the electrostatic deflection plates so further reducing the deflection voltages and enabling a reduction in the distance between the electron gun and the target screen. This approach offers to significantly advance the capabilities of swept-volume volumetric systems in which sequential voxel activation is employed. Figure (b) provides a close-up view of the mesh. (Photographs © 2006 Q. S. Blundell.)

2. **The Peritron (Ref. 6I):** This display unit was discussed in Section 6.4.4 and employs a planar screen moving with translational motion within an evacuated chamber (see Figure 6.11). A single directed electron beam is needed for voxel activation. Opportunities for readily effecting translational motion (at the required frequency and with an appropriate amplitude) in a vacuum should be

re-examined. Furthermore, this approach may be readily adapted to employ a 2-D array of nondirected electron beam sources.

This display provides a single window onto the digital world and if properly developed could support a 100% fill factor. Prototype systems could be readily constructed and the technique offers a low cost volumetric display architecture.

3. **The Cathode Ray Sphere (CRS):** This form of display architecture builds on work conducted by Richard Ketchpel in the early 1960s (see Section 7.2.1). In the late 1980s the author commenced research into the development of the CRS, and over the years a number of successful prototype systems have been developed. The general principles of operation of this display technique are indicated in Sections 1.6.1, 4.6, and 11.2.

Despite the immense amount of effort directed towards the development of this display technology, a number of vital issues have still not been addressed and there remains great scope for further advancement. Some of the areas that need further activity are summarized in Figure 12.4, and several are given a brief mention below:

(a) *Support for PDA* As indicated previously, electron guns able to support PDA enable the beam deflection voltages to be essentially decoupled from

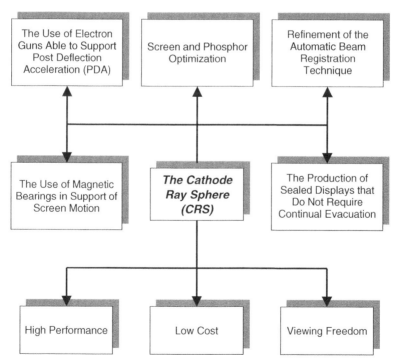

Figure 12.4   Although the CRS has been a subject of the author's research interests for some years, considerable opportunities for further advancement remain. See text for related discussion. (Diagram © Q. S. Blundell 2006.)

the final accelerating potential and additionally may support deflection magnification. The voxel activation capacity of current CRS prototypes is limited by the bandwidth of the DC coupled amplifiers that provide a maximum differential output voltage of $\sim$700 V (see Blundell and Schwarz [2000]).[5] This bottleneck may be alleviated by a move to electron guns supporting PDA, and at the same time the final anode voltage may be increased from 5 kV to $\sim$25 kV (thereby significantly reducing the average voxel activation time and increasing image intensity). In fact the PDA form of electron gun would result in support for a far higher voxel activation capacity (and may even permit exhaustive addressing of the image space volume). Furthermore, this approach would enable a reduction of the distance between electron gun and screen, thereby providing a more compact display unit. The use of electron guns of this type requires that the rotating screen and inner surface of the display vessel be coated with a transparent conductive material.

(b) *Automatic Beam Registration* It is vital that the coordinate system assigned to a directed beam source is accurately related to that associated with the image space. In the case that a single beam source is employed this is a fairly straightforward undertaking but becomes increasingly difficult as a greater number of sources are employed. In the case of all CRS prototypes developed to date, the precise mechanical positioning and alignment has never been considered to be practical, and therefore techniques have been developed to accurately determine the elements required to map between beam source and image space coordinate systems. The use of electron beams can greatly facilitate this process and offers to support an entirely automatic alignment process.

By applying a transparent conductive coating to the screen, it is easy to detect the presence of the beam current (as an electron beam impinges on the screen) as compared to the absence of this current (when the beam fails to strike the screen). Calibration algorithms may then be developed to perform a series of beam deflections that enable the elements within the transformation matrices needed to relate the beam source and image space coordinate systems to be derived.

As previously discussed, the use of one or more directed electron beams for voxel activation supports rapid beam deflection at low cost. Additionally, an electron beam current may be readily detected, and this may be used to facilitate the vital cross-referencing of the coordinate systems applied to each beam deflection apparatus and to the image space. This denotes a key advantage associated with the use of directed charged particle beams (and is not so easily achieved when directed laser beams are employed).

---

[5] For use with electron guns employing a final anode voltage of $\sim$5 kV.

To date, this automatic beam registration technique has not been perfected, and more work is required in this area. The essential difficulty has been caused by charge build-up/secondary emission within the display vessel which introduces noise into the beam current signal derived from the screen. The application of a transparent conductive coating to the inner surface of the display vessel provides a likely solution to this difficulty.

(c) *Continuous Evacuation* All CRS prototypes developed to date have required continuous pumping. This greatly impacts upon display portability and makes it difficult to conduct field trials. The most challenging aspect of developing a "sealed-off" CRS display concerns the need to ensure that all components within the display are able to withstand the "bake-out" temperature (this includes the bearings used in the screen rotation mechanism).

The issues indicated above represent technical advances needed to move a useful and proven volumetric technology out of the laboratory. Although each may appear to represent a relatively straightforward undertaking, in practice a considerable amount of experimental effort is sure to be required. For additional discussion on the CRS, see, for example, Blundell [1991], Blundell et al. [1991, 1993a–bc], Blundell and Schwarz [1992, 1994a,b, 1995a,b, 1999], Schwarz and Blundell [1994a,b]. Additionally, US Patent Numbers 5,703,606 and 6,054,817 focus on aspects of this approach. A CRS prototype currently in development is illustrated in Figure 12.5.

12.4 GAS DISCHARGE DEVICES

In Section 6.3.1, volumetric display units described in John Logie Baird's 1931 patent were discussed. The most interesting of these is the approach employing the rotational motion of panel equipped with a number of gas discharge electrodes contained within a gaseous medium. As indicated previously, from the extensive literature search carried out by the author in the preparation of this book, it appears that this may well represent the first *practical* volumetric display.[6] Furthermore, by removing the viewing restriction (that Baird adopted so as to mate the image capture and display systems), this technique could provide an effective low-cost display offering ~10–20 depth planes and a single window view onto the image space.

Naturally, the re-creation and development of this display technology offers an exciting opportunity and although a commutator would continue to be needed for the passage of the static potentials, the parallel optical link outlined in Section 11.5 could be used for data transfer.

---

[6] An earlier approach described by Luzy and Dupuis (see Section 9.5) and relating to the development of a static-volume display is likely to have suffered from the formation of "ghost voxels". Its usefulness may therefore have been somewhat limited.

Figure 12.5   A CRS prototype currently under development. This display employs two electron guns equipped with post deflection acceleration meshes enabling a final anode potential of 25,000 volts. The screen motor drive is located below the vacuum vessel. (Original image © B.G. Blundell.)

12.5   THE STEPWISE EXCITATION OF FLUORESCENCE

In the development of display units that employ a solid/liquid image space medium, two important difficulties are likely to arise:

(a) The volume of the image space is ultimately limited by its mass.

(b) Boundary refraction may cause unacceptable image distortion.

In Figure 12.6 we indicate possible ways in which we may ameliorate these difficulties. However, through the use of a gaseous image space medium, these difficulties could be avoided altogether, and this is an area that should be actively pursued. In this respect, there is great scope for research that builds on the activities of

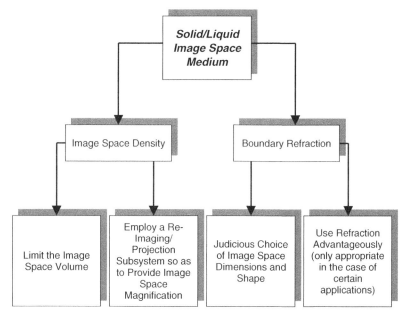

Figure 12.6   Two issues that should be given particular attention in the implementation of an image space that comprises a solid or liquid, are its mass and boundary refraction. Some possible solutions are indicated. Note that although for some applications we may make use of boundary refraction to provide a natural means of supporting image magnification (*cf* a goldfish bowl), this is not appropriate when we wish to visualize complex images, judge spatial relationships, and carry out interactive operations. (Diagram © A. R. Blundell 2006.)

pioneers such as Fajans (see Section 9.5), Zito and Schraeder (see Section 5.6.1), and Kim, Korevaar, Hakakha, and Spivey (also see Section 5.6.1). There can be little doubt that this is an area well worth continued investigation, and the development of a static-volume volumetric display employing a gaseous medium (able to operate at (or close to) room temperature) could offer interesting opportunities. For additional discussion in this area, see, for example, Schwarz and Blundell [1993] and Blundell and Schwarz [1995a,b].

12.6   OTHER APPROACHES

There are many other promising approaches that warrant further research, and several of these are indicated below:

1. *The Generescope (Ref. 7E):* This display technique was outlined in the patent filed by Max Hirsch in 1958 (see Section 7.3.1). Not only is the general technique interesting, but also the display provides an image space divided into two separate viewing zones. The provision of a partitioned image space could have applications in the areas such as medicine and training.

2. *Helix-Based Displays (an ongoing area of activity):* As outlined in Section 7.4, systems employing a helical screen for image space creation date back to the pioneering work carried out by Professor Rüdiger Hartwig and are particularly well able to provide large volume image spaces. Voxel activation may be achieved by means of either directed or nondirected beam sources. In this latter case, the approach indicated in Section 8.6 is worth investigation.

3. *Two Degrees of Freedom (Ref. 7R):* The approach discussed in Section 7.5.5 in which the motion of the screen is determined by two orthogonal drive mechanisms offers some interesting opportunities and should be further studied. Unfortunately, the mechanical aspects of this approach may cause difficulties (especially in terms of the required drive speeds), but such problems are seldom insurmountable.

4. *The Rotating Mirror Technique (Ref. 8F/8G):* The projection of images onto a rotating mirror provides a simple means of implementing a swept-volume volumetric display (although the sweep efficiency is likely to be somewhat limited). Displays of this type can be produced without the need for extensive workshop facilities and provide an opportunity for students to gain direct experience of the volumetric approach.

5. *An Optical Fiber Approach:* The static-volume display paradigm developed by Duncan MacFarlane (see Section 9.2.3) may be simplified through the introduction of rotational motion (resulting in a swept-volume architecture). As discussed in a previous work [Blundell and Schwarz, 2000], this enables a considerable reduction in the number of optical fibers needed (without any increase in minimum voxel separation). Furthermore, by introducing a "hybrid motion"[7] to a central cylindrical core region of the image space (i.e., around the axis of rotation), the density of fibers may be further reduced, and this will assist in improving image space characteristics in relation to the propagation of light.

6. *Beam Intersection in a Dispersed Phosphor:* This static volume approach was proposed by Jack Fajans (see Section 9.5.4) and dates back to the early 1960s. It continues to be of relevance and, by means of techniques such as those devised by Perlin and co-workers, could be developed to necessitate the use of only a single directed beam source.

7. *Voxel Opacity:* Although for many applications the lack of image opacity is not a major handicap (and in some limited number of cases may in fact be advantageous), in other areas opacity is an essential requirement. However, only a relatively small amount of effort has been directed toward the development of volumetric display systems able to support the opacity depth cue. Here is great scope for research, perhaps building upon the techniques devised by Adamson and Jordan in the late 1960s (see Section 5.7).

---

[7] Increased rotational speed plus a *small* amplitude translational motion.

8. *Pointer-Based Interaction:* Volumetric, varifocal, and other forms of creative 3-D display systems offer to support new interaction modalities. There is a great deal of work to be done in this area, not only in terms of developing and refining tools but also in understanding how these tools may best be employed. In this respect, we must not only learn how individual tools can be used but also understand the role that they may play within a highly synergistic interaction environment.

12.7 DISCUSSION

> *The poet's eye, in a fine frenzy rolling,*
> *Doth glance from heaven to earth, from earth to heaven;*
> *And, as imagination bodies forth*
> *The forms of things unknown, the poet's pen*
> *Turns them to shapes, and gives to airy nothing*
> *A local habitation and a name.*[8]

For a number of decades a vast amount of research effort has been directed toward the development of volumetric and varifocal display systems. With the passage of time, the display prototypes are usually no longer in existence and the only legacy left to us takes the form of patents and scientific publications (occasionally containing an intriguing photograph of a display apparatus or 3-D image). The author has sought to outline aspects of this diverse research history and to further develop the concepts and terminology that enable us to discuss volumetric, varifocal, and other forms of creative 3-D display within a common framework.

The reader relatively new to this area of activity may gain from this book a feeling that because so much past research effort has been undertaken, there can be little chance of our continuing to developing novel display architectures. This is far from being the case, and new (and sometimes quite ingenious) display techniques are regularly reported in literature.[9]

If we are to markedly advance the human–computer interaction process, then we must embrace alternative forms of 3-D display and interaction systems. In this respect, volumetric and varifocal displays are, in principle, able to match the *basic* needs of the human visual system,[10] and they offer to support intuitive interaction modalities. Of course, the great diversity of approaches that may be adopted

---

[8] William Shakespeare, *A Midsummer Night's Dream*, Act V, Scene 1.

[9] See, for example, a patent filed in 2005 by Oliver Cossairt and Joshua Napoli (US Patent Application Number US 2005/0180007 A1). These and other current researchers demonstrate that "*steely eyed*" 3-D display designers are still hard at work. Indeed, this is a field that continues to attract highly creative individuals. In respect of this particular patent, the reader is left to decide if this continues to represent a volumetric embodiment, or a hybrid volumetric/multiview approach.

[10] As with other forms of display, they do not offer perfect solutions. In fact, when we consider the profundity of the human visual system, it is readily apparent that we have little (if any) chance of developing the "perfect" display.

has certainly caused the *embarasse de richesse* referred to during discussion of the 1948 Parker and Wallis publication[11] and has made it difficult to judge the most optimal display solutions. Furthermore, there are those who would prefer to advance the human–computer interaction process by simply fine-tuning existing techniques. This outlook is underpinned by the assumption that the mathematically based perspective techniques[12] that were demonstrated some 600 years ago not only provide a sufficient basis for the visualization of 3-D images, *but also are optimal in the support they provide for efficient and intuitive interaction.*[13]

The debate concerning the benefits that may be derived from volume displays that make "space" for the third dimension and thereby enable us to break away from the bounds of Flatlands [Abbott, 1884] therefore continues:

> *In fact, the debate concerning the usefulness of 3-D display techniques parallels discussion in the 1970s on the wisdom of moving from monochrome to more expensive full-colour display technologies for general purpose applications. At that time it was difficult to accurately predict the true benefits of such a move, but with hindsight few would question the need for this development.*[14] *[Blundell, 2006]*

In relation to the benefits to be derived by the proliferation of creative 3-D displays, this continues:

> *Of course, we cannot forecast these benefits with certainty—but if workers in the 1970's had not followed their instincts, the digital world would still be stark and grey. Thankfully, we can view it in Technicolor. The time has now come to liberate it from the confines of the conventional 2-D screen.*

Which provides us with a satisfactory note on which to end!

When you are a Bear of Very Little Brain,
and you Think of Things, you find sometimes
that a Thing which seemed very Thingish inside you
is quite different when it gets out into the open
and has other people looking at it.[15]

---

[11] See Parker and Wallis [1949].

[12] Which give rise to the set of pictorial depth cues.

[13] This assumes that we are able to decouple the visualization and interaction processes and fails to take into account the pivotal role played by our sense of sight in both activities.

[14] A similar debate took place concerning the introduction of stereophonic radio broadcasting.

[15] A.A. Milne, *The House at Pooh Corner.*

APPENDIX
A General Summary of Some Swept-Volume Display Characteristics

Then rose the dumb old servitor, and the dead
Steer'd by the dumb went upward with the flood —
In her right hand the lily, in her left
The letter — all her bright hair streaming down —
And all the coverlid was cloth of gold.

A.1   INTRODUCTION

In this Appendix we briefly bring together some of the characteristics of the various exemplar swept-volume embodiments introduced in this book. In the tables that follow, we highlight various characteristics—not with the intention of forming critical comparisons, but rather to provide the reader with an overview of the broad range of swept-volume architectures.

Where possible, data presented are directly quoted from the literature available to the author. Occasionally, the author has made guesstimates on a "best efforts" basis. Preparing such a summary is not without some difficulty and in examining the summaries provided, it is important to bear in mind the following:

1. The numerical values quoted do not necessarily denote inherent limitations of a technique but, rather, generally relate to specific architectures. Consequently, performance may be limited not as a result of a fundamental weakness of a display unit technique but because of other factors such as limitations in the throughput of the graphics pipeline, the lack of suitable lasers and/or laser scanners, and so on. This is particularly important when considering earlier systems.

2. Numerical values should be viewed with a degree of caution, and in the case where any value associated with an embodiment is significantly different from those assigned to other similar embodiments, one must carefully consider facets of the technology that may give rise to the difference. In the author's experience, patents can on occasion provide unreliable detail, particularly in terms of the quantification of characteristics. Often, the central technology reported in the patent has only been implemented in prototype form and performance characteristics are extrapolated (perhaps over-optimistically). Thus potential problems may not have been envisaged and/or problems may be brushed to one side in a wave of quite natural enthusiasm. Furthermore, in the case of the "alternative methods" that are generally included in patents, these may not have been implemented (even in prototype form) and are frequently included in an attempt to widen the scope and strength of a patent.

3. Finally, we should emphasize that entries dealing with "potential difficulties" reflect the judgment of the author and are certainly not intended to indicate fundamental weaknesses.

In the tables that follow, P denotes the degree of parallelism supported by the voxel activation subsystem, ψ the fill factor, and ξ the sweep efficiency.

TABLE A.1 A Summary of Some Characteristics Associated with the Various Exemplar Display Units that Give Rise to Parallel Image Slices

	Brief Title	Section(s)	Image Space Dimensions (Inches)	Viewing Restrictions	P	ψ (%)	ξ (%)	Distortion and Shadows	Refresh Frequency (Hz)	Strengths and Useful Concepts	Potential Difficulties
6A	Probably the First Swept-Volume System (Rotation) (1931)	6.3.1	~(~5 Depth Planes)	Single face	1	100	Low as described	Very good	—	Potentially able to support 100% sweep efficiency. Use of gas discharge	Limited image space depth
6B	Probably the First Swept-Volume System (Translational) (1931)	6.3.1	—	Single face	1	—	Low	—	—	Insufficient detail to determine strengths and weaknesses	—
6D	Image Slices Cast onto Rotating Planes	6.3.2	Example 4 × 4 × 3	Single face	1	100	Low	Good	—	Simple projection system	Limited image space depth. Low sweep efficiency
6E	Reciprocating CRT (Sperry Corp.)	6.4.1	Depth: ~1	Single face	1	<100	100	Very good	>15	—	CRT mass. Component vibration. Noise at higher refresh rates
6F	Slices Focused onto Moving Screen (Sperry Corp.)	6.4.2	—	Single face	1	<100	100	Very good	—	Novel solution	Two components must move. Lens distortion of image. Noise at higher refresh rates

(continued)

TABLE A.1 (*continued*)

	Brief Title	Section(s)	Image Space Dimensions (Inches)	Viewing Restrictions	P	ψ (%)	ξ (%)	Distortion and Shadows	Refresh Frequency (Hz)	Strengths and Useful Concepts	Potential Difficulties
6G	Slices Reflected by Mirror (non-constant speed) The Sperry Corporation	6.4.3	Depth: 1	Single face (off axis)	1	<100?	200	Good	—	Enhanced depth of image space	Extraneous reflections—limit viewing locations. Noise at higher sweep rates
6H	Slices Reflected by Mirror (non-constant speed) RSRE (Parker and Wallis)	6.4.3	3 × 3 × 1.5	Single face (off axis)	1	100	200	Good	20	Enhanced depth of image space	Dimensions may be inaccurate. Images projected from 3-inch CRT, but a 14-inch square mirror is cited in Parker and Wallis [1949] As in 6G
6I	Peritron	6.4.4 and 4.4	Radius: 4 Depth: 1.4	Single face	1	<100	100	Very good	30 Hz (?)	No noise, no air resistance. Low mass screen, simple solution	Maintenance of moving components
6J	Slices Reflected by Mirror (constant speed)	6.4.5	6 × 8 × 8 cm	Single face	1	100	~190	Very good	~12	Angled mirror avoids extraneous reflections. Enhanced depth of image space	Tilting the mirror reduces image space dimensions
6K	Active SOE (constant speed) Kameyama et al.	6.4.6	9.4 × 3 × 5 cm	Single face	≫1	100	~95	Very good	30	Use of an active SOE—homogeneous image space. Projection of image into "free" space	Noise at higher sweep rates

6L	Active SOE (constant speed) Brotz	6.4.6	—	Single face	$\gg 1$	100	~95	Very good	—	Use of self-reversing screw. Proposed use of FEDs	Noise at higher sweep rates
6M	Rotors with Active SOE	6.5.1	—	Limited freedom beyond a single face	>1	100	~90	Fair	60	Novel approach to the production of image slices	Image occlusion due to axial components. Rotation of electronic circuit components at a high quoted rate
6N	Rotation of Stepped Mirrors	6.5.2	—	Single face	1	100?	~200	Fair	—	Ease of motion. Strength of moving assembly	Image occlusion at some viewing positions due to steps
6O	Rotation of Fiber Optic Bundle (Rotating CRT)	6.5.3	—	Single face	1	100	100	Fair/good	—	Use of fiber bundle	CRT rotation. Electron beam placement accuracy. Beam modulation signal bandwidth
6P	Rotation of Fiber Optic Bundle (Static CRT)	6.5.3	—	Single face	1	100	100	Fair/good	—	Simplicity. Use of fiber bundle	No CRT rotation. Potential of image blurring
6Q	Archimedes' Spiral	6.5.4	—	Single face	1	100	Low	Very good	—	Uniform image space	Low sweep efficiency
4A	Rotation of a Set of Screens	4.3.1 and 6.5	—	Single face	1	100	~6	Very good	—	Uniformity of image space	Size of rotating assembly

(continued)

TABLE A.2 A Summary of Some Characteristics Associated with Exemplar Display Units Discussed in Chapter 7

Code	Brief Title	Section(s)	Image Space Dimensions[1] (cm)	Viewing Freedom	P	ψ (%)	ξ (%)	Distortion and Shadows	Refresh Frequency (Hz)	Strengths and Useful Concepts	Potential Difficulties
7A	Planar Screen and Two Projection CRT's (Parker and Wallis)	7.2	Not indicated	Some limitations: caused by projection apparatus	1	<100	~100	Good	Probably ~20	Amelioration of voxel elongation and placement dead zones by using two projection sources	Maintaining voxel focus as the distance between source and screen varies
7B	Planar Screen and One Electron Guns (Ketchpel)	7.2.1	Ketchpel indicates feasibility of 21-in.-diameter screen. Experimental apparatus: screen appears much smaller in photograph	Good	1	≪100	<100	Poor	~30	Electron gun directly addresses screen. High-speed electron beam deflection	Voxel elongation and placement dead zones limit useful image space
7C	Planar Screen and Two Electron Guns (Ketchpel)	7.2.1	As in 7B, above	Good	1	~100	~100	Good	30	Elimination of voxel elongation and placement dead zones by using two projection sources	Alignment of the electron guns relative to the screen coordinate system

| 7D | Planar Screen and Co-Rotating Electron Gun(s) (Hirsch) | 7.3.1 | Not indicated—perhaps a little larger than Generescope | Excellent | 2 | <100 | ~100 | Very good | Not indicated | Constant geometry between beam sources and image slices. Electron guns directly addresses screen. High-speed electron beam deflection. Radical solution. | Mechanical complexity. Use of traditional commutators (signals could be passed optically—see Section 11.5) |
| 7E | Generescope (Hirsch) | 7.3.1 | Not indicated—perhaps on the order of 8–10 inches in diameter and 8–10 inches in height | Front and rear only | 1 | ~100 | <100 | Good | ~25 | Constant geometry between beam sources and image slices. Electron gun (CRT) rotates around central axis (in fact CRT rotation is not essential) | Projection apparatus interferes with view of the image space and restricts viewing to two zones |

(continued)

399

TABLE A.2 (*continued*)

Code	Brief Title	Section(s)	Image Space Dimensions[1] (cm)	Viewing Freedom	P	ψ (%)	ξ (%)	Distortion and Shadows	Refresh Frequency (Hz)	Strengths and Useful Concepts	Potential Difficulties
7F	Planar Screen and Co-Rotating Electron Gun (Goldberg)	7.3.1	Not indicated	Excellent	1	~100	~100	Good	30 Hz	Constant geometry between beam sources and image slices. Electron guns directly addresses screen. Addition of floor map and graticule (illuminated in red)	High-voltage electronics co-rotates with screen.
7G	CRT Images Projected onto Planar Screen (ITT Labs)	7.3.2	12 inches in diameter, 6 inches in height	Very good	1	<100	<100	Fair	~20	Projection apparatus does occlude the image space	Ensuring that co-rotating optical components are held rigidly and vibration is avoided
7H	Scanned Beam Projected onto Planar Screen (Batchko)	7.3.2	~30-cm diameter, 36-cm height[a]	Very good	1	<100	~100	Very good	20[a]	Projection apparatus does occlude the image space	Ensuring that co-rotating optical components are held rigidly and vibration is avoided
7I	3-D Rotation (Shimada)	7.3.2	30-cm diameter, 15-cm height	Very good	1 or 3	~100	~100	Very good	30	Novel optical arrangement. Projection apparatus does not occlude the image space	Alignment of the three projection tubes. Drive electronics.

7J	Laser addressed helical screen HL3D (Hartwig)	7.4	60-cm diameter 40-cm height	Very good	1	<100	~100	Good	20	Strength of helical structure—suitable for large volume image spaces	Increased gradient toward axis of rotation
7K	Helical Screen within a CRT	7.4.1	Not known—perhaps on the order of 12 inches diameter, 4 inches in height	Single face	1	<100	~100	Good	~20–25	Helix is directly addressed by electron beam. Screen rotates within a vacuum.	Construction. Image space depth is limited. Fixing screen bearings via an unobtrusive support.
7L	HL3D-Based Systems	7.4.2	Various embodiments. Up to 36 inches diameter, 18 inches height	Very good	~4	<100	~100	Good	~20[d]	Large image space dimensions provide good spatial clarity.	Given the excellent large volume image space—limitations in the voxel activation capacity.
7M	Projection of CRT Images onto a Helical Screen (Morton)	7.4.3	Not quoted	Very good	1	<100	~100	Good	~25	Effective voxel generation and activation techniques. The formation of focused voxels. Tracking of user location	The size of the anamorphic lens should match the diameter of the image space.
7N	A Tilted Planar Screen (Garcia and Williams)	7.5.1	Not quoted	Good	1	<100	~100	Good	Not quoted—probably ~20–25	Image data may be projected onto the screen from above (or below)	Image space shape limits the applicability of this technique.

(continued)

TABLE A.2 (*continued*)

Code	Brief Title	Section(s)	Image Space Dimensions[1] (cm)	Viewing Freedom	P	ψ (%)	ξ (%)	Distortion and Shadows	Refresh Frequency (Hz)	Strengths and Useful Concepts	Potential Difficulties
7O	An Alternative Screen Shape (Skellett)	7.5.2	Not quoted	Fair	1	<100	~100	Fair	Not quoted—probably ~20	Screen is directly addressed by electron beam. Screen rotates in a vacuum.	Construction. Voxel elongation. Screen may occlude image.
7P	Augmenting the Planar Screen (Garcia and Williams)	7.5.3	Not quoted	Limited	1	<100	<100	Perhaps poor	Not quoted	Improves the image space shape referred to in 7N, above.	Screen is difficult to address—additional component(s) are at times interposed between beam source(s) and locations on the screen.
7Q	CRT Image Projected via a "Sliced" Fiber Bundle (Garcia and Williams)	7.5.4	Not quoted	Single face	1	~100	100	Good	Not quoted—probably ~20–25	Rugged screen construction	Not all light generated by CRT will enter the intended fibers (possible loss of image sharpness). Image space shape limits the applicability of this technique.

402

| 7R | Two Degrees of Freedom (Garcia and Williams) | 7.5.5 | Not quoted | Very good | 1 | <100 | Possibly 100% | Good | Not quoted | Novel approach with many possibilities. | Mechanical difficulties in implementing a fast and accurate drive mechanism. |
| 7S | A hinged and oscillating mirror (Wolff) | 7.6 | Not quoted | Single face | 1 | <100 | ~100 | Good | Not quoted | Novel approach—discussed in 1938 patent | Nonrectangular image space. Mechanical implementation may be problematic at high sweep speeds |

[a]Figure cited in Clifton and Wefer [1993].

TABLE A.3 A Summary of Some Characteristics Associated with the Exemplar Display Units Discussed in Chapter 8

Code	Brief Title	Section(s)	Image Space Dimensions	Viewing Freedom	P	ψ (%)	ξ (%)	Distortion and Shadows	Refresh Frequency (Hz)	Strengths and Useful Concepts	Potential Difficulties
8A	Planar Screen and Active SOE (Berlin)	4.2 and 8.2	Not indicated—estimate: 13-cm radius, 26-cm height	Good	Depends on addressing scheme (data link serial)	100	~100	Visual dead zone *may* be problematic	30	Beam sources not used—therefore voxel elongation and placement dead zones are avoided	Thickness of rotating screen and light-emitting components impact on visual dead zone. Co-rotating electronics
8B	Planar Screen and Active SOE (Coddington and Schipper)	8.2	10 inches in diameter, 11 inches in height	Fairly good	Depends on addressing scheme	Uncertain: probably ~100	<100	Fair/good	20	Interesting screen implementation.	Connections to screen passed along a central region (occupy a one-inch region) and so visually obtrusive. Use of 100 ring commutator. Resolution of prototype panel ~15 × 15

8C	A Plurality of Scanned Beam Sources (LoRe et al.)	8.3.1	Screen ~4 by 6 inches. Plexiglas with layer of Vellum	Front and rear only	~32 in this embodiment	100	~50 if only 1 set of beams and polygon scanner are used.	Fair/good	Estimate ~30	Use of a multifaceted mirror to simultaneously scan a number of beams	Voxel elongation and placement dead zones limit the region that can be addressed using a single scanning mechanism
8D	Perspecta Display (Actuality Systems Inc.)	8.3.2	10 inches in diameter	Very good	Very high	100	100	Good	~24	Projection apparatus does not occlude the image space. Constant geometry between beams and image space slices. Very high voxel activation capacity	
8E	Images Cast onto a Rotating Mirror (Toshiyuki)	8.3.3	Not indicated	Limited	Depends on addressing scheme	100	Estimate ~30	Fair	~30	Novel approach	Not truly a volumetric technique. Optical arrangement must be designed with care

(*continued*)

405

TABLE A.3 (*continued*)

Code	Brief Title	Section(s)	Image Space Dimensions	Viewing Freedom	P	ψ (%)	ξ (%)	Distortion and Shadows	Refresh Frequency (Hz)	Strengths and Useful Concepts	Potential Difficulties
8F	Images Cast onto a Rotating Mirror (Simon)	8.3.3	Not indicated—estimate fairly small	Fair	1	Low	$\ll 100$	Quite good	Not indicated—estimate 10–20	Simplicity	Low sweep efficiency. Possibility of observer's reflection being visible
8G	Images Cast onto a Rotating Mirror (Simon and Walters)	8.3.3	$\sim 6 \times 6 \times 6$ inches and $4 \times 6 \times 6$ inches	Fair/Good	1	Low	$\ll 100$	Good	~ 10	Simplicity. Possibility of observer's reflection being visible in 8F is eliminated	Viewing freedom is limited
8H	Helical Screen and Active SOE (Brotz)	8.4	Not indicated	Good	Depends on addressing scheme (data link serial)	100	< 100	Shadowing dead zone *may* be problematic	Not Indicated	Beam sources not used—therefore voxel elongation and placement dead zones are avoided	Mass of rotating screen assembly, increased extent of dead zone close to axis of rotation

8I	Helical Screen with Passive SOE; Light Source Spatially Modulated. (Geng)	8.5	Not indicated	Limited in this embodiment	Depends on addressing scheme	100	<100	Good	Not indicated—estimate ~30	The use of a spatially modulated beam for parallel voxel activation.	SLM must be selected with care (perhaps use DMD). Optical arrangement needs to properly focus voxels at different depths within image space.
8J	Helical Screen with Passive SOE: Light Source Spatially Modulated by Reflection. (Thompson/DeMond)	8.5	Not indicated	Good	Depends on addressing scheme and geometry of beams relative to the screen	Possibly 100	<100	Good	Not indicated—estimate ~30	The use of a spatially modulated beam for parallel voxel activation via a DMD	Optical arrangement needs to properly focus voxels at different depths within image space
8K	Helical Screen with Passive SOE, and a moving array of light sources. (Blundell)	8.6	Not indicated	Good	Depends on addressing scheme and number of beam sources	100	<100	Good	30	Exhaustive addressing may be achieved with few beam sources. Use of nondirected beams	Mechanical motion of both the screen and the array of light sources

References

NOTE: Within the body of the text, dates cited in relation to patents indicate the year when the patents were filed. In the references below, we provide the year when the patents were granted. From a historical perspective, the filing date is naturally of primary importance.

U.S. PATENTS

725,567; Ives, F. E. (1903), "Parallax Stereogram and Process of Making Same."
995,607; Kempinski, H. (1911), "Window Display."
1,260,682; Kanolt, C. W. (1918), "Photographic Method and Apparatus."
1,506,524; Hammond, L. (1924), "Stereoscopic Motion Picture Device."
1,552,451; Roach, H. F. (1925), "Optical Instrument."
1,658,439; Hammond, L. (1928), "Stereoscopic Picture Viewing Apparatus."
1,876,272; Bayer, J. V. (1932), "Fog Penetrating Televisor."
2,273,512; Caldwell, G. D., and Hathorn, G. M. (1942), "Viewing Instrument for Stereoscopic Pictures and the Like."
2,361,390; Ferrill, T. M., Jr. (1944), "Stereo Indicator."
2,604,607; Howell, F. S. (1952), "Three-Dimensional Indicator Tube and Circuit Therefor."
2,628,533; Oetjen, R. A. (1953), "Image Forming Optical Reflecting and Converging Mirror Device."
2,749,480; Ruderfer, M. (1956), "Apparatus for Producing Three-Dimensional Visual Patterns."
2,762,031; Fryklund, R. A. (1956), "Three Dimensional Position-Indicating System."
2,806,216; Fryklund, R. A. (1957), "Three-Dimensional Position-Indicating Systems."
2,837,735; Wolff, I. (1958), "Pulse Echo Radio Locator System."
2,967,905; Hirsch, M. (1961), "Three Dimensional Display Apparatus."
3,050,870; Heilig, M. (1962), "Sensorama Simulator."
3,123,711; Fajans, J. (1964), "Luminous Spot Display Device."
3,140,415; Ketchpel, R. D. (1964), "Three-Dimensional Display Cathode Ray Tube."
3,204,238; Skellett, A. M. (1965), "Cathode Ray Tube for Three-Dimensional Presentations."
3,300,779; Sirkis, R. (1967), "Three Dimensional Pictorial Displays."
3,474,248; Brown, M. R, and Waters, G. S. (1969), "Three-Dimensional Visual Display Systems."
3,493,290; Traub, A. C. (1970), "Three-Dimensional Display."
3,541,542; Dugay, M. A., Giordmaine, J. A., and Rentzepis, P. M. (1970), "Display System Using Two-Photon Fluorescent Materials."

Enhanced Visualization: Making Space for 3-D Images. By Barry G. Blundell
Copyright © 2007 John Wiley & Sons, Inc.

3,609,706; Adamson, A. W. (1971), "Method and Apparatus for Generating Three-Dimensional Patterns."

3,609,707; Lewis, J. D. (1971), "Method and Apparatus for Generating Three-Dimensional Patterns."

3,636,551; Maguire, E. T. (1972), "Computer-Controller Three-Dimensional Display."

3,647,284; Elings, V. B., and Landry, C. J. (1972), "Optical Display Device."

3,829,838; Lewis, J. D., Verber, C. M., and McGhee, R. B. (1974), "Computer-Controlled Three-Dimensional Pattern Generator."

4,063,233; Rowe, G. R. (1977), "Three-Dimensional Display Devices."

4,130,832; Sher, L. D. (1978), "Three-Dimensional Display."

4,160,973; Berlin, E. P. (1979), "Three-Dimensional Display."

4,190,856; Ricks, D. E. (1980), "Three Dimensional Television System."

4,692,878; Ciongoli, B. M. (1987), "Three-Dimensional Spatial Image System."

4,881,068; Korevaar, E. J., and Spivey, B. (1989), "Three Dimensional Display Apparatus."

4,922,336; Morton, R. R. A. (1990), "Three Dimensional Display System."

5,042,909; Garcia F., Jr., et al. (1991), "Real Time Three Dimensional Display with Angled Rotating Screen and Method."

5,148,310; Batchko, R. G. (1992), "Rotating Flat Screen Fully Addressable Volume Display System."

5,162,787; Thompson, E. E., and DeMond, T. W. (1992), "Apparatus and Method for Digitized Video System Utilizing a Moving Display Surface."

5,172,266; Garcia, F., Jr. (1992), "Real Time Three Dimensional Display."

5,418,632; Anderson, D. W. (1995), "System and Method for Rotational Scanner Based Volume Display."

5,663,740; Brotz, G. R. (1997), "Display Device Producing a Three-Dimensional Real Image."

5,703,606; Blundell, B. G. (1997), "Three Dimensional Display System."

5,717,416; Chakrabarti, S., (1998), "Three-Dimensional Display Apparatus."

5,745,197; Leung, M. S., Ives, N. A., and Eng, G. (1998), "Three-Dimensional Real-Image Volumetric Display System and Method."

5,815,314; Sudo, T. (1998), "Image Display Apparatus and Image Display Method."

5,854,613; Soltan, P., Trias, J., Dahlke, W. J., Belfatto, R. V., and Sanzone, F. (1998), "Laser Based 3D Volumetric Display System."

5,936,767; Favalora, G. E. (1999), "Multiplanar Autostereoscopic Imaging System."

5,945,966; Acantilado, N. P. (1999), "Computer Program for a Three-Dimensional Volumetric Display."

6,049,317; Thompson, E. E., and DeMond, T. W. (2000), "System for Imaging of Light-Sensitive Media."

6,054,817; Blundell, B. G. (2000), "Three Dimensional Display System."

6,064,423; Zheng, J. G. (2000), "Method and Apparatus for High Resolution Three Dimensional Display."

6,100,862; Sullivan, A. (2000), "Multi-Planar Volumetric Display System and Method of Operation."

6,115,006; Brotz, G. R. (2000), "Rotating Display Device and Method for Producing a Three-Dimensional Real Image."

6,177,913; Whitesell, E. J. (2001), "Volumetric Display."

6,183,088; LoRe A. G., Favalora, G. E., and Giovinco, M. G. (2001), "Three-Dimensional Display System."

6,958,837; Hartwig, R. (2004), "Method for Producing Picture Element Groups by Means of Laser Rays in Space and on a Plane."

U.S. PATENT APPLICATION

2002/0140631 A1; Blundell, B. G. (2002), "Volumetric Display Unit."

2004/0218148 A1; Perlin, K., and Han, J. Y., (2004), "Volumetric Display with Dust as the Participating Medium."

2005/0180007 A1; Cossairt, O. S., and Napoli, J., (2005), "Radial Multiview Three-Dimensional Displays."

EUROPEAN PATENTS

DE2622802C2; Hartwig, R. (1976), "Helix Laser 3D Display."

DE10047695; Hartwig, R. (2002), "Method for Producing Picture Element Groups by Means of Laser Rays in Space and on a Plane."

EP 0 310 928 A2; Garcia Jr, F. (1989), "Real Time Three Dimensional Display and Method."

EP 0 418 583 A2; Garcia, F. Jr. (1991), "Real Time Three Dimensional Display."

EP 0 491 284 A1; Williams, R. D. (1992), "Volume Display System and Method for Inside-Out-Viewing."

FR461 600; Luzy, E., and Dupuis, C. (1914), "Procédé Pour Obtenir des Projections en Relief."

U.K. PATENTS

GB292,185; Television Ltd., and Baird, J. L. (1928), "Improvements in or Relating to Apparatus for Transmitting Views or Images to a Distance."

GB294,671; Baird, J. L., and Baird Television Ltd. (1928), "An Improved Method of Effecting the Optical Projection of Images."

GB373,196; Baird, J. L., and Baird Television Ltd. (1932), "Improvements in or Relating to Television Systems and the Like."

GB552,582; Baird, J. L. (1943), "Improvements in Television."

GB557,837; Baird, J. L. (1943), "Improvements in or Relating to the Optical Projection of Images Exhibiting Relief Effects."

GB592,367; Parker, E., and Wright, C. S. (1947), "Improvements In or Relating to Apparatus Displaying Positional, Numerical or Like Data."

GB634,567; Parker, E., Wallis, P. R., Woroncow, A., and Buckingham, J. (1950), "Improvements in and Relating to Cathode Ray Tube Display Systems."

GB638,274; Keynes, R. D., Parker, E., and Wright, C. S. (1950), "Improvements in and Relating to Radar and Like Systems for Detecting and Locating Objects."

GB652,649; Sperry Corporation, The (1951), "Improvements in or Relating to Systems for Producing Pictorial Displays in Apparent Relief."

GB1,103,861; Sherwood, G. S., and Brown, M. R. (1968), "Three-Dimensional Visual Display Systems."

GB1,167,415; De Montebello, R. L. (1969), "Three-Dimensional Optical Display Apparatus."

GB1,167,416; De Montebello, R. L. (1969), "Three-Dimensional Optical Display Apparatus."

JAPANESE PATENTS

JP60257695; Yasushi, M. (1985), "Stereoscopic Video Image Generating Device."

JP63254647; Hidenori, E. (1988), "Picture Tube for Three Dimensional Image Display."

PUBLICATIONS

Abbott, E. A., *Flatland: A Romance of Many Dimensions*, Seeley (1884).

Abramson, A., *The History of Television, 1880 to 1941*, McFarland and Co. (1987).

Araujo, R. J., "Photochromic Glass," *Journal of Chemical Education* **62**(6), pp. 472–473 (June 1985).

Aviation Week, "New Display Gives Realistic 3-D Effect," pp. 66–67 (October, 31 1960).

Baker, T. T., *Wireless Pictures and Television*, Constable & Company Ltd. (1926).

Balasubramanian, K., Nithiyanandam, N., and Rajappan, K. P., "Analysis of Certain Types of Display Devices for 3-D TV System," *IEEE Transactions on Consumer Electronics* **CE-27**(3), pp. 187–199 (August 1981).

Banchoff, T. F., *Beyond the Third Dimension: Geometry, Computer Graphics, and Higher Dimensions*, Scientific American Library (1996).

Barnes, R. H., Moeller, C. E., Kircher, J. F., and Verber, C. M., "Two-Step Excitation of Fluorescence in Iodine Monochloride Vapor," *Applied Physics Letters* **24**(12), pp. 610–612 (June 1974).

Batchko, R. G., "Three-Hundred-Sixty Degree Electro-Holographic Stereogram and Volumetric Display System," in *Practical Holography, VIII*, S. A. Benton (ed.), paper no. 2176-04, IS&T/Proceedings SPIE International Symposium on Electronic Imaging, San Jose (1994).

Belfatto, R.V., Sr., "The *Commercialization of a Fully Illuminated Volumetric Display,*" *Proceedings SPIE* **3296**, pp. 198–203 (1998).

Berkley, C., "Three-Dimensional Representation on Cathode-Ray Tubes," *Proceedings of the IRE—Waves and Electrons Section,* pp. 1530–1535 (December 1948).

Berman, E., Fox, R. E., and Thomson, F. D., "Photochromic Spiropyrans. I. The Effect of Substituents on the Rate of Ring Closure," *Journal of the American Chemical Society* **81**, pp. 5605–5608 (November 5, 1959).

Bibermanm L. M. (ed.), *Perception of Displayed Information*, Plenum Press, (1973).

Blundell, B. G., "On the Development of Higher Performance Volumetric Display Systems," *Invited contribution to Spring Conference on Computer Graphics and its Applications*, April 23–25, Budmerice, Slovakia (1998).

Blundell, B. G., "3-D Display Systems: Myth and Reality," *ITNow* **48**(1), pp. 32–33 (2006).

Blundell, B. G., and King, W., "Outline of a Low-Cost Prototype System to Display Three-Dimensional Images," *IEEE Transactions on Instrumentation and Measurement* **40**(4), pp. 792–793 (1991).

Blundell, B. G., and Schwarz, A. J., "The Cathode Ray Sphere: A Volumetric Three-Dimensional Display System," *Proceedings Applied Optics and Optoelectronics '92,* Institute of Physics, Leeds, UK, pp. 252–254 (1992).

Blundell, B. G., and Schwarz, A. J., "A Graphics Hierarchy for the Visualisation of 3D Images by Means of a Volumetric Display System," *Proceedings IEEE Tencom,* Singapore, pp. 1–5 (1994a).

Blundell, B. G., and Schwarz, A. J., "The Cathode Ray Sphere: A Prototype System to Display Volumetric Three-Dimensional Images," *Optical Engineering* **33**(1), pp. 180–186 (1994b).

Blundell, B. G., and Schwarz, A. J., "Visualisation of Complex System Dynamics on a Volumetric 3D Display Device," *Proceedings "Visualisierung—Dynamik und Komplexitaet,"* September, 24–26, Bremen, Germany (1995a).

Blundell, B. G., and Schwarz, A. J., "Volumetric Three-Dimensional Displays, Especially Those Based on Gaseous Media or Crystals," in *McGraw-Hill Yearbook of Science and Technology 1996,* McGraw-Hill (1995b).

Blundell, B. G., and Schwarz, A. J., "An Alternative Approach to Human–Computer Interaction," *Interfaces,* no. 41, pp. 12–15 (1999).

Blundell, B. G., and Schwarz, A. J., *Creative 3-D Display and Interaction Interfaces: A Trans-Disciplinary Approach,* John Wiley & Sons (2006).

Blundell, B. G., and Schwarz, A. J., *Volumetric Three-Dimensional Display Systems,* John Wiley & Sons (2000).

Blundell, B. G., and Schwarz, A. J., "The Classification of Volumetric Display Systems: Characteristics and Predictability of the Image Space," *IEEE Transactions on Visualization and Computer Graphics* **8**, pp. 66–75 (2002).

Blundell, B. G., Crombie, G. J., and Schwarz, A. J., "The Development of a Three-Dimensional Display System: The Cathode Ray Sphere," *NELCON Proceedings,* New Zealand, pp. 7–12 (1991).

Blundell, B. G., Schwarz, A. J., and Horrell, D. K., "The Cathode Ray Sphere: A Volumetric Three-Dimensional Display System" (Late news paper), *Proceedings Eurodisplay'93,* Strasbourg, France, pp. 593–596 (1993a).

Blundell, B. G., Schwarz, A. J., and Horrell, D. K., "Visualisation of and Interaction with Spatial Information by Means of a Volumetric Three-Dimensional Graphics Peripheral," *Proceedings SPIE 1993,* Budapest, Hungary, pp. 207–208 (1993b).

Blundell, B. G., Schwarz, A. J., and Horrell, D. K., "Volumetric Three-Dimensional Display Systems—Their Past, Present and Future," *IEE Science and Engineering Education Journal* **2**(5), pp. 196–200 (1993c).

Boff, K. R., Kaufman, L., and Thomas, J.P. (eds.), *Handbook of Perception and Human Performance, Volume I, Sensory Processes and Perception,* John Wiley & Sons (1986).

Boyer, C. B. (revised by Merzbach, U. C.), *A History of Mathematics* (2nd ed.), John Wiley & Sons (1991).

Brinkmann, U., "A Laser-Based Three-Dimensional Display," *Lasers & Applications,* pp. 55–56 (March 1983).

Bruce, V., Green P. R., and Georgeson M. A., *Visual Perception: Physiology, Psychology and Ecology* (4th ed.), Psychology Press (2003).

Burdea, G. C., and Coiffet, P., *Virtual Reality Technology* (2nd ed.), John Wiley & Sons (2003).

Cameron, J. R., Skofronick, J. G., and Grant, R. M., *Physics of the Body,* (2nd ed.), Medical Physics Publishing (1999).

Campbell, F. W., and Westheimer, G., "Dynamics of Accommodation Responses in the Human Eye," *Journal of Physiology* **151**, pp. 285–295 (1960).

Campbell, F. W., Robson, J. G., and Westheimer, G., "Fluctuations of Accommodation During Steady Viewing Conditions," *Journal of Physiology* **145**, pp. 579–594 (1959).

Campbell Swinton, A. A., "Presidential Address," *The Journal of the Röntgen Society* **VIII** (30), pp. 1–13 (January 1912).

Chapanis, A., Garner, W. R., and Morgan, C. T., *Applied Experimental Psychology*, John Wiley & Sons (1949).

Chinnock, C., "Researchers Demonstrate 3-D Volumetric Images," *Laser Focus World*, pp. 28–32 (November 1994).

Chun, W.-S., Napoli, J., Cossairt, O. S., Dorval, R. K., Hall, D. M., Purtell II, T. J., Schooler, J. F., Banker, Y., and Favalora, G. E., "Spatial 3-D Infrastructure: Display-Independent Software Framework, High-Speed Rendering Electronics, and Several New Displays," in "Stereoscopic Displays and Virtual Reality Systems XII," (A. J.Woods, M. T. Bolas, J. O. Merritt, and I. E. McDowall, eds.), *Proceedings SPIE-IS&T Electronic Imaging, SPIE* **5664**, pp. 302–312 (2005).

Clifton, T. E., and Wefer, F. L., "Direct Volume Display Devices," *IEEE Computer Graphics and Applications* **13**(4) pp. 57–65 (1993).

Coddington, J. L., and Schipper, R. J., "Practical Solid State Three Dimensional (3-D) Display," *IRE International Conference Record* **10**(3), pp. 177–184 (1962).

Collender, R. B., "The Stereoptiplexer: Competition for the Hologram," *Information Display* **4**(6), pp. 27–31 (1967).

Computer Graphics World, "Full-Color Display in a Cube," pp. 19–20 (March 1997).

Coren, S., Ward, L. M., and Enns, J. T., *Sensation and Perception*, Harcourt Brace & Company (2004).

Cruz-Neira, C., Sandin, D. J., DeFanti, T. J., Kenyon, R. V., and Hart, J. C., "The Cave: Audio Visual Experience Automatic Virtual Environment," *Communications of the ACM* **35**(6) pp. 65–72 (1992).

Cruz-Neira, C., Sandin, D. J., and DeFanti, T. J., "Virtual Reality: The Design and Implementation of the CAVE," *Proceedings SIGGRAPH 93 Computer Graphics Conference*, ACM SIGGRAPH, pp. 135–142 (1993).

Cutler, L. D., Froehlich, B., and Hanrahan, P., "Two-Handed Direct Manipulation on the Responsive Workbench," *1997 Symposium on Interactive 3D Graphics, Providence RI, USA*, ACM, pp. 107–114 (1997).

De Araújo, L. E. E., Gomes, A. S. L., De Araújo, C. B., Messaddeq, Y., Florez, A., and Aegerter, M. A., "Frequency Upconversion of Orange Light into Blue Light in Pr^{3+}-Doped Fluoroindate Glasses," *Physics Reviews B* **50**(22), pp. 16219–16223 (December 1994).

Dember, W. N., and Warm, J. S., *Psychology of Perception* (2nd ed.), Holt, Rinehart and Winston (1979).

Demel, J. T., and Miller, M. J., *Introduction to Computer Graphics*, Wadsworth (Brooks/Cole Engineering Division) (1984).

Dodgson, N. A., Moore, J. R., and Lang, S. R., "Multi-View Autostereoscopic 3D Display," *Proceedings International Broadcasting Convention* (September 10–14, Amsterdam), pp. 497–502 (1999).

Downing, E., Hesselink, L., Macfarlane, R. M., and Barty, C. P. J., "Solid-State Three-Dimensional Computer Display," *CLEO '94* (1994).

Downing, E., Hesselink, L., Ralston, J., and Macfarlane, R., "A Three-Color, Solid-State, Three-Dimensional Display," *Science* **273**, pp. 1185–1189 (August 30, 1996).

Dudley, D., Duncan, W., and Slaughter, J., "Emerging Digital Micromirror Device (DMD) Applications," *Proceedings SPIE* **4985**, pp.14–25 (2003).

Edgerton, S. Y., *The Heritage of Giotto's Geometry—Art and Science on The Eve of The Scientific Revolution*, Cornell University Press (1991).

Edgerton, S. Y., *The Renaissance Rediscovery of Linear Perspective*, Harper and Row (1976).

EIA (Electronic Industries Association), "Optical Characteristics of Cathode Ray Tubes," TEP 116-B (1987).

Electronics, "Spinning Lens Projects Updatable 3-D Image," pp. 21–22 (October 21, 1985).

English, W. K., Engelbart, D. C., and Berman, M. L., "Display-Selection Techniques for Text Manipulation," *IEEE Transactions on Human Factors in Electronics* **HFE-8**(1) (March 1967).

Enright, J. T., "Art and the Oculomotor System: Perspective Illustrations Evoke Vergence Changes," *Perception* **16**, pp. 731–746 (1987a).

Enright, J. T., "Perspective Convergence: Oculomotor Responses to Line Drawings," *Vision Research* **27**, pp. 1513–1526 (1987b).

Eyal, M., Greenberg, E., and Reisfeld, R., "Spectroscopy of Praseodymium(III) in Zirconium Fluoride Glass," *Chemical Physics Letters* **117** (2), pp. 108–114 (June 1985).

Fajans, J., "Xyzscope—A New Option in 3-D Display Technology," *Proceedings SPIE* **1668**, p. 25 (1992).

Favalora, G. E., "Volumetric 3D Displays and Application Infrastructure," *Computer*, pp. 37–44 (August 2005).

Favalora, G. E., Dorval, R. K., Hall, D. M., Giovinco, M., and Napoli, J., "Volumetric Three-Dimensional Display System with Rasterization Hardware," in *Proceedings SPIE* **4297,** p. 227 (2001).

Favalora, G., Hall, D. M., Giovinco, M., Napoli, J., and Dorval, R. K., "A Multi-Megavoxel Volumetric 3-D Display System for Distributed Collaboration," *IEEE Globecom 2000 Conference, "Application of Virtual Reality Technologies for Future Telecommunication System," San Francisco, CA* (November 2000).

Favalora, G. E., Napoli, J., Hall, D. M., Dorval, R. K., Giovinco, M. G., Richmond, M. J., and Chun, W. S., "100 Million-Voxel Volumetric Display," *Proceedings SPIE* **4712** *(Cockpit Displays IX: Displays for Defense Applications)*, pp. 300–312 (2002).

Foley, J.D., van Dam, A., Feiner, S.K., Hughes, J.F., and Phillips, R.L., *Introduction to Computer Graphics*, Addison-Wesley Norwood, MA (1997).

Geddes, K., and Bussey, G., *The Setmakers: A History of the Radio and Television Industry*, The British Radio & Electronic Equipment Manufacturers' Association (1991).

Girling, A. N., *Stereoscopic Drawing: A Theory of 3-D Vision and Its Application to Stereoscopic Drawing*, Arthur Girling (1990).

Glanz, J., "Three-Dimensional Images are Conjured in a Crystal Cube," *Science* **273**, p. 1172 (August 1996).

Goeppert-Mayer, M., *Annalen der Physik* **9**, p. 273 (1931).

Fritzche, *J., Comptes Rendus Acad. Sci. Paris*, **69**, 1035 (1867).

Goldberg, A. A., "3-D Display System", *Proceedings IRE* **50,** p. 2521(L) (December 1962).

Gordon, J. E. H., "Seeing by Electricity," *Nature* (29 April 1880).

Haken, H., and Wolf, H. C., *The Physics of Atoms and Quanta* (4th ed.) (translated by W. D. Brewer), Springer-Verlag (1994).

Halle, M., "Autostereoscopic Displays and Computer Graphics," *Computer Graphics (ACM SIGGRAPH)*, **31**(2) pp. 58–62 (1997).

Hamagishi, G., Sakata, M., Yamashita, A., Mashitani, K., Inoue, M., and Shimizu, E., "15 High-Resolution Non-Glasses 3-D Display with Head-Tracking System," *Transactions of the IEE (Japan)* **121-C**(5), (May 2001).

Hanson, Captain E.R.T., Jr., "Travel Through the Next Dimension: 3-D Volumetric Display," *Journal of Air Traffic Control*, pp. 24–27 (March 1997).

Harris, L. D., "A Varifocal Mirror Display Integrated into a High-Speed Image Processor," *Proceedings SPIE* **902**, pp. 2–9 (1988).

Harris, L. D., Camp, J. J., Ritman, E. L., and Robb, R. A., "Three-Dimensional Display and Analysis of Tomographic Volume Images Utilizing a Varifocal Mirror," *IEEE Transactions on Medical Imaging* **MI-5**(2), pp. 67–72 (June 1986).

Hecht, S., and Mintz, E. U., "The Visibility of Single Lines at Various Illuminations and the Retinal Basis of Visual Resolution," *Journal of General Physiology*, pp. 593–612 (1939).

Hecht, E., and Zajac, A., *Optics*, Addison-Wesley (1974).

Hecht, S., Shlaer, S., and Pirenne, M. H., "Energy Quanta and Vision," *Journal of General Physiology* **25**, pp. 819–840 (1942).

Helliwell, J., "'Fish-Tank' Display Creates True 3-D Images," *PC Week*, p. 19 (May 8, 1989).

Helmholtz, H. H., *Popular Lectures on Scientific Subjects* (English translation by Atkinson, E.), Longmans, Green, and Co. (1873).

Hesselink, L., and Downing, E., "3D Volumetric Display Using a Non-Moving Medium: End of Phase I Report," in *NRaD Report* (February 1, 1993).

Hesselink, L., Downing, E., and Akella, A., "Proposal to Develop High Efficiency Material Hosts and Fully Integrate a Solid-State 3D Display with RGB Color Capabilities," in *NRaD Report* (February 2, 1995).

Heuring, V. P., and Jordan, H. F., *Computer Systems Design and Architecture* (2nd ed.), Pearson Education Inc. (2004).

Hinckley, K., and Pausch, R., "Two-Handed Virtual Manipulation," *ACM Transactions on Computer–Human Interaction* **5**(3), pp. 260–302 (September 1998).

Howard, I. P., *Seeing in Depth*, Vol. I Basic Mechanisms, I. Porteous (2002).

Howard, I. P., and Rogers, B. J., *Seeing in Depth*, Vol. II Depth Perception, I. Porteous (2002).

IEEE Spectrum, "Innovations, Patents, Processes, and Products: Mental Image," **24**, p. 20 (December 1987).

Inoue, M., Hamagishi, G., Sakata, M., Yamashita, A., and Mahitani, K., "Non-Glasses 3-D Displays by Shift-Image Splitter Technology," *Proceedings 3D Image Conference 2000, Tokyo* (2000).

Ishii, A., "Three-Dimensional Imaging Based on Perfect Projection Using Varifocal Mirror," *Proceedings SPIE* **5202**, pp. 38–49 (2003).

Ives, H. E., "A Camera for Making Parallax Panoramagrams," *Journal of the Optical Society of America* **17**, pp. 435–439 (December 1928).

Ives, H. E., "Motion Pictures in Relief," *Journal of the Optical Society of America* **18**, pp. 118–122 (February 1929).

Ives, H. E., "Parallax Panoramagrams Made with a Large Diameter Lens," *Journal of the Optical Society of America* **20**, pp. 332–342 (1930a).

Ives, H. E., "Parallax Panoramagrams Made with a Large Diameter Concave Mirror," *Journal of the Optical Society of America* **20**, pp. 597–600 (1930b).

Ives, H. E., "Optical Properties of a Lippmann Lenticulated Sheet," *Journal of the Optical Society of America* **21**, pp. 171–176 (March 1931).

Johnston, J., Roberts, T. L., Verplank, W., Smith, D., Irby, C. H., and Beard, M., "The Xerox Star: A Retrospective," *IEEE Computer* **22**(9), pp.11–29 (September 1989).

Kaiser, W., and Garrett, C.G. B., "Two-Photon Excitation in CaF_2: Eu^{2+}," *Physics Review Letters* **7**(6), pp. 229–231 (September 1961).

Kameyama, K., Ohtomi, K., and Fukui, Y., "Interactive Volume Scanning 3-D Display with an Optical Relay System and Multidimensional Input Devices," *Proceedings SPIE* **1915**, pp. 12–20 (1993).

Kamm, A., and Baird, M., *John Logie Baird: A Life,* National Museums of Scotland Publishing Ltd. (2002).

Kandel, E. R., Schwartz, J. H., and Jessell, T. M., *Principles of Neural Science* (4th ed.), McGraw-Hill (2000).

Kemp, M., "Science, Non-Science and Nonsense: the Interpretation of Brunelleschi's Perspective," *Art History* **1**(2), pp. 134–161 (1978).

Kennedy, D. N., and Nelson, A. C., "Three-Dimensional Display from Cross-Sectional Tomographic Images: An Application to Magnetic Resonance Imaging," *IEEE Transactions on Medical Imaging* **MI-6**(2), pp. 134–140 (June 1987).

Ketchpel, R. D., "CRT Provides Three-Dimensional Displays," *Electronics*, pp. 54–57 (November 2, 1962).

Ketchpel, R. D., "Direct-View Three-Dimensional Display Tube," *IEEE Transactions on Electronic Devices,* **10**, pp. 324–328 (1963).

Kim, I. I., Korevaar, E., and Hakakha, H., "Three-Dimensional Volumetric Display in Rubidium Vapor", *Proceedings SPIE* **2650**, pp. 274–284 (1996).

King, M. C., and Berry, D. H., "Varifocal Mirror Technique for Video Transmission of Three-Dimensional Images," *Applied Optics* **9**(9), pp. 2035–2039 (September 1970).

Kiss, Z. J., "Photochromics," *Physics Today*, pp. 42–49 (January 1970).

Kollin, J. S., "Collimated View Multiplexing: A New Approach to 3-D," *Proceedings SPIE* **902** *(Three Dimensional Imaging and Remote Sensing Imaging)*, pp. 24–30 (1988).

Land, M. F., and Nilsson, D.-E., *Animal Eyes*, Oxford University Press (2002).

Lang, S. R., Travis, A. R. L., Castle, O. M., and Moore, J. R., "A 2nd Generation Autostereoscopic 3-D Display", *Proceedings 7th Eurographics Workshop on Graphics Hardware (Cambridge, UK, September 5–6, 1992)*, Lister, P. F. (ed.), pp. 53–63 (1992).

Langhans, K., Bahr, D., Bezecny, D., Homann, D., Oltmann, K., Oltmann, K., Guill, C., Rieper, E., and Ardey, G., "Felix 3D Display: An Interactive Tool for Volumetric Imaging," *Proceedings SPIE* **4662** (2002).

Langhans, K., Guill, C., Rieper, E., Oltmann, K., and Bahr, D., "FELIX: A Static Volume 3D-Laser Display," *Proceedings SPIE* **5006** (2003).

Langhans, K., Oltmann, K., Reil, S., Goldberg, L., and Hatecke, H., "FELIX 3D Display: Human–Machine Interface for Interactive Real Three-Dimensional Imaging", in *Lecture Notes in Computer Science,* **3805** (Springer Verlag), pp. 22–31 (2005).

Laser Focus World, "Radial Scanning Produces 3-D Image on a Flat Screen," pp. 41–42 (January 1993).

Lasher, M., Soltan, P., Dahlke, W., Acantilado, N., and MacDonald, M., *"Laser Projected 3-D Volumetric Displays,"* *Proceedings SPIE* **2650**, pp. 285–295 (1996).

Lewis, J. D., Verber, C. M., and McGhee, R. B., "A True Three-Dimensional Display," *IEEE Transactions on Electron Devices* **ED-18**(9), pp. 724–732 (September 1971).

Lindsay, P. H., and Norman, D. A., *Human Information Processing: An Introduction to Psychology*, Academic Press (1972).

Lippman, G., "Epreuves Reversibles Donnant la Sensation du Relief," *Journal of Physics* **7** (4th series), pp. 821–825 (November 1908).

Lipton, L., *"Foundations of Stereoscopic Cinema"*, van Nostrand–Reinhold, (1982). [Also available from http://www.stereographics.com/whitepapers].

Lipton, L., "Selection Devices for Field-Sequential Stereoscopic Displays: A Brief History," *Proceedings SPIE* **1457**, pp. 274–282 (1991). [Also available from http://www. stereographics. com/whitepapers.]

Lipton, L., *Stereographics Developers' Handbook*, Stereographics Corp., San Francisco (1997). [See also http://www.stereographics.com.]

Lipton, L., "The Stereoscopic Cinema: from Film to Digital Projection," *SMPTE Journal*, pp. 586–593 (September 2001). [See also http://www. stereographics.com.]

Loong, K. Y., Jones, G. D., and Syme, R. W. G., "Fluorescence Lifetimes of Pr^{3+} Centers in Mixed $CaF_2{:}SrF_2$ Crystals," *Journal of Luminescence* **53**, pp. 503–506 (1992).

MacDonald, L. W., and Lowe, A. C., *"Display Systems Design and Applications,"* John Wiley & Sons (1997).

MacFarlane, D.L., "A Volumetric Three Dimensional Display," *Applied Optics* **33**(31), pp. 7453–7457 (1994).

MacFarlane, D. L., Schultz, G. R., Higley, P. D., and Meyer, J., "A Voxel Based Spatial Display," *Proceedings SPIE* **2177**, pp. 196–202 (1994).

MacKay, D. M., "Projective Three-Dimensional Displays, Part II," *Electronic Engineering*, pp. 281–285 (August 1949).

MacKay, D. M., "A Simple Multi-Dimensional CRT Display Unit," *Electronic Engineering*, pp. 344–347 (June 1960).

Malinowski, M., Garapon, C., Joubert, M. F., and Jacquier, B., "One- and Two-Photon Spectroscopy of Pr^{3+}-doped $YAlO_3$ Crystals," *Journal of Physics: Condens.Matter* **7**, pp.199–211 (1995).

Mark, H., and Hull, F., "Three-Dimensional Viewing of Tomographic Data—The TOMAX system," *Proceedings SPIE* **120**, pp. 192–194 (1977).

McAllister, D. F. (ed.), *Stereo Computer Graphics and Other True 3D Technologies*, Princeton University Press (1993).

McKay, S., Mair, L. S., Waddell, P., and Fraser, S. M., "Membrane Mirror-Based Display for Viewing 2D and 3D Images," *Proceedings SPIE* **3634**, pp.144–155 (1999a).

McKay, S., Mason, S., Mair, L. S., Waddell, P., and Fraser, S. M., "Stereoscopic Display Using a 1.2-m Diameter Stretchable Membrane Mirror," *Proceedings SPIE* **3639**, pp.122–131 (1999b).

Middleton, H., "Seeing by Telegraph. To the Editor of *The Times*," *The Times,* p. 12 (April 24, 1880).

Miyazaki, D., Lasher, M., and Fainman, Y., "Fluorescent Volumetric Display Excited by a Single Infrared Beam," *Applied Optics* **44**(25), pp. 5281–5285 (September 2005).

Monge, G. (ed.), and Gabay, J., *Geometrie Descriptive*, Broché (1989).

Moseley, S., *John Baird: The Romance and Tragedy of the Pioneer of Television*, Odhams Press Ltd. (1952).

Muirhead, J. C., *Review of Scientific Instruments* **32**, p. 210 (1961).

Mulder, J. D., Jansen, J., and van Rhijn, A., "An Affordable Optical Head Tracking System for Desktop VR/AR Systems," in "International Immersive Project Technologies Workshop," Deisinger, J., and Kunz, A. (eds.), *Eurographics Workshop on Virtual Environments*, pp. 215–223, The Eurographics Association (2003).

Myers, L. M., *Television Optics,* Sir Isaac Pitman & Son Ltd. (1936).

Nithyanandum, N., "A Three-Dimensional Digital Image Display System," *IEEE Transactions on Broadcasting* **BC-21**(4), p. 53 (December 1975).

Okoshi, T., *Three-Dimensional Imaging Techniques,* Academic Press (1976).

Osgood, C. E., *Method and Theory in Experimental Psychology*, Oxford University Press (1953).

O'Shea, D. C., *Elements of Modern Optical Design*, John Wiley & Sons (1985).

Ozawa, L., *Cathodoluminescence: Theory and Applications*, Kodansha Ltd/VCH New York (1990).

Owczarczyk, J., and Owczarczyk, B., "Evaluation of True 3D Display Systems for Visualizing Medical Volume Data," *The Visual Computer* **6**, pp. 219–226 (1990).

Parker, M. J., and Wallis, P. A., "Three-Dimensional Cathode-Ray Tube Displays," *Journal of the IEE* **95**, pp. 371–390 (September 1948).

Parker, M. J., and Wallis, P. A., "Discussion on 'Three-Dimensional Cathode-Ray Tube Displays' " *Journal of the IEE* **96(III)** (42), pp. 291–294 (1949).

Perlin, K., Paxia, S., and Kollin, J. S., "An Autostereoscopic Display," *Proceedings ACM SIGGRAPH* (July 2000).

Perlin, K., Poultney, C., Kollin, J. S., Kristjansson, D. T., and Paxia, S., "Recent Advances in the NYU Autostereoscopic Display," *Proceedings SPIE* **4297** (2001).

Perry, J., and Ayrton, W. E., "Seeing by Electricity," *Nature* **21**, p. 589 (April 21, 1880).

Perry, J., and Ayrton, W. E., "Seeing by Electricity" (paper communicated to the Physical Society, February 26), *Nature* **23**, pp. 423–424 (March 3, 1881).

Petty, M. C., Bryce, M. C., and Bloor, D., *An Introduction to Molecular Electronics*, Oxford University Press (1995).

Pocock, R. F., *German Guided Missiles*, Ian Allan (1967).

Poole, H. H., *Fundamentals of Display Systems*, Macmillan (1966).

Purves, D., and Lotto, R. B., *Why We See What We Do: An Empirical Theory of Vision*, Sinauer Associates Inc. (2003).

Radzig, A. A., and Smirnov, B. M., *Reference Data on Atoms, Molecules, and Ions*, Springer Verlag (1985).

Rawson, E. G., "3-D Computer-Generated Movies Using a Varifocal Mirror," *Applied Optics* **7**(8), pp. 1505–1511 (August 1968).

Rawson, E. G., "Vibrating Varifocal Mirrors for 3-D Imaging," *IEEE Spectrum*, pp. 37–43 (September 1969).

Richter, I. A., *The Notebooks of Leonardo da Vinci*, Oxford University Press (1998).

Saleh, B. E. A., and Teich, M. C., *Fundamental of Photonics*, John Wiley & Sons (1991).

Salmon, R., and Slater, M., *Computer Graphics Systems and Concepts*, Addison-Wesley (1987).

Schiffman, H. R., *Sensation and Perception* (3rd ed.), John Wiley & Sons (1990).

Schmandt, C., "Spatial Input/Display Correspondence in a Stereoscopic Computer Graphic Work Station," *Computer Graphics* **17**(3), pp. 253–259 (July 1983).

Schmitt, O. H., "Cathode-Ray Presentation of Three-Dimensional Data," *Journal of Applied Physics*, **18**, pp. 819–829 (September 1947).

Schwarz, A. J., and Blundell, B. G., "Volumetric Image Presentation on the Cathode Ray Sphere," *Proceedings 7th New Zealand Image Processing Workshop*, pp. 95–100 (1992).

Schwarz, A. J., and Blundell, B. G., "Considerations Regarding Voxel Brightness in Volumetric Displays Utilising Two-Step Excitation Processes," *Optical Engineering* **32**(11), pp. 2818–2823 (1993).

Schwarz, A. J., and Blundell, B. G., "Considerations for Accurate Voxel Positioning on a Rotating-Screen Volumetric Display System," *IEE Proceedings on Optoelectronics* **141**(5), pp. 336–344 (1994a).

Schwarz, A. J., and Blundell, B. G., "Regions of Extreme Image Distortion in Rotating-Screen Volumetric Display Systems," *Computers and Graphics* **18**(5), pp. 643–652 (1994b).

Schwarz, A. J., and Blundell, B. G., "Regions of Extreme Image Distortion in Rotating-Screen Volumetric Graphics Displays," *IEEE Computer Graphics and Applications* **17**(3), pp. 72–88 (1994c).

Schwarz, A. J., and Blundell, B. G., "Optimizing Dot-Graphics for Volumetric Displays," *IEEE Transactions on Computer Graphics and Applications* **17**, pp. 72–78 (1997).

Sher, L. D., "SpaceGraph, a True 3-D PC Peripheral," *SPIE* **902**, pp.10–11 (1988).

Sherr, S., *Applications for Electronic Displays: Technologies and Requirements*, John Wiley & Sons (1998).

Shimada, S., "A New Approach to the Real-Image 3D Globe Display," *SID 93 Digest*, pp. 1001–1004 (1993).

Simon, W., "A Method of Producing a Three-Dimensional Cathode Ray Tube Display," *Behav.Res. Methods & Instruments* **1**(5), p. 179 (1969).

Simon, W., and Walters, T., "A Spinning Mirror Autostereoscopic Display," *SPIE Proceedings,* **120**, pp.180–183 (1977).

Smith, C. J., *Intermediate Physics* (4th ed.), Edward Arnold Publishers (1957).

Smith, D. K., and Alexander, R. C., *Fumbling the Future: How Xerox Invented, Then Ignored, the First Personal Computer*, toExcel (1999).

Smith, F. G., and Thomson, J. H., *Optics*, John Wiley & Sons (1975).

Soltan, P., and Lasher, M., "Non-Moving 3D Volumetric Display Using Upconversion Materials," *NRaD Report* (April 11, 1996).

Soltan, P., and Trias, J., "A Proposal for Research and Development of a Volumetric 3-D Display Using a Non-Moving Imaging Medium," *NRaD Report* (September 1, 1992).

Soltan, P., Trias, J., Robinson, W., and Dahlke, W., "Laser Based 3D Volumetric Display System," *SPIE* **1664,** pp.177–192 (1992).

Soltan, P., Trias, J., Dahlke, W., Lasher, M., and MacDonald, M., "Laser Based 3D Volumetric Display System (2nd Generation)," *SID 94 Proceedings* (1994).

Soltan, P., Trias, J., Dahlke, W., Lasher, M., and MacDonald, M., "Laser Based 3D Volumetric Display System (The Improved Second Generation)," *NRaD Report* (January 5, 1995).

Sullivan, A., "58.3: A Solid-State Multi-planar Volumetric Display," *Proceedings SID'03 Digest*, pp. 1531–1533 (2003).

Sullivan, A., "DepthCube Solid-State 3D Volumetric Display," *Proceedings SPIE* **5291**, pp. 279–284 (2004).

Sutherland, I. E., "A Head-Mounted Three Dimensional Display," *AFIPS Conference Proceedings* **33**, pp. 757–764 (1968).

Sutherland, I. E., "Sketchpad: A Man–Machine Graphical Communication System," in *SJCC*, Spartan Books (1963).

Szilard, J., "An Improved Three-Dimensional Display System," *Ultrasonics*, pp. 273–276 (November 1974).

Takeda, T., Hashimoto, K., Hiruma, N., and Fukui, Y., "Characteristics of Accommodation Towards Apparent Depth," *Vision Research* **27**, pp. 1513–1526 (1987).

Tamura, S., and Tanaka, K., "Multilayer 3-D Display by Multidirectional Beam Splitter," *Applied Optics* **21**(20), pp. 3659–3663 (1982).

The Telegraphic Journal, "Tele-Photography" (1 March 1881).

Tilton, H. B., "Nineteen-Inch Parallactiscope," *Proceedings SPIE* **902**, pp. 17–23 (1988).

Tovee, M. J., *An Introduction to the Visual System*, Cambridge University Press (1996).

Traub, A. C., "Stereoscopic Display Using Rapid Varifocal Mirror Oscillations," *Applied Optics* **6**(6), pp. 1085–1087 (June 1967).

Travis, A. R. L., "Autostereoscopic 3-D Display," *Applied Optics* **29**(29), pp. 4341–4342 (1990).

Travis, A. R. L., Lang, S. R., Moore, J. R., and Dodgson, N. A., "Time-Multiplexed Three-Dimensional Video Display," *Journal of the SID* **3/4,** pp. 203–205 (1995).

Trotter, D. M., Jr., "Photochromic and Photosensitive Glass," *Scientific American*, pp. 56–61 (April 1991).

Tsuboi, T., Ruan, Y. F., and Adachi, G., "Green Luminescence from Er^{3+} Ions in $LiNbO_3$ Crystals," *Physical Status Solidi B* **187**, K75 (1995).

Tufte, E. R., *Envisioning Information*, Graphics Press (1990).

Udupa, J. K., "Display of 3D Information in Discrete 3D Scenes Produced by Computerized Tomography," *Proceedings of the IEEE* **71**(3), pp. 420–431 (March 1983).

Uricchio, W., "Envisioning the Audience: Perception of Early German Television's Audiences, 1935–1944," *Aura Filmvetenskaplig Tidskrift* **2**(4) (1996). [See also http://www.let.uu.nl/~william.uricchio/personal/Sweden1.html (accessed January 4, 2006)].

Valyus, N., *Stereoscopy*, Focal Press (1962).

Wade, N. J., (ed.), *Brewster and Wheatstone on Vision*, Academic Press (1983).

Wade, N. J., "On the Late Invention of the Stereoscope," *Perception*, **16**, pp. 785–818 (1987).

Wade, N. J., "The Chimenti Controversy," *Perception* **32**, pp. 185–200 (2003).

Warren, R. M., and Warren, R. P. (eds.), *Helmholtz on Perception: Its Physiology and Development,* John Wiley & Sons (1968).

Weast, R. C. (ed.), *CRC Handbook of Chemistry and Physics, 1st Student Edition*, CRC Press (1988).

Wehr, D. "Fernsehen Heute," *Die Sendung* (January 7, 1940).

Wheatstone, C., "Contributions to the Theory of Vision—Part the First, On Some Remarkable, and Hitherto Unobserved, Phenomena of Binocular Vision," *Philosophical Transactions of the Royal Society of London* **128,** pp. 371–394 (1838).

Williams, R. D., and Garcia, F., "A Real Time Autostereoscopic Multiplanar 3D Display System," *SID'88 Digest* **19**, pp. 91–94 (1988).

Williams, R. D., Wefer, F. L., and Clifton III, T. E., "Direct Volumetric Visualization," *IEEE Proceedings of the 3rd Conference on Visualization '92*, pp. 99–106 (1992).

Williams, R. W., and Parker, G. M., "A Source of Computing Voltage with Continuously-Variable Output," *Journal of Scientific Instruments* **29**, pp. 322–324 (October 1952).

Wireless World, "Stereoscopic Colour Television," **48**, pp. 31–32 (February 1942).

Withey, E. L., "Cathode-Ray Tube Adds Third Dimension," *Electronics (Engineering Edition)*, pp. 81–83 (May 23, 1958).

Yamada, H., Masuda, C., Nozaki, T., Nishitani, K., and Miyaji, K., "A 3-D Display Using a Laser and Moving Screens," *ICALEO* **48**, pp. 71–77 (1984).

Yamanaka, R., Yamamoto, K., Handa, N., and Yoshikura, H., "A 3-D Display with a Linearly Moving Mirror to Reflect a Series of 2-D Cross Sections and Its Application to Noninvasive Angiography," *IEEE Transactions on Medical Imaging* **7** (3), pp. 193–197 (1988).

Yang, D. K., Chien, J. W., and Doane, J. W., "Cholesteric Liquid Crystal/Polymer Dispersion for Haze-Free Light Shutters," *Applied Physics Letters* **60**, p. 3102 (1992).

Yokokawa, T., Inokuma, H., and Ohki, Y., "Nature of Photoluminescence Involving Transitions from the Ground to $4f^{n-1}\,5d^1$ States in Rare-Earth-Doped Glasses," *Journal of Applied Physics* **77**(8), pp. 4013–4017 (1995).

York House Papers, (24), pp. 1–2 (14 April 1880).

Zito, R., Jr., "Rate Analysis of Multiple-Step Excitation in Mercury Vapor," *J. Appl. Phys.* **34**(5), pp. 1535–1543 (May 1963).

Zito, R., and Schraeder, A. E., "Optical Excitation of Mercury Vapour for the Production of Isolated Fluorescence," *Applied Optics* **2**(12), pp. 1323–1328 (December 1963).

Index

Enhanced Visualization: Making Space for 3-D Images. By Barry G. Blundell
Copyright © 2007 John Wiley & Sons, Inc.

Printed and bound by CPI Group (UK) Ltd, Croydon, CR0 4YY

27/10/2024

14580261-0003